The Novels of
AMITAV GHOSH

The Novels of
AMITAV GHOSH

Edited by
R.K. Dhawan

Prestige
an international publishing house

Published by
Prestige Books
New Delhi 110 058
Ph. 011-25507139
email: prestigebooks@gmail.com
website: asiabookclub.com

Associate Office
60/29-45 Parramatta Road,
Concord, NSW 2137
Australia

ISBN: 81-7551-011-0

2nd Revised Edition, 2010

Rs. 700

Printed at Chaman Offset Press, New Delhi 110 002

Contents

The Calcutta Chromosome

Contributors

Khalid S.T. Abdu, University of Mysore
Madhumalati Adhikari, Rani Durgavati University, Jabalpur
Shyam S. Agarwalla, Ram Manohar Lohia College, Ranchi
Urbashi Barat, Rani Durgavati University, Jabalpur
Seema Bhaduri, Nasik
Shakuntala Bharvani, Bombay
Indira Bhatt, C.U. Shah College, Ahmedabad
Subhash Chandra, S.B.S. College, University of Delhi
R.K. Dhawan, S.B.S. College, University of Delhi
Pradip Dutta, S.V. College, University of Delhi
N. Eakambaram, University of Madras
Leela Gandhi, La Trobe University, Melbourne
Tapan Kumar Ghosh, Tarakeshwar Degree College, W.B.
Babli Gupta, Z.H. College, University of Delhi
Nilanjana Gupta, Jadavpur University, Calcutta
Santwana Haldar, Balasore
Louis James, London, U.K.
Novy Kapadia, S.G.T.B. Khalsa College, University of Delhi
Sharmila Guha Majumdar, Kalyani University, W.B.
Sarvajit Mukherji, University of Allahabad
Alpana Neogy, R.L.A. College, University of Delhi
D.K. Pabby, R.L.A. College, University of Delhi
Murari Prasad, D.S. College, Katihar
K. Damodar Rao, Kakatiya University, Warangal
Nandita Sinha, M.S. College, University of Delhi
S.P. Swain, Municipal College, Rourkela
G.R. Taneja, R.L.A. College, University of Delhi
Pradeep Trikha, Dayanand College, Ajmer
E. Kanaka Bhagya Veni, Stanley Girls College, Hyderabad

The Novels of Amitav Ghosh: An Introduction

R.K. DHAWAN

Indian English writers through Salman Rushdie, Vikram Seth, Vikram Chandra, Anita Desai and Arundhati Roy hold centre-stage in the contemporary literary scenario. They have received national and international recognition, fabulous royalties and prestigious awards. Amitav Ghosh is perhaps the finest writer among those who were born out of the post-*Midnight's Children* revolution in Indian English fiction.

It was in the year 1993 that the Indian English novel came to be associated with big 'monies.' It started with Vikram Seth's *A Suitable Boy* which was a happy marriage of 'money and imagination.' Seth became India's first millionaire novelist. He was paid a fabulous amount of Rs. 2.5 crores as advance royalty for the novel by the British publishers, Orion. His novel was the high watermark of the Indian literary scene of the early nineties. The novel was short-listed for the Booker Award but could not get it in the final round because the Booker Committee Chairman felt that the novel needed editing. Nonetheless, the novel registered a tremendous sale and fired the imagination of many aspiring fiction writers in the country.

The publication of Arundhati Roy's *The God of Small Things* is the latest and most valuable addition to the corpus of Indian writing. It is pre-eminently a novel by a woman, about a woman, seen through the eyes of a woman. Having received the Booker's Award for the Best Novel of the Year, it is the most talked-about novel in the world today. Indeed it has taken the publishing world by storm. The book has shot the newspaper headlines the worldover, and the media is almost hysterical in highlighting the commercial success of the author. No writer has been paid such a fabulous amount for publishing rights of his/her first novel.

Arundhati Roy is an excellent storyteller, and the novel seems to us a literary sport. We may not hesitate to call it a contemporary classic. It is a modern novel in its theme and the treatment of the theme, a postmodern novel in its knotting and knitting of narrative threads, manipulation of expressive literary forms and creative 'play' with words, a feminist novel in the pity and terror that it evokes for the condition of women in a particular cultural milieu, a political novel in its criticism of the hypocrisy of the communist party, an autobiographical novel in the way the facts of the author's life have been distilled into a verbal artefact and so on. In fact the novel is eminently amenable to multiple approaches and interpretations.

There are several reasons for the popularity of recent books published by Indian writers in India and abroad. Of the several qualities a book needs to have, is its capacity to capture the imagination of the reader. In other words, the most pertinent question is whether a book is 'readable.' The fiction of R.K. Narayan, Mulk Raj Anand and Anita Desai has caught the attention of the audience for one or the other reason. Maybe an easy entry into the comic world, a deep concern with social problems, or face to face with the dilemmas of the woman's world. At the turn of the century, however, a new trend seems to be emerging. Marketing strategies are now as important as the contents of a book or its author. Modern technology, especially the media and the Internet, has played a significant role in promoting new books. This has been quite advantageous to the third-world writers, for their books reach the world over in no time. It is no longer uncommon to see a book on the day of its release selling at different places in different countries. Books are now being treated as revenue-generating products that need, apart from other ingredients, an author who has promotion potential and a publisher with wide marketing network. This development has helped an Indian writer in English much more than a regional Indian writer. Works of new writers like Salman Rushdie, Vikram Seth, Vikram Chandra, Gita Mehta, Rohinton Mistry and Arundhati Roy have been published by international book companies. Quality production, effective cost structure and easy mobility have given a boost to the sales: books are treated as products of a corpus culture, to be bought and sold with frenzied efforts. For example, *The Idea of India*, a diasporic book by Indian-born Oxford Professor Sunil Khilnani, has been listed by *The Guardian* among the best ten world books published in 1998.

Many of the regional writers too have been quite visible through translations. The translation phenomenon has become prominent, thanks to the efforts made by the Sahitya Akademi, Katha and other organizations. It has brought into cosmopolitan reckoning some of the brilliant writers in the regional languages. Indeed one of the most popular novels of recent times is U.R. Anantha Murthy's *Sanskara*, written originally in Kannada. The English translation by eminent poet A.K. Ramanujan may be construed as contribution both to traditional Indian literature as also to Indian English literature. The novel won the author many prestigious awards including the Sahitya Akademi and the Jnanpith Awards.

Several of the regional writers have captured the imagination of the English-speaking world. Translations of the plays by Girish Karnad, Vijay Tendulkar, Badal Sircar and Mohan Rakesh, novels by Premchand, R.N. Tagore, Saratchandra, Mahasweta Devi, Qurratulain Hyder, short stories by Sadat Hasan Manto and Krishan Chander have become immensely popular. Some years ago, Pakistani Urdu writer Intezar Husain was given the first Rupa Award of Rs. 50,000. The English translation of his short stories entitled *Leaves* became a favourite of literary world.

India has contributed significantly to the overall world literature. This contribution of India has been chiefly through the Indian Writing in English, novelists being in the forefront in this respect. A good number of novelists on the contemporary scene have given expression to their creative urge in no other language than English and have brought credit to the Indian English fiction as a distinctive force in the world fiction. To attempt creative expression on a national scale in an alien medium has seldom happened in human history; and it speaks of the prolific quality of the Indian mind to assimilate the newly confronting situations and the complex dilemmas of modern world.

It is indeed an irony that the growth and complexity of Indian English literature as a whole, and the novel in particular, is not fully appreciated in India. Its force and vitality is submerged in the literatures produced in the various local languages. Obviously, the literature in a language that is not basic to the country cannot have a wide acceptance in terms of numbers, indeed it would be wrong to judge it solely on this ground. English-speaking people in India cut through class, ethnic and geographical barriers. One may come across a person literate in English in the remote mountains of Ladakh or in the coastal regions of Kanyakumari, three thousand miles away. The correct way to approach this literature would be through its academic acceptance; and academically Indian Writing in English is being increasingly talked about and discussed in the various centres of learning in the country. The purpose of the author is to show that this literature in its scope and achievement has reached far greater heights than conceived by the pioneers in the field.

II

In the recent times, a great body of historical fiction has emerged on the literary scene. Many Indian English novelists have turned to the past as much to trace the deepening mood of nationalism as to cherish the memories of the bygone days. A close study of the contemporary novel reveals writers's preoccupation with our historic past and the unabated interest of the readers in the novels that depict the past or that treat some event of national import that has had wide repercussions. As a critic I have always attached a great deal of importance to the impact on a writer of the historical milieu in which he lives and the historical periods of an earlier time with which the author wishes to associate himself by choice. Writers like Khushwant Singh, Manohar Malgonkar, Chaman Nahal, Shashi Tharoor, Salman Rushdie and Amitav Ghosh amply illustrate this point of view.

It is quite improper to compare historical novel with history proper. The novelist concerned with history is beyond the traditional way of assessing events; he has to blend history with his vision and philosophy. The novel deals with history though a camouflage. P.V. Narasimha Rao's maiden novel *The Insider*, for example, is a fictionalized biography of an ex-Prime Minister. Anand, the protagonist of the novel, is an alter-ego of Rao; the major events of his life run parallel to the author's life history. Also, it is an interesting account of the life and times of this country's politics. The loss of idealism and honesty from public life in India, portrayed candidly in the novel, makes a terrific indictment of the system. It is a historical novel that throws useful light on the slice of the country's socio-political life.

An historical novel is nothing but an evaluation of a segment of historical reality as projected by the novelist whose techniques of writing fiction enable him to describe his vision or world-vision. In all his writing, Amitav Ghosh's engagement with history is not the same kind as that of a historian, but this does not in any way lessen its significance as historical fiction. The fictional framework renders history more readable and lively and he is able to involve the reader more than what history does. Ghosh's fiction reveals that the novelist's involvement with history is his prime obsession. Indeed, he interjects a new dimension into his encounter with history. His fiction is imbued with both political and historical consciousness. Ghosh is a novelist who virtually bends his novels to the needs of history; they largely derive their purpose and shape from it.

A distinction must be made here between the conscious use of history and its sub-conscious presentation. The setting of most novels is in the context of some historical framework unless the novelist wilfully places his action in an imaginary locale hoping to highlight a special metaphysical or political point of view, e.g. William Golding's *Lord of the Flies*, George Orwell's *Nineteen Eighty-Four*. Sometimes, he creates the country, as does Joseph Conrad in *Nostromo*. It is my contention that whatever be the perfection of craftsmanship in this type of novel, such works are accepted by the public as nothing more than utopias.

Modern deconstructionists would easily discuss them as exercises in self-deception. Utopias make fine reading; their relevance to the immediate problem is more of an escapist nature suggesting remedies neither available nor practical. The historical novel represents no surface wave of escapism, but a deep, unconscious movement towards national homogeneity. It is in the historical novel only that the actual day-to-day problems of life can be encountered, examined, exposed, challenged and rectified. Entertainment and instruction are, by common consent, most valued virtues of historical fiction. The factual and informational values of history illuminate the subject and increasingly whet the reader's curiosity. In other words, for a true artist history is a hand-maiden which helps him to achieve several purposes. How deft he is in the art of amalgamating the two must be judged only by the finished product. And herein the novelist who makes use of history by choice obviously must be held at a superior level than the one who consciously assimilates it.

A pertinent question that arises is the relevance of history in a work of art. As a matter of fact, historical sense and reality enter into the sphere of art imperceptibly; they are important factors in determining the ultimate value of a given piece of art. In a sense every novelist tries to enshrine a period in a book; in other words every novelist is a historical novelist. This historical reality, in terms of time and space, forms an integral part of a work of art and is transmuted in the process of giving it a creative expression; in the process it achieves wider dimensions of universality and at times a state of timelessness. The historical novelist is none but a historian on whom a talent for imaginative fiction has been happily bestowed.

A writer of historical fiction then is as much a historian as a novelist. But history does impose limitations on him. He is not free to distort history; factual accuracy has to be strictly adhered to. "Herein lies the additional burden," writes Chaman Nahal, "that a historical novelist places on the artist. The novelist is obliged to do careful research into the period he has chosen for presentation and every detail of that period has to be accurate." Detail, not only about the layout of a geographical region, but also about the people living in that region, their mode of speech, their dress, their habits, their peculiar traits and countless other characteristics of that particular community. Indeed every care must be taken to verify incidental details, as a sure guard against anachronism. Before it was published, *Gone with the Wind* was subjected, for a period of eight months, to a rigorous checking of facts; and a systematic verification was made of specific statements contained in the novel. Indeed it is an important reason for the immense popularity of this novel in which Margaret Mitchell makes a serious evocation of the American Civil War.

Again, it is hazardous to infiltrate too much history into the plot of a novel, or to have too many historical figures among the leading characters. History puts the author at a disadvantage since a great majority of characters who have an independent historical reality can hardly be made amenable to the author's designs or the exigencies of the plot. The interaction for historical and fictional characters, and the interaction of the two kinds amongst themselves, is the most challenging part of writing a historical novel.

The historical novel, popularized by Walter Scott, enjoyed immense popularity in the nineteenth century. Dickens, inspired by French Revolution, successfully made use of history in *A Tale of Two Cities*. It is a magnificent novel with a panoramic background representing the dramatic life of a few individuals interwoven with the interest of a catastrophic public event. George Eliot who attempted a historical novel, entitled *Romola,* failed disastrously. The two world wars stimulated the imagination of writers, giving birth to some significant fiction—Eric Maria Remarque's *All Quiet in the Western Front*, Ernest Hemingway's *A Farewell to Arms*, Herman Wouk's *The Cain Mutiny*. Indeed, in the twentieth century the historical novel has largely been the province of Continental novelists for whom themes of revolution or foreign occupation are much closer to the bone than studies of middle-class manners and morals in a relatively stable society such as England's. A case in point is J.G. Farrell's new novel *The Singapore Grip*, a trilogy about the decline of the British Empire. Great political movements, conflicts or revolutions are the warp and woof of a historical novelist and good writers are mediumistic to the deeper stirrings of the life for their time or to an event of the past. Apart from *Gone with the Wind*, the historical novels of the twentieth century which may be termed classics are Leo Tolstoy's *War and Peace* and Boris Pasternak's *Dr. Zhivago*. The first is related to Napoleon's invasion of Russia; the second describes the failure of the Revolution of 1917. Failure of modern Britain to find some great fictional theme could be attributed to history itself than on writers of the age.

As elsewhere, majority of novels in India have been written in response to historical movements or events such as the Gandhian movement, imperial rule, partition of the country, the emergence of the New India. The heroic effort to throw away the foreign yoke was an epic struggle covering the first half of the twentieth century. The nation was in a ferment; a massive movement for liberation from the foreign rule was raging in the country. The British, who were exploiting India the utmost, were in no mood to withdraw. The struggle was long and gruelling.

The freedom struggle caught the imagination of the entire nation, no less the Indian English writers. No significant writer could escape the impact of the mighty movement sweeping the country. The novels written in the Indian languages and English in the thirties and the forties reflect the vitality of a people devoted to a cause. This is amply reflected in the novels of the period—Raja Rao's *Kanthapura*, Mulk Raj Anand's *Coolie*, K.A. Abbas's *Inquilab*, D.F. Karaka's *We Never Die* and C.N. Zutshi's *Motherland*.

The novels dealing with the freedom struggle give vivid pictures of the exploitation and the arrogance of the foreign rulers, as also the portrayal of an awakened people struggling for their birthright. The growth of the historical novel coincided with the intensification of the struggle for Indian freedom, especially after the First World War. Novels written previously had confined to religious aestheticism—now the focus shifted to contemporary socio-political concern.

Indeed it were the English who brought with them enlightenment of the West and inspired the Indians to imbibe the spirit of nationalism. In the early decades of the century, the English system had nearly succeeded in giving the people a unity in law, in public administration, in finance and in education that was hitherto unknown to them and ironically enough all this resulted in generating a sense of national unity which urged them to fight for freedom in later stages.

The intellectuals, be they philosophers, historians or literary artists, have traditionally played significant roles in all national revolutions of the world. Not only do they reach the minds of the people through their writing, they also subject every institution of the society to a specific political philosophy, and through that propagate their point of view.

The Indian English novelists were most responsive to the call of equality, freedom and human rights, for the literary artists have an intrinsic quality and ability to look beyond their time. It is they who hold before the common man a lense, as it were, through which he could see what threatened him socially, culturally or politically, and which made him aware of the precipice that lay ahead. As it was, a number of novels were written during the period that portrayed the unjustness of the British rule and the grim fight the people were determined to give to get rid of it. Politics became synonymous with nationalism.

No doubt, the most important historical event of our age, as is evident from the writings of Indian English novelists, was the partition of the subcontinent. The English in 1947 left the country with bag and baggage, after dividing it into two parts. The religious and political differences between Hindus and Muslims which climaxed with this event led to widespread disturbances, causing destruction of human life on a scale unprecedented in the recent history of the subcontinent. There was let loose a communal fury which caused a great havoc and misery. In the massacres, which immediately preceded the partition and continued for several months afterwards, at least one million Hindus and Muslims lost their lives. There was large-scale migration of people from one country to the other. In the process, thousands were massacred; women were raped, children were flung on spears and property was looted on a vast scale.

The Indian English novelists, like their counterparts in Indian languages, responded to these happenings with a sense of horror. A number of novels were written on the theme of partition, the destruction it brought and the plight of the refugees. They faithfully record the reign of violence that characterized the period and provide a sad, telling commentary on the breakdown of human values. A strain of despair and disillusionment is predominant in these novels. Our freedom movement is the greatest historical fact of contemporary India. Whatever we may regard to interpret it, no one had conceived, not even the shrewd British, the dimension this movement would acquire in a matter of few decades. E.M. Forster, publishing his *Passage to India* in 1924, is completely silent about this movement. George Orwell has written of the imperialism in Burma and Leonard Woolf, in his three-volume autobiography, of imperialism in Sri Lanka. There are scattered memoirs of the Britishers who lived in India but they are mostly in the form of nostalgia that depict the comforts they enjoyed here. None of these writers, not even Kipling, who is said to have identified himself so closely with India, foresaw that in a few years's time this empire, the greatest jewel in the British Crown (to borrow a title from Paul Scott), would come to an end.

With the emergence of Gandhi on the scene, the political situation in India took a turn. From the 1920s the national struggle acquired the spectrum of a broad river which kept on expanding until the British were thrown out of India. The manner in which country achieved its independence is debatable; division of the country could perhaps have been avoided. All the same, by the end of the 40s, in a matter of three decades, India had emerged as a nation in its own right with its cultural heritage unscathed.

III

As a writer, Amitav Ghosh has been immensely influenced by the political and social milieu of the country. Also, the stories and events he heard from his parents during his childhood made an indelible impression on his mind. He was born several years after India's independence. His mother grew up in Calcutta and her memories were of Mahatma Gandhi, non-violence and disobedience, and the terrors that accompanied Partition in 1947. His father worked in the British colonial army in India and his stories were of the war and of his fellow-Indians who fought loyally beside the British. The image of the changing India, politically and socially, cast a deep shadow on Ghosh's mind.

Now in his early forties, Ghosh spent his childhood days in Calcutta, Dhaka and Colombo. He graduated from St. Stephen's College, University of Delhi. For a short period during the Emergency, he worked with *The Indian Express*. Later he joined the Delhi School of Economics as a lecturer in the Department of Anthropology. After some time, he received a scholarship to do a D.Phil. in social anthropology at Oxford University. It is this anthropological study which took him to Alexandria University and consequently to the villages of Egypt. He admits that his campus life and travels within and without the country contributed to his development as a creative writer.

IV

Amitav Ghosh published his first novel *The Circle of Reason* in 1986 when he was teaching at the Delhi School of Economics, University of Delhi. This novel has been translated into many European languages; its French edition received the *Prix Medici estranger*, a prestigious literary award in France. *The Circle* is a skilfully constructed novel with the folk tale charm of Arabian Nights. Stretching from a remote village in Bengal to the shores of the Mediterranean, this is a neatly sculpted work of a master craftsman. It marks a break from the traditional themes of the Indian English novel and the form and structure of the well-made novel. In "Magic and Irony as Principles of Structure: A Reading of *The Circle of Reason*," K. Damodar Rao shows how the immediacy of experience of the reality is conveyed to the readers by a medley of devices: ironic mode of narration, recreating a magical world, and an uninhibited exhibition of narcissistic tendencies. The all-embracing structural principles of magic and irony eloquently weave the total pattern of the novel. Pradip Dutta, on the other hand, analyzes *The Circle* as an epic of restlessness. Around the bare outlines of the plot which moves over continents, are clustered an infinite number of stories ranging back and forth in time. By showing life as a journey larger than death, *The Circle* makes death find its identity in the horror and sadness which embalms this process.

V

The year 1984 was in some ways a turning point in the writing career of Amitav Ghosh. Certain events that took place that year had a deep impact on his mind. In an article that appeared in *The Guardian* in 1995, Ghosh admits:

> Nowhere else in the world did the year 1984 fulfil its apocalyptic portents as it did in India. Separatist violence in Punjab; the military attack on the great Sikh temple of Amritsar; the assassination of the Prime Minister, the gas disaster in Bhopal—the events followed relentlessly on each other. There were days in 1984 when it took courage to open the Delhi papers in the morning.

Of the year's many catastrophies, the sectarian violence following Mrs. Gandhi's death had the greatest effect on Ghosh's life. Looking back, Ghosh realizes that the experiences of that period were profoundly important to his development as a writer. Being a witness himself, he never mustered courage to write about these events directly, even later.

Indeed he gives a graphic description of the gruesome events that followed the murder of Mrs. Indira Gandhi. He tells us how as he went to Delhi University campus to take his classes, he witnessed violence and riots. Throughout the city, Sikh houses were being looted and then set on fire, often with their occupants still inside. Such horrible events had a stifling effect on the creative mind of Ghosh. When he went back to his desk, he found himself confronting decisions about writings that he had never faced before. How could he write, he felt, about what he had seen without reducing it to mere spectacle? His next novel was bound to be influenced by his experiences but he could see no way of writing directly about these events without recreating them as a panorama of violence, an act of reporting or re-creating.

Within a few months, Ghosh started his new novel which he eventually called *The Shadow Lines*, a book that led him backward in time to earlier memories of riots, once witnessed in childhood. It became, says Ghosh, "a book not about any one event, but about the meaning of such events and their effects on the individuals who live through them."

The Shadow Lines is, by common consent, Ghosh's best work. It is a family saga which is also a roller-coaster ride through the currents of history. The novel covers a large span of period; it tells the story of the three generations of the narrator's family spread over Dhaka, Calcutta and London. Chronologically, the story begins with a passage about the time in colonial India when the narrator was not even born. The novel begins thus: "In 1939, thirteen years before I was born, my father's aunt, Mayadebi, went to England with her husband and her son, Tridib." (3) In the first section of the book titled "Going Away," Ghosh recaptures London on the eve of, and during, war. This knowledge of war was gained by the adolescent story-teller not from books but from the experienes of his uncle who exercised an indelible impression on him. The uncle tells him stories which give him "the worlds to travel in and eyes to see with." In the section "Coming Home," Ghosh shifts his focus to the Indian subcontinent, mainly to Calcutta and Dhaka where he tries to find the meaning of political freedom. Indian nationalism, which was the chief weapon of the freedom fighters in their struggle against the British rulers changed its meaning after the Partition and tended to exclude people on the other side of the border. Communal frenzy, violence and destruction are the obsession now. Ghosh brings out the futility of drawing lines across a nation to form two nations. The novel rejects the very concept of Partition. The implication of the story is the need for co-existence and strong humanitarian ties across cultures, overlooking personal, regional and political considerations.

The Shadow Lines, in the opinion of the eminent critic A.N. Kaul, is concerned with the theme of crossing of frontiers—especially those of nationality, culture and language. While the theme is an old one in fiction, Amitav Ghosh gives it a new twist in his novel which covers three countries—India, East Pakistan and England. However, *The Shadow Lines* is not an *inter*-national novel in the sense E.M. Forster's *A Passage to India* is which involves the study and confrontation of two different cultures—those of the east and the west. In *The Shadow Lines*, Amitav Ghosh acknowledges no separate national or cultural realities because for him, all such demarcations are shadow lines, arbitrary and invented divisions. While crossing the border, the grandmother cannot see the line dividing the countries. A.K. Ramanujan aptly remarks: "He evokes things Indian with an inwardness that is lit and darkened by an intimacy with Elsewhere."

The apparently simple narrative is in fact a complex jig-saw puzzle of varied time and place segments as also new thematic dimensions. No wonder, the novel has been subjected to rich and varied interpretations. In her article "Some Recent Trends in Modern Indian Fiction: A Study of Shashi Deshpande's *That Long Silence*, Shashi Tharoor's *The Great Indian Novel* and Amitav Ghosh's *The Shadow Lines*," Shakuntala Bharvani concentrates on theme, language and innovative technique in the three novels mentioned in the title. The analysis shows how the three authors have successfully harnessed a foreign language to a sensibility that is essentially Indian as well as modern. In "Shadow Lines:

Cross-Cultural Perspectives in the Fiction of Amitav Ghosh," Louis James analyzes Ghosh's first two novels and points out how they radically de-construct traditional novel forms. Whileas *The Circle of Reason* introduces a number of "languages," including those of the Indian folk tale, the *Mahabharata*, journalism and the memory patterns of the extended family, *The Shadow Lines* has sharper unifying focus and brings together the form of the autobiographical novel and the family chronicle. Both the novels end with a ritual—a religious intimation of the cycle and continuation of life.

Partition of the Indian subcontinent was the most traumatic experience in our recent history. The event has been the focal point in many Indian novels. Novy Kapadia's article "Communal Frenzy and Partition: Bapsi Sidhwa, Attia Hosain and Amitav Ghosh" deals with the genre of partition novel. Bapsi Sidhwa's *Ice-Candy-Man* presents the ambivalent attitude of the Parsis towards Partition which relentlessly divided friends, families, lovers and neighbours. Attia Hosain's *Sunlight on a Broken Column* reveals the trauma of Partition through the narrator-heroine Laila's memories and insights. Both the novels show the communal responses to the horrors of violence. Similar patterns of violence are depicted by Amitav Ghosh in his novel *The Shadow Lines*. In his article "Theme of Partition and Freedom in Khushwant Singh's *Train to Pakistan* and Amitav Ghosh's *The Shadow Lines*," D.K. Pabby points out that the real sorrow of the partition as portrayed in the two novels was that it brought to an end a long and communally shared history and cultural heritage. In *Train to Pakistan*, Khushwant Singh describes how the feeling of guilt arose from the maddening violence by the Hindus and the Muslims precipitated by reports of the proposed division of the country into "a Hindu India and a Muslim Pakistan." In *The Shadow Lines*, Amitav Ghosh brings out the futility of drawing lines across a nation to form two nations, one having an East wing, which is separated from its West wing by over a thousand miles. Alpana Neogy in her article "The Partition of Bengal: A Comparative Study of Amitav Ghosh's *The Shadow Lines* and Sunil Gangopadhyay's *Purba Paschim*," points out that both the novels focus on the Partition of India and the consequent trauma of the East Bengali psyche. The common themes in both the novels are the agonies of displacement, the sense of alienation in the adopted land and the constant dream of a return to one's land.

Amitav Ghosh evokes postcolonial situations, cultural dislocations and anxieties in the period between 1962 and 1979 and interprets the issues of fractured nationalities in close and telling encounters. The narrator, with his expanded horizons and imaginative understanding of the world caught up in the vortex of violence and murderous rampage stresses on the urgency preserving the memories of saner and humane transactions for cultural self-determination and inter-personal communication. In his article "*The Shadow Lines:* A Quest for 'Indivisible Sanity'," Murari Prasad points out that the media and public memory must keep alive the 'indivisible sanity' of communities to prevent recurrence of insane frenzy.

The war-time London, the burning Dhaka of the post-Partition period and Calcutta of the riots are vividly created in the novel. Discussing the theme of violence, N. Eakambaram examines how violence cracks the mirror of life in the fictional world of *The Shadow Lines*. Tridib, the narrator, is killed in a communal riot. As in Greek tragedies, the violence comes through in a terrible manner because it is conveyed through choric characters.

Seema Bhaduri's article "Of Shadows, Lines and Freedom: A Historical Reading of *The Shadow Lines*" focuses on Ghosh's treatment of the changing middle class ethos in India during the pre- and post-Independence era. The lives of the characters in this novel are determined largely by their idea of freedom and this idea, in its turn, is shaped by the history of the times.

The Shadow Lines as a novel resists classification. It is basically a memory novel that weaves together past and present, childhood and adulthood, India and Bangladesh and Britain, Hindu and Muslim. It is a social document and a political novel, a bildungsroman and a postmodernist work of fiction. In her article "Imagination and Reality in *The Shadow Lines*," Urbashi Barat points out that the novel belongs to that long tradition of fiction which examines its symbiotic relationship with fact and explores the role of the imaginations creating and evoking reality.

In *The Shadow Lines*, the overall focus is on the meaning and shades of political nuances in contemporary life. In "Contrasting Strands of Political Nuances in *The Shadow Lines*," Novy Kapadia points out that the quest for political freedom, the violence in modern life, the role of rumour in riots are aptly delineated in the novel. Amitav Ghosh boldly tackles political themes, both national and international.

S.P. Swain in his article "The Quest for Meaning: A Study of *The Shadow Lines*" argues that the silent quest of the narrator for meaning in life, for filling up the inner void in him with words forms the focus of the novel. The narrator's story unfurls itself through fragmentary streams of consciousness where the private turmoil of the individual is reflected in the public chaos and crises. The need to articulate silence throws the notions of secularism, nationalism and freedom into disarray and the quest for meaning continues without finality.

In his article "Silence as Possible Mode of Response in *The Shadow Lines*," K. Damodar Rao points out that the novel creates a rich tapestry of eloquence and silence. Since the text is studded with myriad possibilities and multiple points of view, Rao feels that silence is employed by means of subversion as a possible mode of response.

The Shadow Lines has an extraordinary density of narrative texture. The story emerges in layers and each layer is a fusion of private lives and public events, all linked into a thematic unity. In her article "Perspectives in Time: The Narrator as Child in *The Shadow Lines*," Nandita Sinha shows how Ghosh uses first-person narrative from a dual viewpoint—that of the child and the adult "I". By putting the child in the centre of the narrative and surrounding the events of the past with later interpretations, Ghosh leads the reader through the same deepening of perception that the narrator experiences.

Writing a short note on the novel, G.R. Taneja points out that Ghosh has strengthened the new English novel in more than one way. *The Shadow Lines* takes in the war-devastated London, civil strife in post-Partition East Bengal, and the riot-hit Calcutta and embodies a major critique of the psychological make-up of the contemporary man that thrives on violence.

VI

Amitav Ghosh's third book *In an Antique Land* shows that he is not a mere fictionist but an indefatigable researcher, a social anthropologist and a keen traveller as well. It bears testimony to Ghosh's interaction with at least four languages and cultures spread over three continents and across several countries. Unlike some of the other contemporary writers, his canvas keeps on conquering new images, giving expression to new ideas and themes. In an interview, Ghosh talks about the book's theme and form: 'No this time I am not writing a novel. Not even sociology, history or belles-lettres based on historical research. My new book cannot be described as any one of these. It's a strange sort of work. Within the parameters of history, I have tried to capture a story, a narrative, without attempting to write a historical novel. You may say, as a writer, I have ventured on a technical innovation.' The anthropologist Ghosh is at his best in weaving a complex pattern of fact and fiction. It was in 1978 while going through manuscripts in Oxford library that Amitav Ghosh read about Abraham Ben Yiju, a Tunisian Jewish merchant who came to India via Egypt around 1130 A.D. and Ben Yiju's slave Bomma who is from Tululand of ancient India. Says Ghosh:

> I was a student, twenty-two years old, and I had recently won a scholarship awarded by a foundation established by a family of expatriate Indians. It was only a few months since I had left India and so I was perhaps a little more befuddled by my situation than students usually are. At that moment the only thing I knew about my future was that I was expected to do research leading towards a doctorate in social anthropology. I had never heard of the Cairo Geniza before that day, but within a few months I was in Tunisia learning Arabic. At about the same time the next year, 1980, I was in Egypt, installed in a village called Lataifa, a couple of hours' journey to the south-east of Alexandria.

In his scholarly article "Beyond the 'Shadow Lines': Amitav Ghosh's Quest for the Remains of an Antique Civilization," Tapan Kumar Ghosh argues that the book clearly defies the "shadow lines" of language, religion and culture, and explores some basic traits of human character and some fundamental human feelings and attitudes that persist through the ages despite socio-political upheavals and geographical changes. One finds a successful resuscitation of medieval Egypt and Mangalore. The novelist makes a comparative study of the two oldest cultures and civilizations of the two most important continents—Asia and Africa, that of India and Egypt. The novelist's inquisitive mind reconstructs the historical Egypt-India relations over a period of time.

In her article "The Shadow Lines and *In an Antique Land*: Some Thematic Considerations," Sharmila Guha Majumdar concentrates on the two novels dealing with history. World War II, Indian Independence and the partition of the country provide Amitav Ghosh with raw material against which he studies the historical truths—the meaning of nationalism and political freedom in the modern world—in *The Shadow Lines.* The 1964 riots are described in *In an Antique Land* from the other side of the border. Ghosh has drawn parallels between war and riots, Europe and Indian subcontinent to show how all violence whether committed in the name of nationalism or freedom is to be given no other colour. Yet another scholar Shyam S. Agarwalla shows how Ghosh draws and reworks a number of sources and traditions that span a varied range of concerns and historical situations. Agarwalla also deals in detail with Ghosh's art of characterization in the book *In an Antique Land.* Towards the end of his article, he traces incidents of compassionate humour in the book.

Amitav Ghosh describes himself as a traveller interested in men, places and scenery. Travel is man's primordial quest to expand his awareness into realization. In his article "*In an Antique Land:* A Traveller's Tale," Pradeep Trikha points out that *In an Antique Land* is a travel book for it records people and their manners. Ghosh has the travel writer's infallible eye for the quirk that lays bare the soul of a people.

Through his imaginative interrogation of the past, Ghosh animates the dead letters of libraries and archives with living voices. In her short note "*In an Antique Land*: A View," the eminent scholar Leela Gandhi finds the book rather heavy and unreadable. Nevertheless, she finds that Ghosh's sensitive amplification of unrecorded lives and voices successfully personalizes history and makes it more personable.

In an Antique Land focusses on the interrelationships of the people rather than of nation-states and their rulers. In the article "*In an Antique Land*: A Counter-Narrative of Coloniality," Nilanjana Gupta points out that Ghosh's text is a combination of autobiography, history, anthropology, travelogue and fiction. It presents us with a subversive look at history while suggesting possibilities of an alternative discourse of dialogue, rather than domination.

The book, it may be noted, has very few women characters and none of them has a significant role to play. In fact, woman here is always mentioned in connection to the male—be it her father, brother, son or husband. E. Kanaka Bhagya Veni's article "The Image of Woman in *In an Antique Land*" focuses on the few women characters—Yiju's wife Ashu, Khamees's sister Busaina, Khamees's wife, Yiju's daughter and the three women in Shaikh Musa's house besides the girl dancer and servant girls. Veni concludes by saying that Ghosh has the antiquated attitude of the patriarchal society towards women.

VII

In his next novel entitled *The Calcutta Chromosome* (1996), Amitav Ghosh makes a unique experiment by combining various themes and techniques. He amalgamates here literature, science, philosophy, history, psychology and sociology. The result is a complex, fascinating and highly imaginative story of quest and discovery that weaves past, present and future into an intricate texture. The novel has two major strands of story-line: the first narrates the life-story of Antar, an Egyptian computer clerk working on his super-intelligent machine Ava in the early twenty-first century to locate the whereabouts of Indian-born American scientist L. Murugan who had mysteriously disappeared in Calcutta in August 1995; the second revolves around Ronald Ross's discovery of the malarial parasite in 1902. The novel is divided into two sections: "August 20, Mosquito Day" and "The Day After." It reads like science fiction with multiple characters and swift turns in the plot. The novel however is no mere thriller, for a fuller reading reveals that it is the work of a social anthropologist than that of a detective novelist. In order to render an entertaining tale into a serious one, Ghosh pushes in arguments and ideas which are forever knocking and undermining the rational view of science and the universe. His treatment of history in this novel is unique. He succeeds in evoking the places and times with touching details. Antar's New York exists in an apocalyptic twilight; Ross's Secunderabad and Cunningham's Calcutta are colonial. Ghosh is in full control of the intellectual topography and geographical locale.

Attempts to unravel the enigmatic design of *The Calcutta Chromosome* are like unpeeling an onion to find the core. In her scholarly article "Enigma as Ontology in *The Calcutta Chromosome*," Babli Gupta traces the link between Ghosh's two works, *In an Antique Land* and *The Calcutta Chromosome*, and sees the latter as a deliberate inversion of the earlier masterpiece. It is almost as if Ghosh is exorcising the gloom which had crept upon him in the writing of the former book where he recounts the tales of two ancient civilizations, Egypt and India, and chronicles their inevitable decline. In *The Calcutta Chromosome*, Ghosh looks in the direction of magic, conspiracy and silence to overturn the logic of Europe's conquest of the East. Essentially a novel of ideas, it works like a brain teaser undermining conceptual certainties and reads the world as a mighty conundrum, where questions and problems are given conjectural answers.

In her illuminating article "Quest and Subversion: The Empire Strikes Back in *The Calcutta Chromosome*," Urbashi Barat analyzes in detail the thriller form used by Amitav Ghosh in his latest novel. She writes that Ghosh's choice of the thriller pattern for his novel becomes especially interesting when it is seen as an ironic take-off on the way in which stories of medical and scientific discoveries and inventions are popularized in children's books and science-fiction tales. The novel makes a considerable use of the film techniques of crosscut and dissolve so popular in the thriller. Because Ghosh is a fabulist rather than a raconteur, his thriller is a quest-narrative. The colonial world examined in a postcolonial setting turns conventional assumptions about itself, about history and science, inside out and upside down. She feels that Ghosh uses the thriller form, only to subvert it. Through its subversive quest, *The Calcutta Chromosome* celebrates the eternal, celebrates the triumph of the spirit over all that bogs it down in the mire.

Madhumalati Adhikari takes up from where Urbashi Barat concludes. In her article "The Continuity of Life, Mission and Mystery in *The Calcutta Chromosome*," she points out that it is too facile to contemplate that Amitav Ghosh in his latest novel has attempted to inscribe a simple scientific thriller on the fever, delirium and discovery of the malarial parasite. In this novel, Ghosh has universalized the specific through the concept of quest and journey. The notion of delirium, fever and discovery superficially associated with malaria is extended to the meaning of life having identical symbolic and symptomatic significance. She concludes by saying that the novel literally and figuratively rekindles our awareness of the rich Indian heritage to make our future progress inevitable.

In his novel, Amitav Ghosh colours the issue of the malarial fever with mysticism and mystery, supernatural and superstition, calling it the theory of science and counter-science. Indira Bhatt's article "Disappearances and Discovery: A Study of *The Calcutta Chromosome*" examines how this theory of science and counter-science is presented and with what purpose.

Ghosh's *In an Antique Land* and *The Calcutta Chromosome* are steeped in history and social anthropology. Whileas *In an Antique Land* is spun around ancient Indo-Arab trade links where history and myth interweave, *The Calcutta Chromosome* deals with Ronald Ross's discovery of the malaria puzzle in Calcutta in 1889, computer applications, religious cults set against the background of nineteenth and twentieth century India. In "History and Anthropology in *The Calcutta Chromosome*," Shyam S. Agarwalla takes off from quotations from Clifford Geertz's revolutionary article entitled "History and Anthropology" and analyzes in detail the motifs that animate the plot of Amitav Ghosh's novel which joins history and anthropology to produce a fiction.

The blurb of *The Calcutta Chromosome* describes the book as "a medical thriller, a Victorian ghost story and a scientific quest." In his article "A Journey to the Unknown: A Quest for Immortality in *The Calcutta Chromosome*," Tapan K. Ghosh describes the novel as an experimental work that combines literature, science, philosophy and fantasy. It is a novel not only of 'fevers' and 'delirium' but also of discovery, although the object it discovers remains an alluring but elusive mystery. Amitav Ghosh casts the incidents of everyday life in a vortex of Gothic imagination that transforms and transplants them into a weird, uncanny and unfamiliar world.

In the novel, Ghosh approaches human affairs from unconventional points of view like anthropology, medical science, psychology, history and sociology, and has been able to discover a considerable body of information that furnishes the basis for a provisional understanding of human beings. In "*The Calcutta Chromosome*: A Literary Touchstone," Pradeep Trikha opines that the novel is likely to become a literary touchstone for its content and technique.

Postmodernism has been nomenclatured as a mood or a state of mind rather than a movement. In his article "*The Calcutta Chromosome*: A Postmodernist Text," Subhash Chandra approaches the novel through the prism of Postmodernism. He emphasizes the questioning attitude towards the obvious historical fixities and the dissolution of the temporal boundaries in *The Calcutta Chromosome*.

Amitav Ghosh employs in *The Calcutta Chromosome* the impressionistic technique of Henry James and Joseph Conrad where the emphasis is on the "showing" rather than on the "telling." In her brilliant article "Telling and Showing: The Cinematic Narrative Technique in *The Calcutta Chromosome*," Madhumalati Adhikari points out that in recent times, the penetration of the cinematic technique into literature has enabled the writer to manipulate the complex strands of story-line, his design and ideologies more expertly and satisfyingly than ever. In *The Calcutta Chromosome*, Amitav Ghosh uses different cinematic techniques to present the non-linear progression of three different strands of story-line.

VIII

Travel writing, broadly speaking, is of two types, real and fictional. The fictional travel is normally a product of the author's imagination, for instance William Golding's *Lord of the Files*. The other type relates to travel with a purpose. In this case, the traveller is a person who goes in quest of something—money, education or knowledge. Also, there are travellers with a purpose who are searching for their roots. For instance, V.S. Naipaul who undertakes a journey to India in his search for his roots in *An Area of Darkness*. Sometimes, a writer is imperceptibly drawn by the place he visits. In the Prologue to his travelogue *The Jaguar Smile*, Salman Rushdie writes: "I did not go to Nicaragua intending to write a book, or indeed, to write at all; but my encounter with the place affected me so deeply that in the end I had no choice."

Amitav Ghosh is a compulsive traveller: he is an anthropologist who studies life, art and culture as also social and political institutions of the places he visits. His recent publication *Dancing in Cambodia, At Large in Burma* is an excellent work of a socio-historical chronicler. It is a travel book that demonstrates the writer's perceptions about situation in Cambodia and Burma, both countries which practised the politics of extreme isolation in the recent past. Interestingly, the death of the deposed tyrant Pol Pot has aroused international commotion. It has led to many pertinent queries about Pol Pot's motives, his politics of social engineering and the milieu in which he perpetrated one of the worst genocides in the present century. An answer to such queries and an understanding of the factors which led to Pol Pot's politics of isolation are found in Amitav Ghosh's new book, a fascinating travelogue. It is an imaginative rendering of complex responses of a scholarly researcher and sensitive writer of the agonizing process of the evolving of a nation for two South Asian countries—Cambodia and Burma—in their postcolonial phase. In doing so, says D.K. Pabby, "Amitav Ghosh has presented, by implication, a prophetic vision for India in the context of the complex process of national reconstruction." Novy Kapadia in his article entitled "The Politics of Isolation and Resurgence" examines at length the scope and meaning of this book. It is not just another travelogue: it is an important political document that draws its raw material from history, sociology and politics.

Bibliography

Apana, A.B. *The Other Universe of Man: Travel, Biography and D.H. Lawrence*. New Delhi: Prestige, 1998.

Dhar, T.N. *History-Fiction Interface: Mulk Raj Anand, Nayantara Sahgal, Salman Rushdie, Shashi Tharoor and O.V. Vijayan*. New Delhi: Prestige, 1998.

Dhawan, R.K. "History and the Novel: Some Significant Statements in *Imaginary Homelands*," *The Novels of Salman Rushdie*, ed. G.R. Taneja and R.K. Dhawan. New Delhi: Prestige, 1990, 255-67.

Ghosh, Amitav. *The Circle of Reason*. New Delhi: Ravi Dayal, 1986.

______. *The Shadow Lines*. New Delhi: Ravi Dayal, 1988.

______. *In an Antique Land*. New Delhi: Ravi Dayal, 1992.

______. *The Calcutta Chromosome*. New Delhi: Ravi Dayal, 1996.

______. *Dancing in Cambodia, At Large in Burma*. New Delhi: Ravi Dayal, 1998.

______. "A Reporter at Large: India's Untold War of Independence," *The New Yorker*, The Fiction issue, June 23 and 30, 1997, pp. 104-21.

Rao, Parsa Venkateshwar, Jr. "Malarial Maze," *The Indian Express*, 7 April 1996, p. 4.

Singh, Khushwant. "Traveller in the Tortured Orient," *The Hindustan Times*, 16 May 1998.

Thapar, Karan. "Gentle and Subtle," *The Hindustan Times*, 31 May 1998.

Magic and Irony as Principles of Structure: A Reading of *The Circle of Reason*

K. DAMODAR RAO

Amitav Ghosh's first novel, *The Circle of Reason*,[1] marked a break from the traditional themes of the Indian English novel and the form and structure of the well-made novel. In fact, the novel could be taken as the starting point of a whole generation of new writers—often called Ghosh generation[2] or Stephanine school[3]—who have left a lasting imprint on the novel of the eighties setting the tenor for a new thrust in Indian fiction in English. These novelists who have published their first novels in the mid-eighties or early nineties have brought a new internationalism to their fiction, a contemporaneity to their outlook with a daring experimentation in form and structure while at the same time wiping out the linguistic barriers that inhibited the earlier novelists. This group includes Upamanyu Chatterjee, Shashi Tharoor, Allan Sealy, Amit Chaudhuri and Vikram Seth most of whom belong to the urban milieu. Firdaus Kanga, the author of *Trying to Grow* and *Heaven on Wheels*, while analyzing the progress of these writers, comments that the prospect of this new crop of writers making a distinct mark in world literary scene with their rich cultural heritage and language control is not a far-off proposition: "In fact, the two most promising fields for writing in English lie in India and South Africa. Both have the richness of two of the richest of cultures to draw from. Perhaps India has a slight edge over South Africa because of two things—the superb language control of Amitav Ghoshes and Vikram Seths and the inescapable tinge of South Africa's apartheid antecedents."[4] Binoo K. John views this new writing as a new 'literary Renaissance' and pays a glowing tribute to the novelists: "In the history of a country's literature such chapters are seldom written. And when most of it is in the language seemingly alien, the magnitude of the literary Renaissance becomes awe-inspiring. English it seems has finally become the language in which we will tell our stories to the world. And undoubtedly some Indian writers are blitzing their way to find their appointed slots among the galaxy of the immortals."[5] That this was not misplaced faith in the new writers was shown by the remarks offered by Makarand Paranjape in the course of his discussion of the Indian fiction scene in English in the eighties. He says that it is as if two generations of writers have come into their own this decade. With remarkable output and with such brilliant fictional creation behind them the new writers could compete with the best in the world, perhaps the best in their own right: "It would be no exaggeration to say that the best English fiction in the world is being written by Indians or those of Indian origin."[6] Euphoric as these may sound, the fact remains that these novelists have brought an "innovative energy and comic irreverence"[7] replacing the earlier earnestness and realism.

Postmodern fiction could be characterized by its reluctance to make use of psychological model. It no longer considers the penetration into the depths of the characters as the primary goal of fiction and in fact reduces the characters and events to the level of structural strategies. Reality is presented in its mutation and each fragmented part is invested with hyperbolic dimensions: a strategy that resembles the genius of a painter much different from the skills of a photographer. The immediacy of experience of the reality is conveyed/brought to the readers by a medley of devices: ironic mode of narration, recreating a magical world, and an uninhibited exhibition of narcissistic tendencies. This propensity for metafiction urges the reader's attention to its own techniques and processes of creation; the story-telling ability gains control over the subject it handles. It is natural that such a narration should thrive on bizarre happenings and out of world events since, for the narrator, reality itself is surrealistic and defies description. Gabriel Garcia Marquez, Milan Kundera, Thomas Pynchon and Salman Rushdie have all created this magic web of fantasy to capture reality in their novels.

In *The Circle of Reason*, the attempts of the novelist are obviously oriented to floating the events and characters through a medley of metaphors and select ideas. The all-embracing structural principles of magic and irony eloquently 'weave' the total pattern of the novel and ideas, characters and metaphors are explicated through attendant motifs. In fact, the characters themselves are converted into possible metaphors. Their quest is for a specific structuring of their entity in the totality of experience however trivial and absurd it is. The characters achieve this appropriation of their significance through their creative/manipulative capabilities while the novelist himself realizes this through magic and irony and by diverting some of his story-telling abilities to the characters. As the novel progresses from '*Sattva*: Reason' through '*Rajas*: Passion' to '*Tamas*: Death,' it becomes increasingly clear that Alu, the governing metaphor, comes alive only in the company of other live images and other active, associative metaphors/contexts. The novel, as it turns out, is as much a story of Balaram, his idealism and tragic end, as that of Zindi, her pragmatic outlook and her irrepressible instinct for survival. And there are many stories narrated by master story-tellers who thrive on and live by their story-telling abilities. The other associative structural principles of weaving, sewing and the book, *Life of Pasteur* act as catalysts in their attempts at defining, redefining and grafting their outlook as they move from one stage to another and from one place to another in a seemingly endless quest for their significance despite having gone through the trivialities time and again. In the endless monotony of life, the characters find their saving grace in their creative capabilities of narration which is what the novel is about. They use their powers like the magic wand of a sorcerer to conjure up weird things even as they fiercely attempt to grapple with reality.

The novel abounds in weird happenings. These, in turn, spark off a series of stories as told and retold by the characters with unusual relish. The narrator's own description acquires ritualistic connotations in tune with his characters' propensity to mix fact with fantasy. Six months after Alu reaches al-Ghazira, he finds himself buried in the collapse of an immense building called an-Najma, the Star. When it fell, 'it was an avalanche of thousands and thousands of tons of bricks and concrete and cement' (193) and Alu was almost exactly in its centre. The weird happening is described in a prose that is incantatory, deliberately attempted to invoke the impossibility of the happening without losing the immediacy of its experience:

> People said later that the fall shook the whole of al-Ghazira, like an emptying wave shakes a boat. A tornado of dust swirled out of the debris while the rubble was still shuddering and heaving like a labouring beast and for a few moments the whole city was wrapped in the darkness, despite the full mid-afternoon brilliance of the desert sun. (193)

The survival of Alu despite the might of the inanimate cement and bricks is indicative of the victory of creative mind over ruthless mechanisms. The far-off Middle East country, al-Ghazira, is one such mechanism. The cut-throat business interests of the place were already hinted at when Alu lay huddled in a heap in the lap of Zindi aboard 'Mariamma' and observes the lights of al-Ghazira in the distance. The description of the artificial glitter of 'the whims of capital' (189) and its exploitative mechanism is invested with human skills, a metaphor for mercantile activity.

The fall, the debris and the subsequent survival of Alu are sufficient to spark off a series of stories in the Ras. Speculation runs high in the locality and a sense of relief is experienced in telling stories and experiencing them even while they wait for the arrival of Alu. When Hajji Fahmy narrates the story of Nuri the Damanhour he could command a captive audience. Abu Fahl is good at narrating real life experiences with a tinge of magical note. When he first visits Alu beneath the rubble and returns home he too commands an enthralled audience as he starts narrating how he had seen Alu alive beneath the rubble and how two sewing machines had saved his life. Later, on another occasion, when he was attacked by the labour contractors they were brought before Hajji Fahmy to pronounce judgement; Abu Fahl relishes the prospect of narrating the whole incident to an attentive audience. He was more interested in the very act of narration rather than the justice he was entitled to. But it was Zindi who was the master story-teller with her superior powers of narration. She knows her abilities and commands a sure audience even if she repeats the same story any number of times. On hearing the news of Alu's fall she gets ready to tell the story of misfortunes that befell Frowning Abusa and Mast Ram, the inmates of her house, before Alu and others had arrived. The audience, as usual are even more prepared to listen to Zindi yet again. The scene of Zindi holding centre-stage like a presiding deity by her powers of narration is brought in ritualistic terms:

> They crouched on mats around Zindi, listening intently to every word. They had lived through everything Zindi spoke of and had heard her talk of it time and time again: yet it was only in her telling that it took shape; changed from mere incidents to a palpable thing, a block of time which was not hours or minutes or days, but something corporeal, with its own malevolent wilfulness. That was Zindi's power: she could bring together empty air and give it a body just by talking of it. (212-13)

If their creative abilities form one side of their being, their strange obsessions complete the circle. The clearly marked out attitudes are not only indicative of their search for a pattern but even make them conveyors of ideas. Balaram at Lalpukur is obsessed with phrenology and carbolic acid; Toru-Debi, wife of Balaram, is always preoccupied with the world of sewing machines; Alu with weaving; Jyoti Das, the only character to have accompanied Alu through the three parts apart from the structural entities, is called a Bird Man; Zindi herself is obsessed with Durban Tailoring House; and Professor Samuel with theories of queues.

Alu's initiation into the world of weaving is to be viewed as much an act of admiration for the pristine simplicity and creativity of Shombhu Debnath and his daughter, Maya, as a refusal of Balaram's idealism, if not his values. The loom functions as a viable metaphor for Alu's longing for Maya and his mastery over the subtle patterns of weaving including the intricate jamdhani pattern coincides with his winning over the love of Maya which is described in physical and psychological terms. The description of the creative surge of weaving once again defies words and assumes magical incantation:

> So many words, so many things. On a loom a beam's name changes after every inch. Why? Every nail has a name, every twist of rope, every little eyelet, everything of bamboo on the heddle. A loom is a dictionary glossary thesaurus. Why? Words serve no purpose; nothing mechanical. No, it's because the weaver, in making cloth, makes words, too, and trespassing on the territory of the poets gives names to things the eye can't see. That is why the loom has given language more words, more metaphor, more idiom than all the world's armies of pen-wielders. (74)

Alu's search for a new technique on the loom is reflective of his own search for his moorings. The ironic mode of description employed in this context with peculiar intones of different categories drawn from the objective world serves to underline the delicate 'buti work' Alu, of late, has mastered. Initially the patterns were sought to be made in the mould of different experiential realities—Bomb-buti, Refugees-buti and antiseptic-buti—but are found wanting and hence rejected. Ultimately, Alu settles for 'Maya-buti.' This passion for weaving remains with him for the rest of his life long after the house of Balaram goes up in flames in which Balaram, Toru-Debi and Maya are supposed to have lost their lives. In al-Ghazira his constant indulgence in weaving compensates for his silence for, the tons and tons of bales he creates speak eloquently on his behalf.

Carbolic acid, functioning as structural dimension and a metaphor, runs through the novel like a cleansing mechanism. Balaram uses it as an effective disinfectant to keep the settlements of the refugees clean and free from dirt, disease and death. It also works as a psychological therapy, as a means of awakening the dormant villagers against the repressive suffocation unleashed by the village strong-man, Bhudeb Roy. Balaram keeps a constant vigil on the drums of carbolic acid which was taken as an act of sedition and extremist activity and hence the police raid. Alu carries on his uncle's mission of cleanliness and introduces it in al-Ghazira with renewed vigour. Even there, they were chased for their gospel of physical and psychological purity. In '*Tamas:* Death,' in the little town of El Oued on the north-eastern edge of the Algerian Sahara, carbolic acid is converted into Ganga-jal to purify the corpse of Kulfi. "The world has come full circle," wonders Dr. Mishra in the small desert town.

Sewing machines were initially the passion of Toru-Debi. Her flexible attitude in tune with her passion, is shown in her attempts to bring rapprochment between the rival families. She goes to Bhudeb Roy's house and promises Parboti-Debi seven blouses. Later when Parboti-Debi elopes with Shombhu Debnath and takes shelter in their house, she sees that the end was very near. She could see that Parboti-Debi herself has dealt a mortal blow to the bloated ego of Bhudeb Roy and her fears about the imminent attack by him are expressed in the shrouded caution given to Alu: "Can't you see how serious it is? He's coming and it'll be the end of everything if the blouses aren't ready. Only the sewing machine can save us now. Whatever happens, I'll never let your uncle say that it was because of the blouses." (136)

The sewing machines indeed save the life of Alu when he falls beneath the rubble of the Star. Two sewing machines take away the impact of the fall. Zindi's passion for Durban Tailoring House is necessitated by the need to find an alternative source of income as most of the inmates of her house begin to spend their time at Hajji Fahmy's place carrying out the message given by Alu in letter and spirit. She fails to get the Durban Tailoring House for herself but her instinct for survival is proved right when the law-enforcing authorities pounce on the Ras people about to go on a shopping spree. Even Jyoti Das is drawn to the sewing machines and announces that Alu would find good ones back home.

Life of Pasteur has everything in it associated with Balaram and his rational outlook. Balaram considers Pasteur his model and shapes his life since childhood with scientific temper and rationalistic outlook. But the intrinsic contradiction between the internal and external realities throws his plans out of gear on many an occasion. His one ambition in his childhood was to study science and emulate the great masters of science, Pasteur and Jagadish Bose. But his teachers at Dhaka decide that he was good for the study of history and guide him accordingly to Dr. Radhakrishnan, the teacher of philosophy at Presidency College. His favourite pastime, the study of heads, often lands him in trouble but he does not give it up. With his uncompromising stand, he slowly gains control over the Rationalists at the Presidency by weaning it away from Gopal who, of course, was to remain his life-long friend. When he was about to make a point regarding the Rationalists for the first time in the college, Gopal's sense of foreboding warns him that he was a man who could bring disaster to anyone he is associated with: "As he watched Balaram go, Gopal had a premonition: a premonition of the disaster he would call upon himself and all of them, if ever he is allowed to take charge of the society. He decided then, with an uncharacteristic determination, that he would do everything in his power to keep that from happening." (50 His wife also could see that and sets fire to all his books. Alu could retrieve only one book from the flames, *Life of Pasteur*. Balaram's choice of carbolic acid itself has an interesting story. He could have gone for other brands as well but for the fact that they were created by the 'Great Adversary, Robert Koch, who had so tenaciously and falsely opposed Pasteur's 'and is hence drawn to carbolic acid because it was the 'masterly brain-child of Lister's, Pasteur's friend and Great Disciple.' (61)

Inspired by the biography, Balaram starts a school in his village called 'The School of Reason.' He takes it as an ultimate test to his long-cherished beliefs. Even the normally hostile Toru-Debi consents to train the students in sewing and Shombhu Debnath in weaving. For once, their respective obsessions are turned into instruments of supporting education but soon the conflict between Bhudeb Roy and Balaram reaches a crisis-point. Yet again *Life of Pasteur* survives the crisis and with Alu it starts its journey to al-Ghazira. It proves its utility even aboard 'Mariamma' as one of its pages is used by Prof. Samuel to save the life of Karthamma. Once again in '*Tamas*: Death' the book is found in the house of Mrs. Verma, the daughter of Hem Narain Mathur, Balaram's friend and class-mate at the Presidency. Having found no use in its practical utility Alu offers it to the pyre of Kulfi.

The journey as a motif runs throughout the novel and unites its three parts. Characters cross borders "with almost the biological necessity if not always the ease and nonchalance of migratory birds."[8] This motif is particularly associated with Alu who is on the run having been branded an extremist by the police and with Jyoti Das close on his heels always. He moves from Lalpukur to Kerala and then sets off to al-Ghazira in the Middle East along with a number of characters who travel in search of material wealth and more opportunities. Travel itself is converted into a homeland. For Jyoti Das, more than the professional obligations, it was the prospect of seeing more birds on his travels that urges him to move on in his pursuit of Alu. Ironically it was he who causes the journey of Alu once again from al-Ghazira through Alexandria, Egypt, Lisbon, Tunis to the little town of El Oued. He is accompanied by Zindi, Boss and Kulfi, and whenever Zindi says 'We're going West where the sewing machines are' Jyoti Das seems to overhear them for he appears wherever they go. But by this time Jyoti Das is suspended from his service for his sneaking sympathies with the man whom he chases and now he lands even in El Oued to see more birds, rare vultures and atone for previous lapses. But ironically he is viewed as a vulture by Zindi for, she says, he seems to bring death wherever he goes: "That man carries death with him wherever he goes. He can't help it; it's in his eyes. Think of what happened to Jeevanbhai; think of Karthamma and the rest. And this time he's come with a vulture." (393) All alone in the desert, 'terrified of the future, without a past, aware of the prickings of his painful virginal flesh,' (407) Jyoti Das is enchanted by Kulfi but even as he starts wooing her when they rehearse for the dance drama, 'Chitrangada,' Kulfi dies of heart attack. The sense of foreboding of Zindi is proved right once again. Having nothing to fall back in India he sets off to Dusseldorf in Germany to stay with his engineer uncle. When he is informed that Alu and Zindi were moving to Tangier on their way back home he could visualize a sky beaming with different birds over Tangier: a sky alive with "Cory's shearwaters and honey buzzards, white storks and steppe eagles." (421) He takes the permission of the suspecting Zindi to accompany them upto Tangier: "I'm migrating myself—to Dusseldorf. I've got nowhere else to go. Can I come with you, too." (421) While for Jyoti Das his past and future were "continents of defeat—defeat at home, defeat in the world" for Alu the world has come full circle as he settles down to wait for Virat Singh and the ship that would carry them home; despite his hopeful travels on previous occasions, for him, "Hope is the beginning" yet again even at the end of the story.

NOTES

1. Amitav Ghosh, *The Circle of Reason* (New Delhi: Roli Books International, 1986).
2. Rukun Advani, "Novelists in Residence," *Seminar*, 384 (August 1991), p. 16.
3. Harish Trivedi, "The St. Stephen's Factor," *Indian Literature*, no. 145 (Sept.-Oct. 1991), pp. 183-87.
4. Firdaus Kanga, "Three Viewpoints," *Indian Review of Books*, vol. 2, no. 4 (Jan. 16-Feb. 15, 1993), p. 25.
5. Binoo K. John, "A Glorious Chapter," *Indian Express* (Sunday magazine), August 2, 1992, p. 1.
6. Makarand Paranjape, "Indian Fiction in English—A Good Time to be a Writer, But . . . ," *Indian Review of Books*, vol. 2, no. 1 (October 1992), pp. 21-22.
7. Meenakshi Mukherjee, "The New Writers: Short Fiction to the Fore," *Indian Review of Books*, vol. 2, no. 1 (Oct. 1992), p. 24.
8. G.J.V. Prasad, "Really Imagined," *Seminar*, 384 (August 1991), p. 23.

A Voice among Bullet Holes: *The Circle of Reason*

PRADIP DUTTA

Sometimes from a double-decker bus you could see a whole refugee bustee encircled by gun-totting C.R.P. uniforms. Distant cries could be heard, but only vaguely, as they shaded into the hard pop music reccohetting off dangling transistor sets. It was simply another day in Calcutta of the early 70s. There were also evenings when your elders told you of *sonar bangla* of a wealth of fish and land which dissolved in the nightmare of riots, war and exile. And the story continues, unfolding in everyday sights and headlines: the Nellie massacre, burnt houses which once belonged to Sikhs in Delhi, labour contractors leading a flock of rural poor from Orissa to Kashmir, proposals for a boundary wall on the Bangladesh border. . . . The history of our subcontinent, especially of its northern part, has never been able to take its continuities and culture for granted. A life of constant movement and violence has incessantly serrated our roots.

It is not often that we choose to acknowledge the restlessness of our lives. When we do, as in Attia Hosain's *Sunlight on a Broken Column* it is seen simply, as a dislocation from settled childhood. Amitav Ghosh's *The Circle of Reason* presents a much more challenging appreciation. It combines within itself an uncompromising restlessness with a poise and control that suggests peace rather than longing. This is remarkable, for really *The Circle* offers nothing which we would normally call home. Initially located in a refugee village, the story refers back to Bangladesh and Calcutta, finally moving to the Middle East via Kerala where it reaches its denouement in a desert of shifting sand-dunes. And all the while it travels through environments which are never entirely rural or urban. Nor do its ideas provide a stable attitude. Each idea evolves from the story, posing a challenge to the preceding and is itself qualified by a succeeding understanding. Even a basic element like Time is not uniformly patterned. *The Circle* is an epic of restlessness. And yet, the calm. . . .

Science, philosophy, history, politics, culture, art, language, the joy of living, the despair of repeated loss—these are only some of the strands which make the scope of this novel fairly formidable. And like a conjurer, its restless energy provides at each moment and at all levels, a fresh disclosure. The love of the story, for instance. The novel provides not one, but many stories, each equally appealing and important. Basically there are three stories knitted around three characters. The first part unfolds the story of Balaram, a nationalist entranced by the *Life of Pasteur*. His obsessive idealism leads him to treat people as objects, either of observation or of change; a trait which makes him self-destructive as he gets entangled with his alter ego, Bhudeb, a Congressman, who though motivated by cynical considerations looks at people in the same way as Balaram. The second part revolves around Zindi, the earthy, practical, zestful trader whose presence brings together a community of Indians in the Middle East. The second part moves forward through Alu, the nephew and only survivor of Balaram's family. He brings his community to death and destruction by his attempts to create a co-operative community which tries to dispense with money and trade. Finally, the third part structures itself around Mrs. Verma, who in defiance of all rational scepticism, creates in the desert an oasis of Indian community life. The novel, however, moves on as Alu, Zindi and Jyoti Das (a police officer who tracks Alu from the first part, having taken him for an extremist) finally leave Mr. Verma and the desert, bound for destinations which are to be discovered through hope. The main source of continuity is the story of Alu and Das, which is structured on the thriller format, and talks of a relationship which, being based on officialdom and oppressive power, cannot acknowledge its human connections.

A large part of the pleasure in reading this novel is the immense fertility and zest with which it tells stories. Around the bare outlines of the plot which moves over continents, are clustered an infinite number of stories ranging back and forth in time. *The Circle* is specifically a contemporary work. One of the main sources of the freshness of writers like Marquez and Llosa is their genius for story-telling, a facility that has created new possibilities for the novel, while making serious reading a pleasurable, accessible and popular experience again.

The way Ghosh tells stories, makes story-telling itself a way of looking at the world. By letting his stories interplay with time for instance, Ghosh achieves a fairly original synthesis of two different concepts of time. Generally novelists tend to stick either to a chronological narrative or dissolve time into a kind of duration where past and present are indistinguishable. Ghosh chooses to engage in a different, more subtle adventure. The novel starts in the past with Balaram's excitement at exploring the shape of Alu's skull, moves further back in time to Balaram with his friends, all in their mid-thirties, returns to Balaram's relationship with Alu, moves forward to the present with Inspector Das interviewing Gopal, a friend of Balaram and then slips back to the beginnings of Balaram's life and career in Presidency College. Each story unfolds in linear time. Much like the phrases in a *raga*, each maintains its distinctiveness. And like a *raga*, the theme and concerns of the novelist weave them together in a single flowing texture. Each story, whether it moves backwards or forwards in time, continues and explicates the previous one. The final experience is an extraordinary achievement in which past and present coexist while constantly asserting their difference.

But Ghosh does not rest here. In fact *The Circle* does not have a single conception of time. Or rather, it explores the many possibilities offered by its general idea of time. In the second section Ghosh traces a different relationship between the past and present. This shift has nothing gratuitous about it, for the difference flows from the thematic design. In keeping with the tone of vibrant and spontaneous involvement with living (exemplified in Zindi), the distinction between the past and present is emphasized in the second part. While offering the Damanhouri story as a possible interpretation of the star episode, Abu Fahl never loses sight of the fact that the tale he tells is from the past. On the other hand, precisely because the first part is built around Balaram who belongs to the past, the aspect of co-existing time dominates to bring this whole section close to the structure of memory.

The story does not stop even here. A delicate network weaves connections between different phenomena, and removes any claim to absolute autonomy which they may generate. While the overall design patterns time, in its turn the arrangement of time moulds history. *The Circle* presents history as a collective memory embodying a symbiotic relationship between past and present. The past, a reference point for understanding what is happening now, is equally dependent on the present which determines how we look at it. Dantu, Balaram's friend, a secondary character in the first part, surfaces again as Hem Narain Mathur, a crucial presence in the third section, for the immediate concerns of this part demand a greater attention to his history. The mobility with which history traverses past and present is indeed due to the fluid pattern of time; yet time, with the poise and flavour of oral recapitulation coupled with chronological references, never lets us forget that history is situated in the past.

The perception of history evolves from the novel, and Ghosh never attempts to bulldoze history into some other preoccupation. History retains its historicity, as a process which hinges on characters who are representative of important historical tendencies—whether it is Balaram the idealist bhadralok, or Bhudeb the lumpen Congressman who unnervingly talks of mass media and straight lines, or even Damanhouri the one-eyed fantasy of the fledgling bourgeoisie. What does happen however, is that history is refracted through different mediums: in the first part through ideas on science and change, and in the second section, through the Damanhouri story, as a narrative from which earthy lessons are to be drawn. The difference in historical understanding corresponds to the distinction between an intellectually cosmopolitan culture and a more rural one. Being memory, history is fashioned by the way people collectively look at their inheritance. It is subject to culture.

What we have here is a novel that organizes by exploring connections, distinctions and possibilities, rather than putting everything together in a symmetrical design. Each aspect of *The Circle* is gathered into a process of constant change. And despite its formidable array of interests, it never stumbles into chaos. Everything is seen in relationship, both internally and with other areas, being dependent finally on the way the novelist looks at life. The balance *The Circle* achieves through this, creates also an original possibility for the novel itself. By disallowing absolutes, Ghosh is able to break free from the constraints of conventional realism. At the same time, because of the ability to acknowledge the separateness of each area marks many a modernist novel. *The Circle* flourishes in the new space opened up by writers like Marquez, where the style organizes by synthesizing collectively acknowledged categories of reality with the logic and metaphors of the artist's imagination.

But it is not enough to say that Ghosh follows in the wake of these writers. His novel also creates a new style, one which is less lyricized, more responsive to the specificity and multifacetedness of experiene while evincing a constant intellectual curiosity about the life it unfolds. It is this style which provides a rest in the swirling restlessness and violence that pervade the theme and action of the novel for above all, what *The Circle* seems to say is that if there is a home, then it is to be found in the way we perceive and relate to our world. The calm that is affirmed here has within it a great deal of humanism, for through it *The Circle* is able to avoid the obsession with fragmentation and helplessness that has gripped so much of western art.

Equally important is its immediate relevance. The novel has made its appearance at a time when our country seems to be headed towards one of the goriest chapters of its restless existence. Already the battle lines are being drawn. On one hand the discontinuities within our heritage are increasingly being interpreted as negation of any linkages within that tradition. On the other hand the dominant tradition is coming to regard itself as the only legitimate source of our complex culture. The alternatives recall the memory of two terrible possibilities: 1947 and Biafra. The importance of *The Circle* lies in living another process, one which suggests that any relationship must rest on a dynamic and sensitive grappling with similarities and differences and to acknowledge this, given our immediate challenges, would be to explore and create the wholeness immeasurably richer than any narrow nationalist cliche.

Ultimately of course, the seriousness of Ghosh's understanding springs from the fact that it is not easily acquired. *The Circle* takes a lot of beating, tracing a repeated pattern of achievement and loss. In all three parts the novel finds patches of settled community life. Each part is a tale of attempts to better society, efforts (except with qualifications, the law section) which flame into destruction and exile. Yet the novel does not slip into cynicism. The way it looks at its stories ensures that the urge to mould a better life remains undefeated. The style of *The Circle*, the location of its 'home,' also gives it hope.

This hope is important for *The Circle* leads us into a universe which is spectacularly destructive. Even a suicide burns down fifty houses. And Ghosh never lets us find comfort in categorizing these events as 'literary' metaphors. Metaphoric they may be, but then the whole novel *lives* this large, metaphoric existence. The characters too—whether it is Balaram with his carbolic acid, or Zindi frantically trying to buy a shop—becomes metaphoric by the sheer intensity of their obsessions. The metaphor then is not a matter of presentation; it articulates the urgency which the vulnerability of human understanding and life generate in the novel. The fate of whole cultures is involved. The flames of the known world which Alu looks on at the end of part one, are also the flames of positivism which have dominated not merely western but a great deal of international thought. The importance of the issues involved make the metaphors in *The Circle* a grim prophecy.

However, the novel is too assertive of life to make the kind of statement which says that the fate of humanity is inevitable. Its prophecy warns rather than dictates. By displaying life lived at its fullest, it always communicates a sense of alternate possibilities. And in an age that has got accustomed to the prospect of annihilation, this is no small achievement. Nor is it easy to grasp the centrality of human choice, which itself assumes that in any given situation many choices are possible. It liberates the relentless logic of Balaram's actions from any sense of fatalism, and makes it a humanist protest against the myopia of idealistic convictions. For Balaram's inhumanity is inherent in the way he looks at people. By denying people their status as living beings, Balaram has already courted death. Yet the intensity of Balaram's belief and the love with which Ghosh draws his character, makes the cruelty of his destructive absurdities seem directed more at himself, than at others. The novel speaks again of the old tragic anguish, of the fullness of human life and the blindness that destroys it. But then *The Circle* is also an epic novel. Though Balaram's death may be an important moment, it is, after all, only a moment in the course of the novel. Unlike Golding and a host of western authors, Ghosh is able to avoid fetishizing destruction. It is not death which gives meaning to life. On the contrary, by showing life as a journey larger than death, *The Circle* makes death find its identity in the horror and sadness which embalms this process.

The vision of life as a process transforms the restless world of the novel. Restlessness loses its meaning as displacement or instability. It becomes, in Ghosh's hands, a dynamic urge to find a complete relationship with the rich diversity of our world, which is achieved in the organization of the novel. The position, however, can never be final, for by acknowledging the supremacy of life, it has to subject itself to the rush of experience. The world of cotton-weaving, for instance, is initially projected as an alternate ethos to Balaram's universe epitomized in phrenology. Cotton brings together language, art, work, love, giving its practitioners a lively connection with the world. And yet it is pathetic, for the world to which it belonged is gone. Unable to comprehend the new violent world, the language of Jamdani is torn by commerce and destruction until all that is left is Alu's ten fingers to serve as a reminder of what was possible, and a hope that this possibility would be the basis of a fresh, comprehensive language.

The many achievements of the novel make the last part somewhat disappointing. It fails to live the earlier fullness of experience. There is something forced here; the meticulous detail with which the deserts of Arabia are Indianized gives the feeling that a thesis is being imported. In any case, in the light of what had been done, is the search for an obvious resolution necessary? True, the novel leaves Mrs. Verma behind. But the fact remains that she is not questioned at all. By centering the last section on a clear-cut confrontation between Dr. Mishra, the cynical nationalist, and Mrs. Verma, the organic innovator, Ghosh seems to deliberately schematize the structure, so that Mrs. Verma is glorified at the expense of her rival. It is not then as if Mrs. Verma's life is simply one of the many possibilities offered in the novel. It has a larger significance, one that is made to hold hopes of regeneration.

The seriousness of Mrs. Verma's depiction poses serious problems for the approach to the novel. Shadowing her portrait is a danger and a silence, that vitiates much of the wholeness of the novel. The danger lies in the way Mrs. Verma self-consciously creates an oasis of Hindu culture. In a multi-religious and multi-cultural country like ours, this does seem a brittle short-cut to home. For while the obvious point is that religion cannot be completely severed from a culture, the equally important and more interesting problem is to approach the process evolving from the relationship between different cultures. Continuities must be found in the present, and not only recovered from the past. Otherwise Mrs. Verma's efforts—especially at a time when communalism beckons threateningly—can easily be construed as an expression of Hindu zeal. More so, because it leaves a silent space which can only be filled by the denseness of uncritical belief. This area is formed by the tangential view of social change. Mrs. Verma's idea of change rests on a personal recovery of tradition, rather than on making society as a whole more human, a problem which was raised through both Balaram and Alu. Their answers may have been flawed, but the questions they raised, remain. What does one do with the cynicism of Bhudeb, or the inhuman onrush of colonialism shown so vividly in the Damanhouri story? No doubt Ghosh has made an effort to tackle the problem through the figure of Hem Mathur. But the thematic relationship between Mrs. Verma and her Lohatie father does not seem convincing; nor does the celebration of Mathur, whose qualities concern personal integrity and proximity to the oppressed, fully challenge the problem.

However, it is not as if the third section denies altogether the possibilities created in the preceding portion. Ghosh is far too talented a writer to leave us with less than an ambiguous effect, even at his weakest. Despite the liveliness, intelligence, poignancy and zest for affirmation of the third part, the problem remains serious precisely because of the importance of the novel as a whole. And they are not problems with easy solutions, for they have yet to be resolved by our understanding, action and process of living. In brief it is this: the problem of human survival has become dependent on finding the connection between a full conception of relationship and of social change. The problems of our country are also what we share with the rest of the world. For the growing internationalization of the world has, by throwing different cultures and societies together, emphasized their distinctions. How can we prevent these distinctions from becoming antagonistic to a point of no return? And can this be done by simply appreciating distinctions, or does it need a different social perception, which proceeds not by exclusion, but dialectically? *The Circle* provides a direction, a hope and a problem. Need we expect more from a work of art?

Some Recent Trends in Modern Indian Fiction: A Study of Shashi Deshpande's *That Long Silence*, Shashi Tharoor's *The Great Indian Novel* and Amitav Ghosh's *The Shadow Lines*

SHAKUNTALA BHARVANI

The last decade has yielded an abundant harvest in the field of fiction. Expatriate writers, Bharati Mukherjee, Gita Mehta, Ruth Prawer Jhabvala and Rohinton Mistry, too, have been in the limelight; to this list may be added the names of Anita Desai and Nayantara Sahgal, who live in India but have greater appeal to the sophisticated Westernized reader. But it is not possible to discuss so many writers in an overview so limited, thus I will concentrate on theme, language and innovative technique in three recent Indian novels in English: Shashi Deshpande's *That Long Silence*,[1] Shashi Tharoor's *The Great Indian Novel*[2] and Amitav Ghosh's *The Shadow Lines*.[3]

I

Shashi Deshpande's achievement lies in the depiction of her central character, the introspective and inward probing Jaya. She is representative of girls brought up in middle-class families in post-Independent India, a time when most parents strove hard to provide their children with English education and exposure to Western modes of living and thinking. Parents inculcated in their girls a certain duality, sometimes quite unconsciously: on the one hand an impulsive desire to be emancipated and liberated, and on the other, an almost instinctive urge to be traditional and conservative. The woman of today, therefore, speaking in the language of psychology, has a near-schizophrenic personality: one side staidly "accepts" while the other craves to "speak," to think and express the life of the mind. *That Long Silence* presents

Jaya caught in this dilemma: first, trying to be a fit wife to her husband and secondly, struggling to express the kind of emotions women experience, but seldom express in a male-dominated chauvinistic society.

This is not to state categorically that Deshpande is a militant feminist; her work merely reflects the resulting turmoil and vexation. As she herself states: "Innermost feelings come out in my writings. The kind of emotions we know women have but never come out."[4]

The smooth course of Jaya's existence has been disrupted due to her husband's business problems. He moves into an unfashionable Bombay apartment in Dadar relinquishing all company perks. Jaya finds herself free from the round of high-order entertainment. She ponders on her far from successful writing career and her past memories. In the process of doing this she probes inward, thus emerging from her long moments of silence.

The novel is difficult to read as several characters appear and disappear and seem to serve no ostensible purpose. Statements such as, "Deshpande's style needs a lot more exercising and experimentation" and "The plot, too, would be better structured if some of the fringe characters were left out"[5] are valid criticisms. This is the case, too, with Deshpande's earlier novel *Roots and Shadows*, where even a family tree on the introductory page does not really make for a clearer concept of the novel. But Deshpande's convincing portrait of Jaya, with her veneer of middle-class respectability, is commendable. The questions that haunt her, for example, would never haunt a woman from the sophisticated razzle-dazzle jet-set in which divorce and free love are the in-thing; but they certainly bother Jaya who is brought up to regard even film and pop-music as frivolous. I quote a few lines from the last few pages to illustrate the quality of Jaya's thinking:

> What have I achieved by this writing? The thought occurs to me again as I look at the neat pile of papers. Well, I've achieved this. I'm not afraid any more. The panic has gone. I'm Mohan's wife, I had thought, and cut off the bits of me that had refused to be Mohan's wife. Now I know that kind of a fragmentation is not possible. (191)
>
> While studying Sanskrit drama, I'd learnt with a sense of outrage that its rigid rules did not permit women characters to speak Sanskrit. They had to use Prakrit—a language that had sounded to my ears like a baby's lisp. The anger I'd felt then comes back to me when I realize what I've been doing all these years. I have been speaking Prakrit myself. (192-93)

Virginia Woolf's Mrs. Dalloway or Anita Brookner's heroines could not have been more eloquent on the imbalance in such human relationships.

Though Deshpande's work has not created waves, it certainly needs to be taken note of. Born in Dharwar in Karnataka, she is the daughter of the Kannada playwright and Sanskrit critic, Shriranga. She lives in Bangalore, has two children and her husband is a pathologist. Her earlier four novels are: *Roots and Shadows* which was judged the best novel of 1982-83, *The Dark Holds No Terrors* and two detective novels *If I Die Today* and *Come Up and Be Dead.* At prĕsent she is working on a script for Govind Nihalani on man-woman relationships, for which Kishori Amonkar will set the music. *Roots and Shadows* is also being screened by director Prema Karnath.

II

Shashi Tharoor in *The Great Indian Novel*, with superb verve, vivacity and a style eminently readable, adapts the *Mahabharata* story to project the recent political history of India. The ancient epic is retold not by the rishi Vyasa of old but by the venerable and cantankerous politician saint Ved Vyasji to Ganapathi (the scribe, amanuensis and silent bystander). For those familiar with Rajagopalachari's *Mahabharata*, it is necessary only to read the first few pages to realize that Tharoor's is a masterful parody amounting to "a comic epic in prose" which is grotesque and even offensive in parts.

It is little difficult to understand the traditional Indian psyche without understanding our great epic. The Kauravas and Pandavas are archetypal figures, and their experiences are possible patterns of a universal nature. They are relevant today, and refresh our memory at each stage. This is exactly what *The Great Indian Novel* succeeds in doing.

Like Gita Mehta's recent novel *Raj* it is certainly historical, but it is much more. Like Golding's *Lord of the Files*, it is sociological and satirical as well, for it describes history and society of the India of Mahaguru Gangaji, who presents of course, Mahatma Gandhi. The struggle for Independence, the practice of non-violence and satyagraha, the indigo-march, Nehru and "Priya Duryodhani" are part of the scene. Most of the characters are ludicrous, thinly-veiled historical figures, but the identity of several is chameleon-like and shadow-vague. The presentation of the historical ethos of this period is credible and naturally so, for after graduating from St. Stephen's College, Delhi, Tharoor took a doctorate from the Fletcher School of Law and Diplomacy at Tufts University, USA. Since May 1978, he has worked in Geneva and Singapore for the United Nations High Commissioner for Refugees.

Shashi Tharoor's novel is written in pristine Queen's English with an almost Wodehousian tongue-in-cheek manner. The first 100 pages take the reader by surprise at Tharoor's audacity and extremely cavalier attitude to the *Mahabharata* story and his grossly cynical-critical attitude to Indian life and politics. After this, interest wanes as the analogy is stretched and far-fetched. But is it Tharoor's style which reminds the reader how far ahead the Indian novel in English has progressed. A polished sophisticated elegance of a man about town who is Indian in sensibility—and totally at home with words he can mould and bend at will—this is the most distinctive achievement of Tharoor's *The Great Indian Novel.* I quote one example: "But you see, I'm getting ahead of my story again, Ganapathi. You mustn't let me. I haven't yet told you about Kunti, Pandu's faithfully infidelous wife, and how she fulfilled her husband's extraordinary request for progeny." (86)

III

The Shadow Lines by Amitav Ghosh is a remarkable novel by any standards as it transcends the narrow categorization of an Indian novel. The story centres around Tridib, the narrator's uncle. No less vivid and memorable are the portraits of the narrator's grandmother, his cousin Ila and the English girl May Price. The novel creates a wonderful scene of relationships—uncles and aunts are interspersed easily and without any confusion in the course of the narrative, as are also different locations—Calcutta, Dacca, London. We learn that Tridib was born in 1932, had been to England with his parents in 1939, where his father, an important diplomat in the Foreign Service, had received medical treatment. May Price (with whose family they shared a close relationship) had begun a long correspondence with Tridib in 1959. Tridib died in a riot in 1964, while May was on a visit to India.

It is not, however, such events that make up the vital texture of the novel: we are made aware of them only incidentally. What holds our attention is the delicate thread out of which the narrator creates a larger-than-life portrait of Tridib, who used his imagination not to fantasize but to expand his sense of meaning and erase the narrow barriers of lines and partitions. The narrator fondly reminisces: "Tridib . . . who had given me worlds to travel in and eyes to see them with." *The Shadow Lines* takes the reader into the consciousness of several characters, particularly the narrator's grandmother, Ila's parents and May Price. Each consciousness emerges in light and shade, etched with its own individual quirks and idiosyncracies; each character is caught between shadow lines in the wasteland of prejudice, dogma and a narrow nationalism. *The Shadow Lines* ends with the mystery of Tridib's voluntary death—a death symbolic of his sacrifice for humanity.

Time past merges fluidly with time present. At the very start of the novel we have the narrator, a young boy, gazing with respect and admiration as Tridib "makes-up" a story for his group of friends at his *adda* at Gole Park—with a view to impress them about his English connections. This is followed by a long digression about the narrator's own visit to England and his meetings with May Price after Tridib's death. The pendulum swings to the present again at this stage: we are back to the narrator's childhood with his cousin Ila and her mother, nick-named Queen Victoria. Within the first two pages, there are several time-switches, the movement seems natural and easy, making no special demands on the reader. This deft handling of time, in which the "expanded" moment embraces within it, present and past time, gives the novel a Proustian richness and complexity. It is clear that with Ghosh the Indian novel in Englsih has surpassed the rigid barriers of time, place and action, thus making most earlier Indian fiction seem dated and simplistic.

The literary and cultural atmosphere of Calcutta's teashops is quite naturally evoked, and is as easily recognizable as the cigarette which smoulders near Tridib's ashtray when he is engrossed in intellectual activity of a higher kind. The riot and the subsequent events that lead to his death filter through to the reader as the narrator records his research experience while he is sitting one afternoon in 1979 in the Teen Murti House Library, New Delhi. The riots have always remained a mystery to him as he records: "Every word I write about those events of 1964 is the product of a struggle with silence. It is a struggle I am destined to lose." (218) Among the records of January 1964, he reads about the disappearance of the "sacred relic known as the Mui-i-Mubarak"—a hair of the prophet Mohammed, from the Hazratbal Mosque. The cause of the riots, not clear to him earlier, now impinges on his consciousness and he realizes that communal riots which had been sparked off in Kashmir had spread to Pakistan, Bangladesh and Calcutta. He looks at the atlas which once belonged to Tridib, Tridib whose imagination surmounted all barriers and borders. He ruminates: "They had drawn their borders, believing in that pattern, in the enhancement of lines, hoping perhaps that once they had etched their borders upon the map, the two bits of land would sail away from each other like the shifting tectonic plates of the prehistoric Gondwanaland. What had they felt, I wondered, when they discovered that they had created not a separation, but a yet-undiscovered irony—the irony that killed Tridib." (232) As the narrator reads on, he passes on from uncertainty to certainty, he is born anew as it were.

The title of the novel is symbolic of barriers and partitions. Individuals stand divided, as do families, nations and countries. Tridib who had tried to teach the narrator "to use his imagination with precision" meets his death because of the violence of nationalism, ironically enough when he is trying to guard his friend, the English girl, from blind Hindu-Muslim hatred. Ghosh subtly suggests that shadow-lines divide, tear, embitter human beings; this artistically leads to the sudden revelation or Joycean epiphany experienced by the narrator towards the end of the novel. It is a novel with a message and a philosophy—this is unfolded in an intricately and colourfully woven piece of tapestry by a sensitive and skilful artisan.

This probing deep into the consciousness of his characters and at the same time studying them as members of a social community certainly does not come as a surprise. Ghosh, born in Calcutta in 1956, a graduate from Delhi University, is a Social Anthropologist with a D.Phil. in the subject from Oxford. He is also the author of *The Circle of Reason*.

Not very long ago the novelist expressed himself in a language to which he was alien but not quite, a language he had mastered grammatically and correctly as a second language. Uneasy and yet appropriately, he took for his theme and background the Raj, colonial India and post-Independent India. He wrote about his country, either in an idealized manner, or in one which would appeal to a foreign reader. He simplified the complexities of Indian life and culture; his language was English but in thought and sensibility he hovered between two worlds. The trio of the twentieth century—R.K. Narayan, Raja Rao and Mulk Raj Anand—laid the foundation of Indian literature in English, but the "Indianness" of their images can certainly be questioned.

These three novels indicate a major advance. The authors have successfully harnessed a foreign language to a sensibility that is essentially Indian as well as modern.

NOTES

1. Shashi Deshpande, *That Long Silence* (Virago, 1988; Penguin, 1989).
2. Shashi Tharoor, *The Great Indian Novel* (Penguin, 1989).
3. Amitav Ghosh, *The Shadow Lines* (New Delhi: Ravi Dayal, 1988).
4. Ratna Rao Shekhar, "Shashi Deshpande: *That Long Silence* Breaks,' *Society*, Bombay, Dec. 1989.
5. Usha Hemmadi, "A Middle-Class Tale," *The Indian Post*, Sept. 17, 1989.

Shadow Lines: Cross-Cultural Perspectives in the Fiction of Amitav Ghosh

LOUIS JAMES

The novel is the only developing genre and therefore it reflects more deeply, more essentially, more sensitively and rapidly, reality itself in the process of its unfolding. Only that which is itself developing can comprehend development as process. The novel has become the leading hero in the literary development of our time precisely because it best of all reflects the tendencies of a new world still in the making; it is, after all, the only genre born of this new world and in total affinity with it.[1]

Bakhtin was writing in a European context, but could have been addressing with even sharper relevance that of new literatures in English. Bakhtin identified the novel as the "open ended" literary form of the modern age, reflecting and bringing together many languages ("heteroglossia"). These languages are not simply linguistic, but socio-ideological" idioms and forms, voices from different strata of cultural experience.

Amitav Ghosh's work introduces a number of "languages," including those of the Indian folk-tale, the *Mahabharata,* journalism, and the memory patterns of the extended family, radically de-constructing traditional novel forms. In a genre associated in Europe with "realism," Ghosh explores Vedic concepts of Maya (illusion) and transcendence to question the possibility of Western realism. In the opening section of *The Circle of Reason,* the village capitalist, Bhudeb Roy, organizes a festival to Saraswati which Ghosh identifies rather loosely as "the Hindu Goddess of Learning."[2] He has a six-foot image built, with spinning electric lights behind the eyes and a silver-foil halo. During the ceremony the rationalist Balaram leaps onto the platform with defiling sandals and tears off the dyed cotton hair, revealing the clay underneath. "This is not Saraswati, Learning," he cries to the electrified crowd, "it is Vanity." At a deep level, the image of Saraswati *is* "Vanity," for in the Vedic tradition she is a feminine principle and aspect of nature, and only becomes "knowledge" in flowing through the enlightened devotee—Bhudeb Roy is certainly not enlightened. But Balaram is equally benighted—he "exposes" the image not because this misrepresents the tradition, but because it does not represent his concept of Westernized rationalism.

Towards the end of the book there is another festival, the reenactment of Chitrangada's appearance to Arjuna. In the story, taken from the *Mahabharata* via Tagore, the warrior princess Chitrangada is granted the gift of physical beauty for a year in order to attract Arjuna. She becomes his lover, but Arjuna, not knowing the transformation, is drawn by hearsay to Chitrangada's other self. After the year, Arjuna sees her without her beauty, and understands the illusion of the physical. (382) The two episodes are alike and yet opposites. In the first, a religious image is unmasked, showing the crude substance beneath; in the second, physical reality is dissipated to reveal the spiritual.

In both, the real significance of the ritual has been missed. In the first, traditional belief has been prostituted as a means of publicity by the grossly materialistic Bhudeb Roy; in the second, the original legend has been sentimentalized by Tagore and is being played on a gramophone record, in a language the participants cannot understand, in an alien country. Chitrangada is being played by a prostitute, Kulfi. This does and does not invalidate the myths. Misused and misunderstood, the two episodes do have a meaning—the first in the cycle of conflict within which Alu begins his quest for a higher meaning; the second, in the movement that redeems Kulfi (who is given a full ritual burial), and turns Alu back to India. Only through illusion can truth be found.

The concern with the cyclical process of the activity of life underpins the whole book. Reality is Maya, illusion, but only through Maya can reality be understood. The three sections of the novel follow the three Vedic Gunas—Sattva, Rajas and Tamas,—the three aspects of nature ('prakriti') without which no action is possible, taking the development from rising awareness of "Reason," through "Passion," to "Death" or entropy. The process also brings together the divergent stylistic levels of the book—that of an exuberant folk-tale, of the emergence of a human community, and the dialectic between Indian and European consciousness in an alien predicament.

The opening sections focus on a village near the future India-Pakistan border, where Balaram embodies the impact of nineteenth-century scientific reason on India. For Balaram, the modern age began with Pasteur's development of disinfectant and innoculation, and Madame Curie's experiments with radiation to control cancer cells. With these scientific discoveries Balaram believes superstition and ignorance were done away, and the scientific basis of life established. Armed with this knowledge he wages a heroic war against the corrupt commercialism of his arch-enemy, Bhudeb Roy. Yet the inadequacy of this view is hilariously underlined by Balaram's attempt to answer all problems, including war, with buckets of carbolic acid.

Indeed Balaram's concepts of the "new science" were already out of date, Curie and Pasteur being both creators of a new consciousness and the inheritors of the old. Again Ghosh complicates the issue. For Balaram's reliance on a nineteenth-century pseudo-science, Phrenology, in fact approximates to the Indian "superstition" of popular religion and astrology that he opposes. His search for a new Western vision of reality, reflected in the chapter titled "a Pasteurised universe," brings to mind the Vedic legend of the creation of the world, in which the milk ocean of creation was churned by the gods and demons using a snake to separate the poison from the "amrit" (ambrosia). Shiva drank the poison, purifying (pasteurising) the universe. However the outcome was that only the gods drank the "Amrit": Ghosh suggests Balaram also has a one-sided strategy.

Into the story comes Alu, his name, literally "potato." Alu gains his name because his head, of such interest to Balaram, is lumpy like a spud. But Alu, who emerges as the real hero of the book, is also basic, unlovely but ever-renewed, a child of the folk, a creature of the earth. While Balaram pursues his intellectual war against Bhudeb Roy in a landscape scarificed by the internecine India-Pakistan conflict, Alu becomes a master-weaver. Weaving is a central image of the book, bringing together its many paradoxes and opposites. A craft, using the cotton indigenous to India from prehistoric times, it is a paradigm Indian culture. Yet as a mechanical process, it embodies the commercial exploitation that undermine all human societies. "When the history of the world broke, cotton and cloth were behind it; mechanical man in pursuit of his own destruction . . . millions of African and half of America were enslaved by cotton." (57)

When a misdirected flare ignites Balaram's defensive arsenal, Alu escapes with a sewing machine and Balaram's *Life of Pasteur*. Pursued south to Kerala by the police detective Jyoti Das, who becomes a figure of death as the book progresses, Alu crosses the Indian ocean to the imaginary Gulf State of Al-Ghazira with a boatload of Indian women, destined for the town's brothels by Zindi. Sexual, predatory and physically dominating, Zindi is an ambivalent figure of womanhood whose machinations continue whatever quest idealism may pursue. Al-Ghazira is an oil state, a chaotic meeting of the traditional folk, the old tyranny of the Emirs, and the Western pressures of colonial administration and post-colonial exploitation.

A huge economic centre has risen in the desert as a monument to a progress no one wants: when it collapses, Alu is buried in the dead-centre, the rubble arrested by a fallen beam inches from his nose. When he emerges after days of meditation, it is with the inspiration that money, not germs, are destroying civilization. The vision is as flawed as that of Balaram, and when the revolutionary society led by Abu Fahl is crushed by the state, it is with Zindi, Kulfi (an inmate of Zindi's brothel) and an orphan child called Boss that Alu escapes. Following in reverse the routes by which European culture travelled to India, they reach Tunisia, chosen by Ghosh as an instance of a political integration of European and African cultures. Here the trio meet up with an expatriate Indian doctor, Dr. Verma.

The "circle" is closing. For if Balaram came to his vision of reason through biology, attacking deviant microbes with his panacea of carbolic acid, Dr. Verma comes to a Hindu reverence of life also from a basic in microbiology. Dr. Verma even has a *Life of Pasteur*. In it she points out to Alu that the germ both brings death and makes the possibility of life. "It says without the germ 'life would be impossible because death would be incomplete.'" (356) It is Dr. Verma who organizes a dramatic reenactment of the play by Tagore, already mentioned, where the princess Chitrangada, returned to her plain appearance, is seen in her essence by Arjuna. Dr. Verma has to take what Indian actors she can find, and as noted above, when the scene is enacted, within the costumes Kulfi the prostitute takes the part of Chitrangada, while the warrior Arjuna is played by the police-agent Jyoti Das. Kulfi expresses a moment of intense sexual desire and crashes to the ground, clutching her heart, dead.

"Heavenly. Her fathers have gathered her to their heavenly abode" intones Dr. Verma, dressed as Madana, the God of Love. (400) The cycle of death and regeneration is almost complete. After Alu has gone to great lengths to give Kulfi a proper Indian burial, he is told by Dr. Verma that this will give him a reason for going home, and the book ends with Alu, Boss and Zindi, turning back towards India, while the death-bearing Jyoti Das looks towards Europe.

The Circle of Reason is an extraordinarily accomplished first novel. It combines wit, intelligence and creative innovation to explore new possibilities for the novel form in the Indian context. Yet it is not wholly successful. The different narrative strategies pull apart, and the substructure, of knowledge working its way through the stages of the three Gunas, does not sufficiently unite the divergent sections. Moreover the work suffers from being *too* complex for its imaginative integrity: at times one becomes aware of Ghosh's manipulation.

II

In *The Shadow Lines,* Ghosh finds a sharper unifying focus. The novel brings together the forms of the autobiographical novel and the family chronicle, to subvert both. "I am born" begins Dickens' *David Copperfield.* "In 1939, thirteen years before I was born," begins *The Shadow Lines.* Ghosh's novel introduces a family "tree," but it is not the legally-defined family of European society, of Galsworthy's *Forsyte Saga* or Thomas Mann's *Buddenbrooks*—rather, it is the Asian extended family of loyalties, affections and associations. This becomes so complex that even the narrator confesses confusion and the novel is to some extent about the meaning of family relationships in a distintegrating world. "Shadow Lines" of the title refers both to lines of separation, and the invisible links which bind.

There are several lines of family introduced—that of the narrator, based in Calcutta; that of his grandmother's sister, associated with Dhaka, and two further lines bringing into the story Robi and Ila. But the blood relationships merge with those forged by intimacy, as with the British family, linked through domicile in India, of Lionel Tresawsen. The narrator's closest links are with Mayadebi, his grandmother's sister, and with her son Tridib, the enigmatic older friend through which the "I" narrator experiences much of his life.

For if *Circle of Reason* is about "Knowledge," *Shadow Lines* is about "Knowing." The novel moves through an intricate weaving backwards and forwards in time. Narrative sequence is constantly frustrated by the intrusion of memory—memory working not, as in James Joyce's *Ulysses*, as a stream-of-consciousness, so much as remembered family histories, restructured in a search for meaning. Memories sharpen into focus, then blur: "Although I cannot remember when it happened any more than I can remember when I first learnt to tell the time or tie my shoelaces."[3] "I don't know, I can't tell: that world is closed to me, shut off by too many years spent away." (13) Can we ever be sure? One of the most vivid episodes in the novel, a sexual encounter in a bombed theatre, is related by Tridib to May and so taken at third hand by the narrator. But even Tridib cannot be certain of how far his memory has been accurate: "he didn't know whether it had really happened or he had imagined it." Yet this does not invalidate memory. "Reality" for its own sake does not have any specific truth." Ila who claims to be "objective" remembers the cities she has visited by the airport lavatories.

(26) Tridib gives meaning to his experience through his imagination, but not wilfully. He teaches the narrator to "use [his] imagination with precision." (29)

Not that the ostensibly "practical" Ila is free from illusion. One of the recurrent motifs in the book is the mental creation of a house from another, secret, place—a vivid expression of the relationship between real and imagined "homes." Arriving in the Tresawsen's house in London, the narrator knows the position of every room. This is because when a child he had been taken to hide in a cellar below Ila's family home in Dhaka, where they had "played houses." Ila had traced out for him an imaginary house, which we discover is identical in form to the London house where Ila had spent her childhood. In the cellar, as they play at having a family, it becomes clear their doll-child represents the earlier Ila. Yet the doll is blue-eyed and flaxen-haired, befriended and protected by the son of the house, Nick Price. In reality Ila was dark, and Nick deserted her: Ila's underground imagination evades reality rather than clarifying it.

The novel gains stature by placing the individual themes starkly in a contemporary context. The shadow lines divide and link peoples and nations. The novel takes place largely on the newly-created Indo-Pakistan border which divides the family and its past. What is this border? Flying over it, the grandmother expects to see some sign. The father laughs—no, it will not be a long black line with green on one side and scarlet on the other. But the grandmother's question is a serious one. If there are no physical signs, where is the difference? Why cannot people as in the past travel from Dhaka to Calcutta without anyone stopping them? What are the 'shadow lines'? (154-55)

Their dual meaning emerges in the final sections of the book when the grandmothers discover a relative, turning senile, left behind in a hostile Dhaka. They go to rescue him—with Robi, May and Tridib. He is trying to escape from the mob when May and Tridib run to his rescue—May is protected by being English, but Tridib, throwing himself to his own death, drawn by the 'shadow line' of imaginative sympathy. Why he should do it is the mystery left by the book. As May says, "He gave himself up; it was a sacrifice. I know I can't understand it. I know I mustn't try, for any real sacrifice is a mystery." (252)

The profoundly personal ending of the book is different indeed in tone to that of Ghosh's first novel. But both end with a ritual, a religious intimation of the cycle and continuation of life. Ghosh's work to-date extends the scope of the novel, not only within its own narrative, but moving outward and beyond the strategies of words, to an exploration of the past and the future of the culture he has inherited.

NOTES

1. Mikhail Bakhtin, "Epic and Novel," *The Dialogic Imagination* (1981), p. 7.
2. Amitav Ghosh, *The Circle of Reason* (New Delhi: Roli Books International, 1986), p. 29.
3. Amitav Ghosh, *The Shadow Lines* (Black Swan edn., Bloomsbury Publishing, 1989), p. 9.

Communal Frenzy and Partition: Bapsi Sidhwa, Attia Hosain and Amitav Ghosh

NOVY KAPADIA

Throughout history, fanatics as well as ideologues, pushed to the emotional brink of daring their lives, have taken the plunge, which has triggered off a chain reaction of rigid mental fixations and attitudes. Bapsi Sidhwa's novel *Ice-Candy-Man* examines the inexorable logic of Partition as an offshoot of fundamentalism sparked by hardening communal attitudes. First published in 1988 in London, this novel is set in pre-partition India in Lahore. It belongs to the genre of the partition novel like Manohar Malgonkar's *A Bend in the Ganges* (1964), Chaman Nahal's *Azadi* (1975), and Khushwant Singh's *Train to Pakistan* (1956). However in Indian-English fiction it is the second novel on Partition by a woman author. The other novel is *Sunlight on a Broken Column* (1961) by Attia Hosain. Both these sensitive women writers share similar perspectives on the calamities of Partition. The denouement of both novels is quite similar. Both stress a similar vulnerability of human understanding and life, caused by the throes of Partition which relentlessly divided friends, families, lovers and neighbours.

Ice-Candy-Man is a novel of upheaval which includes a cast of characters from all communities. There are Hindus, Muslims, Christians, Sikhs and Parsis, so a multiple perspective of partition emerges as viewed by all the affected communities. Bapsi Sidhwa uses a narrator to tell the tale. A precocious Parsi girl, eight years old with a handicapped foot narrates the story of her changing world with sophistication and wonder. Lenny is like the persona that Chaucer adopts in his Prologue to *The Canterbury Tales*, rendering credibility by being almost a part of the reader's consciousness. With the wonder of a child she is observing social change and human behaviour, noting interesting sidelights, seeking and listening to opinions and occasionally making judgements. Her childish innocence is like the seeming naive display of Chaucer's persona, a source of sharp irony. The device of the child narrator enables Bapsi Sidhwa treat a historical moment as horrifying as partition without morbidity, pedanticism or censure. The highlight of the novel is that the author throughout maintains a masterful balance between laughter and despair. The subtle irony and deft usage of language creates humour which does not shroud but raucously highlights the traumas of Partition. Sensitively the author shows the human toll of Partition, when a concerned Lenny asks: "*Can one break a country?* And what happens if they break it *where our house is?*" (92)

The Parsi paradox of whether to support "Swaraj" or to maintain their loyalty to the British Raj is also humorously delineated. A piquant touch is given to this dilemma. With the impending news of independence, the paranoid feelings of the Parsis, a minuscule minority get accentuated. The Parsis in Lahore at a special meeting at their temple hall in Warris Road, have an acrimonious debate on the political situation. The meeting is interesting as it expresses the insecurity of the Parsis not because of communal antagonism, but the apprehension of their status at the departure of the British. Already the unstinted loyalty to the colonial power is declining. Col. Bharucha and Lenny's father blame the British for bringing polio to India. So at the meeting, India's smallest minority is trying to redefine their strategy which Col. Bharucha claims as "We must hunt with the hounds and run with the hare." (16)

The ambivalent attitude of the Parsis towards Partition and Independence emerged at the main-hall meeting at the Fire-Temple. Col. Bharucha, the President of the community in Lahore, advocates status quo. He warns fellow-Parsis to shun the anti-colonial movement and nationalist agitation spearheaded by Mahatma Gandhi. His reasoning is based on expediency. If there is "Home Rule," political glory, fame and fortune will be acquired by the two major communities, Hindus and Muslims. He considers Home Rule as a power struggle, saying "Hindus, Muslims and even the Sikhs are going to jockey for power and if you jokers jump into the middle you'll be mangled into chutney!" (36) He also advocates caution, because of the Parsis's long-standing attitudes of loyalty to the British. This attitude stemmed from the Zoroastrian religious belief of loyalty to a ruler and a close relationship between state and community. The other cause for loyalty to the British was purely economic. The Parsis primarily traced their secured status as a prosperous minority to British rule, identified as the "good government" of the African prayer. So loyalty was a self-evident precept to the Parsis. Thus Col. Bharucha does not want any Parsi of Lahore to offend British sensibilities by espousing nationalist causes. In a tone of admonition he says, "I hope no Lahore Parsi will be stupid enough to court trouble—I strongly advise all of you to stay at home—and out of trouble." (37)[2]

In her first novel *The Crow Eaters* (1978) Bapsi Sidhwa portrayed the dying businessman Faredoon Junglewalla vehemently protesting against the nationalist movement and exhorting his offspring to remain loyal to the British Empire. Col. Bharucha has a somewhat similar attitude. However with Independence imminent and Partition inevitable, there is a subtle change in the attitude of the Parsis of Lahore. The patriarchal advice of Col. Bharucha is opposed. Dr. Mody promptly poses a plea for involvement in the freedom struggle. He says, "our neighbours will think we are betraying them and siding with the English." (37) The banker Mr. Toddywalla says that the Parsis should support the Indian community which appears to be in a dominant position or will acquire political power after Independence. So he asks the assembled congregation to formulate attitudes and actions on Independence based on self-interest. Finally the assembled Parsis resolve to remain in Lahore and abide by the rules of the land. Wafting in self-esteem they agree to Col. Bharucha's suggestion, "Let whoever wishes rule! Hindu, Muslim, Sikh, Christian. We will abide by the rules of the land." (39)

Some Parsis in the congregation express apprehension about remaining in Lahore after Independence and wish to migrate either to London or Bombay (where majority of their coreligionists live). However such fears get over-ruled and the herd mentality desire of staying only in Bombay is also rejected. The final resolution is one of adaptability and compromise. The President of the Lahore Parsis Col. Bharucha says, "As long as we conduct our lives quietly; as long as we present no threat to anybody; we will prosper right here,—" (40) Through this animated conversation, Bapsi Sidhwa reveals the implicit, lurking fear of the Parsis, a vulnerable minority losing their identity and getting swamped by the majority communities—either Hindus in India or Muslims in Pakistan. So even amongst the Parsis the smallest minority in undivided India, the Partition sparked off an impulse for migration from their homelands. Bombay was opted for, primarily due to safety in numbers rather than the safeguards of democratic India. Historically however the movement to Bombay, as the novelist also indicates, was minimal. The Parsis remained in urban areas of India and Pakistan, trying to preserve their identity by not meddling in political matters. The advice of Mr. Toddywalla is followed, "But don't try to prosper immoderately. And remember don't ever try to exercise real power." (40)

Amidst banter, repartee and humour, Bapsi Sidhwa subtly portrays the underlying fears of the Parsis about Partition and Independence. The depiction of their mental turmoil can be compared to John Masters's depiction of the plight of the Eurasians commonly called Anglo-Indians before the British left the sub-continent. In his novel, *Bhowani Junction* (1954), John Masters aptly depicts the identity crises of the Anglo-Indians. For instance, the loud-mouthed and arrogant Peter Taylor had talked of going "Home" to England (which he has never seen) and wore his solar hat all day to be recognized as an Englishman. Even the anglicized Peter Taylor has a foreboding of impending Independence. He asks Victoria in sheer frustration, "What are we going to do." (42)[3] Knowing that they could become neither English nor Indian, Taylor's conclusion is "we could only stay where we were and be what we were." (21) This shows how Taylor and the Anglo-Indian community have become total prisoners of circumstances. Bapsi Sidhwa shows how the Parsis are similar captives of circumstances in the upheaval of Partition.

Adaptability being part of their social code, the Parsis of Lahore adjust to the changing circumstances after Partition. In *The Crow Eaters,* Bapsi Sidhwa had only hinted at the necessity of changing allegiances after Independence but in *Ice-Candy-Man,* the change in attitudes is depicted. Col. Bharucha and Lenny's father curse the British for bringing polio to India. Lenny suffers from polio and the disease is considered as another example of British treachery. Later in the novel, Lenny's mother, Mrs. Sethi and other Parsi women help Hindu and Sikh families escape in safe convoys to India and assist in rehabilitation of destitute and kidnapped women. Lenny's Godmother rescues the Hindu Ayah forcibly married to her former Muslim friend, the seller of ice-candies. The Godmother helps Ayah return to Amritsar, under police escort. There is already a sense of involvement, with the new reality as Lenny's parents, Godmother and Parsi friends try to bring some semblance of sanity in frenzied Lahore.[4]

With witty remarks and subtle usage of language, Bapsi Sidhwa presents the impact of Independence and Partition in vivid images. The altered social reality becomes even more striking, as narrated by the innocent eight-year-old Lenny. Independence becomes evident to Lenny when she visits the Queen's Garden: "I cannot believe my eyes. The queen has gone! The space between the marble canopy and the marble platform is empty. A group of children playing knuckles, squat where the gunmetal queen sat enthroned." (236) So within her restricted space, Lenny aptly reveals the fading away of an Empire and its value systems. The theme of separation caused by Partition is also revealed in a simple but vividly poignant observation by Lenny. During her romps at the Queen's Garden she notices the absence of the cosmopolitan gathering:

> The garden scene has depressingly altered. Muslim families who added colour when scattered among the Hindus and Sikhs now monopolize the garden, depriving it of colour. The absence of the

> brown skin that showed through the fine veils of Hindu and Sikh women, and beneath the dhoties and shorts of the men, has changed the complexion of the queenless garden. (236)

Through the wondering eyes of the precocious Lenny, the novelist shows the disruption of a settled order and traumatic separations of friends, the legacy of Partition.

The impact of Partition is psychologically understood and narrated through the feelings of a child, who is a member of a minuscule minority. The sense of loss is aptly demonstrated as Lenny and her brother Adi wandering through the garden observe, "Adi and I wander from group to group peering into faces beneath white skull-caps and above ascetic beards. I feel uneasy. Like Hamida I do not fit. I know we will not find familiar faces here." (237) The uprootedness of Partition is revealed as Lenny drifts through the Queen's Garden searching in vain for familiar faces and acquaintances. Even in the child there is a feeling of insecurity. She clings to the hands of her Ayah and cajoles her not to marry the Masseur. A Muslim, the Masseur is one of Ayah's numerous admirers and promises to marry and protect her during the throes of Partition. Overhearing this, Lenny desperately urges Ayah not to get married as it would mean separation. Later when Ayah is abducted it is Lenny who urges her family to search for her. Lenny's responses show the dislocation of life during Partition. The partition novels of Manohar Malgonkar, Khushwant Singh and Chaman Nahal focus on Punjab and the dislocation of life and human feelings in that region. So Bapsi Sidhwa's novel is similar to the novels in this genre. The only difference is that the pointless brutality of communal frenzy is parodied as it is unfurled and narrated by the child-narrator Lenny. She and her younger brother Adi watch "the skyline of the old walled city ablaze and people spattering each other with blood." (134) Fire destroys Hindu, Muslim and Sikh houses and shops at Shalmi. "The entire Shalmi, an area covering about four square miles, flashes in explosions." (137) Fire knows no religion. The shrieks and shouts of "Pakistan Murdabad! Death to Pakistan! Sat Sri Akaal; Bolay so nihaal!" of the Sikh mobs when listening to Master Tara Singh at Queen's Garden and "Allah-O-Akbar! Yaaa Ali! and Pakistan Zindabad!" of the rampaging Muslim mobs gives Lenny as many nightmares as when she recollects the roaring of the lions in the zoo. With such subtle comparisons and ironic exposures, Bapsi Sidhwa shows the brutalization which communal frenzy causes. Even lovers turn hostile. Ice-Candy-Man, the Muslim lover of the Hindu Ayah, watches Shalmi and Mozang Chowk burn with "the muscles in his face tight with a strange exhilaration I never want to see." The transformation of a fun-loving man who frolicked and acted the buffoon in the park into an ogre due to communal frenzy is aptly revealed by Lenny's horror at the sadism in his face. A vivid image which is a stark reminder of the brutality of the times. This is the way Bapsi Sidhwa handles the delicate theme of partition, through subtle insinuations, images and gestures. So the stark horror of loss, bloodshed and separation is portrayed without verbosity, sensationalism, lurid details and maudlin sentimentality. The sensitive portrayal of the horrors of Partition enhances the poignancy and cruelty of the event without the author ever appearing pedantic or pretentious.

Allegory is another literary device used by Bapsi Sidhwa to depict the trauma of Partition. The child-narrator Lenny is also affected by the violence at Lahore: "The whole world is burning. The air on my face is so hot I think my flesh and clothes will catch fire. I start screaming: hysterically sobbing." (137) The scenes of violence and arson and above all the venemous hatred of friends who had months earlier rationalized about the impossibility of violence, have a frightening impact on the young Parsi girl Lenny. Violence breeds violence and Lenny is also a victim. Her age is directed at her collection of dolls. In a frenzy she acts: "I pick out a big, bloated celluloid doll. I turn it upside down and pull its legs apart. The elastic that holds them together stretches easily. I let one leg go and it snaps back, attaching itself to the brittle torso." (138) The destructive urge overcomes Lenny and she is not satisfied till assisted by her brother Adi she wrenches out the legs of the doll and examines the spilled insides. This violent act by Lenny is an apt allegory on the mindless violence of Partition. With a morbid sense of humour, Bapsi Sidhwa reveals how the violence of Partition has serrated the roots of people of different communities, irrespective of ideology, friendship and rational ideas. In such a depiction, Bapsi Sidhwa resembles the horror portrayed by William Golding in *The Lord of the Files* (1954). Golding indicated that there is a thin line between good and evil in human beings and it is only the structures of civilizations which prevent the lurking evil from being rampant. At the end of *The Lord of the Flies*, boys of Jack's tribe like barbarians got a sadistic delight in hunting Ralph. The situation is saved as a Naval officer reaches the island and by his presence curbs the pointless brutality of the abandoned boys. Golding had written this novel after World War II and the allegorical meaning was evident. In the world of fiction, a grown-up stepped in to curb the atrocities and brutality of the boys, but when countries commit atrocities there is no restraining power. Lenny's destruction of the doll also has allegorical significance. It shows how even a young girl is powerless to stem the tide of surging violence within, thereby implying that grown up fanatics enmeshed in communal frenzy are similarly trapped into brutal violence. Lenny breaks down and cries at her pointless brutality, a sombre message by the novelist that unless there is re-thinking, brutality and insensitivity becomes a way of life, such is the conditioning of communalism.

Another partition novel, Attia Hosain's *Sunlight on a Broken Column* (1961), also uses a narrator-heroine to similar effect. Attia Hosain's narrator-heroine Laila reveals the trauma of Partition through her memories and insights of her Taluqdar family disintegrating. Like in the *Ice-Candy-Man*, the enigma of Partition is sensitively shown. When Zohra, her cousin married in Pakistan, returns to Hasanpur, she quarrels with Laila about protection of Muslim culture and language. The disagreements were no longer youthful verbal quarrels but echoed bigger divisions. Laila surmises the most cruel aspect of partition when she says, "In the end, inevitably we quarrelled, and though we made up before we parted I realized that the ties which had kept families together for centuries had been loosened beyond repair." (303)[5] Like Lenny, the grown-up Laila is also both nostalgic and restless. Laila ruminates and wanders in her disbanded ancestral home Ashiana after Partition. Memories come flooding back. However her nostalgia is controlled. Whilst walking through the rooms of Ashiana, she remembers the past, but does not wish for the old order to return. Her new-found identity and struggle to be Ameer's lover and wife, curbs any desire for a return to the cloistered feudal order. Instead it broadens her horizons of life. She comes to detest dogmatism, either in the name of religion or radicalism. Her views and perspective of life developed after intense personal struggle enable Laila to tackle the loss of her husband Ameer and the trauma of Partition. So both narrator-heroines, Lenny and Laila react against communal responses and the horrors of violence. The mature Laila rationalizes against communal tension whereas the young Lenny instinctively reacts against the horrors of communal violence.

There are other similarities between the two novelists, Bapsi Sidhwa and Attia Hosain. Both realize there are no easy solutions to communal holocausts except intense struggle against dogmatism. Laila's concerted attempts at breaking from traditional customs, the negation of despair and recognition of struggle are upheld by Attia Hosain. Her narrator-heroine does not lapse into a glorification of the past or take refuge in mysticism, epicureanism or jingoism. Similarly Bapsi Sidhwa shows there are no winners in the communal holocausts of Partition. This is revealed by clever juxtapositioning of images. Gramophones and speakers mounted on tongas and lorries pour out the melody of Nur Jehan's popular film song,

> Mere bachpan ke sathi mujhe bhool na jana—
> Dekho, dekho hanse na zamana, hanse na zamana. (159)

Ironically the sentiments of the song are not followed and instead there is turbulence and violence. At the festival of Holi, instead of splattering friends with bright colours, people are splattering each other with blood. Bapsi Sidhwa shows the human loss in Partition:

> Instead, wave upon scruffy wave of Muslim refugees flood Lahore—and the Punjab west of Lahore. Within three months seven million Muslims and five million Hindus and Sikhs are uprooted in the largest and most terrible exchange of population known to history. The Punjab has been divided. (159)

Bare facts present the horror of the greatest communal divide in history. Bapsi Sidhwa aptly shows the inexorable logic of Partition which moves on relentlessly leaving even sane people and friends helpless and ineffective. Jagjeet Singh with a furtive group of Sikhs visited a Muslim village Pir Pindo under cover of darkness to warn them of an impending Akali attack. Pir Pindo is attacked at dawn and swamped by Sikhs. Men, women and children are killed. Similarly Sikh families are attacked in Lahore. The neighbour of the Sethis, Mr. and Mrs. Singh leave with their two children and a few belongings. Other goods are left behind with Lenny's parents. Sher Singh the zoo attendant flees from Lahore, due to insecurity, after his brother-in-law is killed. Similarly the student fraternity of King Edward's Medical college is disrupted. Prakash and his family migrate to Delhi and Rahool Singh and his pretty sisters are escorted to a convoy to Amritsar. In Lenny's household the gardener Hari is circumcised and becomes Himat Ali, and Moti becomes David Masih, the politics of compromise and survival. Ayah's lover the Masseur's mutilated dead body is found in a gunny sack. The money lender Kirpa Ram flees leaving guineas and money behind. Even middle-class families like the Shankers flee in haste. Partition is shown as a series of images and events depicting human loss and agony. The dislocation of settled life is aptly revealed by Lenny's understanding of the demographic change in Lahore. In awe she observes, "Lahore is suddenly emptied of yet another hoary dimension: there are no Brahmins with caste-marks—or Hindus in dhoties with bodhis. Only hordes of Muslim refugees." (175) Lahore is no more cosmopolitan. Even the Sikhs have fled. The child-narrator senses the difference and pain caused by the huge exchange of populations.

Bapsi Sidhwa also subtly delineates the psychological impact of the horrors of Partition on the lives of people. The communal frenzy has a distorting effect on people and leads to feelings of suspicion, distrust and susceptibility to rumours. Even the children, Lenny, Adi and their cousin are intrigued and suspicious of any minor deviations from normal behaviour. Mrs. Sethi and Aunt Minnie travel all over Lahore in the car but do not take the children with them. Deprived of long drives, Lenny and her cousin are intrigued at the movements of their mothers. Ayah enhances the sense of mystery when she states that the dicky of the car is full of cans of petrol. The author shows that in a highly surcharged atmosphere, suspicion and distrust become inevitable. The Ayah is also suspicious about the movements of cans of petrol by the two Parsi ladies. If she suspects they are distributing petrol to the arsonists she does not state so. The three children are stupefied by this revelation and let their imagination run wild. Finally they come to the same conclusion. "We know who the arsonists are. Our mothers are setting fire to Lahore!—My heart pounds at the damnation that awaits their souls. My knees quake at the horror of their imminent arrest." (173)

Bapsi Sidhwa cleverly parodies the feelings of suspicion and distrust of the children for their mothers. The imaginary fears of Lenny, Adi and their cousin are a source of humour but also a grim reminder of how rumour becomes institutionalized in a highly surcharged atmosphere. The children only fantasize about their mother's dangerous acts but the author shows how rumour preys upon the frenzied minds of men vitiated by communal hatred. On the radio there is news of trouble at Gurdaspur, which the Ice-Candy-Man and his friends at once interpret as "there is uncontrollable butchering going on in Gurdaspur." (148) There are further rumours of a train full of dead bodies coming to Lahore from Gurdaspur. The Ice-Candy-Man returns panting after a frantic cycle ride and adds to the horror, by describing atrocities on women and stating that the dead are all Muslims. The acquaintances of Queen's Garden believe this rumour and harbour revenge against Sikhs. They now look with hatred on long standing friend Sher Singh, compelling the latter to flee from Lahore.[6]

In the vitiated communal atmosphere, insanity prevails as ordinary men lose their rationality. Such a degradation is best exemplified in the rage of Ice-Candy-Man who says: "I'll tell you to your face—I lose my senses when I think of the mutilated bodies on that train from Gurdaspur . . . that night I went mad, I tell you, I lobbed grenades through the windows of Hindus and Sikhs I'd known all my life! I hated their guts." (156)

Revenge becomes the major motivation for the Ice-Candy-Man and his friends. The role of rumour and the consequent pattern of violence as depicted by Bapsi Sidhwa is compact and realistic. It is also very contemporary as similar patterns of violence are depicted by Amitav Ghosh in his novel *The Shadow Lines* (1988).[7] Using the narrative technique of unnfurling events, by reading old newspaper reports, Amitav Ghosh shows how communal violence spread in Calcutta and cities of erstwhile East Pakistan in 1964. As he stresses, rumour took over. The poisoning of water, the trains of dead bodies, all incredible rumours, further vitiated the communal frenzy and increased the violence. Amitav Ghosh's novel is very contemporary and relevant as it shows how communal fanatics thrived on the spread of rumours which intensified feelings of anger and triggered off violence. The bland newspaper reports and memory technique of Amitav Ghosh remove the impact of time. It is implied that the riots are contemporaneous. The 1964 Calcutta riots could be the 1984 Delhi riots, the 1987 Meerut riots or in recent times the 1989 Bhagalpur killings. They all follow a similar pattern, suspicion, distrust and rumour activating conditioned minds, all sources of terrifying communal violence.

Very perceptively Amitav Ghosh shows how different cultures and communities are becoming antagonistic to a point of no return. Hence in *The Shadow Lines* he effectively uses political allegory to stress the need for a syncretic civilization to avoid a communal holocaust. Bapsi Sidhwa's concerns are also similar. The message in Bhisham Sahni's novel *Tamas,* that "those who forget history are condemned to repeat it," is applicable to *Ice-Candy-Man* also. Sidhwa's novel written at a period of history when communal and ethnic violence threaten disintegration of the subcontinent, is an apt warning of the dangers of communal frenzy. Bapsi Sidhwa shows that during communal strife, sanity, human feelings and past friendships are forgotten. At the Queen's Park in Lahore, friends and colleagues had argued endlessly about the impossibility of violence against each other and of fleeing from their homeland. Yet ironically, whilst the elders—Masseur, Butcher, Ice-Candy-Man, Sher Singh and Ayah—gossip about national politics the child-narrator senses the change in the days before Partition: "I can't put my finger on it—but there is a subtle change in the Queen's Garden." (96) The admirers of Ayah, in the pursuit of love temporarily sidetrack communal feelings and "Hindu, Muslim, Sikh, Parsi are as always, unified around her." (97) The others without such motivations are deliberately sitting with members of their own community, huddled together preserving cultural and religious identities. The Brahmins form their own circle of exclusivity. Burkha-clad Muslim women and children have their own group. The saddest fact as observed by Lenny is that even the children do not mix whilst playing.

Lenny attempts social interaction with a group of Sikh children but Masseur tries to pull her away. Sikh women ask her name and the name of her religion. When the child states that she is a Parsi, the Sikh women express amazemant at the discovery of a new religion. It is then that Lenny instinctively realizes the social divide between communities. Rationalizing her feelings she says, "That's when I realize what has changed. The Sikhs, only their rowdy little boys running about hair piled in topknots, are keeping mostly to themselves." (96) The author implies that the events at Queen's Garden are a reflection of a crystallization of feelings at a larger scale in Lahore and other cities of India. Cultural and religious exclusivity leads initially to indifference and later to contempt which becomes the breeding ground for communal violence and bigotry. With a subtle parody, Bapsi Sidhwa conveys the dangers of social exclusivity. The Ice-Candy-Man, in striking attire, enters the Queen's Garden, "Thumping a five-foot iron trident with bells tied near its base." (97) He is in the guise of a holy man and chants "Ya Allah!" With his ash-smeared face and eccentric manner he pretends to be Allah's telephone. The author implies that in an atmosphere which encourages religious bigotry, even charlatans emerge as holy and godmen. The difference between appearance and reality is slim. The Ice-Candy-Man pretends to talk to God on telephone. The scene is ludicrous and a source of rich humour. However amidst laughter the real meaning of such clowning emerges. The Ice-Candy-Man's antics provoke amusement but it is a pointer to the duplicity of people in the name of religion. Their sheer gullibility is exposed in a scene vividly described:

> Suddenly he springs up. Thumping his noisy trident on the ground, performing a curious jumping dance, he shouts: Wah Allah! Wah Allah! so loudly that several people who have been watching the goings-on from afar, hastily get up and scamper over. Sikhs, Hindus, Muslims form a thick circle round us. I can tell from the reverent faces around me that they believe they are in the presence of a holyman crazed by his love of God. And the madder the mystic, the greater his power. (99)

The message is clear. If charlatans can arouse such fervour, then obscurantism needs little prodding to slide into bigotry.

The secular group, Ayah's admirers maintain a facade of unity by cracking ribald jokes on community characteristics. However they also become vicious and prey to communal frenzy in the near future. The Ice-Candy-Man is part of the frenzied mob which abdicates Ayah and keeps her in the brothels of Hira Mandi. So even the passion of love is powerless against religious bigotry. Later in the novel, the Ice-Candy-Man attempts to make amends. He forcibly marries Ayah, changes her name to Mumtaz, and recites love poetry to her. But even here love is shown as powerless. Ayah has a revulsion for her newly-acquired Muslim identity. With the help of Lenny's Godmother she is taken to a Recovered Women's Camp and then sent to her family in Amritsar. The Ice-Candy-Man, now a "deflated poet, a collapsed pedlar" follows her to Amritsar in vain. Their relationship is serrated forever, one more victim of communal frenzy and Partition. Love does not conquer all, when communal and obscurantist passions are aroused.

With a sprinkling of humour, parody and allegory Bapsi Sidhwa conveys a sinister warning of the dangers of compromising with religious obscurantism and fundamentalism of all categories. Otherwise a certain historical inevitability marks this historical process. Though her novel is about the traumas of Partition, Bapsi Sidhwa like Amitav Ghosh reveals that communal riots are contemporaneous and that those who do not learn from history are condemned to repeat it.

NOTES

1. Bapsi Sidhwa, *Ice-Candy-Man* (London: William Heinemann, 1988)
2. The sentiments and ideas of Col. Bharucha represent a prominent social code of behaviour amongst the Parsis. They have always venerated loyalty. Dr. Homi B. Dhalla in his essay, "The Zoroastrian Moral Imperative: Its Relevance in the Late 19th and Early 20th Centuries" published in the Delhi Parsi Anjuman's *Dar-E-Meher* (fire-temple) silver jubilee celebrations souvenir (1986) gives instances of loyalty. He states: "Large gatherings of Parsis have over the years, assembled for public acts of worship or thanksgiving (jashan). To cite a few: on July 16, 1854, a jashan was performed where about 6,000 Zoroastrians offered prayers for Britain during its war with Russia. As a mark of celebration, a mammoth jashan was organized on Queen Victoria's Golden Jubilee on Feb. 16, 1887 and again on June 20, 1897 to commemorate her Diamond Jubilee." Also cited in James Boyd and Firoze Kotwal, "Worship in a Zoroastrian Fire Temple," *Indo-Iranian Journal*, 26, 1983, pp. 308-10. Col. Bharucha was thus just following a Parsi moral imperative.
3. John Masters, *Bhowani Junction* (New York: The Viking Press, 1954), p. 42.
4. Charity and social usefulness is a Parsi moral code, based on the teachings of the prophet Zarathushtra. This is amply revealed in Eckehard Kulke's scholarly book, *The Parsis in India: A Minority as*

Agent of Social Change (Delhi: Bell Books, 1978). Kulke states that Parsi charities are cosmopolitan and communal as the ancient scriptures and daily prayers extolled philanthropy. Kulke states "This charity system was made possible and furthered by the basic attitude of the Parsis, motivated by their religion, that wealth is fundamentally positive, that it brings, however certain social obligations along with it." So charity is part of the Parsi ethos.

5. Attia Hosain, *Sunlight on a Broken Column* (Delhi: Arnold Heinemann, 1979).
6. The role of rumour in both the nationalist movement led by Mahatma Gandhi and the traumas of Partition is best explained in Sumit Sarkar's book, *Modern India* 1885-1947 (Madras: Macmillan India, 1983) In his chapter "The Role of Rumour," Sumit Sarkar shows how peasants and workers responded to institutionalized rumours.
7. Amitav Ghosh, *The Shadow Lines* (Delhi: Ravi Dayal Publisher, 1988)

Theme of Partition and Freedom in Khushwant Singh's *Train to Pakistan* and Amitav Ghosh's *The Shadow Lines*

D.K. PABBY

As the plot of Khushwant Singh's novel *Train to Pakistan* progresses towards its concluding part, one of the main characters viz. Hukum Chand, the magistrate of Chundunnugger, is a disillusioned man as he feels the sting of his helplessness to do much to stop the communal violence that had erupted in the wake of the partition of the country. Political freedom had been achieved apparently through 'non-violent' means but Hindu-Muslim riots had erupted in several parts of India and also in the newly-created Pakistan. Hukum Chand's words of self-introspective rumination quietly proclaim the futility of this political freedom without proper orientation of the people: "What were the people in Delhi doing? Making fine speeches in the assembly! Loud speakers magnifying their egos; lovely-looking foreign women in the visitors' galleries in breathless admiration: 'He is great man, this Mr. Nehru of yours. I do think he is the greatest man in the world today. And how handsome!' Wasn't that a wonderful thing to say? 'Long ago we made a tryst with destiny and now the time comes when we shall redeem our pledge, not wholly or in full measure but very substantially.' Yes, Mr. Prime Minister, you made your tryst. So did many others."[1] The two novels, Khushwant Singh's *Train to Pakistan* (1956) and Amitav Ghosh's *The Shadow Lines* (1988) attempt to grapple *inter alia* with this question of 'the tryst of others' i.e. 'the tryst of the common people' caught between the greed of self-seeking politicians, fanatic religious leaders and their cohorts, power-wielding corrupt bureaucrats and anti-social elements always looking for opportunities to exploit any situation to their own advantage; and the unseemly haste with which the labour government in Britain decided to transfer power. It is on record that Lord Mountbatten, the then Viceroy of India and later the first Governor General of free India, got his reforms commissioner, Mr. V.P. Menon, to draw up the plan for the transfer of power and the division of India in just a few hours. With this plan, he himself flew to London and got Mr. Atlee the Prime Minister of England and his cabinet to accept it in exactly five minutes. The subsequent hasty implementation of this plan without much foresight, farsightedness and the much-needed preparedness at several levels, led to an unprecedented holocaust of communal frenzy. Before the people could realize the political and social implications of the partition, they were swept off their feet by a wave of violence that swiftly became a tide. Hundreds of people were killed, raped and butchered on either side of the border, and for those who survived the catastrophe, the experience was so traumatic that the memories of those grief-stricken days haunted them for years to come. For millions of people, the independence of the country brought terrible but avoidable suffering and humiliation, a loss of human dignity and a frustrating sense of being uprooted. This is not what they had aspired for in the name of freedom—the partition was a dirty trick.

In *Train to Pakistan*, Khushwant Singh brings to the centre stage the fact of the partition of the Punjab and the question of the subsequent violence on both sides of the border in a very effective, vivid and graphic manner. In a brief preface to the novel, Arthur Lall aptly comments: "Its intrinsic qualities as a novel grip the reader. Throughout, the action sweeps one along. The characters are vivid and highly credible, and Khushwant Singh keeps them going magnificently on two levels: in their quotidian matrix compounded of their passions of love and revenge, their tremendous sense of belonging to a village community, and their insolence and heroism; and then again on the wide stage set by the tornado that breaks on their lives in the shape of the cataclysmic events of the partition of India in 1947." In fact, the novel opens with forebodings of ill omen: "The summer of 1947 was not like other Indian summers. Even the weather had a different feel in India that year. It was hotter than usual, and drier and dustier. And the summer was longer. No one could remember when the monsoon had been so late. For weeks, the sparse clouds cast only shadows. There was no rain. People began to say that God was punishing them for their sins." (1)

Khushwant Singh goes on to describe how the feeling of guilt arose from the maddening violence by the Hindus and the Muslims precipitated by reports of the proposed division of the country into 'a Hindu India and a Muslim Pakistan.' The riots had first broken out in Calcutta and then spread north and east and west engulfing a vast segment of population. Though the novelist does hold the Britishers and the political leaders responsible for the avoidable communal riots, he does not take any sides: "Muslims said the Hindus had planned and started the killing. According to the Hindus, the Muslims were to blame. The fact is, both sides killed. Both shot and stabbed and speared and clubbed. Both tortured. Both raped. . . . The riots had become a rout. By the summer of 1947, when the creation of the new state of Pakistan was formally announced, ten million people—Muslims and Hindus and Sikhs—were in flight. By the time the monsoon broke, almost a million of them were dead, and all of northern India was in arms, in terror or in hiding." (1-2) The massacres and brutalities unleashed by the partition are then juxtaposed against the harmonious bonds of friendship, brotherhood and good-neighbourliness in an obscure, sleepy and tiny village Mano Majra situated near the border and inhabited by only seventy families out of which "Lala Ram Lal's is the only Hindu family. The others are Sikhs or Muslims, about equal in number." (2) Simplicity and calmness of the lives of the Mano Majrans can be gauged from the fact that all the activities of villagers are closely related to and measured in terms of the arrival and departure of various trains from early morning till late in the evening. The shattering of the peace and harmony of this small helmet with the brutal murder of the village moneylender Lala Ram Lal and the daring dacoity at his house by the gang of Malli and his men, is a kind of foregrounding of the communal violence and the anarchic chaos that was to be let loose later. "Ram Lal uttered a loud yell and collapsed on the floor with blood spurting from his belly. The dacoits jumped off the roof to the lane below. They yelled defiance to the world as they went out towards the river. 'Come' they yelled. 'Come out, if you have the courage! Come out, if you want your mothers and sisters raped, Come out! brave men!'" (10)

A close reading of the novel clearly reveals that the dacoity at his house and murder of the moneylender are not merely accidental—these are a prelude to the swelling acts of murder and violence across the frontier which do not remain unretaliated. Though the conversation between the police sub-inspector and the District Magistrate of Chundunnugger about the communal situation in the district town, in the border village of Mano Majra, and the general situation on both sides of the border, is subsumed with gentle irony, it does articulate the general mindset as is clear from the following:

> "Do you know," continued the magistrate, "the Sikhs retaliated by attacking a Muslim refugee train and sending it across the border with over a thousand corpses? They wrote on the engine 'Gift to Pakistan'!"
>
> The subinspector looked down thoughtfully and answered: "They say that is the only way to stop killings on the other side. Man for man, woman for woman, child for child. . . . Here we are

> on the border with Muslims living in Sikh villages as if nothing had happened. Every morning and evening the muezzin calls for prayer in the heart of a village like Mano Majra. You ask the Sikhs why they allow it and they answer that the Muslims are their brothers." (19-20)

But the calmness of the atmosphere in this 'oasis of peace' gets shattered when the 'ghost trains' start arriving in Mano Majra. The tense situation is evocatively articulated by the novelist in the opening paragraph of the chapter titled *Kalyug*: "Early in September, the time in Mano Majra started going wrong. Trains became less punctual than ever before and many more started to run through at night. . . . children did not know when to be hungry. . . . Goods trains had stopped running altogether, so there was no lullaby to lull them to sleep. Instead, ghost trains went past at odd hours between midnight and dawn, disturbing the dreams of Mano Majra." (77) And as days passed by, there were more news as well as rumours about the brutalities by the Muslims and Sikhs against each other on this and that side of the border. These obviously led to suspicions between the two communities which had lived together as family members for decades. "Quite suddenly every Sikh in Mano Majra became a stranger with an evil intent. His long hair and beard appeared barbarous, his kirpan menacingly anti-Muslim. For first time, the name Pakistan came to mean something to them—a haven of refuge where there were no Sikhs." (120-21) And the Sikhs too became sullen and angry and some of them started saying "Never trust a Mussulman." The young were particularly unhappy and agitated especially after the arrival of some 'refugees' from across the border. Yet the feeling and spirit of mutual welfare and brotherhood endured and after a long meeting Imam Baksh said: "What have we to do with Pakistan? We were born here. So were our ancestors. We have lived amongst you as brothers." (126) But when the Muslims feel compelled by the circumstances to leave for Pakistan in spite of all the good intentions of the local Sikhs, another aspect of partition/freedom is revealed. Infamous Malli and his gang who had looted the village moneylender and murdered him in defiance of the law, not only now align themselves with the instigators but are also officially appointed 'custodians' of the Muslim property left behind and proceed to loot in broad daylight. On the instigation of the young Sikh boys, quite a few of the Mano Majran Sikhs volunteer to aid and abet the destruction of the train stealthily at night so that the Muslims of Chundunnugger and Mano Majra among others, would not go alive and safely to Pakistan. The young Sikh, ironically of course, swears by the Gurus and inflames the fellow Sikhs of Mano Majra with the words "By the Grace of God/We bear the world nothing but good will" (152) on his lips. It is, however, the sagacity of the shrewd and wily but good-intentioned District Commissioner who heaps all kinds of abuses on the new political bosses for creating the traumatic situation, that saves the Muslim passengers from being butchered not with the help of the police but with the help of the village Budmash Jugga who was released from the jail and who was told that his beloved Nooran was also travelling by the same train. Jugga, though a dus-numbri (a proclaimed offender) had his mind and heart fired with the noble sentiment of love for Nooran. No sooner is he released than he rushes to cut the thick rope stretched and tied tightly across the railway bridge, after seeking Guru's word from Bhai Meet Singh even without understanding the meaning of that word. In the process of ensuring safe passage of the train to Pakistan, he has to make the supreme sacrifice of his own life: "He went at it with the knife, and then with his teeth. The engine was almost on him. There was a volley of shots, the man shivered and collapsed. The rope snapped in the centre as he fell. The train went over him, and went on to Pakistan." (181) Though some critics have labelled this ending of the novel as 'somewhat melodramatic' due to the lack of sufficient foregrounding of Jugga from a budmash, an anti-hero, into a hero, Jugga's sacrifice can be probably viewed as a form of wish fulfilment for the writer to achieve in fiction what on his own admission, he could not achieve in real life at the time of partition. Referring to the questions raised at the Press Conference after the screening of the film version of *Train to Pakistan* directed by Pamela Rooks at the recently concluded International Film Festival in New Delhi (11-20 January 1998), Khushwant Singh made the following comments which seem to be very pertinent even today i.e. fifty years after the unfortunate tragedy of Partition took place:

> Should the partition be forgotten? Has it any relevance to us today? My answer to both the questions is an emphatic yes. We must not forget the partition because it is relevant today. We must remember that it did in fact happen and can happen again. That is why I keep reminding people who clamour for an independent Kashmir, Khalistan or Nagaland to remember what happened to Muslims when some of them asked for a separate Muslim state. I keep telling my fellow Sikhs that the worst enemies of Khalsa Panth are Khalistanis, and of the Nagas those who ask for an independent Nagaland. Reminding ourselves of what happened in 1947 and realizing the possibilities of its recurring, we should resolve that we will never let it happen again.[2]

In *The Shadow Lines* the development and growth of Tha'mma's character encapsulates the futility and meaninglessness of political freedom which was otherwise supposed to usher in an era of peace and prosperity for all. During the days of her childhood and youth, she had her sympathies with all those who were fighting for the cause of freedom. In fact, she too wanted to earn small portion of the glory enjoyed by some of her classmate 'terrorists' by running secret errands for them or even cooking for them and washing their clothes. The aim was to be associated with such a group of persons, actively involved in fighting for a 'pious cause.' In response to a question by the narrator, "Do you really mean Tha'mma, that you would have killed him?"[3] we are told thus:

> She put her hands on my shoulders and holding me in front of her, looking directly at me, her eyes steady, forthright, unwavering: 'I would have been frightened. . . . But I would have prayed for strength, and God willing, yes, I would have killed him [the English Magistrate.] It was for our freedom: I would have done anything to be free.' (39)

Her formative years have taught her the need, necessity and desirability of political freedom which is a sort of pre-requisite for economic, social, cultural and intellectual freedom and development. As Novy Kapadia points out, the theme of the novel encompasses all these experiences: "By exploring connections, distinctions and possibilities, Amitav Ghosh shows that in a changing world, different strands of nationalism and ideology will exist and even compete. The force of nationalism in the quest for freedom or ideology is often a source of violence. . . . So the 'shadow line' between people and nations is often mere illusion. The force and appeal of nationalism cannot be wished away (so easily), just as death by a communal mob in the bye-lanes of old Dhaka."[4] Dhaka has been Tha'mma's place of birth, but her nationality is Indian. As a young girl, she had thought of fighting for freedom in East Bengal. But those very same people for whom she had been willing to lay down her life are enemies now in 1964. Feelings of nationalism had after all motivated the fight against the British in Khulna. But in 1964, the group of Indians travelling in the embassy car are the enemies to be hunted down and killed.

However, Tha'mma's disillusionment increases when she has to mention her birthplace on the passport-form during her visit to Dhaka. Home ought to be the place where one was born and brought up, sealed by an emotional bond, where one can claim one's right without a thought and without any hesitation. And if there was a basic confusion on this score—about the very roots of one's origin—an individual's identity would be in question. Leaving Dhaka during the Partition had obviously meant severing old roots and groping for a new kind of stability and identity. Therefore, years later, on her visit to Dhaka, she is distressed to write 'Dhaka' as her place of birth: "She liked things to be neat and in place—and at that moment she had not been able to quite understand how her place of birth had come to be so messily at odds with her nationality." (152)

Finally, the fact that "The border isn't on the frontier: it's right inside the airport" (151) puzzles Tha'mma all the more and she feels that her sacrifice has been in vain: "But if there aren't any trenches or anything, how are people to know? I mean, where's the difference then? And if there's no difference both sides will be the same; it'll be just like it used to be before, when we used to catch a train in Dhaka and get off in Calcutta the next day without anybody stopping us. What was it all for then—partition and all the killing and everything—if there isn't something in between?" (151) Tridib's death bewilders her further. She finds her idealism fast turning into helplessness as the anarchic tendencies within and without her gather force. There is obviously need for an order, a new order, but what kind of an order, remains an unanswered question. Tha'mma lies in bed, weak and helpless. Even as she realizes that war, partition and violence are meaningless if they create no visible borders between two countries; she never accepts and understands Ila's desperate urge to settle in England. Her orientation may be apparently that of a 'war-mongering fascist' as Ila terms it, it is nevertheless a harsh truth or at least a harsh partial truth that marks the psyche of the modern nation-states. The likes of Tridib have to die so that a comprehensive view of real freedom may find favour and flourish with the help of personal relationships. Ultimately, the responsibility of achieving and sustaining real freedom rests with every individual as it lies with every nation too within the larger framework. In fact, *The Shadow Lines* questions prevailing precepts and ethics which man inherits blindly. The value of political zeal and social freedom is no longer stable, exclusive, permanent and immutable as Tha'mma and Ila had believed. The apparent stability which is offered by such ideas often proves to be illusory. With Tridib, however, the novel emphasizes the relevance and significance of human relationships. This alone can lead to an attainment of genuine freedom. Man is free to decide on a course of action which is found to affect a whole group of people, a nation, mankind. Every individual shares the responsibility of establishing a code of values which would ensure peace and solidarity for mankind. As Sartre said: "Every one of our acts has at its stake, the meaning of the world and place of man in the universe. Through each of them, whether we wish it or not, we set up a scale of values which is universal."[5]

It has to be remembered that freedom is not just the absence of external pressure, it is also the presence of something else. The struggle for freedom is not without its darker side. If the fight for political freedom aims at ensuring peace for a particular community, it may also arouse and mobilize diabolical forces in man—forces which one would have believed to be non-existent, or at least to have died out long ago. If social and moral freedom is unlimited, it may unleash the numerous problems of excess and the lack of restraint. Taking all this into account, the question that arises is whether there is such a condition as complete freedom? Are freedom for the individual and for the society linked to and compatible with each other? And is absolute freedom a possibility for an individual, a community or for a nation? Should there be sufficient essential preparation, orientation and education of the individuals and of the society to enable them to digest their freedom, realize its full potential and cope with this freedom with dignity and with rationality? Fortunately both the novels *Train to Pakistan* and *The Shadow Lines* raise these significant questions in all their various dimensions and the narratives of the two obliquely explore and subtly answer these questions with the much needed flexibility of interpretation especially with reference to the pluralistic, multilingual, multicultural, multireligious and multiethnic character of the vastly-spread society of India in its widespread regions and teeming with paradoxes and contradictions at several levels.

In conclusion, it can be said that the partition of the Indian sub-continent was the single most traumatic experience in our recent history. The violence it unleashed by the hooligan actions of a few fanatics, the vengeance that the ordinary Hindus, Muslims and Sikhs wreaked on each other worsened our social sense, distorted our political judgements and deranged our understanding of moral righteousness.

The real sorrow of the partition, however, as portrayed in the two novels under review, was that it brought to an abrupt end a long and communally shared history and cultural heritage. The relations between the Hindus and the Muslims were not, of course, always free from suspicions, distrust or the angry rejection by one group of the habits and practices of the other; but such moments of active malevolence and communal frenzy were a rare and transient exception to the common bonds of mutual goodwill and warm feelings of close brotherhood. Even if there were some disruptions on some rare occasions, the rich heterogeneity of the life of the two communities was never seriously threatened. The Hindus never ceased from paying homages at dargahs; the

Muslims continued to participate in Hindu festivals; and traders of both the communities continued their usual exchange of goods and services in the bazars, etc. Indeed, one can assert with confidence that the dominant concerns of the Hindu and Muslim intellectuals throughout the nineteenth century and till about 1935, were more with creating free spaces for enlightened thought than with confining people within their narrow religious identities. Organizations which nurtured violent hatred towards each other and incited communal passions did exist, but at the very margins of the solidly and healthily functioning social and cultural order. It is the unthoughtful decision of partition and hollow love of 'nationalism' that let the mischief off and out.

NOTES

1. Khushwant Singh, *Train to Pakistan* (1956; New Delhi: Time Books International, 1989), p. 176.
2. Khushwant Singh, "A Forgetful Nation" in "With Malice towards One and All," *The Hindustan Times*, January 31, 1998, p. 13.
3. Amitav Ghosh, *The Shadow Lines* (Delhi: Ravi Dayal Publishers, 1988), p. 39.
4. Novy Kapadia, "Imagination and Politics in Amitav Ghosh's *The Shadow Lines*," ed. Viney Kirpal, *The New Indian Novel in English: A Study of the 1980s* (New Delhi: Allied, 1996), p. 205.
5. Sartre, *Le Sursis*, qtd. Henry Peyre, *French Novelists of Today* (New York: Oxford University Press, 1967), p. 267.

The Partition of Bengal: A Comparative Study of Amitav Ghosh's *The Shadow Lines* and Sunil Gangopadhyay's *Purba Paschim*

ALPANA NEOGY

In this paper, I am attempting a comparative study of two novels, one written in English, *The Shadow Lines* by Amitav Ghosh and the other a Bengali novel, *Purba Paschim*, by Sunil Gangopadhyay.

Both the novels have as their centre of focus, the Partition of India and the consequent trauma of the East Bengali psyche. Gangopadhyay's protagonist is Pratap Mazumdar, a Hindu from Malkhanagar in East Bengal, and the novel traces his life and times. The narrator of Ghosh's novel is a young boy who grew up in Calcutta and Delhi in post-Partition India. The trauma of Partition continues through three generations. The agonies of displacement, the sense of alienation in the adopted land, the constant dream of a return to one's land—these are the common themes in both the novels.

Fifty years have passed by since India became 'free.' The Bengali diaspora has been dispersed to distant lands. Some have gained successes in new associations and developments. Yet the sense of loss of one's identity, the connection with one's *baari* remains. *Baari* is where one's ancestors have lived for generations. *Baasha*, on the other hand, is a temporary residence no matter how long one has stayed there.[1]

For the East Bengali, 15 August 1947 is the Partition day, not India's independence day, a day that deliberately bifurcated the Bengali community. If the purpose of Partition was to gain freedom, then that freedom is a 'mirage.' Observing the front pages of newspapers which give details of terrorist activities, Amitav Ghosh is driven to ask: "Why don't they draw thousands of little lines through the whole subcontinent and give every place a new name?"[2]

Despair is the dominant note struck by Amitav Ghosh in *The Shadow Lines*. Ghosh brings out the futility of drawing lines across a nation to form two nations, one having an East wing which is separated from its

West wing by over a thousand miles.

Tha'mma, the narrator's grandmother, belongs to the generation that had to uproot itself in 1947. When she is all set to go to Dhaka to rescue her Jethamoshai, she inquires if she would be able to see the border between India and East Pakistan from the airplane. "But surely there's something—trenches perhaps, or soldiers, or guns pointing at each other, or even just barren strips of land. . . . But if there aren't any trenches or anything, how are people to know? I mean, where's the difference then? And if there's no difference, both sides will be the same; it'll be just like it used to be before. . . . What was it all for then—Partition and all the killing and everything—if there isn't something in between?" (151)

Subconsciously she has rejected the historical act of Partition. History perhaps could explain the events leading up to this event, perhaps even explain why it happened when it did. It is her memory of her ancestral home (which actually reaches out far beyond any historical fact) which inspires her to go to Dhaka on that tragic mission. Earlier on, when told that Jethamoshai was still alive in Dhaka and that the whole house had been occupied by Muslim refugees from India, she exclaims, "You mean our house has been occupied by refugees?" (135)

This nostalgia for the past, the refusal to accept historical realities, is evident in Sunil Gangopadhyay's Bengali novel *Purba Paschim*[3] published in two volumes, as well. Its vast canvas covers events and occurrences in both East and West Bengal. The novel progresses through the recent history of the two Bengals. Starting in the mid '50s, the novel becomes a living documentation of how political and social change in the two Bengals has affected the lives of the people of Bengal. The novel concludes in the '80s. There is a constant reference to the halcyon days of pre-Partition Bengal. The Nehru days, the Indo-Pakistan war, the rise of Indira Gandhi, the steady economic decline, the increase of revolutionary feelings amongst the youth, the Naxalbari movement, the demands for political freedom in Bangla Desh, the despair of the youth, the murder of Sheikh Mujibur Rehman, all these political facts form the backdrop to this story.

Ghosh's novel, on the other hand, concentrates on one event that triggers off a whole series of events. On 27 December 1963, a relic, believed to be a hair of the Prophet Muhammad, disappears from the Hazratbal mosque at Srinagar in Kashmir. Hindus, Sikhs and Muslims demonstrate throughout the Valley in protest. No animosity existed between the various religious groups in the Kashmir Valley at that time. Indeed, not one incident involving religious discord surfaced after the theft.

Yet, in Khulna, a small town in the distant east wing of Pakistan, a demonstration taken out in protest against the theft, turns violent. Riots spead outwards from Khulna towards Dhaka. Tridib, who had gone to "rescue" his mother's Jethamoshai at Jindabahar Lane, Dhaka, is caught in the midst of one of these riots and is killed. He did not realize that the masses of the subcontinent has "an unregenerate side always prone to violence."[4] Tridib had dreamt of a "better place, a place without borders and countries." When May comes down from England as a stranger, he wants to meet her in a ruin, far from friends and relatives, in a place "without a past, without history, free, really free, two people coming together with the utter freedom of strangers." (144)

The name *Purba Paschim* denotes the two Bengals; in a sense it could denote the Eastern and Western Hemisphere, or the two ends of the horizontal axis. Gangopadhyay traces the genesis of the Hindu-Muslim rift in this novel. A close friend of Pratap Mazumdar, a Hindu student at Rippon College, Calcutta was a Bengali Muslim, Syed Mojammul Haque, affectionately called Mamun who came from a village in Coumilla, East Bengal. All well-to-do families in East Bengal would send their sons to study in Calcutta in those days. Mamun takes Pratap to this ancestral home one day, knowing full well that his father is a rigid Muslim who would not tolerate even a Hindu shadow to fall on his doorstep. The father takes one look at Pratap's clean-shaven face and remarks, "You look like a Hindu." While the young man shivers in his rain-drenched clothes, he has to answer questions about his home, his father, his profession, his property.

Thereafter, Pratap is permitted to change out of his wet clothes and offered a bowl of puffed rice and a glass of milk. Syed Hakim, Mamun's father, then tells him with deep regret and with the utmost humility that no Hindu could take shelter in his home just as no member of his family could take shelter in the house of a Hindu: this was the unwritten code of the family laid down by *his* father, who had been insulted many years ago at the house of a Hindu brahmin family in Sylhet. He had but entered the brahmin's house when he was asked to go and stand outside. All the potable water of that house was thrown away and the earthen pitchers broken. Pratap, naturally, finds no reason why he should be insulted because some Brahmin, so many years ago had behaved in such a crude fashion.

The prejudices in the Hindu mind, largely due to the strong caste-system, had coalesced through the years. Once Mamun had overheard his friend's mother remark: "Is the boy a Muslim? I had thought him to be a Bengali." As Mamum muses: "If Muslims cannot be Bengalis, then Muslims cannot be Indians too. Only Muslims."

Gangopadhyay attempts to analyse the Hindu-Muslim discord. The prejudices on both sides had hardened their relationships. Mamun believes that both in the field of education and work, the Hindus had been the favoured ones in Bengal. Pratap, very agitated, had replied that he was not even aware that he was a Hindu. Perhaps the majority Bengali Hindu population, secure in the knowledge of being Hindus, had not fully appreciated the depths of insecurity in the Muslim psyche. But these social differences were not insurmountable, Gangopadhyay believes.

It was the chicanery of the politicians that permanently divided the land purely on the basis of religion. The Communal Award of 1937 laid the foundation of communalism. In the Bengal Assembly of 250 seats, according to the Award, 117 seats were to be allotted to the Muslim Bengali, 52 to the Bengali Hindus and the rest to the other categories. Under these conditions, there was no way by which Bengal could have a Bengali Hindu government. The Bengali Hindu was the first Indian to acquire western education and the western political system, and also the first to take up the call of freedom. From the Bengali Hindu community had emerged the revolutionaries and the terrorists. Their literature and music had kindled in the masses the desire for freedom. Small wonder then that the British Government felt it necessary to teach the Bengali Hindus a lesson!

The tragedy of Bengal lay in the fact that at the time of Partition she had no leader—C.R. Das, who had dreamt of a Bengal free of communalism where Hindus and Muslims would stand side by side and face the common enemy, the British, had passed away; Subhash Bose had disappeared; and Aurobindo Ghosh had relinquished politics for a spiritual life at Pondicherry.

After Partition, Pratap Mazumdar finds himself a job as a sub-judge in Calcutta and settles down in a small rented flat in one of the poorer colonies. Had he sold off his family estate in East Bengal (and not abandoned it) the money accrued from the sale would have fetched him a mansion in one of the posh localities of Calcutta.

Living in cramped conditions, he and his mother are often swamped by waves of nostalgia as they remember their coconut and mango groves in East Bengal. When it rains in Calcutta, he remembers Malkhanagar. In an enclosed rickshaw in the rain he imagines he is once again in a covered boat in his pond at Malkhanagar. When he sees some fresh *illsh* fish in the market, he buys not one but four of them.

Both Ghosh and Gangopadhyay express a stunned disbelief that Partition could happen at all. For Gangopadhyay it is a cry from the heart—suddenly and in such a cruel manner the Mazumdar family had been cut adrift from a familiar and loved world. The native village is pictured as both sacred and beautiful. Something of value to Bengali culture and the understanding of what home was had been destroyed by the Partition.

Life becomes difficult as the Mazumdar family copes with the changed circumstances. A certain way of life, a certain kind of decency seems to have passed away. Pratap's brother-in-law is a lover of music. The landed gentry had suddenly become "declassed" with Partition. He has spent his youth acquiring a knowledge of music and had not learnt how to earn a living. He gradually fades away unable to cope with the changed circumstances.

Pratap's eldest sister Supriti is introduced to emphasize the tremendous divide between the East Bengali Hindu (the Bangaal) and the West Bengali Hindu (the Ghoti). The Ghotis have always considered East Bengal to be a land of muddy villages and believed that a Bangaal is civilised only when he moves to Calcutta.

Supriti is married to a West Bengali Hindu. After her marriage, she is forced to wipe out the Bangaal lilt in her speech; it takes her even longer to learn the West Bengali idiom. She is never accepted and when her husband is killed, allegedly by the land-grabbing refugees (her "country cousins" according to her in-laws) she is driven out of the family home, penniless.

After Partition, the East Bengali Hindu found that he had very little in common with the West Bengali Hindu. He had a greater affinity of mind with those he had left behind on the other side of the border-line—the East Pakistani Muslim! His food habits were different, his tastes were different, he even spoke differently.

And this confusion about one's identity runs through both the novels. In London, Tutul, Pratap's niece, often meets Bengalis settled there who ask her about her "desh" (that is, one's place of origin). When she replies "Calcutta," she is asked to be more specific in order that she may be identified as an East or West Bengali.

Ila in *The Shadow Lines* rejects everything that is Indian and tries to seek an identity for herself in an alien land. "Do you see now why I've chosen to live in London? It's only because I want to be free. Free of your bloody culture and free of all of you," (88) she yells, as she is dragged out of the hotel dance-floor where she has started dancing with an unknown businessman. Her cousin Robi checks her outrageous behaviour by saying that "Girls don't behave like that here. . . . There are certain things you cant do here; that's our culture." (88) Ila, brought up outside India, travels all over the world with her diplomat father. But she is rootless: she doesn't find a sense of belonging anywhere and fantasizes an existence where she is the cynosure of all eyes. In reality she is lonely and miserable. In an attempt to reject her roots and identify herself with the West, she marries Nick but finds him cheating her for the sake of "variety." Rootless and lost at the end of the novel, she clings to the arms of the writer and Robi, members of her family. Her attempt to adopt an alien culture proves abortive and, at the end, she finds the need to go back to one's family.

Both the novels reject the very concept of Partition. They scoff at national leaders who had believed that problems could be solved by drawing lines across the land. Both Bengals are historically, culturally and geographically one and a division was not a solution to the traditional Hindu-Muslim animosity.

Ghosh believes that freedom in the truest sense is an impossibility even in a "free state." One can be enslaved by memories so powerful that a chance remark can set one's hand shaking like a leaf. There was a time when "sensible, good-intentioned people had believed that once they had etched their borders upon the map, "the two bits of land would sail away." (233) They had created not a separation, but a yet undiscovered irony: "the simple fact that there had never been a movement in the four thousand year old history of that map when the places we know as Dhaka and Calcutta were more closely bound to each other" (233) than ever before.

Sunil Gangopadhyay, through the character of Mamun, reveals the loss of the Bengali Muslim in the newly created land now called East Pakistan to wipe out its Bengali identity. He misses his contact with Shantiniketan, with Murshidabad and with all the culture associated with united Bengal. When he seeks shelter in Calcutta during the Bangla Desh war, he is told not to refer to water as "paani" but to ask for "jal." He remembers a word coined in the earlier days "jalpaani" which was a synthesis of both cultures, Hindu and Muslim. Perhaps herein lay the answer to the problem—find avenues for synthesis. A division of a land purely on the basis of religion was no answer to the problem.

NOTES

1. See Dipesh Chakravarti, "Remembered Villages: Representation of Hindu Bengali memories in the aftermath of the Partition," *Economic and Political Weekly*, Vol. 31, No. 32, Aug. 10, 1996.
2. Amitav Ghosh, *The Shadow Lines* (Delhi: Ravi Dayal Publisher, 1988), p. 247.
3. (Calcutta: Ananda Publishers, 1981).
4. See Nirad C. Chaudhuri, *Thy Hand, Great Anarch* (Chatto and Windus, 1987), p. 806.

The Shadow Lines: A Quest for 'Indivisible Sanity'

MURARI PRASAD

> The novel is not required—even assuming the task is within the realm of possibility—to describe the specific historical forms of a society; that is not where the truth lies. Nor of course is it a matter of saying that the author's ideas are necessarily correct. But literature is always an attempt to reveal to us "an unknown side of human existence," as Kundera says somewhere, and thus although it has no privileged access to truth, it never stops searching for it.[1]

Amitav Ghosh's *The Shadow Lines* is one of the most readable and least frivolous of the recent Indian novels in English. An effective fiction, it emanates from a particular historical moment which intersects the narrator and the nation at a crucial point of their evolution and growth. While capturing the high points of the historical moment in credible and efficient narrative action, the novel eventuates into a search for the vibrant concerns essential for the survival of central strength and sanity in society. The novel is rich in signifying transactions that do not depend for their effect on "solid slabs of continuous experience" but on the potentiality of materiality marshalled by the author to anchor his perception of reality. It quickens our conscience and triggers our response to the mingled frenzy of violence, idealism, passion and intrigue that has amputated the narrator's intimate history and geography. By skilfully manipulating the narrator's developing sociological consciousness and his interaction with multicultural representatives in a fictional construct, Ghosh makes his novel a supple medium of sophisticated comment on current realities. Although the situations are bound by their historical and geographical co-ordinates, they enlarge the spatial and temporal axes and offer a melange of insights into a kind of 'reality' that can sustain inter-personal bond across cultural boundaries and contain the threats flowing from the absurdities of borders and frontiers.

The novel tells the story of the three generations of the narrator's family spread over Dhaka, Calcutta and London and lines up characters from different nationalities, religions and cultures in a close-knit, palpable fictive world. Written against the backdrop of the civil strife in post-partition East Bengal and riot-hit Calcutta, the events revolving around itinerant Mayadebi's family, their friendship and sojourn with their English friends, the Prices, Tha'mma, the narrator's great mother, ties with Dhaka and the later wrench from her roots, spontaneous communal combustion in 1964 in Dhaka claiming the lives of Jethamoshai, Khalil and Tridib pose the challenge of intercultural understanding and friendship in contemporary society divided by arbitrary demarcations of national boundaries. The narrator's mnemonic fund is enriched by his uncle and mentor, Tridib, who lets him in on the creative powers of memory and imagination. On one hand is the narrator's family consisting of his grandmother, Mayadebi's elder sister, and his parents; on the other are Mayadebi, her husband, a diplomat, and their three sons, Jatin, an economist with the UN, Tridib and Robi. Jatin's daughter, Ila, is always away with her parents. While the narrator's family is settled in Calcutta where his grandmother is a schoolmistress, Mayadebi's family except Tridib keeps on going around the world. Tridib, who lives in his ancestral house in Ballygunge place, is seen at a loose end at Gole Park among his *adda* acquaintances. Stay in close vicinity brings the narrator and his uncle Tridib together, although much to the dislike of Tha'mma, who is stern middle-class matriarch.

Tridib saw May Price as a little baby when he went to England with his parents in 1939. The friendship between the families began when Mrs. Price's father, Lionel Tresawsen, and Tridib's grandfather, Mr. Justice Chandrashekhara Datta-Chaudhury, met in Calcutta at seances. By the time Tridib meets May in India in 1962, their friendship through correspondence since 1959 has ripened into love. The narrator who is Ila's age and is drawn to her apparently liberated charms loses his chance to Nick Price, May's younger brother. It is May-Tridib relationship which is central to the thematic concerns of the novel. The narrator's close interaction with May who accompanied Tha'mma, Mayadebi and Tridib to bring his grandmother's uncle, Jethamoshai, from Dhaka to Calcutta and was witness to the killing of Tridib, is the most moving part of the novel. The narrator recalls his meeting with May at crucial point in the chronology of the novel: "I met May Price for the first time two years after that incident, when she came to Calcutta on a visit. The next time I met her was seventeen years later, when I went to London myself."[2] (19) The stretch of history during these seventeen years between 1962 and 1979 is the effective background of the novel against which the author evokes postcolonial situations, cultural dislocations and anxieties, and interprets the issues of fractured nationalities in close and telling encounters.

The historical baggage shouldered by the novel includes the freedom movement in Bengal, the Second World War, the partition of India and the miasma of communal hatred breaking out into riots in East Pakistan (now Bangla Desh) following the Hazratbal incident in Srinagar in 1964. The novel is not a recapitulation of these historical upheavals; it catches alive the trauma of emotional rupture and choked human relations as also the damaging potential of the siege within people sundered by politics. The materiality of Ghosh's novel constituted by the web of material relations at a certain time in a certain location binds the narratives and authenticates the nexus between the historical moment and the fictive world. The reconstruction of the past through houses, photographs, maps, road names, newspapers, advertisements and other concretizations allows the reader to examine the text with diverse co-texts and validate the author's perception of the time and milieu covered by the novel. A close look at the principal episodes with reference to their historicity and materiality is significantly revealing in that the author's insight into the issues troubling the consciousness of characters can be identified and gleaned. "In *The Shadow Lines,*" writes Nivedita Bagchi, "the very materiality of objects plays a vital role in validating the narrative. Tridib, we are told, is an archaeologist, and the chief narrator is a history research fellow. The importance of material objects to the archaeological-historian for validation of oral narratives, for dating and establishing chronology in the reconstruction of history, cannot be overstated."[3]

The looping, non-linear progression of the narratives underpinned by the narrator and the historical sweep entail active and alert audience participation. In the opening lines, the narrator refers to his grandmother's sister's visit to England and establishes the narrative framework: "In 1993, thirteen years before I was born, my father's aunt, Mayadebi, went to England with her husband and her son, Tridib." (9) We gather that Mayadebi was born in 1910 and Tridib in 1931. The novel also telescopes the political ferment in Bengal and the upbringing of Tha'mma, who was born in 1902, and Mayadebi in the revolutionary decades of the present century. As soon as we infer the details of Mayadebi's visit to England, the narrative shifts to 1960 when Tridib first shared his experience of London with the narrator:

> Over the years, although I cannot remember when it happened any more than I can remember when I first learnt to tell the time or tie my shoelaces, I have come to believe that I was eight too when Tridib first talked to me about that journey. I remember trying

> very hard to imagine him back to my age, to reduce his height to mine, and to think away the spectacles that were so much a part of him that I really believed he had been born with them. It wasn't easy, for to me he looked old, and I could not remember him looking anything other than old—though, in fact, at that time he could not have been much older than twenty-nine. In the end, since I had nothing to go on, I had decided that he had looked like me. (9)

Thus the narrative spills back and forth but all the episodes are held in simultaneous focus nonetheless to illuminate the major burden of the novel.

Chronologically, the story begins with a passage of time in colonial India when the narrator was not born. The year 1939 is historically significant for the outbreak of the second world war and phenomenal changes caused by that agonizing epochal event. Mayadebi's visit to London around this time, her warm and consequential contact with the Price family and Tridib-May component of the story is recounted by Tridib to the narrator twenty-one years later when the latter is an eight-year-old inquisitive child. Although May was a little baby when Tridib saw her in London—and they have not met since then—a romantic relationship develops through correspondence between them, transcending the shadow lines of nationality and cultural boundary. Amitav Ghosh explores the mysterious pull between Tridib and May and the abiding intimacy between the two families, when the countries were pitted against each other. This search for invisible links ranging across the realities of nationality, cultural segregation and racial discrimination is the central theme of *The Shadow Lines*. The author questions the validity of geographical boundaries and celebrates the union of aliens pulled together by self-propelling empathy and attachment. Tresawsen and Mayadebi, Tridib and May, Jethamoshai and Khalil rise above the prevailing passion of war, hatred and communal bad blood and vindicate the political logic of partition and border demarcation to define national and cultural particularities. Ghosh's maturer view of reality was missed glaringly by Bruce King in his review of *In an Antique Land* in *World Literature Today*. The reviewer notes: "Amitav Ghosh's novels *The Circle of Reason* and *The Shadow Lines* are somewhat difficult to place on the current literary map; they have an unusual perspective and cover unexpected territory. *In an Antique Land* fills in some of the picture of how Ghosh sees the world and, besides the interest of the book itself as social anthropology and what it tells us about Ghosh, might be a starting place for future discussion of his fiction."[4] Without questioning the merit of *In an Antique Land*, the present writer differs with Bruce

King's comments on *The Shadow Lines* in that the latter, as a seminal piece of fiction, does bring out the rare and remarkable talent of Ghosh who passionately searches for strategies for survival in a violent, hate-filled world of narrow divisions and finds in love the enabling and productive action to tide over separatist propensities of communities and nationality groups. The novel addresses the challenge of geographical fluidity and cultural dislocations with a new consciousness and firm grasp of socio-cultural and historical material. The experience of aliens and immigrants in postcolonial setting furnish us with the clue to the novel's larger project of cultural assimilation, friendship across borders and adjustment with the altered face of the world. The theme is first sounded when in a conversation with the narrator in London in 1978 May Price shares her growing intimacy with Tridib:

> Smiling at the memory, she told me how his card had reached her just when she was trying to get over an adolescent crush on a schoolboy trombonist, who had had no time for her at all and had not been overly delicate about making that clear. It was nice to feel that someone wanted to befriend her. She had written back, and after that they had written to each other regularly—short, chatty letters, usually. Soon, pen-friendship, they had exchanged photographs. (23)

The narrator recalls that Tridib's made-up story of his English relatives through marriage recounted to his *adda* acquaintances at Gold Park around 1960 sprang from his passionate longing for May:

> Where have you been all this while Tridib-da! somebody said. It must be three or four months. . . .
>
> I've been away, I heard him say, and nodded secretly to myself.
>
> Away! Where!
>
> I've been to London, he said. To visit my relatives.
>
> His face was grave, his voice steady.
>
> What relatives!
>
> I have English relatives through marriage, he said. A family called Price. I thought I'd go and visit them.
>
> Ignoring their grunts, he told them that he had been to stay with old Mrs. Price, who was a widow. Her husband had died recently. She lived in north London, he said, on a street called Lymington Road; the number of their house was 44 and the tube station was West Hampstead. Mrs. Price had a daughter, who was called May. (17)

Tridib realizes May concretely and warmly in his imagination with all the attendant excitement stored in his senses. He can visualize her shape and appearance precisely even without meeting her. Their love has instrinsic reality; it crosses all borderlines and shadow-lines. The narrator also owes his broadened horizons to Tridib's influence. He has become an imaginative traveller of distant locations beyond the limits of his mind and experience at a fairly young age. He is verily enamoured of the Tridib who had pushed him to "imagine the roofs of Colombo" for himself and "had said that we could not see without inventing what we saw, so at least we could try to do it properly." (37) The narrator's psyche absorbs cross-cultural interactions and sheds particularity of his origin and narrow nationalism fostered and instilled in him by his grandmother. Unlike Ila's pragmatic cosmopolitanism, either lukewarm or lacking in vibrant reciprocity, the narrator learns the lesson of love and sacrifice untrammelled by exclusionary nationalism and spatial limits, first under the spiritual tutelage of Tridib, and later, in the warm embrace of May towards the close of the novel. He contrasts the cross-cultural perspectives of Tridib and Ila at several places in the novel. For instance:

> I tried to tell her, but neither then nor later, though we talked about it often, did I ever succeed in explaining to her that I could not forget because Tridib had given me worlds to travel in and he had given me eyes to see them with; she, who had been travelling around the world since she was a child, could never understand what those hours in Tridib's room had meant to me, a boy who had never been more than a few hundred miles from Calcutta. I used to listen to her talking sometimes with her father and grandfather about the cafes in the Plaza Mayor in Madrid; or the crispness of the air in Cuzco, and I could see that those names, which were to me a set of magical talismans because Tridib had pointed them out to me on his tattered old Bartholomew's Atlas, had for her a familiarity no less dull than the lake had for me and my friends; the same tired intimacy that made us stop on our way back from the park in the evening and unbutton our shorts and aim our piss through the rusty wrought-iron railings. (26)

Yet the narrator is hooked on to Ila's exotic appeal. It is her striking foreignness, her western ways and easy informality that attract him. Her liberated gestures and overtly off-beat demeanour arouse Tha'mma's contemptuous dislike for her. While the narrator develops a mesmeric fascination for Ila in the flush of adolescence, his grandmother hates her vulgar transgressions. Ila's preference for Nick Price and her later disappointment expose her wobbly transplantation in the western culture. Her dislocation stems from her penchant for illusions devoid of any real understanding of the cultural interface. The adult narrator sees through Ila's hidden anxieties and discomfiture. Her last words in the novel are aimed at consoling the narrator and her cousin that everything is all right between her and Nick. Commenting on Ila's role in the novel, Suvir Kaul notes that she is central to the narrator's coming-of-age and functions "as a narrative scapegoat, a figure who acts as a lightning-rod for a great many sexual and cultural anxieties, and the telling of whose unhappy and even sordid itinerary, especially her relationship with Nick, takes on all the cautionary tones of a modern fable."[5] Nick-Ila pairing is a counterpoint to Tridib-May kinship in the thematic framework of the novel. When the narrator looks at Ila's seductive foreignness with unstinted eye in his mature stage, he notices her snooty ways and cultural contradictions. Significantly, the novel ends with May and the narrator lying in close embrace after the former has recounted Tridib's tragic killing in Dhaka. May interprets Tridib's act as sacrifice and defines the manner of his giving up his life while rushing to Jethamoshai for his unsuccessful rescue from the frenzied rioters. Tridib appreciates May's ideals of humanitarianism and acts like her soulmate. Jean Sudrann makes a perceptive comment on the thematic concerns of Amitav Ghosh: "As in his first novel, *The Circle of Reason,* where Ghosh pitted rationality against emotion as warring forces within and among people, so here the conflict has been resumed in epistemological terms. Knowledge can set us free, but only if it is bred of heart as well as head. May's love—of the narrator, of Tridib, of the cycle-rickshaw man, of the hate-filled lawyer—which prompts her to reveal her innermost thoughts to the narrator, releases him from the silence which is outside his intelligence into the perhaps equally unspeakable mystery of love."[6] The novel insists on the imperatives that assure empathy and unimpeded flow of friendship, and mock the conception of militant nationalism, exclusive national pride and identity. The outbreak of communal strife in Dhaka following the disappearance of the prophet's hair in Srinagar exposes the fragile demarcation of political frontiers. The author's postcolonial angst for the disrupted subcontinental commonality and snapped cultural bonds is evident in the instant communal reaction to the Hazratbal incident in Calcutta and Dhaka. Tha'mma's ideals of nationalism nurtured since the Swadeshi movement do not stand the test of time. Hers is a misplaced sense of pride reminiscent of the 'tardy late-bourgeois world.' Drawing national borders with blood is bound to be undone by the inherent logic of and propensity to separateness and divinations. Her senile old uncle has a grasp of ambiguous and tenuous geographical boundaries: "Once you start moving you never stop. That's what I told my sons when they took the trains. I said: I don't believe in this India-Shindia. It's all very well, you're going away now, but suppose when you get there they decide to draw another line somewhere! What will you do then! Where will you move to! No one will ever have you anywhere. As for me, I was born here, and I'll die here." (216)

The message of the novel underlines the need of friendly ambience for co-existence and humanitarian ties across cultures independent of political managers. The 'indivisible sanity' of people beyond borders has the potential to ensure warm and wholesome international amity and exorcise divisive streaks and madness. Mayadebi and Tresawsen realize the palpable evidence of this desire among people both in England and Germany even as the second world war is looming ahead:

> Well, she said, laughing, the couple of months she had spent in London had been so exciting—the atmosphere had changed so dramatically, even within the last few weeks. People were becoming friendlier; in the shops, on the streets, she couldn't help noticing. Everyone was so much nicer now; often when she and Tridib were out walking people would pat him on the head and stop to have a little chat with her; the shopkeepers would ask her how her husband was, and when he was to have his operation. But it wasn't just her—everyone was being friendly with everyone; why just that morning his sister, Elisabeth, had said that old Mrs. Dunbar who lived down the road had actually been civil for the first time in living memory. . . .
>
> Yes, he said, that's true—there's a kind of exhilaration in the air.
>
> Yes, that's the right word, said Mayadebi: exhilaration.
>
> I've been lucky, I've been lucky to watch England coming alive. I wouldn't have seen that if I hadn't been here now.
>
> Tresawsen laughed. People don't believe me, he said, but it's the same over there—in Germany—though of course in a much more grotesque way. It was odd coming back here—like stepping through a looking glass. (70-71)

The narrator with his expanded horizons and imaginative understanding of the world caught up in the vortex of violence and murderous rampage stresses on the urgency of preserving the memories of saner and humane transactions for cultural self-determination and inter-personal communication. The media and public memory must keep alive the 'indivisible sanity' of communities to prevent recurrence of insane frenzy. Ghosh has edged up his novel to confront the memory of traumatic events and shake up our indifference to the gathering potential of tragedy. All in all, the novel is "an eloquent critique of colonial hangover and cultural dislocation in postcolonial situation as also the psychological make-up of the contemporary man who thrives on violence."[7] Amitav Ghosh projects these genuine Indian vibrations with remarkable competence.

NOTES

1. Tzvetan Todorov, "A Dialogic Criticism," *Literature and Its Theorists*, trans. Catherine Porter (London: Routeledge and Kegan Paul, 1988), p. 164.
2. Amitav Ghosh, *The Shadow Lines* (London: Black Swan, 1988), p. 19.
3. Nivedita Bagchi, "The Process of Validation in Relation to Materiality and Historical Reconstruction in Amitav Ghosh's *The Shadow Lines*," *Modern Fiction Studies*, 39 (Winter 1993), pp. 187-201.
4. Bruce King, "*In an Antique Land*," *World Literature Today*, 68:1-2, 1994, p. 430.
5. Suvir Kaul, "Separation Anxiety: Growing Up Inter/National in Amitav Ghosh's *The Shadow Lines*," *The Oxford Literary Review*, 16 (1994), pp. 125-45.
6. Jean Sudrann, "Goings and Comings," *Yale Review*, 79 (1990), pp. 414-38.
7. G.R. Taneja, "*The Shadow Lines*," pp. 149-50 of this book.

The Theme of Violence in *The Shadow Lines*

N. EAKAMBARAM

Amitav Ghosh's *The Shadow Lines*[1] is a complex novel interweaving memory and contemporary life, more memory than contemporary life. It converges on the traumatic life of a family in Calcutta and Dhaka in 1964 when a member of the family, Tridib was killed in a communal riot. Ghosh employs the technique of the narrator, an educated young man who travels between Calcutta and London in 1981, to tell the story which contains multiple stories of his grandmother and her sister, of his uncles—Tridib and Robi, of his cousin Ila who marries an Englishman, and of May Price, a family friend in London. Many stories that belong to the oral sphere in the extended family memory get their validation by being written in the novel—a feature of most postcolonial writing.

Ghosh depicts the urban middle class in India to whom education and professional jobs are important. Living and partly living they drift from one day to another, and so for a whole lifetime. The reward, if one is lucky, may be one's own house and a pension to lean upon. The environment of the school and/or office encourages the cultivation of the virtues of hard work, contentment, obedience, and conformity to the norms of society. Amitav Ghosh's characters inhabit this realm of life. But when misfortune strikes their lives in an unforeseen manner, they are left baffled. If it is, at least, death or disease, they may try to comprehend it. But when violence erupts like a volcano in the public sphere, they are totally disoriented. Life seems to lose its significance. The present paper examines how violence cracks the mirror of life in the fictional world of *The Shadow Lines*.

The narrative of *The Shadow Lines* is in two parts: "Going Away" (3-112) and "Coming Home." (115-252) The words "going" and "coming" are used in relation to 'home,' a place of one's birth and upbringing, a place to which a person is deeply attached, especially if one lives in another place. Though in the growth of a human being, it would be ideal to feel that all places are one's place and all people one's people, and he/she is 'a citizen of the world', most people are circumscribed by the contexts of their life. They either 'go away' or 'come home.' Ghosh's characters go as far as Delhi or London on work or travel, and come home to Calcutta or Dhaka only to learn that peace is as elusive as ever.

One disturbing feature of life in Calcutta/Dhaka and such cities is the increasing tension between the Hindu and Muslim communities and the eruption of violence which takes its toll of innocent lives and destruction of public as well as private property. As long as one learns about death and destruction in newspapers and other media, one is not touched by them. But when someone in the family is caught in the carnage, then one realizes what it is. In fact, this exactly is what happens to the characters of Amitav Ghosh.

The narrative structure of *The Shadow Lines* is fragmentary. There are sixteen sections in the first part, and fifteen in the second part, but the sections do not add up to an organic whole with a proper beginning, middle and ending. Nivedita Bagchi observes: "The 'story' or the chief narrative line evolves sporadically and is constantly interrupted and diverted by other narratives. The only fixed center is that of the chief narrative voice through whom the other narratives are filtered."[2] Ghosh's narrator shuttles not only from Calcutta to London to collect material for his Ph.D. thesis, but across the loom of time from 1981 to the 1960s onto the 1940s and earlier. Especially his mind is drawn on the troubled time of the 1960s when Tridib, his uncle, was killed in a Hindu-Muslim riot in Dhaka. At the time this tragedy took place, the narrator, a twelve-year-old boy, had been told that Tridib had died in an accident. It is only in 1981 that he learns from Robi, another uncle, an eyewitness, how Tridib had been killed, also from May Price, an English family friend, also an eyewitness to the tragedy. The oblique manner of the revelation of Tridib's death is more effective than a direct presentation. It is a timeless moment in the tortured consciousness of the family. The narrator—whose name is not given—is the bearer of this troubled memory.

The narrator's grandmother, Tha'mma is the central character in the novel. In fact, *The Shadow Lines* is very much her story. The narrator remembers how Tridib had called her "a modern middle-class woman. . . All she wanted was a middle-class life in which, like the middle classes the world over, she would thrive believing in the unity of nationhood and territory, of self-respect and national power: that was all she wanted—a modern middle-class life, a small thing that history had denied her in its fullness and for which she could never forgive it." She has lived a quiet life for a whole lifetime in Calcutta, but when she goes to Dhaka (her native city) on a visit, she is the unwitting witness to the most horrendous act in her life when a rioting mob kills her aged uncle and her young nephew. She is left totally disoriented as she cannot comprehend the meaning of what happens. She is the dangling woman suspended by the quirk of history.

Amitav Ghosh presents the grandmother's early life as a story told by her to the narrator. (121-26) Born in 1902 in Dhaka, she grew up as a member of "a big joint family, with everyone living and eating together." (121) But when her grandfather died, the ancestral house had to be partitioned because of the strife that broke out between her father and her uncle. While at college for her B.A. in History in Dhaka, she had known the terrorist movement amongst nationalists in Bengal: "about secret terrorist societies like Anushilan and Jugantar and all their offshoots, their clandestine networks, and the home-made bombs with which they tried to assassinate British officials and policemen; and a little about the arrests, deportations and executions with which the British had retaliated." (37)

In her own class there was a shy young man who was a member of a terrorist organization. One day as the lecture was going on, the police entered the class and arrested the young man as they had learnt that he planned to kill an English magistrate in Khulna district. He was tried and later deported to the cellular jail in the Andaman Islands. In her youthful enthusiasm she had dreamt of terrorists like Kudhiram Bose and Bagha Jatin who had been betrayed by treacherous villagers who in turn had been bought with English money. "She'd been expecting a huge man with burning eyes and a lion's mane of a beard, and there he was, all the while, at the back of her class, sitting shyly by himself." (39) She had wanted to work for the terrorists, to run errands for them, to cook their food, to wash their clothes and to render some help. After all, the terrorists were working for freedom. When the narrator asks her whether she would have killed the English magistrate, she replies: "I would have been frightened. . . . But I would have prayed for strength, and God willing, yes, I would have killed him. It was for our freedom: I would have done anything to be free." (39) But her romantic notion of terrorism and freedom went like a bubble with her marriage. Her short married life, mostly lived in Burma, was punctuated by the birth of a son in 1925, and the unfortunate death of her husband in 1935 when she was just thirty-two.

A new phase of life began in 1936 when she took up the job of a school teacher in Calcutta. Amitav Ghosh omits this part of the grandmother's life except dropping hints from which the reader may construct the story. Starting life in Calcutta in a one-room tenement in Bhowanipore, she would dream of "the old house, her parents, Jethamoshai [her uncle], her childhood" (125) in Dhaka, but she could never go there. The big political events, the partition in 1947 and Dhaka becoming the capital of East Pakistan, divided her from her native city. But these public events did not have a direct impact on her so much as the demands of her personal life. As a school teacher she educated her son on her own, declining the help of her rich sister. The son's employment in a private company, his marriage, the birth of a grandson in 1952, her own retirement in 1962 as the headmistress of the school she had joined in 1936 are abbreviated and revealed in an oblique manner. The focus of the novel is on the grandmother from her retirement in 1962 to her death in 1965.

One feature that may be noted is the kind of house in which the grandmother lives: from the large house in Dhaka to a succession of houses in Burma with her husband onto the one-room tenement in Calcutta after her husband's death, then to a cramped little flat in Gole Park (119) where she spent most of her life. She had grown up with the school where she was a teacher and became the headmistress in the last six years of her service. But the school disappeared from her life with her retirement, and around the same time her son was promoted as the General Manager of his firm. The family moved to a large new house on Southern Avenue, opposite the Lake—with "rooms upstairs, rooms downstairs, verandas, a garden as well as a roof big enough to play cricket on." (119) She was given the best room in the house, but she dreamt of her old house in Dhaka where she was born and had grown up to adulthood.

The grandmother's younger sister, Mayadebi, is the fortunate girl in the family. Born in 1910, she grew up into a beauty and married Datta Chaudhuri, the son of the wealthy judge, who became a diplomat in the Indian Foreign Service. She lived mostly abroad, moving from one country to another, wherever her husband had his posting. Mayadebi had three sons. The eldest was Jatin, born in 1929, who had a job as an economist with the U.N., working most of the time in Africa or South-East Asia. He lived with his wife and his daughter, Ila who was of the age of the narrator. Tridib was the second son, born in 1931, who lived in the 1960s in the family's large ancestral house in Ballygunge Place in Calcutta with his aging grandmother. He was supposed to be working for his Ph.D. in Archaeology. The youngest son was Robi, born after a long break, almost the age of the narrator. By 1981 Robi is in the Indian Administrative Service and he stops in London to be with the narrator and Ila for a few days. On leave from his job, he is on his way to Harvard where he has a fellowship to study administration and public affairs for six months.

London figures in a prominent way in the life of Mayadebi's family.

She and her husband with their eight-year-old son, Tridib, had stayed with Mrs. Price, a family friend in London in 1939 for a whole year when the war had started. Tridib had told the narrator about their life at 44, Lymington Road and other places. People in London had started living with the terror of German air raids and the Prices suffered when Mrs Price's brother, Alan Tresawsen, and his three friends were killed in an attack. They were young intellectuals whose life had been snuffed out all of a sudden. Though they were in the photograph that Tridib had shown, "nobody can ever know what it was like to be young and intelligent in the summer of 1939 in London or Berlin." (68) After more than forty years the narrator explores these places as "I wanted to know England not as I saw her, but in her finest hour every place chooses its own and to me it did not seem an accident that England had chosen hers in a war." (57)

But England comes through in a different light in the life of Ila, the narrator's cousin. After roving round many places with her parents, she had come to London to school. There was so much racism that one day she was beaten up while returning from school and she had never gone to school again. Later she did B.A. in History at the University College in London, took up a job in an office and married Nick Price whom she had known over the years. Of course, the narrator is in love with his beautiful cousin. On one occasion the narrator's grandmother is angry that Ila was living in London. She had said:

> Ila has no right to live there. . . . She doesn't belong there. It took those people a long time to build that country; hundreds of years, years and years of war and bloodshed. Everyone who lives there has earned his right to be there with blood: with their brother's blood and their father's blood and their son's blood. They know they are a nation because they've drawn their borders with blood. . . That's what it takes to make a country. Once that happens people forget that they were born this or that, Muslim or Hindu, Bengali or Punjabi: they become a family born of the same pool of blood. That is what you have to achieve for India, don't you see? (77-78)

The narrator disagrees with his grandmother when she says that Ila lives in London for the money and the comforts of British life. He had known Ila to live a simple life and spend her spare time going on demonstrations and acting in radical plays for Indian immigrants in east London. (79) It is a mystery why Ila who can live like a princess in Calcutta should live in London like a martyr. Probably it is the romance of freedom in an alien land. Also she seems to be the kind of person who is not attached to any particular place.

The heart of *The Shadow Lines* is the death of Tridib and it is only towards the end of the novel the narrator approaches this experience. It is a struggle with silence as he has no words to communicate what happened: "it lies outside the reach of my intelligence, beyond words . . . it is simply a gap, a hole, an emptiness in which there are no words." (218) A little later he writes: "I can only describe at second hand the manner of Tridib's death: I do not have the words to give it meaning. I do not have the words, and I do not have the strength to listen." (228) The narrator loved and admired Tridib as a hero. So he finds it difficult to accept the fact of Tridib's death. "So complete is this silence," the narrator declares, "that it actually took me fifteen years to discover that there was a connection between my nightmare bus ride back from school, and the events that befell Tridib and the others in Dhaka." (218) The narrator's struggle with the presentation of Tridib's death makes it all the more agonizing.

The trouble started when the sacred relic known as the Mu-i-Mubarak—believed to be a hair of the Prophet Mohammed himself—disappeared from its place on 27 December 1963 in the Hazratbal mosque near Srinagar, two hundred and sixty three years after it had been installed. "Over the next few days life in the valley seemed to close in upon itself in a spontaneous show of collective grief. There were innumerable black flag demonstrations, every shop and building flew a black flag, and every person on the streets wore a black armband." (225) But surprisingly there was not a single incident of Hindu-Muslim animosity in the valley. Probably it was the gifted leadership of Maulana Masoodi who "drew the various communities of Kashmir together in a collective display of mourning." (226) While India was deeply agitated, Pakistan fanned communal passion, and spoke of 'genocide.' Fortunately the Mu-i-Mubarak was 'recovered' on 4 January 1964 by the officials of the Central Bureau of Intelligence, and Kashmir heaved a sigh of relief.

The narrator is concerned with the impact of this event on life in Calcutta and Dhaka. Novy Kapadia rightly points out: "Amitav Ghosh's greatest triumph is that the depiction of communal strife in Calcutta and erstwhile East Pakistan, and its continuation in contemporary India, is very controlled and taut. There are no moralizing or irrelevant digressions. Lucidity and compactness is achieved primarily by his unusual narrative device."[3]

The narrator remembers how on a certain morning in early January 1964 the school bus, which would normally be overcrowded, came with only a dozen boys. No sooner he got in than the other boys told him that 'they' had poisoned the water in the Tala Tank, which catered to the entire city of Calcutta. Everyone knew who 'they' were. At school, the classes were cancelled half-way through. On their way home the boys saw that the streets "were eerily empty now except for squads of patrolling policemen." (202) At a particular point an unruly mob had thrown stones on their bus and chased it from its normal route. The boys began to sob as they could not go home. "It would not be enough to say we were afraid: we were stupefied with fear." (204)

This fear grips the thousand million people who inhabit the Indian sub-continent and sets them apart from the rest of the world. The narrator comments upon the quality of this fear in the following manner: "It is a fear that comes of the knowledge that normalcy is utterly contingent, that the spaces that surround one, the streets that one inhabits, can become, suddenly and without warning, as hostile as a desert in a flash flood. . . . it is the special quality of loneliness that grows out of the fear of the war between oneself and one's image in the mirror." (204) This is a very evocative account of the fear that has rocked the people of our sub-continent since the partition and that threatens to engulf us any moment.

It was at the time the narrator suffered the worst of fears in Calcutta, that his grandmother had gone on a visit to her sister, Mayadebi, who was in Dhaka. Her husband had his posting in East Pakistan. When the idea was mooted that she should visit Dhaka, she had wondered whether the border between India and East Pakistan was marked by trenches or something. What could be the dividing line between the two countries? Then her son explains: "This is the modern world. The border isn't on the frontier: It's right inside the airport. You'll see. You'll cross it when you have to fill in all those disembarkation cards and things." (151-52) She was worried because "she had not been able to understand how her place of birth had come to be so messily at odds with her nationality." (152) When she flew into Dhaka on 3 January 1964, accompanied by Tridib and May Price, who had come on a visit to India, and met her sister, the grandmother's question was: "Where's Dhaka? I can't see Dhaka" (193) for the dream image of her native city had vanished long ago.

One important reason for the grandmother to go to Dhaka was her desire to see her old house and bring her uncle, Jethamoshai, to India. No sooner she had spent a few days in her sister's house than the grandmother accompanied by Mayadebi, Tridib, May Price, and Robi set out in the Mercedes car with the driver and a security guard of the High Commission. The car had to stop at a particular point in the by-lanes of

Dhaka, and they had to walk to the old house. They discovered to their dismay an automobile workshop in what was a garden in their house. Their house was crumbling and a large number of families were living there. Their uncle Jethamoshai, now called Ukilbabu, was decrepit and bedridden, looked after by Khalil, a cycle-rickshaw driver, and his family. The old man failed to recognize them, and spoke ill of his relatives when they were mentioned. As for going to India, he had not believed in that. In fact, he had told his India-bound sons: "but suppose when you get there they decide to draw another line somewhere? What will you do then? Where will you move to? No one will have you anywhere. As for me, I was born here, and I'll die here." (215) The old man would have gone on with his talk, but the car driver intervenes to say that they must leave immediately as "there's going to be trouble outside." (216) So the grandmother and Mayadebi and others depart, arranging with Khalil that he should bring their uncle to their house in his cycle-rickshaw telling him that he is taking him out. It is then that "trouble" starts. In a book-review, Girish Karnad makes the following observation on this episode: "The grandmother's visit to the ancestral home . . . is surely one of the most memorable scenes in Indian fiction. Past and future meet across religious, political and cultural barriers in a confusion of emotions, ideals, intentions and acts, leading to a shattering climax."[4]

The "climax" occurs as the grandmother and her sister are returning in their Mercedes from their ancestral home and their uncle is following them in the rickshaw (Robi's narrative 243-47, May Price's recollection 250-51). When they come to the bazaar area, they find that the shops are closed and the street is deserted, but for stray people. It was as if they were waiting for the car. In no time a lot of men surround the car, break the windscreen and the driver suffers a cut across his face. The car lurches and comes to a halt with its front wheel in a gutter. Then the security guard jumps out and fires a shot from his revolver and the crowd begins to withdraw from the car. At the same time the eerie silence is broken by a creak, and the attention of the crowd turns to the sound of a rickshaw—Khalil's rickshaw—with their uncle in it, and the people surround the rickshaw. Though the sisters could have driven away, May Price and Tridib leave the car to save the old man and they get lost in the whirlgig of the crowd. The mischief takes less than a moment and the crowd begins to melt away. The dead bodies of Khalil, the old man and Tridib lie on the road. The horror of the act is branded with fire on the memory of May Price and Robi who see the whole thing.

Amitav Ghosh dramatizes the violence that is at the heart of *The Shadow Lines*. Characters in the novel—Robi, May and the narrator (Ghosh's alter-ego)—tremble "like a leaf" to recollect the scene of

Tridib's death, "fifteen years later, thousands of miles away, at the other end of another continent." (247) As in Greek tragedies, the violence comes through in a terrible manner because it is conveyed through choric characters. Robi, May and the narrator perform such a role of mediation. True, the violent bear it away. But for what? People kill for freedom. But do they achieve it? It seems to be a mirage, as the shadow lines that divide one people from another keep ever-changing.

NOTES

1. Amitav Ghosh, *The Shadow Lines* (Delhi : Ravi Dayal Publishers, 1988), p. 78.
2. Nivedita Bagchi, "The Process of Validation in Relation to Materiality and Historical Reconstruction in Amitav Ghosh's *The Shadow Lines,*" *Modern Fiction Studies,* 39.1 (Winter 1993), p. 188
3. Novy Kapadia, "Imagination and Politics in Amitav Ghosh's *The Shadow Lines,*" *The New Indian Novel in English: A Study of the 1980s*, ed. Viney Kirpal (New Delhi: Allied, 1990), p. 208.
4. Girish Karnad, "Worlds within Worlds: Book Review of *The Shadow Lines,*" *Indian Express Magazine*, December 18, 1988, p. 5.

Of Shadows, Lines and Freedom: A Historical Reading of *The Shadow Lines*

SEEMA BHADURI

This paper focuses on Ghosh's treatment in *The Shadow Lines*,[1] of the changing middle class ethos in India during the pre- and post-Independence era. It advances the thesis that the lives of the characters in this novel are determined largely by their idea of freedom and that this idea is, in its turn, shaped by the history of the times.

This paper highlights how in this novel, the failures of nationalism and nationalist governments find voice in the characters's memories and views of the partition, militancy, and the riots. The major characters here move towards a global humanitarianism, coming to grips with the realization that freedom cannot be geo-politically defined or delimited.

Finally, Ghosh's prescription for freedom in the context of the dubious meaning which political independence holds and the distortion of perspectives the individual inevitably undergoes in an increasingly heterogeneous world, is closely scrutinized.

It would be interesting at the outset to look at collectively, three articulations in the novel:

> I gave it to the fund for the war. I had to, don't you see? For your sake, for your freedom. We have to kill them before they kill us; we have to wipe them out. (237)

> I don't believe in this India-Shindia. It's all very well, you're going away now but suppose when you get there, they decide to draw another line somewhere? What will you do then? Where will you move to? None will have you anywhere. As for me, I was born here, and I'll die here. (215)

> Tridib . . . had said that we could not see without inventing what we saw, so at least we could try to do it properly. . . . We had to try because the alternative wasn't blankness—It only meant that if

> we didn't try ourselves, we would never be free of other people's inventions. (31)

These three extracts represent the different ideas of freedom underlined by different world-views that, in *The Shadow Lines,* unfold vis-a-vis one another in the commonplace rounds of middle-class life. The ramifications of the nationalist ethos essentialized in the first quote, surface in the lives and memories of the older generation—the narrator's grandmother and her fellow relatives—who lived their prime lives when nationalism rode the world's politics. Evolving from its denouement are the imperatives, in the younger generation i.e. in the narrator and in Robi, Tridib, and May, for yet another world-view, a global humanitarian approach to counter the war, riots and militancy-ridden political atmosphere of the present-day world.

Spanning roughly four decades from the forties to the eighties, the narrative builds on the life and interaction of two families—the one, the narrator's (including Tridib's) and the other, the Prices of London who have been closely associated with Tridib's family throughout this period.

The narrative is an impressionistic rendering of a perceptive middle-class youth's world of these changing times. It evolves in the stream-of-consciousness tradition, through sketchy, disjointed outlines of memories, associations and fancies as they pool into the narrator's mind and consciousness by way of reminiscence, fusing gradually into a coherent pattern of stories mutually interrelated yet disparate, intersecting only laterally, spatialized in their simultaneity the profile of a multilateral world. In the fragmentary pieces—the random diversions of the narrator's memory—is captured the socio-cultural ambience of Calcutta and partly, of London. One finds encoded here the larger patterns of Indian society locked in its internal affiliations and antipathies.[2]

It is a world of memories and reminiscences with the narrator recalling his past associations in order to trace the gradual shaping of his vision under the guiding voice of Tridib who is relationally an uncle doing research in anthropology but functionally a friend and guide full of abstruse knowledge from whom the narrator learns how "to see." For, for the narrator (as for Ghosh) reality lies not in the obvious but in what is evoked and understood by memory and imagination over changing laps of space and time. This novel is all about 'seeing' and 'not seeing.'

To 'see,' as the narrator learnt from Tridib, is to appropriate imaginatively all things seen or heard of—to make the vicarious one's own. It is to embody the world in one's consciousness. It is a multiple vision that emerges, and an acute sense of locale i.e. of the present. End result—in the currents of quotidian living are deciphered the larger drifts of history—national as well as international. To 'see' these currents that hold individual lives in such abeyance for what they are, is to tide them—to be free. And freedom is what almost all the characters in the novel are groping for.

Ghosh's characters have to deal with two types of servility—the one is to ideas spawned by history viz. the ideas of nationalism. These ideas hold sway even after the times to which they were relevant, have passed. The other is servility to one's personal fantasies that distort one's vision, 'Thamma'—the writer's grandma—personifies the first type while Ila, the writer's cousin personifies the second. Thamma essentializes the spirit of European nationalism. She is a typical neo-Victorian figure in her progressive view of the future and her Puritan sense of work and discipline. Nationalism, the product of those times, carries for her the earnestness of religion, informing her every thought and deed. So her grandson must run rather than walk, that he might be strong enough to face the impending challenges to the nation. She opposed any Indian's opting for a life in England on the grounds that the English had earned their liberty and prosperity by incorporating military valour with their religion. Indians she felt, had no right to enjoy what they hadn't earned. (77-78) Her preferences likewise are for men like Robi (Tridib's brother) who have an unintellectual moral impulse and a commitment to action—the type that made the firebrand nationalists of her own youth—the type she admired and had wanted to join. (36-37) Tridib's indisposition to money-earning (he was without a job), his aversion to the Bengali middle-class discipline and snobbery (he frequented street-side talk-shops and guzzled unlimited cups of tea which spoilt his constitution) threatened her Puritanical commitment to work progress and discipline.

But Grandma wasn't the only Indian type to be found during the nationalist period and Ghosh is interested in the totality of impressions of the object/time-span he is depicting. So there is grandma's foil in the anglicized elite, Tridib's father, whom Grandma disparagingly called the Sahib and thought incapable of any achievement.

But here lies Ghosh's pronouncement—Grandma could never get the type of freedom she had dreamt of from India's independence: she had had to eke out the difficult connotations of widowhood in the class-ridden Hindu society that political independence little altered. She became a foreigner to her own home in Dhaka, more foreigner than the English May who didn't need a visa to visit East Pakistan. (195) Besides, her visit there brought the greatest disaster imaginable—her uncle and nephew were killed by rioters close to their home. The responsibility was largely hers—she had insisted on going there and bringing away her uncle to India. Her nonagerian uncle's views on this issue of nationhood and migration, expressed just before he was coaxed into leaving his house, strike at the essential unsoundness of nationalist principles: "I don't believe in this India-Shindia. It's all very well, you're going away now, but suppose when you get there, they decide to draw another line somewhere? What will you do then? Where will you move to? None will have you anywhere. As for me, I was born here and I'll die here." (215)

With her imagination enslaved to the idea of nationalism, Grandma couldn't see what was so obvious, namely, nationalism had destroyed her home and spilled her innocent kin's blood. The extent of her subjectivity can be grasped by the fact that even after this tragedy which affected her mental balance, he gave away her gold chain, the only ornament she had retained with her after her widowhood as a momento of her dead husband. Unable to either reconcile herself to Tridib's death or to understand its fundamental causes, she clung faster for faith to that very idea that had let her down. She tells the narrator: "I gave it [the chain] to the fund for the war. . . . For your sake, for your freedom. We have to kill them before they kill us: we have to wipe them out." (237) She could not understand that national liberty in no way guarantees the individual's liberty.

The new generation in the new era of internationalism must view liberty differently, and one of the easily available methods which the narrator's cousin Ila adopts, is escape—escape to the West, to England. For, to her, freedom means liberty from the restrictive customs that delimit the individual's activities in India. (89) Ila represents the vast majority of the Indian youth who, enamoured of the West, tap impatient heels at their Oriental anchorage. No wonder her mother prefers butler English to plain Hindi while speaking to her Indian maid and has been nicknamed Queen Victoria by Grandma. But freedom is not an external condition merely and Ila is not really free. She is victim to the fantasy her child's mind had built to mentally escape the racial discrimination she has faced in the European schools. She had fancied herself to be a princess whom the white girls didn't like because she was extraordinarily beautiful and intelligent and because all the boys wanted her. She ends up marrying the same Nick who had once let her be beaten by a racist gang from his class. As a child, Ila lived out that fantasy in the form of her beautiful doll Magda for whom she was inordinately jealous. (71-76) She fantasized that Nick, Mrs. Price's son, was in love with Magda. Soon after her marriage however, she discovered that Nick had been and was ever going to be unfaithful to her. And this, as the narrator puts it, made her realize that "The squalor of the genteel little lives she had so much despised was a part too of the free world she had tried to build for herself." (188)

The longing for freedom is universal and primitive to man but the method of its realization varies with the times. Amitav Ghosh sets his narrative in the current age. The narrator's and Tridib's world is global. Hence, when in Calcutta, the young narrator's mind roamed in the London of Tridib's memories and vice versa, and Delhi seemed about as far from Calcutta as London. It is the present-day world besieged with militants in India (246) and famines in Africa. (162) Every age is distinguished by a distinct set of problems. If geo-political sovereignty was the aim of grandma's age, intellectual independence is under threat in the present with colonizers casting their technological nets for the 'third world' mind. In such a setting Tridib's insistence upon 'seeing' remains the only way to preserve one's intellectual integrity.

The story, or whatever there is of it, eddys around the characters's first hand yet scattered experiences of war, violence and riot, their edges deceptively softened by commonplace occupations love and envy, memories and dreams. The conventional hero of the traditional novel, who leads the action that affects others, is absent. And yet in this age when peoples, cultures, truths, whirl together uncomfortably, one of the most thrilling acts is perhaps to look beyond imposed assumptions, discover realities for oneself and then 'act' in full knowledge and responsibility, as Tridib does in the end. But before coming to that, one must know better what seeing according to Ghosh involves.

Memory and imagination occupy prime place in this business of 'seeing' for memory enlivens the present with the past while the imagination helps to ingest the vicarious, the distant and thereby widen one's world. For those like Ila who cared for neither memory nor imagination, 'the current was the real.' For her therefore, London was only the "busy, bustling town" of the present. Tridib explained to the narrator that even Ila invented places like London, for every place "has to be invented in one's imagination" but as she had all along travelled with her father—a U.N. employee, from country to country, "the inventions she lived in moved with her so that although she had lived in many places, she had never travelled at all." (21) As a result, she identified exotic places like Cairo and Adis Ababa only by the position of the 'Ladies' in the Departure Lounge of the airports for "those were the only fixed points in the shifting landscapes of her childhood." (20)

Ila dismisses imagination as fancy. But Tridib, the narrator says, was an archaeologist not interested in "fairy tales." Imagination must be used with "precision," he said. (24) The faraway must be so vividly recreated as to bring up the feel of the place. Hence the narrator, when in London for the first time, locates with little trouble or help its different streets and the buildings that had stood there during the world war II and also identifies Mrs. Price's house, showing a surprising familiarity with its internal structure. And all this because he had first "seen it with Tridib's eyes [so that] its past seemed concurrent with its present." (31) This historical vision makes to the narrator the bombed and gutted streets that Tridib had seen, seem somehow simultaneous with their present peaceful settlements. (57) And it was the former reality, the narrator realizes, that seemed truer than the latter. Tridib had captured for the narrator something precious. "I wanted to know England not as I saw her, but in her finest hour—every place chooses its own and to me it did not seem an accident that England had chosen hers in a war." (57)

History leaves its mark not only on a place. Every object howsoever trivial, has for Ghosh its relevance to the greater reality of its times. The Citroen parked on an English roadside, the huge table in Ila's Calcutta home—everything becomes an artefact of the times. A simple photograph taken at the Prices' during the II World War encapsulates the entire history of England of the times. There was in it the freshly dug pit to serve as an emergencey trench: there was Alan Tresawsen a free lance journalist writing for socialist papers. Of the remaining figures in the photograph, one was a Trotskyist who had fought the Spanish Civil War and now wrote for left wing papers, another was an Irish nationalist, the third was the academic, Snipe—Mrs. Price's husband, the fourth was Tridib's father—the suited booted Anglicized Indian. Then there was Tridib's mother standing with baby Tridib in her arms, and with the veil on her head. There was also the lady Francesca Halevy who shared the house with the three men. Mrs. Price didn't know who she shared it with. (60-65) There was another photograph—of Lionel Tresawsen, Mrs. Price's father. This photograph is equally significant because he was a globe-trotter, inventor, humanist (51-52)—a Renaissance figure, who summed up the spirit of European History. The need for a historical vision in which memory and imagination are incorporated is essential because, for Tridib every image/situation/personality is inherently complex—its apparent clarity he thinks, is a sign of one's own ignorance. (67) This means that every such image—be it Ila then, or a London street—incorporates multiple layers of reality. For instance, the present always includes the 'presences' from the past. The narrator says that the figures from the past are all around us, "their ghostliness is merely the absence of time and distance . . . a ghost is a presence displaced in time." (181)

"Seeing" with imaginative precision leads one to freedom for it has the force of detachment. To know a thing especially an idea or concept in the totality of its context is to 'place' it; to assimilate it in one's mental framework and thereby to become free of it. Such detachment from things external gradually leads to the coming face to face with oneself, with one's image in the mirror. (29) This union of one's public and private selves is freedom. It means the reconciliation of one's desires which belong to the public field, with one's knowledge and consciousness, which are private. To act then in such a state is to act in free will. Tridib's death while trying to save his granduncle from the rioters in Dhaka is such an act, possibly. Its motives, no doubt, are complex. To the narrator it remains a mystery. (252) And yet, slowly over the years, chance discoveries coupled with his propensity for looking beyond the apparent, for contradicting general assumptions born of the skill of 'seeing,' leads the narrator on to discover the larger truths this act signifies. An analysis in some detail, of Tridib's death is essential for several reasons. It is the only 'act' proper in the novel since it shows independent determination and an awareness of the possible outcome on part of the agent. Besides, it is of great structural significance in the novel. It would indeed be right to look at it as an epiphany, a full illustration of the narrative's major concerns viz. the idea of individual and political liberty in the context of growing internationalism.

It was no doubt clear to Tridib as it was to everyone else in the car that fateful hour that his going out unarmed into the murderous gang meant sure death. (250) Nor could he have risked his life solely for that nonagerian granduncle, who despised them all so (214) and who was dead against arbitrary political divisions that robbed one's homeland. (215) It is more likely that he ventured out of the car in order to save May for Tridib's act surely included his concern for her, born of his love. She had been the first to move out of the car. He loved her dearly. (144, 175) He had compared himself to Tristan who loved the lady from beyond the seas. (186) Ironically he had also desired to make love to her against the backdrop of a historical ruin. (144) What better ruin then, of modern history than the riots—the ruin of nationalism—its most notable achievement? But a voluntary death, where it could achieve nothing for his love was most unbecoming of Tridib. Surely it was more than a mere capricious suicide. Besides, he must have known as May did, that the rioters wouldn't harm her for she was English. (251) He moved into the mob leaving her behind.

The larger implications of the death dawned very gradually on the narrator through the years. Initially he had been told that Tridib died in a car accident (239); later that he was killed. (238) But the more shocking aspect of the tragedy opens up when, fifteen years later, the narrator digs out old newspapers to show his doubting colleagues that serious Hindu-Muslim riots did occur in Bengal in 1964. What those papers revealed was shocking—that these riots had first begun in Dhaka and had spread to Calcutta from there. Tallying dates, the narrator now realized that Tridib had lost his life in these riots. (227)

It was the horror of this realisation—why should the likes of Tridib, who would hurt none, be killed in the riots?—that had led the narrator on to scan the papers of those days for detailed information on the nature and causes of those riots and thereby, to the true import of Tridib's death. He found that the cause had been the loss of the holy relic from the Hazratbal Shrine in Kashmir. But there the Hindus, Muslims and Sikhs had led a unified protest against the Government and the Police. Soon, the Government took steps, the relic was reinstalled and the people responded with celebration and joy. But the Pakistani Govt. declared that the theft was "an attack upon the identity of Muslims," (226) and warned of retaliation. Consequently, rioting began in East Pakistan and surprisingly, gathered force after the relic had been re-installed. (228-29) What was more shocking to the narrator was the Calcutta newspapers on the days immediately preceding the riots here had given no hint at all of the trouble in East Pakistan, and very little indeed, of the events in Kashmir. Or else, the narrator's father would never have allowed his people to go to Dhaka at that time. The narrator says that these papers, like all common men and women, had believed in the power of distance. (227) Srinagar being 1200 miles away from Calcutta, and Dhaka being in another country, were both distant, so what happened there could not probably affect life in Calcutta! This piece of news led the narrator to discover a momentous truth: national frontiers create a false sense of distance and of reality. Though Dhaka and Calcutta are at the same places nearly, and Srinagar so far away, the latter had been supposed closer, simply because it belonged with Calcutta in the same country! Experimenting now with a compass on Tridib's old atlas, he made some startling discoveries. Chiang Mai in Thailand, he realized, is closer to Calcutta than Delhi is, yet he had never heard of the place before. And further, that within a radius of 1200 miles from any city of the world as the centre, lay different cities of different countries and that the only event with the power to draw all the various citizens together, was war! So that the world was left only with "states and citizens: there were no people at all." (231-33)

While the narrator was making these discoveries on the atlas on which "the smudges left by [Tridib's] fingers were clearly visible, he had Tridib . . . watching over [him]." (231-32) So he was discovering only now with the gift of sight Tridib had given him, what the latter had already known and acted on: that riots are born of gross political manipulation of communal sympathies and nationalist passions; that political lines cannot separate people or their common land and realities. (233) Dhaka and Calcutta, the narrator now realized, were the "inverted images of one another"—what happened at one place was sure to spread out into the other. And, most interestingly, it was the indivisible sanity of people like Tridib on both sides of the border, who often at the cost of their lives, tried to rescue their brethren of opposite religions, that really helped to quell the riots. (229-30)

So Tridib's had been the normal humane gesture of one whose vision had transcended the shadow lines—and the shadow realities these lines imposed upon minds that stuck by them—of national frontiers and distances. Interestingly it is Tridib—the laid-back, lazy object of grandmother's scorn who rises to an act that turn out to be tragic-heroic while Robi the man of action and grandma's pet cowers inside the car paralyzed in fear. (245-46) Equally significant is the fact that May and Tridib are not the only ones whose vision and therefore, emotions have not been constricted by nationalist fervour. The writer observes, "As always, there were innumerable cases of Muslims in East Pakistan giving shelter to Hindus, often at the cost of their own lives, and equally in India of Hindus sheltering Muslims." (229-30) These men and women demonstrated "that indivisible sanctity that binds people to each other independently relationship is the natural enemy of government, for it is in the logic of states that to exist at all they must claim the monopoly of all relationships between peoples." (230)

NOTES

1. Amitav Ghosh, *The Shadow Lines* (New Delhi: Ravi Dayal Publisher, 1989).
2. Nandita Sinha, "Perspectives in Time: The Narrator as Child in Amitav Ghosh's *The Shadow Lines*," pp. 143-48 of this book.

Imagination and Reality in *The Shadow Lines*

URBASHI BARAT

> The novel is no more the work of imagination than it is a reflection of reality: its essence, its necessary quality, lies in the expression of the connection between the real and the imaginary.[1]

Amitav Ghosh's *Shadow Lines* resists classification. It is 'basically a memory novel'[2] that weaves together past and present, childhood and adulthood, India and Bangladesh and Britain, Hindu and Muslim, story and happening, through the 'coil within coil of memories [that] unfurl within it'[3]; it establishes its socio-historical situation through its careful observation of concrete social reality and as such can be regarded both as a social document and a political novel[4]; it is also in many ways a bildungsroman, tracing the growth and development of the narrator from childhood to maturity. It is part of the Indian experiment with the non-fiction novel whose first significant landmark was Salman Rushdie's *Midnight's Children;* it is as postmodernist a work of fiction as Farrukh Dhondy's *Bombay Duck*.

Several more labels can be affixed to *The Shadow Lines*, each as valid as the others; after all, as Henry James noted in *The Art of the Novel*, 'the Novel remains still, under the right persuasion, the most independent, most elastic, most prodigious of literary forms.'[5] But one of the most rewarding ways of reading the novel is, I believe, to see it as belonging to that long tradition of fiction that includes *Don Quixote* and *Tristram Shandy* on the one hand and *Travels with My Aunt* and *Haroun and the Sea of Stories* on the other: fiction, that is, that examines its symbiotic relationship with fact and explores the role of the imagination in creating and evoking reality, which, 'in the artist's sense,' in the words of A.A. Mendilow, 'is always something created: it does not exist *a priori*.'[6]

This theme is established in *The Shadow Lines* through the use of the geographical metaphor and the journey motif implicit in its title—derived, significantly, from Conrad—and in the titles of its two parts, 'Going Away' and 'Coming Home.' This metaphor pervades the book and enables it to extend and to expand spatially and temporally (a journey, after all, takes place sequentially and in time). This is of course a traditional method for the novel that sets out to discover the relationship between imagination and reality; indeed, even Edward Said uses it when he observes of the novel, 'stories are at the heart of what explorers and novelists say about strange regions of the world.'[7] It is through its imagination, perception and rendering of human experience in everyday life, through what Proust calls the 'gross dimensions of social phenomena,' that the novel is able to 'evoke the essentially non-finite quality of existence.'[8] Ghosh's approach has in fact a close affinity with Graham Greene's in *Travels with My Aunt* and *The Captain and the Enemy*, which are likewise concerned with this relationship and which are similarly based on the metaphor of the journey.

Appropriately, *The Shadow Lines* begins with a statement about a journey, one that Mayadebi, the narrator's great-aunt, her husband and Tridib, her son, undertook in 1939, from India to England: a journey which will be undertaken again and again, and by other characters in the novel, too, both physically and in the imagination, sometimes, however, from England to India as well. Tridib's father is a diplomat, living abroad or in Delhi and only occasionally visiting Calcutta; but Tridib himself prefers to stay on in their family house in an upper-middle-class neighbourhood of Calcutta with his elderly grandmother. Why he has rejected his parents's peripatetic lifestyle is not known, but the narrator's grandmother (and Tridib's aunt) puts it down to incompatibility with his father. The fiercely bourgeois old lady disapproves not of her nephew's estrangement from his father but of what she considers his flippancy in letting so trivial a matter stand in the way of his material prospects. In her eyes Tridib is an untrustworthy and dangerous nonconformist, though outwardly he may seem the quintessential middle-class Bengali, living staidly in Calcutta and looking after his grandmother, and engaged in research for his doctoral degree. The apparently everyday quality of his life, paradoxically, only emphasizes his uniqueness, and he is a source of perennial fascination for the boy who as a young adult is the narrator of the 'story' of the novel.

Tridib, too, is a story-teller, 'happiest in neutral, impersonal places—coffee houses, bars, street-corner addas—the sort of place where people come, talk and go away without expecting to know each other any further,'[9] for it is detachment and objectivity that allow the imagination to soar. He spends much of his time in gossip with young ne'er-do-wells at street corners and tea-stalls, much to the distaste of the grandmother, who has a Gradgrind-like belief about time: 'For her time was like a toothbrush: it went mouldy if it wasn't used,' and stank. Tridib, however, 'never seemed to use his time, but his time didn't stink.' (4) For he is caught up with the non-essential, the non-material, the imaginary and the imaginative: the world of story, the world of the creative imagination. He himself, like his tales, constantly skirts the border between truth and falsehood, reality and the imagination, so that it is difficult to say whether it is fact or fiction that prevails with him. Sometimes his imagination creates a story that is truer than reality; once he speaks gravely of visiting his English relatives by marriage in London, describing them in graphic and truthful detail—the only caveat being that they are not his relatives at all, nor has he been to London to meet them. The boy blurts out what he believes is the reality, and Tridib's exciting story falls apart, so that the truth of his account of the Price family is dismissed: the irony being, of course, that they do literally become his relatives by marriage in course of time.

Tridib's niece Ila sometimes comes to Calcutta, and the boy tries to remind her of their shared experiences of her uncle's stories. She is surprised by the vividness of his memories, for she cannot understand how, sitting in a little room in Calcutta, 'Tridib had given me worlds to travel in and . . . eyes to see them with.' (20) Ila has travelled all over the world with her parents, but too great an exposure to reality has erased the magic from her eyes, so that all those places on the map which are to him 'a set of magical talismans' are for her merely familiar, commonplace, dull, significant only by virtue of the position of Ladies toilets in the airport lounges, which become for her the signs of stability, 'the only fixed points in the shifting landscapes of her childhood.' (20) She is therefore irritated by the narrator's enthusiasm for the London Underground: 'To her the Underground was merely a means of shifting venue,' and he comments: "I could not persuade her that a place does not merely exist, that it has to be invented in one's imagination; that her practical, bustling London was no less invented than mine, neither more nor less true, only very far apart. It was not her fault that she could not understand, for as Tridib often said of her, the inventions she lived in moved with her, so that although she had lived in many places, she had never travelled at all." (21)

Ila believes that her emphasis on reality has had a salutary effect on the narrator: 'at least you learnt that those cities you saw on maps were real places, not like those fairylands Tridib made up for you.' But Tridib, the archaeologist who makes the past come alive for the present, has never believed in fairytales: what he had taught the boy was 'to use my imagination with precision.' (24) For instance, when Ila's mother described an encounter with a snake in Colombo, the boy tries to earn his mentor's approval by asking what kind of snake it was. Tridib, however, is disappointed. The snake has little to do with real life, and what kind it is is merely factual information; what is interesting, rather, is to imagine life under a sloping roof, so unlike the flat ones of Calcutta. This is what reality is; something that must be seen and known through the imagination, which works out of 'real desire,' 'a longing for everything that was not in oneself, a torment of the flesh, that carried one beyond the limits of one's mind to other times and other places, and even, if one was lucky, to a place where there was no border between oneself and one's image in the mirror.' (29) The mirror-image, repeated later in the novel too, is especially significant, for it is the traditional symbol of art. Art is expected to represent or reflect reality, and the novel is a mirror walking along a highway, in Stendhal's picturesque phrase; but how far a mirror-image is 'real' and how far a distortion of 'reality' is to be questioned. As Michel Zeraffa observes, 'the "real" is what fate must reveal, sooner or later, for us to know. Fiction, on the other hand, consists in what can never be brought to our knowledge except through "splendidly wandering" thoughts and desires' (57)—through, that is, the imagination, which is thus no less 'real' than so-called 'reality.'

Indeed, even the apparently unimaginative Ila cannot do without imagination. As a child her only souvenirs of the faraway places she has lived in are the Yearbooks of her schools—'the places themselves went past her in an illusory whirl of movement' (23)—with photographs of her fellow-students, about whom she weaves many stories. So the most beautiful and talented among them are her special friends, and yet she herself is never photographed with them; and when she finds that her cousin has discovered a photograph of a boy she has claimed to be her boyfriend with his arms around other girls, while Ila herself stands a little apart from everybody else, the page with the incriminating photograph is torn from the book. The boy realizes then that the exotic and unapproachable Ila is like him after all, creating her own reality, her own space, out of her imagination.

Similarly, when Ila teaches her cousin to play Houses with her in the dark basement (note the significance of this setting) of the family house in the village, she talks about Nick Price, with whom she has evidently played this game before and whom she describes as coming to her rescue when she is attacked by a group of racist children in London. It is only later that the adult narrator learns what the reality was like: that Nick was ashamed of her and had certainly not gone to her aid at all. Ila is obviously in love with Nick, and she inveigles him into marrying her, with her father's money as bait; but she soon discovers that Nick does not care for her and is openly unfaithful. The only way in which she can cope with the situation is by pretending to herself and to her cousin that the reality is actually imaginary and that the imaginary world of well-being she creates is the reality.

Everyone in the novel, in fact, hovers over the shadow lines between imagination and reality; everyone has his or her stories and memories that are based partly on imagination, partly on reality, and when they are retold they are relived as well. They interlink and participate in each other, so that in the end the boundary between fact and fiction, imagination and reality, disappears, and everything becomes part of an imaginatively perceived experience of real life. The shadow lines between people and between the countries they inhabit and call their own, too, merge and become one. When, therefore, Ila shouts out that she has chosen to leave India and live in London because she wants to be free of her past, of her people and of the inhibitions they impose on her, the narrator shouts back at her, 'You can never be free of me. . . . If I were to die tomorrow you would not be free of me. You cannot be free of me because *I am within you* . . . [sic] just as you are within me.' (89)

Imagination is not just a part of reality, it can and does create its own reality. Rumour can start a riot; so that the story of the loss of the Prophet's hair in faraway Srinagar can kill Indian Hindus in Dhaka and make vast crowds of people believe that their water supply has been poisoned and break up a friendship in Calcutta. For it is imagination that links a people together, not the fact of geographical contiguity. The Bengali feels closer to what is happening on the Indian subcontinent than to events in Chiang Mai in Thailand or Chendu in China, which are closer to Calcutta than Delhi or Srinagar; while places in Europe as far away from each other as Khulna and Srinagar in South Asia remain uninvolved with each other, for there is no imaginative connection between them. Indeed, the physical fact of geographical boundaries between nations is of no real importance: the border drawn between the two Bengals has in fact pulled them even closer together, 'So close that I, in Calcutta, had only to look into the mirror to be in Dhaka; a moment when each city was the inverted image of the other, locked into an irreversible symmetry by the line that was to set us free—our looking-glass border.' (233)

Facts can in fact distort reality much more than imagination can. Thus the intensely felt horrors and the betrayals of the riots in Bengal following the theft of the Prophet's hair hardly find a mention in the newspapers outside Bengal, and when the narrator recalls the event his friends suggest that he might have imagined it all. He is naturally 'unnerved by the possibility that [he] had lived for all those years with a memory of an imagined event,' (222) until he remembers that the riot had coincided with a Test Match in Madras. Searching through the papers of that day he finally discovers a brief mention about them—except that the report is about Khulna, not about Calcutta or Dhaka. The riots in these two cities of Bengal have 'dropped out of memory into the crater of a volcano of silence' (230) because neither the newspaper nor the reader was at the time or later imaginatively involved with what had happened then. To bring them back to light now requires the narrator to make the 'strangest journey' of all: 'a voyage into a land outside space, an expanse without distances; a land of looking-glass events.' (224) Zeraffa's comments about what he calls the 'documentary novel'—the non-fiction novel, as it is most commonly known—are of relevance here: "This idea of reality is suited to a mass society whose eyes and ears are daily assailed with innumerable aspects of the world so that the imagination is clogged, instead of being inspired. The idea of society and social structures is beginning to disappear under an increasing flood of social facts, always being revised, which are represented as instances." (147) Reality is as subjective as the imagination; facts are not, and so cannot be as true as imaginatively comprehended experience.

Perhaps the character who most clearly illustrates this is the narrator's grandmother, posited from the beginning of the novel as Tridib's opposite. She may disapprove of Tridib's unconventionality, but Tridib can sympathize imaginatively with her, and sums her up as "a modern middle-class woman—though not wholly, for she would not permit herself the self-deceptions that make up the fantasy world of that kind of person. All she wanted was a middle-class life in which, like the middle classes the world over, she would thrive believing in the unity of nationhood and territory, of self-respect and national power: that was all she wanted—a modern middle-class life, a small thing that history had denied her in its fullness and for which she could never forgive it." (78) For her nationality is not something nebulous and ambiguous but a reality built over 'hundreds of years, years and years of war and bloodshed. . . . They know they're nation because they've drawn their borders with blood. . . . That's what it takes to make a country. Once that happens people forget they were born this or that, Muslim or Hindu, Bengali or Punjabi: they become a family born of the same pool of blood.' (77-78) As a young girl in the turbulent years of the freedom struggle she had seen for herself what shedding blood for the sake of the country had meant, and she had been inspired enough by the freedom-fighters to join the terrorist movement, even to kill, for her cause, and she retains this fierceness till the end. That is why she believes Ila is wrong to make England her country; if she does so, it is 'because she's greedy; she's gone there for money.' (79) The grandmother knows that Ila's claim to be free outside India is false; freedom cannot be bought 'for the price of an air ticket,' for it is much more than being 'left alone to do what [one] pleases.' (89) Ila's horizons are shrunken because she does not use her imagination to find out the real meaning of freedom. The narrator knows, however, that freedom lies in being bound and in living with 'the clamour of voices within [him]' that his imagination gives rise to: the freedom to imagine and to feel.

The grandmother is so angry about her grandson's defence of Ila that she believes he shares the young woman's view of freedom and that, accordingly, he must visit prostitutes in Delhi, where he is studying; she even writes to the dean of his college complaining about his character and demanding his expulsion. The narrator easily denies the charges; but the fact remains that her imagination has not run too far away from reality. (93) As she sinks into dementia following her retirement, she lives more and more in her imaginary world and rejects the 'real' one.

The grandmother's memories of the Dhaka of her childhood are so sharp, vivid and concrete that her grandson can easily visualize it for himself, in another kind of imaginative reconstruction of reality. When she gets an opportunity to go there again as an old woman, she is at first a little reluctant, for reality often destroys memories and dreams. But she convinces herself that she has a mission ahead, to rescue her old uncle living alone in their old family house, although he and her father had long been estranged. She is full of excitement when her plans are finalized, but not because, as the boy thinks, of the prospect of her first flight, but because, she hoped to see the border between India and East Pakistan from the plane. She cannot believe that there are no lines or marks to separate the two countries; obviously, then, partition has failed, if things are as they used to be before with no definite boundaries; it has merely made her, and thousands like her, aliens in their own home.

Dhaka itself no longer seems the same Dhaka, but it is only when she and Mayadebi see their old house that reality overtakes memory and imagination. The house is changed beyond recognition, but the uncle has not: he clings to the only reality he knows, the old family feud, and refuses to go with them: "Once you start moving you never stop. . . . It's all very well, you're going away now, but suppose when you get there they decide to draw another line somewhere? What will you do then? Where will you move to? No one will have you anywhere." (215) And when he does agree to move, it is the end for him. The stay-at-home can survive, because his imagination keeps him alive; reality can kill.

The old uncle's end is the end also for Tridib, who had accompanied the two elderly ladies to their ancestral home to rescue their recalcitrant relative. On their way back, the riots break out and their car is attacked by a frenzied mob. They would have got away had it not been for May, the girl he is in love with, the kind considerate girl whose honesty is assailed so scornfully as barren by her brother Nick and who is distressed by what the Victoria Memorial symbolizes, the harsh reality of power games. On the Indian streets she had once killed a dying dog, run over by Tridib's car, with her penknife; now in Dhaka she re-enacts what she had done then with Tridib as her victim. For she sees coming behind them the old uncle in a rickshaw pulled by his trusted Khalil; and when 'the mob [goes] after them instead,' (250) May jumps out of the car, against everybody's advice, to help them, and Tridib runs after her to help her, as he had always done. She herself is untouched, for she is 'an English memsahib,' (251) but the old man, the rickshaw-puller and Tridib are slaughtered. May realizes now that her earlier kindness had been insensitive, and that it was because of her that Tridib died. Clearly, then, kindness is not enough if it is not accompanied by understanding, which is the gift of imagination. For years May has blamed herself for his death. But now she has seen the reality behind Tridib's death: 'He gave himself up; it was a sacrifice. I know I can't understand it, I know I mustn't try, for any real sacrifice is a mystery.' (251-52) Ultimately, then, it is imagination which triumphs, for it gives her and the narrator and the reader a 'glimpse' of 'a final redemptive mystery' that must remain distanced from reality.

NOTES

1. Michel Zeraffa, *Fictions: The Novel and Social Reality* (Harmondsworth: Penguin, 1976), p. 20.
2. Novy Kapadia, "Imagination and Politics in Amitav Ghosh's *Shadow Lines,*" *The New Indian Novel in English: A Study of the 1980s*, ed. Viney Kirpal (New Delhi: Allied, 1990), p. 201.
3. A.K. Ramanujan, pre-publication comment on the back of the jacket of the novel.
4. A political novel is one 'in which political ideas play a dominant role or in which the political milieu is the dominant setting,' according to Irving Howe's definition in *The Idea of the Political Novel* (NY: Fawcett, 1967), p. 19.
5. Qtd. Damian Grant, *Realism* (London: Methuen, 1985), p. 1.
6. *Ibid.*, p. 16.
7. *Culture and Imperialism* (NY: Knopf, 1993), p. xii.
8. Zeraffa, p. 20.
9. *The Shadow Lines* (Delhi: Ravi Dayal, 1988), p. 9.

Contrasting Strands of Political Nuances in *The Shadow Lines*

NOVY KAPADIA

In Amitav Ghosh's second novel, *The Shadow Lines* (1988), the overall focus is on the meaning and shades of political nuances in contemporary life. The universal urge for political freedom, the response to violence and strident nationalism are some important aspects of contemporary life in the sub-continent, stressed in this novel. The vision of life presented is a dynamic desire to find a harmonious and complete relationship with the rich diversity of the modern world. The quest for political freedom, the violence in modern life, the role of rumour in riots are all aptly delineated in this novel.

It is basically a memory novel, which skilfully weaves together personal lives and Bangladesh. The focus is on story telling. Coil within coil of memories unfurl in the narrator's story. Conventional chronological narrative is not used. The narrator is a young boy who at the start of the novel listens to the variety of stories by his perceptive and scholarly cousin Tridib. These stories create new vistas of experience for the narrator, a young school boy in Calcutta. However the novel never becomes too esoteric. Amitav Ghosh, with his subtle humour and awareness of contemporary politics, ensures that private turmoil and crises are mirrored and intermeshed in public turmoil and crises. Amitav Ghosh uses this technique to unveil the political theme in the novel. The first instance of different strands of political nuances in this novel appear in the memories of the grandmother of the narrator about her old hometown Dhaka. The grandmother is a displaced person and had to leave her ancestral home Dhaka and settle in Calcutta after Partition. She returns to Dhaka and her homeland in 1964. Dhaka is a different city yet in her mind; the place of her childhood remains as real as ever. Her memories are passed on as vivid stories to the narrator. The idyllic vision of the ancestral home at Dhaka is shattered by political events like communal riots in both India and Pakistan in 1964. The political theme of this novel gets highlighted as the narrator shows the contrasting responses to violence and concept of nationalism that are revealed by his grandmother and Tridib.

Most of the grandmother's vision is nostalgic. There is no rancour about Partition and Muslim refugees occupying her ancestral home. Yet this is a novel which acknowledges the restlessness and political turmoil of the times. The communal riots in 1964, in both India and Pakistan, lead to the untimely death of Tridib, by an impassioned mob, in old Dhaka. The death of her nephew changes her perception. She talks now of fighting for freedom, "We have to kill them, before they kill us." (237) Her home in Dhaka, which was like a pastoral retreat, a golden vision, is now a reminder of death and communal violence. The idyllic vision is shattered. The desire now is changed. To use the phraseology of social psychology, the grandmother also now thinks in terms of 'us and them.'

The death of Tridib is the climax of the political theme in the novel. The overall focus is on the meaning and nuances of political freedom in contemporary life. Communal strife and the irresistible urge of nationalism, are also highlighted by the author. Characteristic of many Indian novels in English in the 1980s, politics national and international, is the most important theme of Amitav Ghosh's *The Shadow Lines*. Political freedom, communal strife and nationalism, important aspects of contemporary life in the subcontinent, are some of the strands which make the scope of this novel formidable. Like in his previous novel, *The Circle of Reason*, there is immense zest in story telling. The narrative technique of uncoiling memories and private turmoil mirrored by public turmoil, creates curiosity and makes the style interesting. The vision of life presented is a dynamic urge to find a complete relationship with the rich diversity of the modern world.

Political insights never obtrude or impede the flow of the story. They become an intrinsic part of the story, because of the memory technique. This is what makes the novel distinctive. For instance, the grandmother lying in bed, during her final illness, is told a story about a communal experience Ila underwent in London. The private crisis mirrors public turmoil. The grandmother's response to Ila is not sympathetic. She tells the narrator,

> Ila has no right to live there. . . . She doesn't belong there. It took those people a long time to build that country . . . years and years of war and bloodshed. Everyone who lives there has earned his right to be there with blood. . . . War is their religion. That's what it takes to make a country. (77-78)

The grandmother is not in a state of hallucination. Her insights are sharp and full of clarity. In her conversation, she reveals an alarming prospect, that feelings of nationalism can only develop through the process of war and sustained bloodshed. The novel moves backwards and forwards in time, which makes political issues more realistic. When the narrator had told Ila about the ranting grandmother's reaction, the latter a University graduate in history had promptly categorised the response as that of "warmongering fascists." The narrator aptly rejects such easy generalisations and recalls the more worldly wise Tridib's observations.

> All she wanted was a middle class life in which, like the middle classes the world over, she would thrive believing in the unity of nationhood and territory, of self respect and national power: that was all she wanted—a modern middle class life, a small thing that history had denied her in its fullness and for which she could never forgive it. (78)

So as Tridib had observed, the grandmother was not a fascist, but a modern middle class person not living in a world of fantasy and self-deceptions. The grandmother was nurtured in an environment of police raids in the colleges and universities of Dhaka. It was the time of British rule and the terrorist movement in Bengal in the first few decades of this century, "clandestine network and home-made bombs." Her motivation was a desire to be free and so feelings of nationalism got linked to self-respect and national power. So the grandmother can never fathom Ila's desire to live in London, rootless but free of middle class constraints and taboos or May's urge to collect money for worthy causes like famine relief in Africa. There are also Ila's radical friends in London, who picket on politics issues. Dan the Trotskyite who wrote anti-Nazi pamphlets and Tresawsen who edited a left wing newsletter. Another facet of nationalism is revealed in Nick Price, who later marries Ila. Nick gave up a lucrative chartered accountant's job in Kuwait because of outdated management practices and interfering Arab business partners. He still clings to Britain's colonial past, as it provided greater opportunities for exercising power and travel. The grandmother's desire to even kill for freedom, May's internationalism, Nick's colonial hangover, Ila's Trotskyite friends picketing for political causes and Ila striving for personal freedom, are either strands of nationalism or political commitment which the novel brings forth. By exploring connections, distinctions and possibilities, Amitav Ghosh shows that in a changing world, different strands of nationalism and ideology will exist and even compete. The force of nationalism in the quest for freedom or an ideology is often a source of violence. So the 'shadow line' between people and nations is often mere illusion. The force and appeal of nationalism cannot be wished away, just as death by a communal mob in the bye-lanes of old Dhaka. Robi an IAS officer, in charge of a district, philosophises to Ila and the narrator near a derelict church in Clapham, London.

> You know, if you look at the picture on the front pages of the newspapers at home now, all those pictures of dead people—in Assam, the north-east, Punjab, Sri Lanka, Tripura—people shot by terrorists and separatists and the army and police, you'll find somewhere behind it all, that single word; everyone's doing it to be free. (246)

This is the hallmark of the novel, it recognises and acknowledges the violence in our lives. There is state terror, there is majority communalism and minority communalism violence. The novel makes no distinctions, takes no sides. Amitav Ghosh shows that even characters like the grandmother and Ila, who do not indulge in violence are on the fringe of it. The grandmother, even though afraid, was willing to run errands for the Bengal terrorists and kill the English magistrate at Khulna during her student days. There is a certain cruelty in the way Ila breaks from her family to adapt to the more cosmopolitan life style of London. The quest for political freedom in *The Shadow Lines* makes the novel very contemporary.

The complexities of majority and minority communalism are also very sensitively handled by Amitav Ghosh. Using the memory technique, he links two events, riots in Calcutta and mob violence in Dhaka which led to Tridib's death. The violence in Calcutta started on 10 January 1964, the day the first cricket test match of the 1964 series against England at Madras commenced. The narrator, by recalling wicketkeeper batsman Budhi Kunderan's maiden Test Century, is able to focus on other eventful happenings on that day. The schoolbus was nearly empty because of a rumour circulated that the whole of Calcutta's water supply was poisoned. The dozen old schoolboys in the bus, do not doubt or question the authenticity of the information. As the narrator remembers, even the young minds were conditioned to assume and believe that it was 'they' the Muslims who had poisoned the water. The most poignant expression of the communal divide is shown in two actions. The narrator disowns his best friend, a young Muslim boy, named Montu: "I lied, I haven't met Montu for months." (200) Before reaching school "We unscrewed the caps of our bottles and poured the water out." (200) Amitav Ghosh, with his sensitive use of language and unique narrative technique, highlights that such irrational behaviour was not confined to that particular incident. He shows that in the highly surcharged atmosphere of suspicion and distrust, rumour has become institutionalised. The narrator is recalling these events as a research student in the 1980s. The author very subtly conveys that events in the novel are also contemporaneous and can be linked to similar incidents in the 1980s.

Amitav Ghosh stresses that due to social conditioning, the role of rumour in riots or mass movements is deep rooted. The young schoolboys willingly believe that a certain community has poisoned the water in Calcutta. Later as a research student, reading newspaper reports in the Teen Murti House library in Delhi, about the 1964 events the narrator recalls the motivations for riots in Calcutta.

> In Calcutta rumours were in the air—especially that familiar old rumour, the harbinger of every serious riot—that the trains from Pakistan were arriving packed with corpses . . . with refugees still pouring in, rumours began to flow like floodwaters through the city and angry crowds began to gather at the stations. (229)

The author's views on the impact of rumours are authenticated by the distinguished historian Dr. Sumit Sarkar, Professor of History at Delhi University. In his scholarly book, *Modern India 1885-1947*, Dr. Sumit Sarkar projects the role of rumour in the growing popularity of the Gandhian movement. He shows the effectiveness of rumour in any mass movement especially during periods of acute strain and tension.

> From out of their misery and hope, varied sections of the Indian people seem to have fashioned their own images of Gandhi, particularly in the early days when he was still to most people a distant, vaguely-glimpsed or heard-of tale of a holy man with miracle working powers . . . peasants were giving vague rumours about Gandhi a radical, anti-zamindar twist.[4]

Sumit Sarkar notes that the currency which Gandhi's name acquired in the remotest villages was primarily due to the impact of rumour, perpetuated by a desire to be represented by a saviour from above.[5]

Awareness of the growing internationalisation of the world is highlighted by the author. He shows the coming together of different societies and culture, which has also emphasized their distinctions. *The Shadow Lines* aptly reveals that the cultural divide, communal struggle and misunderstanding is in a state of crisis in India. The political allegory, the contemporaneousness of the motivations for riots is very sensitively handled. The rumour of water being poisoned by a particular community and of a train full of dead bodies, is not confined to particular incidents of certain decades but has become a recurring feature. In the novel, Amitav Ghosh reveals that on 27 December 1963, two hundred and sixty-three years after the Mu-i-Mubarak, believed to be a hair of the Prophet Mohammed, was brought to Kashmir, it was stolen. The newspaper reports, read by the narrator, indicate that "there was not one single recorded incident of animosity between Kashmiri Muslims, Hindus and Sikhs." (225) The targets of the rioters were properly identified with the government and the police. The purveyor of sanity was the wise leader Maulana Masoodi "who persuaded the first demonstrators to march with black flags instead of green and thereby drew the various communities of Kashmir together in a collective display of mourning." (226) Amitav Ghosh rightly regrets that in the hysteria that prevails in the subcontinent now, the sane and secular Maulana Masoodi has been forgotten.

Using the narrative technique of unfurling events, by the reading of newspaper reports, it is shown that in both wings of Pakistan, there were protest demonstrations. Certain disgruntled bigots hinted at attacks upon the identity of the Muslims. However on 4 January 1964 the Mu-i-Mubarak was recovered by the officials of the Central Bureau of Intelligence.

The protests in Pakistan subsided. Only in Khulna, a small town in the distant east wing of Pakistan, a demonstration turned violent. "Some shops were burnt down and a few people killed." (226) Headlines in newspapers of 7 January 1964 were, "Fourteen die in frenzy off Khulna." (228) Riots spread from Khulna to the outskirts of Dhaka. It is now that rumour took over. The poisoning of water, trains full of dead bodies, all incredible rumours, further vitiate the communal frenzy, and add to the violence. However what makes the novel very contemporary and relevant is the subtle implication by Amitav Ghosh that the lessons of history have not been learnt.

The deplorable violence unleashed upon the Sikhs in Delhi, from 31 October to 4 November 1984, shows history repeating itself. The report of the Citizens' Commission (1985) indicates that the motivation for the Delhi riots, after the assassination of late Prime Minister Indira Gandhi, followed a familiar pattern, insidious spread of rumours. The report prepared by five senior and responsible citizens of Delhi says,

> The basic provocation [for the riots] was provided by the spreading of rumours, some of them of a most incredible nature. . . . On the night of 1/2 November numerous citizens received telephone calls or were told otherwise that the city water supply had been poisoned, by Sikh extremists. Allegations circulated like wildfire

> that truckloads and a train full of dead Hindus had arrived from Punjab and that Sikh students danced the Bhangra on hearing of Smt. Gandhi's death.[6]

The difference between fiction and reality is thus shown as marginal. *The Shadow Lines* shows how rumour mongerers thrived and intensified feelings of anger, which triggered off violence in Calcutta in 1964. Amitav Ghosh's greatest triumph is that the depiction of communal strife in Calcutta and erstwhile East Pakistan, and its continuation in contemporary India, is very controlled and taut. There are no moralising or irrelevant digressions. Lucidity and compactness is achieved primarily by his unusual narrative device.

Violence is never described. It is depicted in several ways. The cause of the riots of 1964 and the violence at Khulna are presented as newspaper reports. The narrator reads these reports, at the Teen Murti House Library, sixteen years later, after a discussion with his friend Malik. A mature, research student, the narrator is still shocked by the needless violence, the motivations which triggered off the violent incidents and the sudden realisation that this was how his cousin Tridib died. The news item narrative technique, with its emphasis on facts, eliminates any digression or gory details. Sheer stark reality is presented, which adds to the horror of the event. Also the bland newspaper reports, just concerned with detail, remove the impact of time. It is implied that the riots are contemporaneous. The 1964 Calcutta riots could be the 1984 Delhi riots or the 1987 Meerut riots. They all follow a similar pattern, suspicion, distrust, rumour activating conditioned minds, all sources of terrifying communal violence. The newspaper reports technique hints at a continuity of the lurking danger of communal strife, which can be sparked off by both marginal and recalled major events. The violence in Calcutta is not narrated, but is presented as the memories and images of the narrator. Again the role of rumour and overall distrust is stressed, facets which have a bearing on communal trouble in the current decade also. Such treatment adds to the immediate relevance of *The Shadow Lines*.

Precise details of the death of Tridib are conveyed by May to the narrator, years later at a dinner in London. May narrates the story to exorcise her feeling of guilt, that she was responsible for Tridib's untimely death. The narrator, being a young boy, had been told that Tridib's death was due to an accident. On learning the truth, both May and the narrator realise they cannot rationalise the motives for Tridib's sacrifice. As May says, "any real sacrifice is a mystery." (252) As a political action, Tridib's reckless act is not redemptive. He had saved May and could have returned to the safety of the car himself. Plunging into the berserk mob just leads to his death. As a political act, it is revealed that individual valour or action cannot stem the upsurge of communal strife. Tridib dies as he lived, an iconoclast, a mystery.

The absence of pessimism, despair and ambiguity makes *The Shadow Lines* a very convincing and effective work of art. The author boldly tackles political themes both national and international. The meaning of political freedom in the modern world is shown as complex and without any easy solutions. For human survival, a new perception of relationships must emerge. On the national level, Amitav Ghosh shows how different cultures and communities are becoming antagonistic to a point of no return. This is revealed as a major issue in contemporary India. The author realises that with the dominant tradition slowly regarding itself as the only legitimate source of India's complex culture, communal antagonism will grow. Hence in the novel he effectively uses political allegory to stress the need for a syncretic civilisation, to avoid a communal holocaust. Above all, the use of imagination and the memory technique make *The Shadow Lines* a compact novel. The narrative is controlled, is not too digressive and does not give the impression of a collection of stories yoked together. Imagination and politics are the binding force of Amitav Ghosh's second work of fiction.

NOTES

1. Amitav Ghosh, *The Shadow Lines* (Delhi: Ravi Dayal Publishers, 1988), p. 7.
2. Plato, *The Republic* (Middlesex, England: Penguin, 1955), p. 421.
3. Philip Sidney, *Defence of Poetry*, ed. Dorsten Jan Van (Delhi: Oxford University Press, 1978).
4. Sumit Sarkar, *Modern India 1885-1947* (Madras: Macmillan India, 1983), p. 181.
5. *Ibid.*, p. 182. In the section. "The Role of Rumour," Sumit Sarkar reveals that peasants would imagine that Gandhi would end zamindari exploitation. For instance agricultural labourers in U.P. believed he would provide holdings for them. Assam tea coolies left the plantations en masse in May 1921, saying they were obeying Gandhi's orders and hoping for a better deal. Gandhi became a historical necessity. Even local achievements like illegal eviction being restricted in Pratapgarh, due to a peasants' struggle is attributed to Gandhi.
6. *Delhi 31 October to 4 November 1984, Report of the Citizens' Commission, January 1985* compiled by Justice S.M. Sikri, former Chief Justice of India, Badr-ud-Din Tyabji, former Commonwealth Secretary, Rajeshwar Dayal, Govind Narain and T.C.A. Srinivasvadaran (Delhi: Citizen's Commission, 1985), p. 36.

The Quest for Meaning: A Study of *The Shadow Lines*

S.P. SWAIN

Basically a memory novel, Amitav Ghosh's *The Shadow Lines*[1] presents a dexterous blending of private lives and public events into a desultory mosaic of history. The narrator's story unfurls itself through fragmentary streams of consciousness where the private turmoil of the individual is reflected in the public chaos and crises. It is through the stories narrated by Tridib that the narrator, a young boy, validates his experiences: "Tridib had given me worlds to travel in and he had given me eyes to see them with." (20)

The question that Amitav Ghosh raises or seems to ask his readers is that whether or not one can draw a demarcating line between imagination and reality and the implied response that he offers is "No." There indeed cannot be a dividing line between imagination and reality. Ghosh seems to suggest that there can only be a "shadow line" between imagination and reality, since reality is too vast and complex a concept to be circumscribed within historical chronology or geographical contours. A place is more than its geographical and historical features. It carries a deep imaginative meaning. The narrator disapproves of Ila's down-to-earth perception of reality. He says: "I could not persuade her that a place does not merely exist, that it has to be invented in one's imagination; that her practical bustling London was no less invented than mine, neither more nor less true, only very far apart." (21)

The interpretation of reality in mundane terms, as does Ila, is a falsification of it, since such a perception of reality is shorn of its true meaning. It lacks imaginative perception of feeling. It is gross. But Ila is obsessed with such feelings and hence the narrator's failure to persuade and convince her to a meaningful imaginative interpretation of reality. Amitav Ghosh seems to say that it is imagination alone which can portray a lucid and an enduring picture of reality. Hence he gives more emphasis to the creative role of imagination in delineating the uncoiling of memories through the stream-of-consciousness of Tridib and other characters in the novel like the grandmother. Exploration of meaning occurs at two planes—the private and the public. In the first section of the novel—"Going Away," the novelist focusses on London on the eve of, and during the war. London is vividly portrayed through the narrator's deft dispensation of his historical imagination. The significance of war is explored both at the personal and the human level. At the personal level there is a feeling of pity and sympathy, of fellow-feeling brought about by the shadow of an impending death and at the national (public) level, there is a feeling of masked and counterfeit exhilaration across national borders, and both in England and in Germany. Sharmila Guha Majumdar opines that this sense of exhilaration is "the defence mechanism that people developed to combat the sense of doom."[2] The personally experienced reality of Tridib colours the imagination of the storyteller. It is through Tridib and the grandmother that the narrator views reality and lends meaning to his meaningless infantile fancy. The title "The Shadow Lines" becomes an ambivalent symbol. It suggests the dichotomy of one's mind, the shadow lines that pervade the minds of the people. Grandmother's son says: "This is the modern world. The border isn't on the frontier; it's right inside the airport. You'll see. You'll cross it when you have to fill in all those disembarkation cards and things." (151-52)

In the absence of any clear-cut division, the meaning of nationalism as described in the novel becomes quite blurred and vague. The narrator, unable to vividly comprehend "these physical equivalents of the division,"[3] says: "They had drawn their borders, believing in that pattern, in the enchantment of lines, hoping perhaps that once they had etched their borders upon the map, the two bits of land would sail away from each other like the shifting tectonic plates of the pre-historic Gondwanaland." (233) Amitav Ghosh aims to drive home the meaning of nationalism, in the minds of the readers, through the characters in the novel. The narrator's grandmother thinks nationalism a holy and sacred word which has become the focus of political thinking in the nineteenth and twentieth century. It suggests everything that is anti-British. Sharmila Guha Majumdar observes: "In her desire to win political freedom she dreamt of killing English officials. She even considered war as a necessary evil which inspired the idea of nationalism and thus strengthened the foundation of a nation." (146)

Nationalism in the late twentieth century degenerated into political animosity between the Indians and the Englishmen. Such was the narrowmindedness of the grandmother that she viewed nationalism as a belligerent and recalcitrant attitude held by the Indians towards the Englishmen. She failed to have a proper grasp of nationalism in her mind. Not only the grandmother but also Irishmen like Mike thought that "for a person to be righfully Indian, it was necessary to kill Englishmen." Such is the individual enmity between the Indian and the Englishman, that they fail to form a meaningful interpretation of nationalism. In the section "Coming Home" Ghosh explores the meaning of political freedom. Indian nationalism, a manifestation of political freedom fails to guarantee the territorial integrity of the coutry. The historic event of Partition gave a jolt to the Indians' sense of nationalism. Majumdar holds that "Nationalism in the Indian context changed its meaning to exclude people on the other side of the border but could not include everybody on this side of paradise." (146) But I feel that the characters fail to form a cogent picture of nationalism because of the lack of an inner harmony, or rather the lack of a mutual sense of love and regard for each other. After all what is nationalism and political freedom without the element of love and regard for oneself as well as others? But the grandmother, with her perspicacity and clarity of vision gives her own views of nationalism. She thinks that the sentiments of nationalism can only develop through war and bloodshed. Her feelings of nationalism are related to the ideals of self-esteem and national power. The grandmother tells the narrator: "It took those people a long time to build that country . . . years and years of war and bloodshed. Everyone who lives there has earned his right to be there with blood. . . . War is their religion. That's what it takes to make a country." (77-78)

In a bid for political freedom, people have frenziedly and madly given themselves to terrorism and communal violence. "Even characters like the grandmother and Ila who do not indulge in violence are on the fringe of it."[4] Her willingness to run errands for the Bengal terrorists and kill the English magistrate at Khulna during her youth bears testimony to her love of violence and war. If in the grandmother the quest for political freedom manifests in her belligerent and violent motives, in Ila it manifests in her personal freedom, her breaking away from her family for a cosmopolitan way of life in London. It is this quest for freedom—personal and political—that imparts a realistic touch to the novel. With a dialogic narrative approach Ghosh reveals the motive behind everyone indulging in violence and mutual hatred. Robi, the IAS officer, philosophises to Ila and the narrator: "You know, if you look at the pictures on the front pages of the newspapers at home now, all those pictures of dead people—in Assam, the North-East, Punjab, Sri Lanka, Tripura—people shot by terrorists and separatists and the army and police, you'll find somewhere behind it all, that single word: everyone doing it to be free." (246)

Amitav Ghosh does not elaborate the meaning of concepts and ideologies. On the other hand, he insinuates the readers into the world of history through the mind of characters, their painful and nostalgic re-callings and recollections and it is these psychic intrusions that destroy the narrative sequence of the story. The novel, therefore becomes a se-ries of random reflections, for it reflects "reality itself in the process of its unfolding . . . tendencies of a new world still in the making."[5] Per-sonal histories, family histories and the history of the nation are weaved into a thin and transparent gossamer of imagination. They are restruc-tured in a quest for meaning, a quest for knowledge since what the char-acters reminisce has the touch of inaccuracy. Hence Tridib is not sure as to the accuracy of his memory: "he didn't know whether it had really happened or he had imagined it" (29) to make it sensible and meaning-ful. It is through imagination that the "I" narrator experiences much of his life in the process of knowing through a search for meaning:

> I shook my head violently. . . . You're lying. I shouted at her. That can't be a staircase because it's flat, and staircases go up, they aren't flat. And that can't be upstairs because upstairs has to be above and that isn't above; that's right beside the drawing room. I dropped to my knees and began to scrabble around in the dust, rubbing out the lines, shouting: You're lying, you're mad, this can't be a house. (70)

This is nothing but the travesty of a quest by the half-knowing young narrator who makes a fancifully naive approach to validate materiality. But the narrator, despite his imaginative skill fails to comprehend the real when his childhood hero, Tridib, falls a prey to the "seamless si-lence," (270) that meaningless violence in Dhaka. It was May Price who finally recounted the incident that gobbled Tridib. K. Damodar Rao ob-serves: "The silence that preceded and followed the revelation was a moving statement on the actualisation of internal violence. The search and the revelation together cause a harrowing experience for the narra-tor." (65) In fact, the search for meaning amidst communal frenzy and political chaos is motivated by the awareness of a need, that is the need to know the cause and nature of silence that permeates the life of the in-quisitive young narrator:

> Every word I write about those events of 1964 is the product of a struggle with silence. It is a struggle I am destined to lose—have already lost—for even after all these years I do not know where within me, in which corner of my world, this silence lies. . . . It is simply a gap, a hole, an emptiness in which there are no words. (218)

The silent quest of the narrator for meaning in life, for filling up the inner void in him with words forms the focus of the novel and it is this search for words, the need to articulate silence that "throws the notions of secularism, nationalism and freedom into disarray."[6] But could the narrator fill the gap, the silence in him with words and voice? All voices seem to be stifled in that traumatic psychic state where uncertainty and horrific apprehensions make our otherwise peaceful existence on this earth meaningless. Look at Ghosh's graphic account of the communal situation in the subcontinent where all forms of quest for meaning are rendered futile: "It is like the fear of the victims of an earthquake, of people who have lost faith in the stillness of the earth. . . . It is a fear that comes of the knowledge that normalcy is utterly contingent, that the spaces that surround one, the streets that one inhabits, can become, suddenly and without warning, as hostile as a desert in a flash flood." (204)

Such a psychological situation alienates man from man and even sets apart the subcontinent from the rest of the world. It is this that has "the special quality of loneliness that grows out of the fear of the war between oneself and one's image in the mirror." (204) Such meaningless absurdity of our shaky existence where, in the words of Matthew Arnold, "ignorant armies clash by night," where incertitude rules our life, man's quest for meaning and value turn into a cry in wilderness.

The novel urges the reader's involvement in actively constructing for himself an interpretive framework that runs parallel to the characters' traumatic and anguished recounting of the past. Especially the grandmother's remembrances of her painful and haunting past have been vividly and dramatically presented. They give validity to her existence, meaning to her chaotic and tense life. The grandmother, the narrator, Tridib, Ila and many other non-Indian characters present a multiplicity of voices characterised by variegated discourse and language to recount their experiences. This is nothing but a striving after meaning and reason for the stifled thoughts of the past tormenting their psyche. Replete with interpretive potential, an appealing aspect of the novel is its multivocal dimension, and a structure fragmented and episodic, successfully leading to a conclusion that the historical events of the past, political rivalry, religious and communal strife and even personal trauma and nostalgia are beyond objectification. Through multivocal narrative, Ghosh lends meanings to social and political chaos reflected in the individual's search of a meaningful existence personified in memory as a relived experience.

The meaning of political freedom in the modern world is for Ghosh a complicated and an intricate one. It is without a clear solution. In a land where culture and communities thrive on mutual hatred and antagonism, the quest for meaning is liable to end in failure. The 'journey motif' which runs through the fabric of the story like the grandmother's journey to Dhaka in the second part of the novel and the narrator's journey backwards in time is symbolic of the quest for meaning in life. It is the quest for wholeness, an attempt to impose a pattern on our otherwise chaotic experience. It is a shadow line. The novel which depicts violence and crude barbarity through the recounting of riot memories seems to convey the message that man's running after self-esteem, his search for an authentic selfhood through freedom to act the way he likes, is a mirage. It would only come to a point of no return. Hence the futility of the quest for the validation of one's existence. Hence it is difficult to say why Tridib gave up his life, why he threw himself to his own death. Louis James maintains that he was "drawn by the 'shadow-line' of imaginative sympathy."[7] But the question that crops up in our mind is why he did it. It is a mystery. Ghosh does not give any clear answer to this and so Tridib's death, though a real sacrifice, becomes a mystery, an absurdity for the common man who fails to find any meaning in it. The quest for meaning thus continues without finality.

NOTES

1. (New Delhi: Ravi Dayal Publisher, 1988).
2. "Amitav Ghosh's *The Shadow Lines* and *In an Antique Land*: Some Thematic Considerations," pp. 178-88 in this book.
3. K. Damodar Rao, "Silence as Possible Mode of Response in Amitav Ghosh's *The Shadow Lines*," pp. 136-42 in this book.
4. Novy Kapadia, "Imagination and Politics in Amitav Ghosh's *The Shadow Lines*," in Viney Kirpal, ed., *The New Indian Novel in English* (New Delhi: Allied, 1990), p. 205.
5. Mikhail Bakhtin, "Epic and Novel," *The Dialogic Imagination*, ed. Michael Holquist, trans. Caryl Emerson and Michael Holquist (Austin: Univ. of Texas Press, 1981), p. 7.
6. Rao, p. 65.
7. "Shadow Lines: Cross-Cultural Perspectives in the Fiction of Amitav Ghosh," p. 58 in this book.

Silence as Possible Mode of Response in *The Shadow Lines*

K. DAMODAR RAO

Amitav Ghosh's second novel, *The Shadow Lines*,[1] creates a rich tapestry of eloquence and silence. It offers a vintage formula of sketches, memories, and glimpses in an intricate pattern of past and present gushing through the prismatic view of the personal and the historical. With its axis on the Indian subcontinent's specified context, the novel's breath-taking compass coils together geographical distances and deliberately attempts to break many myths while taking the country's history, culture and political situation in its stride. Amitav Ghosh's first novel, *The Circle of Reason,* is about eloquence, search for metaphor, and the narrative capabilities of the narrator and his characters. The story-teller-audience interaction is marked by understanding, expectancy and involvement. While the zest for narration is evident in *The Shadow Lines,* it allows just enough space, and in it lies its eloquence, to see the limitations of the normally accepted notions of love, history, violence, freedom, communication and justice. The text, as such, is important for things eloquent as much for things left unsaid. The metaphors, in themselves all-pervading and eloquent, with all their contours of language and creation, are oriented towards capturing the possibilities and nuances of silence. Since the text is studded with myriad possibilities and multiple points of view, an attempt is made in this paper to view silence as employed in the text by means of subversion as a possible mode of response.

The novel puts to test some of the personal experiences, relations, memories and historical processes in which the realization of the futility of metaphor on the one hand and an awareness of the 'illusion of knowledge created by deceptive weight of remembered detail' (67) are evidenced at many levels. This process of testing is achieved by constant juxtaposition of silence with powers of communication, and of experiential realities with those notions supposed to have been theorized, defined and categorized. The pathetic situation of finding oneself beyond or below the categorized parameters throws into relief some seemingly undefined, vague and unreal conditions. This incongruous element is approached by the novelist from different angles by applying different frames of reference covering different areas of human experience. If irony is one mode of reference, silence is the other mode of reference as well as response, a strategy to probe deep into the validity or otherwise of words and notions. The questions dealt with are both experience and eloquence.

The division of the novel into two parts—'Going Away' and 'Coming Home'—is in itself a conscious attempt on the part of the novelist to dismantle some of the time-tested notions of experience and eloquence. These words, all by themselves, cannot encompass the subtleties of coming and going which overlap any number of times. In an on-going process of continuity, strict compartmentalization of the notions of coming and going might become arbitrary as the text testifies to the intricacies of these in both the parts. And when national boundaries are constantly drawn and re-drawn, the meaning could take an ambiguous turn while the processes of coming and going get marginalized.

The grandmother of the narrator, born and brought up in Dhaka and now living in Calcutta, recalls her childhood days and mentions to her son that in those days before partition there were no forms to be filled up and says: "I could come home to Dhaka whenever I wanted." (152) At this the narrator who was a child then jumps up at the ungrammatical expression of his grandmother-headmistress and wonders why she could not make out the difference between coming and going: "Tha'mma, Tha'mma! I cried. How could you have 'come' home to Dhaka? You don't know the difference between coming and going!" (152) The question involved here is twofold: one of capturing in words the actual processes of coming and going and the other relates to national boundaries, notions of patriotism and the like. Words and meanings have got to be defined and re-defined in accordance with the changing physical boundaries and political affiliations. Even for the grandmother, a mental division must entail a physical division. Now it is her turn to pose a question, not a childish one by any means. She thinks that there were 'trenches perhaps, or soldiers, or guns pointing at each other, or even just barren strips of land' that would give an indication of the thing happened, the division of physical borders as it happened in the minds of the people of the subcontinent. But, to her dismay, much like her grandson's, she learns that the mental equivalent of the division was not physically visible on the frontiers, and the natural question would be: 'What was it all then—partition and all the killing and everything—if there isn't something in between.' (151) Her son's remark brings to the fore the dichotomy, the shadow lines, that existed in the minds of the people: "This is the modern world. The border isn't on the frontier; it's right inside the airport. You'll see. You'll cross it when you have to fill in all those disembarkation cards and things." (151-52) The myth of nationalism gets broken in the absence of these physical equivalents of the division. The narrator himself is worried about the problem when he grows up and broods on this: "They had drawn their borders, believing in that pattern, in the enchantment of lines, hoping perhaps that once they had etched their borders upon the map, the two bits of land would sail away from each other like the shifting tectonic plates of the prehistoric Gondwanaland." (233)

The conspicuousness of words and logic is presented, in the first instance, in the case of the narrator's love for Ila. He thinks aloud on the futility of metaphors in this context of a love, unreciprocated:

> Perhaps those miles and yards are my own living metaphors, my attempt to claim a share of justice. For I had already thrown everything else I had on the scales; not insubstantial things after all, for I was a human being too, with my own worth and weight, not ugly, not without substance, educated, and with other qualities too, like patience and good humour—what more could a human being have, in fairness—I had thrown in all of that, everything I had, and by not so much as a tremor had the scales acknowledged their weight. (96)

One may, in fact, go on heaping the metaphors and still not find the state itself and there is also the danger of finding its opposite. Hence, the virtue of the other extreme, silence. For Ila, the current, cut off from the past and future, alone was the real. It was as though she was completely overwhelmed by the present which was like "an airlock in a canal, shut away from the tidewaters of the past and the future by steel floodgates." (30) The narrator has not travelled extensively around the world as Ila did since her childhood. Yet he could invent these places in his imagination on the basis of the described places and narrated events first by Tridib, by Ila's parents and then by Ila herself. But when he goes to London years later—to collect data from the India Office Library on the textile trade between India and England in the 19th century—and mentions 'Cairo' to Ila, what all she could remember was 'Ladies' in the airport which she says was on the other side of the departure lounge. Probably, the 'tired intimacy' (20) made her forget the aspects which precisely held a magic aura for the narrator. As Tridib would say of her, "the inventions she lived in moved with her, so that although she had lived in many places, she had never travelled at all." (21)

The worlds they had essentially belonged to were understood by Ila in the first place. The narrator could not help loving her and it was in the very personality of Ila not to spare a loving space for the likes of him. Even as the narrator feels that his invented England was no less real and concrete than the actual base of Ila and leads her and Nick Price, based on memory of description, to the old building in which Nick Price's maternal grandfather, Mike Tresawsen, and others of a socialist outfit carried on their activities on the mid-thirties, Ila's slight comes as a shocker:

> You wouldn't understand the exhilaration of events like that—nothing really important ever happens where you are . . . well of course there are famines and riots and disasters. . . . But those are local things after all—not like revolutions or anti-fascist wars, nothing that sets a political example to the world, nothing that's really remembered. (104)

The thoughts that cross the mind of the narrator at this would provide a fitting commentary on the 'mystery of difference' (32) between the two, on the futility of metaphors and of a life that fits in with such an ability of communication only: "She seemed immeasurably distant then, in her serene confidence in the centrality and eloquence of her experience, in her quiet pity for the pettiness of lives like mine, lived out in the silence of voiceless events in a backward world." (104)

Ila's love for Nick Price, by the same token, defies logic. Even as a child she hides the essentially mean and the timid in Nick Price whom she was to marry later on, and presents a cosy picture of an incident supposed to have taken place at school in London in which Nick Price does the rescuing act while in reality he runs away from the scene of action for fear of being seen with a non-native. She persists with her illusion and does not hesitate to marry him in later years despite his proven qualities of inconsistency and waywardness. The narrator whose love was unreciprocated ('You were always the brother I never had'—Ila) soon establishes his superiority but the agony, the silence, that made him do away with metaphors remains much the same.

The shadow lines, queer turns, absence of logic, sheer absurdity, and defiance of well-defined systems of thought and ordering might often prove to be the hallmarks of the notions of governance, excellence, freedom and justice as in the case of a purely personal experience of love. Tridib was the narrator's childhood hero. Apart from the fact of Tridib being at the centre of things, the narrator also accepted his influence as part of his own being. Tribid, he feels, has given him "worlds to travel in and . . . eyes to see them with." (20) One thing of substance he had learnt from Tridib was to use his imagination with precision. He knew that what Tridib could see in his imagination "was infinitely more detailed and more precise" (29) than he could ever possibly hope for. All the same he could not forget his advice that if he didn't try it himself he would never be free of other people's imagination and invention.

Despite the art of imagination the narrator has assiduously cultivated, he fails to grasp the actual when his childhood hero and mentor becomes a victim of meaningless violence in Dhaka. It was only much later that he finds himself, despite the promise he had made to his father that he would not be interested in knowing the cause of Tridib's death, on the look out for the bits and pieces that would connect him to the cause of Tridib's death. It was May Price who at the end actually recounts the incident of communal frenzy that engulfed Tridib. The silence that preceded and followed the revelation was a moving statement on the actualization of internal violence. The search and the revelation together cause a harrowing experience for the narrator. The stoic understatement of the entire narration is informed by this awareness, an awareness of the need and result of silence: "Every word I write about those events of 1964 is the product of a struggle with silence. It is a struggle I am destined to lose—have already lost—for even after all these years. I do not know where within me, in which corner of my world, this silence lies . . . it is simply a gap, a hole, an emptiness in which there are no words." (218)

The silent search of the narrator which forms the core of the novel throws the notions of secularism, nationalism and freedom into disarray. In effect, it implies a search, a probe that has been orientated towards the prime cause for the creation of illusions, the shadow lines. Political domain which has thrown many such illusions is sharply contrasted with a sensitive individual's attitude that rises above narrow considerations and shallow confines of the political exigencies. Hence, the basic problem one is confronted with in this sphere is not merely that of eloquence, but that of communication which comes to the fore any number of times. So complete is this silence—"of an absolute, impenetrable banality" (218)—in the life and mission of the narrator that it took nearly fifteen years to discover that there was a connection between the theft of the Prophet's hair from the Hazratbal shrine in 1964, the nightmarish bus ride back from his school and the events that befell Tridib and others in Dhaka.

The communal riots follow their own 'grotesque logic' (229) fed by rumours, devoid of the basic human streak, as evidenced in the life of the subcontinent at frequent intervals since independence. The carnage let loose on such occasions is beyond description. The loss of life, the manner in which people get killed and the animal instincts that come to the fore in an atmosphere of frenzy and violence convert human life into a huge pretension or an accidental freak. Before the riots erupt there would not be 'any hint or augury' that would suggest the impending carnage. The situation would be 'replete with the fullness of normalcy.' (227)

And then all the mayhem would follow as if by design, in a pattern. Unable to measure the 'stirrings of silence' Tridib had fallen a prey to that 'seamless silence.' (227) The grandmother of the narrator and May were witnesses to the ghastly scene of Tridib's murder at the hands of a fanatical mob. What could be reactions of the intimate ones of the victims or the actual witnesses to such gory deaths? The grandmother of the narrator attempts to wreak psychological revenge at the time of the war with Pakistan in 1971 by offering blood in a frantic hurry, as if in a fit of madness. As for May, she thinks that she was, to some extent, responsible for the thing happened, as it was she who wanted to rescue the old man and Khalil, the rickshaw puller, who were following their car. She applied the same previous logic of stopping the car and requesting Tridib to relieve the dog, that fell under their car, of its pain. But to her dismay, as she herself revealed it to the narrator in the last pages of the novel in a vivid manner as if she could not forget the tragic event, as if she has been living with the painful experience ever since, she becomes a witness to the murder of three persons: "When I got there, I saw three bodies. They were all dead. They'd cut Khalil's stomach open. The old man's head had been hacked off. And they'd cut Tridib's throat, from ear to ear." (251) She feels she could have gone right into that mob—'they wouldn't have touched me, an English memsahib'—and saved them all. But an understanding of the strange dynamics of the communal tension peculiar to the subcontinent makes her conclude that Tridib had given himself up. She considers it 'a sacrifice.' (252)

The day Tridib and others were murdered in Khulna on the outskirts of Dhaka, the narrator himself, as a school-going boy, was undergoing a traumatic experience as the riots erupted in Calcutta also. The narrator could remember it vividly, more so because only the previous day the cricket match with England had started in Madras and the wicket-keeper-batsman, Budhi Kunderan, scored a century on debut. The school was closed abruptly and he could remember, on their way back home in the school-bus, how 'the streets had turned themselves inside out,' and how 'the city had turned' against them all, children. Tublu, one of his school-mates, wept all the way—'for all of us' (204)—and all the others gathered around him. At any other time they would have laughed, but that day they remained silent. The 'texture' of the fear, although indescribable, could still make a lasting and powerful impact on the mind of the narrator, and in later years he tries to reconstruct his mental state which must be regarded as, perhaps, the most eloquent statement on the communal situation in the subcontinent:

> It is like the fear of the victims of an earthquake, of people who have lost faith in the stillness of the earth. And yet it is not the same. It is without analogy, for it is not comparable to the fear of nature, which is the most universal of human fears, nor to the fear of the violence of the state, which is the commonest of modern fears. It is a fear that comes of the knowledge that normalcy is utterly contingent, that the spaces that surround one, the streets that one inhabits, can become, suddenly and without warning, as hostile as a desert in a flash flood. (204)

This psychological state is peculiar to our cultural and political context. This is a peculiarity that sets us apart from the rest of the world: "It is this that sets apart the thousand million people who inhabit the subcontinent from the rest of the world—not language, not food, not music—it is the special quality of loneliness that grows out of the fear of the war between oneself and one's image in the mirror." (204)

What could be the attitudes of the governments involved in this peculiar geographical and political context? In fact, the theatre of war, 'where generals meet, is the stage on which states disport themselves,' where violence is considered justified by the state. They have no use for 'memories of riots' (230) that bring feelings of oneness among sections of society independent of the state intervention that might be detrimental to the interests and welfare of the state mechanism. Hence, the governments follow a fairly predictable line. Initially they start with 'rhetorical exchanges' such as symmetrical accusations for remaining passive in the face of a 'frenzy of looting, killing and burning.' And when the riots get subsided on their own, congratulatory notes are exchanged 'over their respective successes in quelling disturbances.' The measure of governments's success or failure depends on the number of deaths occurred. When only a few people get killed, governments have no use for them. The irony that killed Tridib and others was conveniently forgotten and the murderous frenzy itself disappeared from the collective imagination "into the crater of a volcano of silence." (233) Conversely, the impact on the consciousness of the concerned individual could be a shattering one. The best course would be to take recourse to silence, as the novel eloquently does.

NOTE

1. Amitav Ghosh, *The Shadow Lines* (New Delhi: Ravi Dayal Publisher, 1988).

Perspectives in Time: The Narrator as Child in *The Shadow Lines*

NANDITA SINHA

On reading *The Shadow Lines* one is struck by the extraordinary density of its narrative texture. The story emerges in layers and each layer is a fusion of private lives and public events, all linked into a thematic unity. This paper proposes to show how Ghosh uses first-person narrative from a dual viewpoint—that of the child and the adult "I," thus giving us a sense of inhabiting both past and present simultaneously. The narrator as child comes into close contact with the protagonists of the story and thus serves to weave together its multiple facets—through his grandmother with her East Bengal background and memories of her girlhood days in Dhaka in a sprawling house with its idiosyncratic occupants, the narrative takes us to the odyssey of her search for an old uncle left behind in what was by then East Pakistan and its tragic consequences; through his relationships with his uncle Tridib and cousin Ila and their connections with the Price family in London, the narrative takes us back in time to war-torn London and doubles back again to a time when he is a student in London himself. And once again, through Tridib, whom the child hero-worships, we have an authentic vista of Calcutta life—the streetside addas, the strollers round the Lake, the squalid tenements—as well as a lovingly drawn portrait of childhood in a middle-class Bengali family. The child observes and assesses his world—a world in which "children were sent to school to learn how to cling to their gentility by proving themselves in the examination hall"; where the women possess a "peculiar manipulative worldliness which comes from dealing with large families," where there is a subtle balance of power between the mother and grandmother. His intuitive insights give a grounding to what is one of the novel's most appealing features—its remarkable air of authenticity.

The personal drama in each case is played out against a canvas of sweeping historical events—the freedom movement and the rise of insurgency in Bengal, England's war against Hitler's Germany, the Chinese aggression and the Indo-Pak war, the desecration of the Hazratbal shrine in Srinagar in 1963, and the communal riots in Khulna and Calcutta in 1964—each of which directly or indirectly impinges on the child's experience.

The Shadow Lines is a novel about time, about growing up, not so much in years as in understanding. It is not what happened, but the meaning of what happened that is the central concern and the meaning emerges when the past and the present are considered together. Ghosh discards linear narrative in favour of multiple perspectives and here the narrator as child plays a significant role. People and events encountered in childhood are once again brought into focus when the adult narrator views them from a perspective of cumulative knowledge. The narrative voice, now that of the child's, now the adult's criss-crosses the novel. The juxtaposition of an incident as it appeared to the child while he was experiencing it with a later view of it from an unexpected angle is one of the recurrent devices of the narrative and introduces an effect that is almost cinematic. The movement back and forth in time is not merely a structural device, it serves to image a central theme—that the line dividing past and present is only a shadow, that the past lives in the present and that the present is shaped by the past or, as the novel puts it, "the past is concurrent with the present."

The inseparable tie between past and present manifests itself in the two love relationships that develop in the novel—Ila's infatuation with and later marriage to Nick Price and Tridib's love for May. Each is a bid for freedom from the past, but the irony lies in the fact that such freedom is an illusion. Ila desires freedom from a petty middle-class orthodoxy, but she discovers that the free world she had tried to build for herself was not free from the squalor of betrayal. Tridib wants to meet May as "the completest of strangers, far from their friends and relatives—in a place without a past, without history, free, really free, two people coming together with the utter freedom of strangers." But both are caught up inexorably in the backlash of history.

The child's involvement in these relationships takes him to the threshold of awareness, but his understanding remains partial till adulthood, when fresh perspectives heighten his sensitivity to the deeper meaning of his earlier experience. In the beginning it is his fascination for his cousin Ila that forms the core of his existence. To the boy, brought up in the humdrum routine of a "small, puritanical world" Ila appears as an exotic butterfly, with her easy intimacy with places which are magic names in the boy's atlas. But his love for her makes him vulnerable and with the clarity born out of despair he sees himself defenceless in her power and faced with the adult truth—"that need is not transitive, that one may need without oneself being needed." At age nine jealousy enters his world in the form of Nick Price, whom he has never seen, but who appears bigger and better and more desirable, because he was so in Ila's eyes. But the boy is puzzled at the way she bursts into tears while recounting the story of Nick's heroic rescue of a girl in distress. Much later, he learns from May what really happened—that the story was only make-believe, the truth was Nick Price's rejection of Ila because he was ashamed to be seen by his friends walking home with an Indian, an act of betrayal that reveals its full implications when the adult narrator is confronted with the reality of Nick's later betrayal of Ila, now his wife. This incident surfaces into the memory of the adult narrator many years afterwards when Ila takes him down to Mrs. Price's cellar in London and weeps as she tells of Nick's unfaithfulness. It is a telescoping of time and the two images appear to coalesce. But now he sees things differently. He sees Nick Price as vulnerable and fallible as he himself once was, "facing in future of helpless dependence coupled with despairing acts of rebellion." "I wanted to get up then and hold him, chest to chest, his shoulders to mine. But of course I didn't—he did not know of the part he had played in my life, standing beside me in the mirrors of my boyhood." (189)

The relationship between May and Tridib, too, unfolds from the child's point of view; he instinctively knows that there is something between them which he could never understand or share. "I was jealous, achingly jealous, as only a child can be, because it had always been my unique privilege to understand Tridib and that day, at the Victoria Memorial, I knew that I had lost that privilege, somehow May had stolen it from me." Understanding comes seventeen years later, when bits of information fall into place to create a pattern of meaning. He becomes aware of the true nature of their unique bond. The values that May cherishes and which motivate her to put a helpless dog, hurt in an accident out of its misery at personal risk are the same values that inspire Tridib's act of selfless heroism. Cutting across the superficial barriers of nationality, gender and similar divisions is human nature's "indivisible sanity."

The image of the journey is central to the novel—its two parts being entitled "Going Away" and "Coming Home." Tridib goes away from India to England with his family and the child relives the experience vicariously through Tridib's imaginatively vivid descriptions, so that when he himself grows up and goes to London, it is an effortless transition, a "coming" rather than a "going." It is Tridib who expands the frontiers of his boyhood world, giving him "worlds to travel in" and "eyes to see them with." It is Tridib who explains to him how one could be carried beyond the limits of one's mind to other times and other places "and even if one was lucky, to a place where there was no border between oneself and one's image in the mirror." Thus the boy learns to value the imaginative as revealing a world as concrete and real and infinitely more exciting than the world experienced through the senses. His journeys into the past with Tridib leave him with a vivid recollection of war-torn London and later, though he does not see the "uprooted trees or splintered windows or buckled flagstones "that have been lost in a forty year old past" he realizes that he has been shown something more valuable—England in her finest hour. As the adult voice puts it, "despite the clear testimony of my eyes it seemed to me still that Tridib had shown me something truer about Solent Road a long time ago in Calcutta." (57) In contrast, the narrow limits of Ila's imagination baffles the boy and makes him aware of the mystery of difference between people, a difference that is not based on distance in time and space, but on attitudes of the mind, as for instance between himself and Ila "who lived in a present which was like an airlock in a cánal, shut away from the tide-waters of the past and the future by steel floodgates, so that though she had lived in many places, she had never really travelled at all."

In the second part, the grandmother's journey to Dhaka becomes a symbolic search for a point of fixity. The prospect of a return to a home where she has inexplicably become a foreigner bewilders her. The child innocently misinterprets her confusion as anxiety at the prospect of travelling in a plane and his naive response strikes a note of touching humour: "I could see, then, that she was going to land up in a hopeless mess. I was sure, for example, that she would roll her window down in midair unless I warned her not to." Many years later, he comes to understand the true source of her mental conflict—her inability to understand how her place of birth had come to be so messily at odds with her nationality. The irony of this situation permeates the account (told to the now adult narrator) of her encounter with her old uncle who does not recognize her. In her bid to resurrect the past that memory has so indelibly imprinted in her mind, she fails to take into account the realities of the present, so that it is she who is the alien, the Muslims Khalil and Saifuddin who have befriended the old man are his family in the truest sense of the word. Her total allegianee to her past (symbolized by her changing into a red-bordered saree at the moment of departure) limits her vision, so that in the end, she remains isolated in the Mercedes, while the mob butchers the old man in his rickshaw as well as Tridib who sacrifices his life in trying to save him.

The meaning of political violence is one of the major themes of this novel. Violence is seen as destructive, but also as redemptive, for it can bring out heroism in unexpected ways. Ghosh draws a parallel between the heroism of ordinary Englishmen like Alan Tresawsen, Dan and Mike in facing the knowledge that "their world and in all probability, they themselves, would not survive the war" and Tridib's act of foolhardy courage, reinforcing thereby his belief that people are not so different after all, that geographical lines of division cannot change human values.

The child's experience touches both these situations at second-hand—through an old photograph in Tridib's room taken in London in 1939, and through his parent's reluctance to speak of Tridib's death to him as other than an accident. The child accepts their explanations unquestioningly: "for me, 'dead' was just a word, associated vaguely with films and comic books. That was all. I had no means of attaching that word to a real presence, like Tridib's. I felt nothing—no shock, no grief. I did not understand that I would never see him again, my mind was not large enough to accommodate so complete an absence." The boy is more concerned with his own immediate experience of violence when an ordianry school day turned into a nightmare with rioting mobs on rampage in the streets giving his school bus chase. He understands the terrifying power of rumour and its frightening ability to demarcate a division between "we" and "they." He also experiences a gut-wrenching fear, which is translated into a perception about the nature of this sort of fear by the adult narrative voice: "It is a fear that comes of the knowledge that normalcy is utterly contingent, that the spaces that surround one, the streets that one inhabits, can become, suddenly and without warning, as hostile as a desert in a flash flood. It is this that sets apart the thousand million who inhabit the subcontinent from the rest of the world—and language, not food, not music—it is the special quality of loneliness that grows out of the fear of the war between oneself and one's image in the mirror." (204)

The boy's experience is juxtaposed with the adult experience when the narrator, now in London as a student, hears two separate accounts of the violence that led to Tridib's death from Robi and May, both of whom had been present there. For Robi, the memory is a nightmare from which there is no deliverance, for his experience as an administrator has by now shown him how human nature remains unchanged, that the concept of freedom has become a catchword to condone killing, and that political freedom is an illusion, so that to draw thousands of little lines through the whole subcontinent and give every little place a new name would not change anything at all. For May, who is guiltridden at the thought that in some way she is responsible for Tridib's death, it is a luminous mystery that defies understanding a sacrifice and a martyrdom, an idealist's heroic stand against the tide of madness and bloodshed.

All these perceptions radiate from the focal incident of communal violence in Calcutta which the narrator experienced as a child, and which he later realizes is the obverse side of the same violence in Dhaka that took Tridib's life. These separate insights coalesce into a final awareness which forms the core of the novelist's vision. What matters is people and especially, as far as the subcontinent is concerned the indivisible links between them. The relationship could be positive as Ghosh records in his documentary account of the disappearance of the Mu-i-Mubarak from the Hazratbal shrine in Srinagar—that there was not one single recorded incident of animosity between Kashmiri Muslims, Hindus and Sikhs. It could as easily flare up at a moment's notice into the "pathological inversion" of communal riots in places as far apart as Khulna in East Pakistan and Calcutta. This indivisible tie governs the paradox that while the people of Khulna did not care about the fate of the mosques in Vietnam or South China which were much nearer in terms of geographical distance than Srinagar, in the other direction (i.e. Calcutta) it took no more than a week to rouse a frenzy of looting, burning and killing. Thus the irony of our political processes, which seek to give people separate identities by drawing boundary lines, is highlighted. As the novel puts it in a major setting forth of theme: "They had drawn their borders, believing in that pattern in the enchantment of lines, hoping perhaps that once they had etched their borders upon the map, the two bits of land would sail away from each other like the shifting tectonic plates of the prehistoric Gondwanaland. What had they felt, I wondered, when they discovered that they had created, not a separation, but a yet-undiscovered irony—the irony that killed Tridib: the simple fact that there had never been a moment in the four-thousand-year-old history of that map, when the places we know as Dhaka and Calcutta were more closely bound to each other than after they had drawn their lines—so closely that I, in Calcutta, had only to look into the mirror to be in Dhaka; a moment when each city was the inverted image of the other, locked into an irreversible symmetry by the line that was to set us free—our looking-glass border." (238)

The novel can therefore be described as the narrator's journey backwards in time in quest of a fuller meaning in life. It is an attempt to impose a pattern on experience. By putting the child in the centre of the narrative and surrounding the events of the past with later interpretations, Ghosh leads the reader through the same deepening of perception that the narrator experiences.

The Shadow Lines: A Note

G.R. TANEJA

The new Indian English fiction of the eighties is free from the self-consciousness, shallow idealism and sentimentalism that characterized the work of the older generation of novelists such as Raja Rao, R.K. Narayan or Mulk Raj Anand who started writing in the thirties. The fiction of the eighties takes a maturer view of Indian reality. There is freshness and vitality and the writers betray remarkable confidence in tackling new themes, and experiment with new techniques and approaches to handle those themes. Amitav Ghosh, whose first novel, *The Circle of Reason* appeared in 1986, has strengthened the new English novel in more than one way.

The Shadow Lines takes us into the mnemonic fund of a young narrator who as a wide-eyed adolescent hero-worshipped Tridib, an uncle, who fed him on his memories of his one visit to London during the war; and his grandmother, who shared with him her nostalgic memories of East Bengal where she was born and spent her childhood. And then there is Ila (his cousin, for whom he nurtures a secret passion), who travels all over the world with her diplomat glob-trotting parents and occasionally comes home to tell a wonderstruck boy accounts of her peregrinations abroad. Their memories "form a part of my secret map of the world, a map of which only I know the keys and coordinates, but which was not for than reason any more imaginary than the code of a safe to banker."

From the three whose memories form his own consciousness, he learns to see in different ways. Ila sees much but experiences little. With her superficial response to life, she only remembers how one airport differed from the other by its less or more conveniently located ladies'. Tridib teaches him to see with precision because he teaches the boy to see with imagination ("we could not see without inventing what we saw"). He evokes for the young boy "the worlds to travel in and . . .

Published in *World Literature Today*, University of Oklahama, Spring 1991.

eyes to see them with." The grandmother establishes to him the oneness of the memory for according to her neither space nor time can divide it.

The Shadow Lines spans three generations of the narrator's family spread over in East Bengal and Calcutta: the English family-friends, the Prices, whose histories include the two Wars and contemporary London. And the web of life in *The Shadow Lines*, which encompasses many countries, many religions, is a collage of memories, the narrator's own, and others, dusty photographs, yellowing newspaper clippings, but strengthened above all by imagination. While nations, religions, war, violence and partition divide people, memory does not. Imagination creates a world that cannot be divided, any more than nations break and float away when geographical boundaries are arbitrarily recreated. Life in *The Shadow Lines* loses its chronological logic. Past invades the present and enriches and transforms it and in the process strengthens the narrator's ability to encounter and even reshape his own future when it invades his present at a later date. (In that sense one of the major concerns of the novel is about growth and experience and maturity.) The very structure of the novel—coil within coil opening up vistas of new worlds, new experiences—reflects this giddying whirl of life, memory and imagination. His remarkably brilliant handling of his linguistic medium is one of his major achievements. He writes fluently, and his narratives move with grace, ease and understatement.

Ghosh's evocation of the city of his birth and adolescent years, Calcutta, depicted in remarkably vivid details, is comparable only with Anita Desai's re-creation of Bombay in *Baumgartner's Bombay* (1988). His experience as a social anthropologist at the Universities of Delhi and Oxford shows in his handling of the characters and the context in which they exist. He reveals a sense of history and a firm grasp of socio-cultural and historical material that underlies his narrative. He confesses to one of his earliest memories of Calcutta as that of a mob surrounding his house, a memory that he decided to "exhume" and confront after he witnessed the 1984 riots (the most traumatic event in contemporary Indian history) which spread through the country after Indira Gandhi's assassination. *The Shadow Lines* takes in the war-devastated London, civil-strife in post-Partition East Bengal, and the riot-hit Calcutta and embodies a major critique of the psychological make-up of the contemporary man that thrives on violence.

Beyond the 'Shadow Lines': Amitav Ghosh's Quest for the Remains of an Antique Civilization

TAPAN KUMAR GHOSH

Amitav Ghosh holds a place of singular distinction in contemporary Indian fiction in English. He has written only two novels so far,[1] but this small oeuvre has ensured him international renown. A profound historical sense, a strong humanitarian drift that defies geo-cultural boundaries and moves towards cosmopolitanism, a witty but compassionate insight into man and his society, an attempt at interlacing the time past and the time present in the crucible of memory—these are the essentials of Amitav Ghosh's fiction. These, together with his brilliant art of construction that weaves together private lives and public events, and balances complex sets of issues with a rare deftness, his ingeniously structured web of history and mythology, politics and philosophy, and, above all, his evocative use of an indefectible prose that stands out for its lyrical grace and transparent clarity, have established him as a significant new voice among the recent Indian authors crafting fiction in English.

But Amitav Ghosh, as one finds him in his third book, *In an Antique Land,* is not a mere novelist but an indefatigable researcher, a social anthropologist and a clear-sighted traveller as well. The very first thing that strikes a reader about the book is its subject. It is unusual in contemporary Indian writing in English, as is the sort of painstaking international research that has gone behind the book. Those who have read *The Circle of Reason,* will realize Amitav Ghosh's close knowledge of and intimate relation with the Middle East and the Arab world. The fascination began with his study of Arabic. Egypt, specifically her judaeo-Arabic culture, was the area of his doctoral research at Oxford. The creative writings of this world, its culture and thought have deeply influenced his attitude and his works.[2] His third book bears testimony to his interaction with at least four languages and cultures spread over three continents and across several countries. Indeed, the book, like the earlier ones, clearly defies the "shadow lines" of language, religion and culture, and it attempts to explore, at a deeper level, some basic traits of human character and some fundamental human feelings and attitudes that persist through the ages despite socio-political upheavals and geographical changes.

It is not easy to categorize *In an Antique Land,* for the book has a certain je ne sais quoi. What sort of a work is it? A travelogue with a strong narrative drive? A study in social anthropology? An authentic historical document presented in the form of fiction? Amitav Ghosh's latest tour-de-force may at once be described as a socio-historical document with an abundance of varied facts, a travelogue enriched by first-hand experience and exuberant details, and of course, a close and extensive research work. It is, in brief, a work that easily diminishes, sometimes even wipes out, the bounds of the time-honoured division of literary forms. When, at the fag end of the twentieth century, fiction writing ceases to conform to any fixed norms, *In an Antique Land* can be described as an experimental milestone in contemporary Indian writing in English. There is, in every layer of the book, memory, real life experience, history and imagination, indivisibly and inextricably linked.

In an Antique Land is not a novel like *The Circle of Reason* and *The Shadow Lines.* Amitav Ghosh himself admits in an interview with a Bengali daily: "No, this time I am not writing a novel. Not even sociology, history or belles-letters based on historical research. My new book cannot be described as any one of these. It's a strange sort of work. Within the parameters of history, I have tried to capture a story, a narrative, without attempting to write a historical novel. You may say, as a writer, I have faced a technical challenge."[3] (My translation)

It is the technical novelty as well as the unique art of construction that marks the book as a distinctive work. There are three parallel stories in *In an Antique Land.* First, the story of a Jewish merchant, Abraham Ben Yiju, who came from Aden to Mangalore for trade eight hundred years ago, and his Indian slave. He married a slave girl named Ashu, belonging to the matrilineal community of Nairs, and lived in Mangalore for nearly two decades. Secondly, the story of modern Egypt that Amitav Ghosh relates from first-hand experience in two Egyptian villages. The third story is about Amitav Ghosh's search for a story, i.e. his search for the antique world of Ben Yiju and his slave and the story he builds up from the disconnected and fragmentary medieval documents including the letters exchanged between Ben Yiju and his friends and correspondents in the twelfth century. The three stories interpenetrate and form an intricate texture. It makes the conscious reader alert; one has to pause and ponder which level of the narrative serves as the functional device.

The book is divided into four sections: "Lataifa," "Nashawy," "Mangalore" and "Going Back," beginning with a prologue and rounded off with an Epilogue. It is almost a circular journey. En route, the past easily infiltrates into the present and vice versa. There is an expansion of time, place and persons, but the bonds of interconnections between the varied events in the book never slacken. Because, in the first person narrative, the "I" is not simply a narrator or a chronicler but a witness and a participant as well; the all-pervasive presence of this "I" has tied together all the facts and events in the book.

But the major source of the book's distinction lies, perhaps, in its inherent theme, and the origin of this theme can be traced to the deeper layers of history and civilization. The author's perception of the basic character of man and his elemental feelings and emotions has added an extra dimension to the book. On the one hand, there is a sketch of the antique civilization of the twelfth century; on the other, there is an account of the fast changing twentieth century world—there is a bridgeable gulf between the two. But the accounts of these two completely different worlds reflect some attitudes and behavioural patterns which are identical. They reveal some human relationships that efface the distance between the Middle Ages and the Modern times, between antiquity and modernity, and that remains unchanged in the eternal tension between the old and the new. Indeed, it is the author's success in conveying to the readers a valuable insight into some abiding aspects of human life and human character which are never carried away by the flowing currents of history and civilization, that makes the book a remarkable achievement.

To a large extent, the narrative is based on history. Thus, the historical dimension of the book excels all the others. Characters and events are viewed from the perspective of historical research. Minutely, and with a remarkable single-mindedness, Amitav Ghosh has unveiled the multiple strata of the interrelationships between the Indian, Egyptian, Jewish and Islamic cultures and their histories.

The central background is twelfth century, around 1130 A.D. The history centres round Abraham Ben Yiju and his slave. One finds a successful resuscitation of medieval Egypt and Mangalore. A few disconnected clues, a few scraps of paper including some of Ben Yiju's letters preserved as medieval documents in various universities and research centres are all with which Amitav Ghosh has built up the complete story of Yiju's life. The transcriptions of the letters written by a merchant in Aden named Khalaf ibn Ishaq to Ben Yiju in Mangalore which Amitav Ghosh, as a student of social anthropology at Oxford, came upon in the winter of 1978, provided him with the clues to the story of the slave of "MS H. 6" (the catalogue number given to one of Khalaf's letters in the National and University Library in Jerusalem). The first letter, written in the summer of 1148 A.D. when Palestine had turned into a "thoroughfare for European armies"[4] preparing for a crusade against Islam, appeared in an article written by the eminent scholar, E. Strauss. It was published in the 1942 issue of a Hebrew journal, *Zion*. The second letter of Khalaf ibn Ishaq was included in a collection entitled *Letters of Medieval Jewish Traders* (1973), translated and edited by Professor S.D.Goitein of Princeton University. This letter was prefaced with a few words about Ben Yiju and it contained a footnote about the slave. Ben Yiju was introduced as

> a Jewish merchant, originally of Tunisia, who had gone to India by way of Egypt, as a trader, and had spent seventeen years there. A man of many accomplishments, a distinguished calligrapher, scholar and poet, Ben Yiju had returned to Egypt having amassed great wealth in India. The last years of his life were spent in Egypt, and his papers found their way into his synagogue in Cairo; they were eventually discovered in a chamber known as the Geniza. (19)

The footnote, very brief, merely described the slave as Ben Yiju's Indian 'slave and business agent, a respectable member of his household.' (18)

The letters made Amitav Ghosh restless because they spoke not only of two merchants but also of a slave. In each of his letters addressed to his friend Ben Yiju, Khalaf ibn Ishaq had singled out the slave, mentioned him by name and sent him "plentiful greetings." (16) This was something unimaginable in the Middle Ages. An amazed Ghosh explains:

> That is all: no more than a name and a greeting. But the reference comes to us from a moment in time when the only people for whom we can even begin to imagine properly human, individual existences are the literate and the consequential, the wazirs and the sultans, the chroniclers and the priests—the people who had the power to inscribe themselves physically upon time. But the slave of Khalaf's letter was not of the company: in his instance it was a mere accident that those barely discernible traces that ordinary people leave upon the world happen to have been preserved. It is nothing less than a miracle that anything is known about him at all. (16-17)

Amitav Ghosh came to learn from Strauss's article and Goiten's book that the letters had been recovered from a 'Geniza' in the biggest Palestinian synagogue in Cairo, known as the Synagogue of Ben Ezra. They were written in an unusual hybrid language. Known today as Judaeo-Arabic, it was, in fact, "a colloquial dialect of medieval Arabic, transcribed in Hebrew script and liberally strewn with Hebrew and Aramaic." (103) Most of the Geniza documents were written in it and there was only a handful of scholars in the world who could decipher this bafflingly esoteric language. But Amitav Ghosh was determined to trace the "antique" world of the Jewish merchant and his slave. With a view to verifying the authenticity of the available material, Amitav Ghosh had gone to Tunisia and learnt Arabic; in 1980, he was in Egypt, "installed in a village called Lataifa, a couple of hours journey to the south-east of Alexandria." (19) He returned to Egypt twice again, in 1988 and then in 1990. The search continued in Mangalore and culminated in Annenberg Research Institute, Philadelphia, where the 'last testament' of the Slave's life—a handwritten document stating that Ben Yiju owed a sum of money to his slave for household purchases—was preserved. Thus, what one finds in the story of Ben Yiju is not an imaginary picture, but an authentic account of the twelfth century. Hence it is history. In fact, it is the abundance of verified facts that reinforces the historical dimension of Amitav Ghosh's book. For instance, in the first section of the book ("Lataifa") one finds an introduction of historical facts about "the Egyptian Babylon" and a description of Ben Ezra's Synagogue and its Geniza in Cairo, as mentioned by the British historian A.J. Butler. The tenth chapter of this section (that details the loot of the Geniza documents by European scholars from eighteenth century onwards) is pure history. Again, in the second section entitled "Nashawy," one finds historical documentation of the author's childhood in post-Partition Dhaka. The third section, "Mangalore," contains the accounts of Ibn Batuta, the folk life of Tulunad, the history of Tulu language and culture, and the life story of the Mogera fishermen. In this section, there is plenty of information about the trade relations between India and the Middle East during Ben Yiju's lifetime. Each and every information is supported by corresponding historical documents mentioned in the end-notes.

Side by side, the stream of the narrative flows on smoothly. The story of Abu Ali and Shaikh Musa in Lataifa and that of Ustaz Sabri and the Imam in Nashawy introduce a number of unforgettable characters. It is not mere narration but delightfully presented stories within story. Along with the rise and fall of the larger society, one notices the progression of the major characters. Gradually, the narrative part of the book assumes a self-sufficient form.

At the historical level, as at the temporal, Amitav Ghosh's narrative runs on parallel lines. There were tremendous political disturbances in the Middle East when Ben Yiju left for India. The European superpowers were uniting for a Crusade against Islam. Ben Yiju's return to Aden after seventeen years's stay in Mangalore coincided with the political turmoil over large areas in the Middle East and North Africa. The raids of Ifriqiya, Yiju's homeland, by Sicilian armies and the forceful conversion and largescale massacre of the Jews were followed by famine and disease, leading to the exodus of a substantial section of the Jewish population. Then, in the twentieth century, there were the two world wars and the Holocaust. When Amitav Ghosh visited Egypt in 1980 and 1988, the Iran-Iraq war was going on. His last visit to Egypt took place soon after the Iraqi invasion of Kuwait in 1990. The newspapers were talking of vast flood of Egyptian workers pouring out of Iraq and his co-passengers in the taxi from Cairo to Damanhour "talked randomly of disaster, killing and vengeance" (350) in confused apprehension. Hundreds of thousands of American and European troops were being mobilized for an all-out attack on Iraq. It was the greatest army ever assembled in the Persian Gulf since the days of the Crusades. But amidst "this tornado of grand designs and historical destinies," (15) the lives of the common people continued uninterrupted. The Indian Ocean trade that brought the Jewish merchant from Tunisia to Aden and then to the Malabar Coast, and that gave rise to a unique culture of accommodation, mutual trust and compromise, had flourished amidst these political upheavals. Amitav Ghosh peeps through the "foxholes" (16) of history to trace that singular tradition that had brought Ben Yiju and his Indian slave into close contact, and their "small, indistinguishable, intertwined histories" (339) which "prevailed until some centuries ago, but which then became partitioned in several areas where they had once existed."

The historical narrative of *In An Antique Land* centres round Abraham Ben Yiju and his Indian slave named Bomma. It is not easy to present facts of history in a narrative vein. But, like a master craftsman, Amitav Ghosh has interwoven history and narrative with a rare dexterity in the story of Ben Yiju. The task was stupendous: arranging the varied materials in historical sequence and building up the complete account of the twelfth century out of fragmentary documents. Although at a few places Amitav Ghosh had to have recourse to imagination to fill in certain gaps (for instance, his remark about Bomma cheering Adenese soldiers with a flask of wine to fight against a group of pirates raiding merchant vessels, in page 259, is not supported by historical document), he remained more or less faithful to the available material. He did not sacrifice historical authenticity to the claims of fiction.

The most intriguing part of Ben Yiju's story is his relationship with his slave, the slave of MS H. 6. The slave, called Bomma, appears frequently in the letters written to and by Ben Yiju. Amitav Ghosh's search for the origin of the slave provides the readers with a wonderful study in social anthropology and a valuable "insight into the uses of History." (270) The story takes the reader back to an antiquated world in the Middle Ages when, despite religious, social and geographical divisions, "a culture of accommodation and compromise" (288) had spread over a wide area in the Middle East and the Indian subcontinent that made the crossing of the paths of the Jewish merchant and his Hindu slave possible.

The name "Bomma," which had once "had a wide currency within Tulu Culture," (250) relates the slave to the "Bhuta-cult," the worship of spirit deities which is still practised in certain areas of Tulunad. The name was derived from the name of a deity of the Tulu myth, "Berme" or "Bermeru," the "principal figure in the pantheon of Tuluva Bhuta-deities." (254) "Bermeru" was not the same as the Brahma of classical Sanskritic mythology. But in course of time, "with the growth of Brahminical influence, the Tulu deity "Berme" had slowly become assimilated to the Sanskritic deity, "Brahma"! (254) Bomma had been born in one of the several matrilineal communities of Tulunad that played an important role in the Bhuta-cult. The Bhuta-cult was not considered to be religion at all. In fact, "it fell far beneath the Himalayan gaze of canonical Hindu practice" and it was "dismissed as mere 'devil worship' and superstition." (264)

Although most of the Geniza documents, in which Bomma figures, refer to him as Ben Yiju's slave, the actual terms of his service were completely different from those which the word "slavery" suggests today. The medieval concept of slavery was, as Amitav Ghosh tells us, totally different from the contemporary notion:

> In the Middle Ages institutions of servitude took many forms, and they all differed from "slavery" as it came to be practised after the European colonial expansion of the sixteenth century. In the lifetimes of Bomma and Ben Yiju, servitude was a part of a very flexible set of hierarchies and it often followed a logic completely contrary to that which modern expectations suggest. (259-60)

In the Middle East, as in a large part of North India, "slavery was the principal means of recruitment into some of the most privileged sectors of the army and the bureaucracy." (260) It was also used by merchants and traders as a means of recruiting apprentices and agents. The "slaves" recruited in this way were often given a share of the firm's profits and they "could generally be sure of obtaining manumission." (260) Again, servitude was used, over a large part of the medieval world, "as a means of creating fictive ties of kinship between people who were otherwise unrelated." (260) The slaves were often inducted into the household of their masters and regarded as their family members.

But the most elusive aspect of the medieval concept of slavery was its role as a "spiritual metaphor." During Bomma's own lifetime, a group of "pietist and fiercely egalitarian" (260) poets of south India, who were known as "Vachanakara Saint-poets," used slavery as a poetic image,

> to represent the devotee's quest for God: through the transforming power of metaphor the poets became their Lord's servants and lovers, androgynous in their longing; slaves, searching for their master with a passion that dissolved self-hood, wealth, caste and gender, indeed difference itself. In their poetry it was slavery that was the paradoxical embodiment of perfect freedom; the image that represented the very notion of relationship, of human bonds as well as the possibility of their transcendence. (260-61)

The Arabic speaking religious world in the Middle East, which Ben Yiju had hailed from, was also being rocked under the tremendous impact of the Sufis—the mystics of Islam. In spite of the wide gulf separating the medieval Sufis from the Saint-poets of Southern India, there was, in fact, "a commonality in the nature of their quest" and "a similarity in their use of poetic imagery." (262) To the Sufis, as to the Vachanakaras, the notion of slavery constituted "one of the central metaphors of religious life"—"metaphors of perfect devotion and love strung together in an intensely charged, often erotic, spiritual imagery." (262)

The poetic imagery and spiritual metaphors might well appear remote from the mundane relation between a merchant and his agent. Bomma was probably not familiar with the teachings of the contemporary saint-poets. But since he belonged to a community, which had long been relegated to the fringes of the orthodox and hierarchical Hindu society, he must certainly have been intimately aware of the "great range of popular traditions and folk-beliefs which upturn and invert the categories of Sanskritic Hinduism." (262) As a well-educated person, Ben Yiju, for his part, might well have been acquainted with the teachings of the

Sufis. At the same time, he might have "shared in some of the beliefs and practices that have always formed the hidden and subversive counter-image of the orthodox religions of the Middle East: the exorcism cults, the magical rites, the customs of visiting saints's graves and suchlike." (263) And it was, in all probability, those "inarticulate counter-beliefs" that formed a common ground between the patriarchal Jew and the matrilineal Tulu, "who would otherwise seem to stand on different sides of an unbridgeable gulf." (263)

This unique culture, which had been born of the subversion of the categories of Hinduism, Islam and Judaism and was nurtured by the "peaceful traditions of the oceanic trade" and the "pacifist customs and beliefs" (287) of the merchants—irrespective of their religious faiths—in Malabar and the Middle East, collapsed after the appearance of the maritime powers of Europe on the Indian Ocean. The arrival of Vasco da Gama on the Indian Coast on May 17, 1498—about three hundred and fifty years after Ben Yiju left Mangalore—and the consequent political developments sounded the knell of the strange world of Ben Yiju, Ashu and Bomma and marked the beginning of the European supremacy in the Indian Ocean trade. The European aggression put an end to the singular traditions in which the Eastern trade, itself the product of a "rare cultural choice," (287) had flourished for centuries.

In a sense, *In An Antique Land* is the story of two Indians in Egypt. The first one is Bomma, the slave and business agent of the medieval Jewish merchant, Ben Yiju, who followed his master when the latter returned to Aden around 1148 A.D. and remained faithful to him till the end of his life. The other Indian is Amitav Ghosh who, in 1980—about eight hundred and fifty years after Ben Yiju's voyage to India—travelled to Egypt to trail the story of the slave of MS H. 6, a story "miraculously preserved in the footnotes of history."[6] It is a strange, colourful world—at once medieval and modern—presented in the garb of a traveller's tale. It is here, in the Egyptian backwater, that Amitav Ghosh sought to retrieve the remnants of the antique civilization of the twelfth century. His guides in both the villages were his neighbours: Abu Ali, his obese, gargantuan landlord; Shaikh Musa, the gentle and good-humoured village elder; Jabir, the son of Ali's cousin; Amm Taha, Amitav Ghosh's caretaker in Nashawy, who had a rare skill "in ferreting out . . . the most jealously guarded of household secrets" (127); the self-reliant and individualistic Busaina; Zaghloul, the superstitious weaver who was very fond of stories and "had a manner of telling them that was marvellously faithful to the metaphorical resonances of his chosen craft," (137) Ustaz Sabri, the well-educated and knowledgeable school teacher, battling, with the other youngmen of his neighbourhood, against ignorance, poverty and exploitation and fashioning post-Revolution Egypt into the path of Islam; the college students, Ismail and Nabeel; Khamees the Rat, the beady-eyed local wit; and the village Imam with whom Amitav Ghosh had a serious quarrel. It is almost a pageant of characters carefully observed and faithfully presented. Amitav Ghosh narrates, from the viewpoint of a social anthropologist, the lives of these people—their dialects, manners, social and religious customs—and points out the commonalities and differences between medieval Masr and the post-Revolution Egypt. One learns about the exploitation of the poor, landless "fella-heen" (the unlettered peasants) by the Pashas and the British, the Revolution of 1952 under the leadership of Jamal Abd Al Nasir, the redistribution of land, the massive co-operative movement that sought to organize the land-owning farmers, and the Suez crisis of 1956. Apart from the history of modern, developing Egypt, there is an account of another Egypt, teeming with poverty, superstition, miracles, blood-feuds and exorcism rituals—a world not far removed from the antique world inhabited by Ben Yiju and Bomma. Although Amitav Ghosh found there men like Ustaz Sabri who were aware of the age-old and intimate ties between India and Egypt and of the similarity of the problems "that had been bequeathed to them by their troubled histories," (134) most of the villagers had no clear idea about the country where Ben Yiju spent seventeen valuable years of his life. But it was with these simple and largely unlettered fellaheen, who were devoutly religious but had no interest in politics, that Amitav Ghosh felt at home since they seemed to belong to "a familiar world." (167) In spite of their ignorance of India and her people and religion—which is evident from the barrage of questions they asked him: questions invariably about cow-worship, the burning of the dead, circumcision of men and clitoridectomy of women that often non-plussed him—they befriended Amitav Ghosh and provided him with the information he needed for his research. Someone like Busaina even earnestly proposed: "You had better not go back. Stay here and become a Muslim and marry a girl from the village." (172)

When Amitav Ghosh revisited the villages seven years later, he was astonished by the changes that had overtaken them. There was no electricity at Lataifa in 1980. Someone had bought a diesel water pump from a nearby town. Such machines were "generically known as 'al-makana al-Hindi,' the Indian machine, for they were all manufactured in India." (72) The whole village had gathered on the courtyard of the owner, waiting expectantly as Amitav Ghosh, the "doktor al-Hindi," who had been invited to give his expert opinion, examined the machine. But in 1988, he found refrigerator in every other house, new brick buildings in place of adobe houses, calculators, TV sets, cassette players, and even food processors. The people owed their prosperity to the Gulf money. Most of the young men of the villages had left Egypt by that time to find jobs in Saudi Arabia and the Gulf countries, but mostly in war-riven Iraq whose own men had gone to the borders to fight with Iran. The "gleanings from that distant war" (299) had worked a silent economic revolution in rural Egypt and changed the lives of the fellaheen. People were sending their children to schools and colleges and were talking about "development." But ignorance, fanaticism and superstition still prevailed. Amitav Ghosh was asked the same embarrassing question about Hinduism, the burning of the dead and the "purification" of women in India over and over again. It was one such question from the Imam of Nashawy that made Amitav Ghosh flare up and enter into an angry altercation with the religious fanatic who publicly humiliated him for the burning of the dead in his country.

As they, the "delegates from two superseded civilizations, vying with each other to establish a prior claim to the technology of modern violence," (236) were locked in a fierce combat, a sad Amitav Ghosh reflected:

> it seemed to me that the Imam and I had participated in our own final defeat, in the dissolution of the centuries of dialogue that had linked us. . . . We had acknowledged that it was no longer possible to speak, as Ben Yiju or his slave, or any one of the thousands of travellers who had crossed the Indian Ocean in the Middle Ages might have done; of things that were right, or good, or willed by God; it would have been merely absurd for either of us to use those words, for they belonged to a dismantled rung on the ascending ladder of Development. (236-37)

And Amitav Ghosh felt himself "a conspirator in the betrayal of the history that had led [him] to Nashawy; a witness to the extermination of a world of accommodations that [he] had believed to be still alive, and, in some tiny measure, still retrievable." (237)

But his backward journey to Ben Yiju's world was not altogether unrewarding. Despite ignorance and superstition, religion and politics, and the seemingly unbridgeable gulf of time and culture, Amitav could trace points of contact with the ancient civilization Ben Yiju had come from. It was still alive both in Egypt and in India—in the inarticulate beliefs and religious practices of the people.

One major discovery of Amitav Ghosh in Mangalore was a shrine devoted to a spirit-deity known as "Bobbariya-bhuta," "deemed by legend to be the spirit of a Muslim mariner and trader who died at sea." (271) The deity was venerated by a small group of fishermen along the Malabar Coast, known by the name of "Magavira" or "Mogera" who had traditionally belonged to the margins of the caste structure of the orthodox Hindu society, and had long been closely linked with the foreign merchants and mariners who came to trade in Malabar. Their links with foreign merchants were "commemorated in the traditional symbol of their distinct identity," (271) the Bobbariya-bhuta cult. The shrine Amitav Ghosh visited was "a large modern building, modelled after a classical Hindu temple." (273) It was situated in a rapidly developing village of fisherfolk that owed its prosperity to the Gulf money. The temple bore the posters of a "fundamentalist Hindu political organization, an upper-caste group notorious for its anti-Muslim rhetoric." (273) But the real surprise awaited him inside the remodelled temple whose main place was reserved for the most Brahminical of Hindu gods, Vishnu:

> Once we went inside, however, it turned out that one small aspect of the past had ingeniously escaped reinvention: the spirit of the Bobbariya-bhuta still remained in the temple although in a wholly altered guise . . . he stood beside the image of Vishnu, but at slightly lower level. The old symbols, the mace and the pillar, had been dispensed with: he was now represented by an image, like a Hindu god. (274)

And an awe-struck Amitav Ghosh remarks:

> I had to struggle with myself to keep from applauding the ironies enshrined in that temple. The past had revenged itself on the present: it had slipped the spirit of an Arab Muslim trader past the watchful eyes of Hindu zealots and installed it within the Sanskritic pantheon. (274)

The antique world is not entirely lost. The Bhuta-cult, itself a subversion of the categories of Sanskritic Hinduism, still exists among the fisherfolk of Mangalore; and, despite the sincere efforts of enlightened people like Ustaz Sabri, exorcism rituals, blood-feuds, beliefs in ghosts and miracles, and the practice of visiting the saints's graves (as the tomb of Sidi Abu-Hasira, a Jewish holyman and mystic who later converted to Islam and earned great renown for his miracles, is visited by both the Muslims and the Jews at Damanhour, in Egypt [329-42])—which constitute "the subversive counter image" of the orthodox religions of the Middle East, like Judaism and Islam, are not removed from the minds of the people of Nashawy and Lataifa. The partitioning of the past and of the intertwined histories of the two countries notwithstanding, these "superstitions," which had given rise to the unique culture of accommodation and co-existence, still linger in the psyche of the people. "Development" and the all-consuming influence of politics and religion could not totally efface them. In defiance of the enforcers of History, small remnants of Bomma's world have survived in both Egypt and India, and it is these remains that Amitav Ghosh explores with painstaking thoroughness in his unusual book.

NOTES

1. *The Circle of Reason* (New Delhi: Roli International, 1986), *The Shadow Lines* (New Delhi: Ravi Dayal Publisher, 1988) and *The Calcutta Chromosome* (New Delhi: Ravi Dayal Publisher, 1996).
2. In an interview with Subho Ranjan Dasgupta, published in the Bengali daily *Ananda Bazar Patrika* dated 14.8.94, Amitav Ghosh acknowledged the influence of the writers of the Arab world on his writings. He specifically mentioned, in this connection, the Sudanese writer, Tayeb Salih (the author of *Season of Migration to the North*), the Egyptian Nobel laureate, Naguib Mahfouz, and also Taufiq al-Hakim whose works had direct influence on *In an Antique Land*).
3. Interview with Ranjan Banerjee in the *Ananda Bazar Patrika*, 13.12.92.
4. Amitav Ghosh, *In an Antique Land* (New Delhi: Ravi Dayal Publisher, 1992), p. 14.
5. See the blurb.
6. *Loc. cit.*

In an Antique Land: A Critical Study

SHYAM S. AGARWALLA

Montesquieu's *The Persian Letters* "is a combination of oriental, philosophical essay, and epistolary fiction. The seventeenth century spirit of exploration stimulated the publication of many new accounts of what to Europeans was the mysterious East. Fascinated by cultures that in many instances equalled their own, Europeans came to scrutinize their own standards and to analyze general patterns of social behaviour. The philosophical essay, with its tone of reasonableness, was a natural vehicle for the thoughts of the rationalist writers, but for the popularization of these ideas epistolary prose fiction served better."[1]

Amitav Ghosh's *In an Antique Land*,[2] in my opinion a demi, oriental tale and epistolary fiction on the one hand, and, on the other, a contemporary novel, delineating some ordinary characters, in their daily encounters, with religious rites and social customs, personal whims and eccentricities, sometimes grave, solemn and other times humorous, antiquarian, *in esse*, helps contemporaneity, tale grows into story, ordinariness assumes historicity and anthropology becomes the half-sister of history. This led Clifford Geertz to say, "a change in the ecology of learning, like so many migrant geese, has driven anthropologist and historian into one other's territories."[3]

In an Antique Land, a tour de force, is first book of its kind, written by an Indian-English writer. Ghosh makes a comparative study of the two oldest cultures and civilizations of the two most important continents—Asia and Africa, that of India and Egypt. Unlike other historians, he researches on an Indian slave Bomma and his master Abraham Ben Yiju, plying a flourishing overseas trade in Mangalore, in the twelfth century. It is just a small incident on all accounts when Ghosh chanced to discover in a letter written by a merchant of Aden to Ben Yiju, a Tunisian, during his research work in Oxford. This letter seems "to open a trap-door into a vast network of foxholes whose real life continues uninterrupted." (16) He "knew nothing then about the Slave of MS H. 6 except that he had given me a right to be there, a sense of entitlement." (19)

A "sense of entitlement" led Ghosh to go to Egypt and the USA, following trails left by a Hebrew journal, *Zion, Letters of Medieval Jewish Traders*, translated and edited by S.D. Goitein of Princeton University. Ben Yiju's "origin lay in a region that was known as Ifriya in the Arabic-speaking world of the Middle Ages—an area centred around what is now Tunisia." (55) Following the migration of traders to Egypt, Ben Yiju also migrated to Egypt, joined the 'Synagogue of the Palestinians,' the building destined to last until a good seven hundred years after Ben Yiju's lifetime. "A man of many accomplishments, a distinguished calligrapher, scholar and poet," (19) Ben Yiju, a born trader, migrated from Egypt to Aden, the port that sat astride the most important searoutes connecting the Middle East and the Indian Ocean. His paper shows that his acquaintance with a wealthy and powerful trader Madmun ibn al-Hasan ibn Bundar proves to be a turning point in the life of Ben Yiju. It is possible that Ben Yiju was introduced to Madmun, by letters of introduction by his friends and relatives.

Ghosh, by deft sleight of hand, introduces the term 'Geniza,' "a word that is thought to have come into Hebrew from a Persian root, ganj, meaning 'storehouse'—a common element in place-names in India and Iran, particularly beloved of the British who sprinkled it liberally across their Indian settlements in odd anglicized forms like 'Ballygunge' and 'Daltongunj.'" (57) Geniza, in the synagogue, was the depository of all writings of the Jews, intended to present the accidental desecration of any written form of God's name. By another sleight of hand, he says: "I found that some of the usages of the dialect of Lataifa were startlingly close to those of North African Arabic spoken by Ben Yiju." (104) There was startlingly a similarity of certain words and turns of phrase in the Ben Yiju document with Lataifa and Nashawy. Ghosh cleverly and linguistically first brings the ancient Egypt closer to India, and then, the twelfth-century Egypt to the contemporary Egypt.

After Ben Yiju settled as a trader in the Malabar before 1932, there was a continuous exchange of letters between Madmun, Yusuf ibn Abraham and Khalaf Ibn Ishaq from Aden and Ben Yiju from India. Yusuf was "a judicial functionary as well as a trader: a man of a somewhat self-absorbed and irritable disposition, on the evidence of his letters. The other was Khalaf Ibn Ishaq—the writer of MS H. 6, and possibly the closest of Ben Yuri's friends in Aden." (156-57) What is more interesting is the fact that, unlike other traders cum travellers, Abu Said Halfon and Abu Zikri Sijlmasi, Ben Yiju "does not seem to have travelled back to Aden or Egypt even once in the nineteen or twenty years that he was in India." (159)

Once he had settled in Mangalore, according to a document available, he married Ashu, a slave girl. She is not mentioned anywhere in the entire corpus of Ben Yiju's documents except in a set of accounts scribbled on the back of one of Madmun's letters. "It links her to the matrilineal community of Nairs, who still form a substantial section of the population of the southern part of the Malabar coast." (229) The document reveals that in India "concubinage is permitted between everyone, so long as it is not with married woman." A couple of centuries before Ben Yiju's lifetime, a chronicler in the Persian Gulf part of Siraf had professed shock upon hearing duties of Indian temple dancers. "Let us thank God," he had written in pious disapproval, "for the Quran which he has chosen for us and with which he has preserved us from the sins of the infidels." In *The Persian Letters* Montesquieu also writes about the "nature of European and Asiatic religions in one subject of continuing interest. The Mohammedan rules against the eating of pork, for example, are made to seem as unreasonable as the Catholic veneration of the Virgin birth."[4] (64)

Indian temple dancers, devadasis in Sanskrit term, literally means "servant or slave of god." Their tradition was matrilineal, as situation which inevitably led to the unusual valuing of the female over the male. Not to talk of the chronicler mentioned above, even Europeans like Domingos Paes, Abbé Dubois and Beryl De Zoete have written disparaging comment on them. So far as history reads, devadasis were given their due status and prestige during the Chola and Pallava dynasty. They were skilful in art and dance and they dedicated their lives to the cause of God by saying regular prayers, chanting hymns and cleaning the temple precincts. When Ben Yiju married Ashu, Europeans were far behind his time, in writing derogatory language about devadasis and Indians, following the writings of these Europeans, had started campaigns against this system. R.K. Narayan, in his novel *The Man-Eater of Malgudi*, introduces a devadasi character, Rangi. Although never actually called a devadasi, she is alternately identified as a "public woman,"[5] "a woman of the temple," (115) "a temple prostitute," (149-50) "a dedicated woman" (116) and "a dancing woman," (147) all of which epithets point to this South Indian profession and heritage.

The devadasi system is linked with a Hindu myth. Parasuram, the legendary saint-warrior, beheaded his mother Renuka on the order of his father saint Jamadanga. Then, Parasuram wanted to get his mother's life back. The saint agreed on condition that Renuka would get back her life with the head of a harijan woman. Then that harijan woman was rewarded with the status of a Goddess to be worshipped by people in recognition of her noble contribution.

The name of Malabar is linked with its Arabic nomenclature and the "name was applied loosely to the southern third of the west coast, an area that shares many aspects of a common culture." (244) Ghosh connects the past with the present. Before and after the arrival of Ben Yiju in Mangalore, the Middle Eastern travellers and traders found the economic opportunities here in the form of industrial craft, apart from one of the richest spice-producing territories of the medieval world. History takes its revenge. Today, Jure divino or Jure humano, thousands of Mangaloreans migrate to the Persian Gulf, in search of employment and trade.

In one of his regular exchanges of letters with Ben Yiju, Khalaf Ibn Ishaq makes a point of singling the slave (Bomma) out and sending him 'plentiful greetings.' This letter bears the catalogue number MS H. 6 of the National and University library in Jerusalem. In another letter, Bomma gains a brief footnote. It merely explains him as Ben Yiju's Indian slave and business agent, a respected member of his household. 'According to a specialist in history,' Bama is 'vernacular for Brahma.' Professor Vivek Rai corrects 'Bama' for 'Bomma.' The research of Ghosh on Bomma reveals one more aspect of Indian culture, centred in and around Mangalore, embedded in the Tulu culture of the area. First of all, there were various groups and clans in Tulunad. Secondly, despite diversity in social hierarchy, they spoke Tulu for one, and "they also followed matrilineal rules of inheritance for certain kinds of property." (251) Thirdly, they shared in the worship of certain spirit-deities known as Bhutas. There were also many untouchables among them. The Indian history speaks of the assimilation of the Dravidians and Aryans, their living in peaceful co-existence, in South India, since time immemorial. Ghosh is in trail of religious and cultural roots of the slave. The Aryans (Brahmins) practised the folk-region of the high Sanskritic tradition and the Dravidians followed Bhuta-cult, the local form of worship. There were Brahmin temples as well as Bhuta shrines. "There was no contradiction in this, of course, for to them Bhutas and Sanskritic deities represented aspects of divine and supernatural power that shaded gently and imperceptibly into each other. Indeed, under the benign cover of that shade, there was a good deal of trafficking between the two pantheons: some Bhuta deities would occasionally appear within the mists of high Sanskritism, while others fell from favour and vanished into the nether world." (252) The origin of the name of the slave 'Bomma' is, in all likelihood, a diminutive of 'Berme,' the principal figure in the pantheon of Tuluva Bhuta-deities and this Tulu deity, over time, with the growth of Brahminical influence, is slowly assimilated to the Sanskritic deity 'Brahma.'

This is a synthesis at the cost of historic memory. Suniti Kumar Chatterjee says: "the Dravidians of the south, by accepting the philosophy and religion of this composite culture (Austrico-Mongolo-Dravido-Aryan), together with the language that was its authoritative repository, viz., Sanskrit, made an outstanding contribution to its development and enrichment."[6] When Ghosh, accompanied by Father D'Souza, visited a village near Mangalore, he was told by a lady that "not now, never: everybody had good Sanskritic names nowadays names like 'Bomma' belonged to a time when very few people in the community had been educated and fisherman had ranked at the bottom of the social order." (272) The walls of the houses were painted prominently with the letter 'Om' and an old shrine was remodelled after a classical Hindu temple, its walls bore the posters of a fundamentalist Hindu political organization.

Ghosh, in a parallel study of history, reveals that in the time of Ben Yiju, there was no sectarian and religious clash between the Jews and the Muslims in the Middle East. In *The Persian Letters*, dismayed by the sectarian nonsense that he meets with in religious matters, Usbek concludes, "whatever religion a man lives under, the observation of the Laws, love of our neighbour, duty to our Parents, are the chief Acts of Religion." (151) In Middle East, the Jews were strongly aware of their distinctive religious identity but they, simultaneously, living in the Arabic-speaking world, shared the everyday language of their religious life with the Muslims of that region; "when they invoked the name of God in their writings it was usually as Allah, and more often than not their invocations were in Arabic forms, such as inshâ allâh and al-hamdulillâh. Distinct though their faith was, it was still a part of the religious world of the Middle East—and that world was being turned upside down by the Sufis, the mystics of Islam." (261)

The Sufis influenced Judaism as they influenced the orthodox Islam in the Middle East. One Jew Sufi, Abraham Maimonides, is known to have remarked once that the Sufis were "worthier disciples of the Prophets of Israel than were the Jews of his time." (261) In Bomma's time in India, as Ben Yiju's time in the Middle East, Vachanaka the saint-poet taught an egalitatian culture, creating fraternal communities of artisans and working people. For the Sufis as for the Vachanakas, the notion of being held by bonds was one of the central metaphors of religious life. "They too draw some of their most powerful images from the institution of slavery: metaphors of perfect devotion and love strung together in an intensely charged, often erotic, spiritual imagery." (262) Therefore, it is possible that the meaning of slavery, in the time of Bomma and Ben Yiju, means the ties "that bound an apprentice to a master craftsman, an accountant to a merchant . . . as links that were in some small way ennobling human connections, pledges of commitment, in relationships that could just as well have been a matter of a mere exchange of coinage." (263) Bomma is, therefore, a slave and business agent, a respected member of the household of Ben Yiju.

The older versions of Judaism showing the bond of linguistic and cultural identity with Muslims, like Hindus and Muslims in India, in course of time, became mutually antagonists and, then, fundamentalists. The writings on the walls of houses of a village by a fundamentalist party is as glaring as the fundamentalism of Muslims and Jews, in the present-day world. The sufism of the Arabic-speaking people of the middle East, the religious tolerance of the time of Ben Yiju, on the one hand, and, the egalitarian preaching of Vachanaka on the other have yielded place to Hindu, Muslim and Jew fundamentalism. How similar is the religious, cultural history of Ben Yiju and Bomma?

The linguistic diversity and similarity of the Ben Yiju's time ought to be explored. It is likely that Ben Yiju corresponded with his friends in Aden in Arabic. But the question still nags us: how did Ben Yiju communicate with Ashu and Bomma or with his business associates, hailing from various regions in India. There is no evidence that he ever acquired fluency in Tulu or any other south Indian language. Indeed, the linguistic diversity was formidable. The Arab geographer Masûdi refers to a language called 'Lâriyyá,' which he describes as being spoken along much of the length of the Malabar coast. It is possible "he was referring to a pidgin, one that was possibly compounded largely of Perso-Arabic and north Indian elements, and was in use amongst merchants and traders all along the coast." (28)

In the matter of dress, diversity persists. Ben Yiju continued to wear the customary garments of the Middle East—robes, turbans and the like. During his business tour of Aden, Bomma brought back to India two 'gowns' for Ben Yiju. "The people of Malabar, on the other hand, generally left the upper part of their bodies bare, men and women alike—their preferred markers of class distinction being ornaments and jewellery rather than articles of clothing." (267) Ghosh, once again, by sleight of hand, says that Ben Yiju received delicacies such as raisins, nougat, dates and "Middle Eastern cane-sugar." India produced palm-sugar but Egypt had pioneered the production of cane-sugar which were exported to many parts of Asia, including India. And, "the Arabic Wordsukkar (hence the English 'sugar') is itself ultimately derived from a Sanskrit source: today, throughout north India, crystallized sugar is still known as misri in commemoration of traders like Ben Yiju and the tastes they imported from Masr." (269)

The religious, cultural, social and linguistic studies, gleaned from the letters, are the images of Oriental life, fruits of the herculean research work of Amitav Ghosh. William Graves, writing an introduction for *The Persian Letters*, observes: "Although there is minimal plot development in the first volume, the personal and social concerns of the personae insure thematic unity. Usbek and Rica observe the manners of European history—principally French—relate their impressions to life in Persia, and finally comment generally on the significance of their discoveries." The plurality of the Oriental culture was destroyed by the advent of Europeans in both the continents. Some three hundred and fifty years after Ben Yiju left Mangalore, Vasco da Gama landed in India, in the Southern coast. "Within a few years of that day the knell had been struck for the world that had brought Bomma, Ben Yiju and Ashu together." (286) The concept of plurality, for European historians, is but a fatal weakness, since "the dignity of nuances of choice and preference" (287) is not allowed to the vanquished.

The same fate awaited the Geniza documents. The Western cultural predators since 1864 cast their evil eyes on them. First, Jacob Saphir took only a 'few leaves from various old books and manuscripts.' Then, Abraham Firkowitch, a Crimean Jew of the Karaite sect, pillaged the precious oriental documents, now collected in the State Public Library in St. Petersburg. The dispersal of documents went on. By the first world war, the geniza had finally been emptied of all its documents. Egypt is left with not a scrap of paper to remind her of that aspect of her past. "It was as though the borders that were to divide Palestine several decades later had already been drawn, through time rather than territory, to allocate a choice of Histories." (95)

Bomma's story ends in Philadelphia. The documents are kept in the Annenberg Research Institute, a creation of America's television magazines, 'TV Guide' "cared for the spin-offs of 'Dallas' and 'Dynasty' and protected by the awful might of the American police." (349) It provides proof that Bomma was with Ben Yiju when he went back to settle in Egypt in the last years of his life.

Ghosh thus draws and reworks a number of sources and traditions that span a varied range of concerns and historical situations. Like Michael Ondaatje, a Canadian, he bases his tale on characters and records retrieved from the archives. Ondaatje's own assertion about his shaping of a guiding or organizational principle in his novel, *In the Skin of a Lion*, "The first sentence of every novel should be; 'Trust me, this will take time, but there is order here, very faint, very human'"[7] could as well be the pronouncement of Ghosh, also. The personal and social concerns of the personae insure thematic unity.

While the pursuit of Ben Yiju and Bomma is impressive not only for its scholarship but also for building a bridge between the two most ancient cultures and civilizations, it's the second strand that brings to the fore Ghosh's special skills, displayed in *The Circle of Reason*, viz., strong characterization, compassionate humour and convincingly translated dialogue. These special skills are preserved in the two sections, "Lataifa" and "Nashawy" named after the two Egyptian villages where the author stays for his field work. His intimate relationship with the villagers, their religious practices, social patterns and mentality is a source of education to us. It is a wonder that these villagers, unaffected by the Muslim fundamentalists, have cultivated a catholicity, an insatiable urge to know the Hindu India, despite the fact that a vast tract of land separates Egypt and India.

II

Characterization is evidenced in the "Lataifa" and "Nashawy" sections. In the former, the most impressive character is Abu-Ali. Then, there is Jabir, a foil to Abu-Ali, Shaikh Musa and Ustaz Mustafa. All of them live a pious pastoral life, untouched by the evil of modern civilization and crass materialism, except Abu-Ali. All of them, living thousands of miles away from India, unacquainted with newspapers, books, televisions, lived in the belief: Ignoti nulla Cupido. Ghosh unsettles them. Ustaz Mustafa, in one way, is their spokesperson, asking many questions on 'Hinduki' business.

> "What is this "Hinduki" things? I have heard of it before and I don't understand it. If it is not Christianity nor Judaism nor Islam what can it be? Who are its prophets?" (47)
>
> "I know—it's cows you worship—isn't that so?" (47)
>
> "What is your God like?" (48)
>
> "Now that you are here among us you can understand and learn about Islam, and then you can make up your mind whether you want to stay within that religion of yours." (48)

Ustaz Mustafa is a learned, devout specialist in civil and religious law. He is now practising in a court in Damanhour. His scanty knowledge about India and Hinduism was gained when he was a student of law at the University of Alexandria. Like a Hindu Brahmin, he would walk carefully lest any impure matter would touch his jallabeyya. He read his namaz four or five times a day, ready to espouse Islam not out of fanaticism but out of ignorance of Hinduism.

Abu-Ali is a small trader who hurt his leg in his childhood and is excused "for not working on the land and as a result his father had allowed him to go through school . . . he had cultivated contracts with students from influential families . . . he succeeded in getting a permit to set up a government-subsidized shop for retailing essential commodities at controlled prices." (25) As a man he was miserly and greedy and as a businessman, a good bargainer: "he had a remarkable talent for squeezing the last piastre from everything that came his way. People often said that it was useless to bargain with Abu-Ali: in the end he would get exactly what he wanted." (28) He was overbearing, haughty, possessive but, at times, timid also, especially, in the presence of Jabir.

Jabir is impulsive, friendly, shy though sharp tongued for Abu-Ali, a boy in his late teens. Jabir's father was a cousin of Abu-Ali in the paternal line, and thus Jabir belongs to an extended family, or lineage, of which Abu-Ali was nominally the head. Besides, Jabir was also the best friend with one of Abu-Ali's sons.

Shaikh Musa, in his mid-fifties, a contemporary of Abu-Ali, is a kind-hearted, moderate and matured man, unlike Abu-Ali. He inspires trust, again unlike Abu-Ali. Once or twice, obliquely, he warned Ghosh against Abu-Ali and his unfettered greed:

> "Things are cheap in the countryside," he said, "much cheaper than they are in the city. . . . You should not expect to pay as much here as you would in the city. . . ."
>
> I was taken aback for a moment, and then I realized that he was referring obliquely to Abu-Ali. (43)

Ghosh was a lodger in Abu-Ali's house.

All these characters, with the exception of Mustafa who does not appear afterwards, develop into three-dimensional mould of a conventional novel in the section "Going Back." The "Lataifa" section is concerned with the first visit of Ghosh in 1981. This second visit, exactly seven years later, in 1988, is mentioned in "Going Back." In 1981, even a purchase of 'al-makana al-Hindi,' the Indian machine was a novelty, a matter of rejoicing and exultation. The Iraq-Iran war has changed the material and human face of Lataifa. In 1988, the people have refrigerators, washing machines, television sets, Toyota pick-up trucks, food-processors, calculators, exotic pens and watches. It is a story of migration and metamorphosis. Characters grow, materially, mentally and spiritually. We are presented with an account of its linear and cumulative progression. Ghosh's description of the plight of the worker, in Iraq, does not necessarily involve the advocacy of a teleological Marxist vision which projects the downfall of that "bare-knuckle capitalism."

Jabir, a shy young man of acid tongue, is now a great orator in colleges and universities. He had sported a beard for a while but had to shave it because a secular Egypt, though a Muslim country, "isn't safe to look like a Muslim." (309) Is not the same complaint uttered by a devout Hindu, in India? He grows out of his past, matures. His boyish shyness "sharp-tongued ferocity" (307) has been replaced by "a kind of quiet hopelessness, an attitude of resignation." (307)

Shaikh Musa develops hilarity and pride and awe. He gleefully tells about refrigerators and iced water. There was a time when he looked through the window of a showroom but did not have the heart to enter it. "It had come as a shock to think that boys like Mabrouk thought nothing of going into places like that." (292) There was a time when he overawed others in his family, by his knowledge of religion. Now, Jabir overawes him by the profundity of his knowledge on matters of religion: "he would not have dreamed of entering that milieu: he considered himself far too ignorant to enter into learned arguments on matters of religion." (295)

Abu-Ali, clever and imaginative, is the first man in Lataifa "to become aware of the opportunities that were opening up in Iraq, during the war with Iran." (297) His foresightedness pays him rich dividends. His material possessions awestrike Shaikh Musa and Ghosh "like helots gazing at the spoils of Pharaoh." (298) His inbred bad temper gives way to a MGM lion's roar. His accessibility to his relatives and friends has changed as "Abu-Ali had now risen to an estate where neither his family nor his neighbours were fit to use his furniture." (298-99) Characters like Ustaz Sabry, Imam Ibrahim, Khames the Rat, Yasir, Nabeel, Busaina and Taha people the section "Nashawy," like the characters in the section "Lataifa," have distinct identities, growth, both material and mental. It was a part of a great desert till 1820 when two young, belonging to Bedouin and Abu-Kanaka origins settled in Nashawy. Imam Ibrahim belonged to the latter lineage.

Ibrahim, in his youth, had the gift of baraka. Now, he looks older than Shaikh Musa, his contemporary, and always lives in seclusion. He was a barber and healer. "He had shown remarkable skill in curing the sick . . . was very learned in the classical arts of learning . . . could do miracles with herbs and roots. . . . He had also become known for his learning in the scriptures, and at one time he had been much sought after for his opinions on points of theology and matters of religious law and jurisprudence." (119-20)

Ustaz Sabry is a young teacher, a too-much-talk and a well-informed man, known in the surrounding villages. He is religious but not superstitious. On one occasion, "in a speech . . . he had condemned the custom that the women observed, of leaving offerings at the graves of dead relatives. . . . He and the other teachers had even succeeded in uniting the villagers against a man who was known to perform exorcism rituals for women, secret Ethiopian rites called zâr." (146) He was also a social worker. They "had even hatched a plan to start a consumer's co-operative . . . so that people of Nashawy would no longer have to put up with the sinful profiteering of the village's shopkeepers. In time, with the help of God, they would succeed in rooting out all exploitation and unbelief from the village, and people would see for themselves where the path of true Islam lay." (147-48)

Khamees the Rat is in his mid-twenties, scrawny, with a thin mobile face, deeply scorched by the sun. He has the brightness of eye and the slightly sardonic touch to his mouth. Unlike Mustafa in Lataifa, Khamees has a kind of appalled admiration of Hindus. He is eccentric in most things because he is ignorant and "the world outside was still replete with the wonders of the unknown." (174) He marries twice but remains childless and it could be one of the reasons for his eccentricities.

Yasir is a pleasant, cheerful-looking person, in his early forties or so, a tall, deep-chested man who, like his father, always wears a large white turban. Like his father Ibrahim, he has learnt to cut hair; even his father later on derives no satisfaction in his craft. Again, unlike his father, he sets up a small barber shop, the first in the entire area. He is meek, docile, dutiful and non-interfering. He neither sulks like his father nor projects himself like Ustaz Sabry.

Busaina, the sister of Khamees, has been married off years ago to a man from Nakhlatain, not far from Lataifa. A self-respecting woman, she walks out of her husband's house with two fine and healthy children when he decides to marry another girl. Shaikh Musa comments: "The Jammal are all like that, difficult and quarrelsome, and it's best to keep them at a distance." (165) She does not mourn her exile nor does she find it difficult to adjust, once again, among her brothers.

Nabeel graduates from an Agricultural training college in Damanhour. Ambitious, sharp and intelligent, he ultimately lands in Iraq. Taha, in his late fifties or thereabouts, known as uncle, is a vendor. Ate is also a kind of witch, a sâhir and he occasionally earned a bit of extra money by casting the odd spell.

III

There is compassionate humour in *In an Antique Land*. Like Swift, it is not the air and body of the novel, you merely catch glimpses of it as you might catch the flashes of a sword waved in the sunlight. J.B. Priestley says: "In order to be a humorist, you must have a needle eye for the incongruities, all the idiocies and antics of this life, but you must also have—strange and contradictory as it may seem—an unusual quickness and warmth of feeling, an instant affection for all that is lovable."[8] Amitav Ghosh is one such humorist.

The first instance of Ghosh's humour is Abu-Ali, his driving a delicate and sturdy Japanese moped:

> He would hitch up the hem of his jallabeyya and then, lifting up his leg, he would mount the vehicle with a little sidelong hop, while his son held it steady. To me, watching from the roof, it seemed hardly credible that so delicate a machine would succeed in carrying a man of Abu-Ali's weight over that bumpy dirt track. But to my astonishment it invariably did: he would go shooting off down the road, his jallabeyya ballooning out around him, while the moped, in profile, diminished into a thin, sharp line—it was like watching a gargantuan lollipop being carried away by its stick. (28)

Abu-Ali's vehicle is the pitiful beast—the "lean hack" of Don Quixote of Cervantes, all skin and bone. His jallabeyya is like Quixote's old suit of armour. Then, there is his hilarious ride on his moped which makes him a laughable and lovable character in this story.

Another example is that of Mabrouk, his father and other relatives. They, like the Shandies of Sterne's *Tristram Shandy*, may not understand Hindu customs, religious rites and rituals. Nevertheless, they exult at their purchase of an 'al-makana al-Hindi,' the Indian machine. Their exultation causes bewilderment to Ghosh for he has been asked to verify whether they have got a good one or not. He knows nothing at all about water pumps; indeed, "I would not recall ever having noticed one before coming to Lataifa." (72) Yet, he has to justify the confidence reposed in him by the family of Mabrouk.

> A hush fell upon the courtyard as I walked up to the machine. . . . I went up to the machine's spout, stopped beside it and peered knowledgeably into its inky interior, shutting one eye. Standing up again, I walked around the pump amidst a deathly silence, nodding to myself, occasionally tapping parts of it with my knuckles. Then placing both hands on the diesel motor, I fell to my knees and shut my eyes. When I looked up again Mabrouk's father was standing above me, anxiously awaiting the outcome of my silent communion with this product of my native soil. (73)

We have here not only the Shandy bewilderment but also the Shandy affection.

Ghosh may not have his compeer in this genre of novel-writing in India but he has A.S. Byatt as his compeer in the British fiction. Her *Possession: A Romance* (1990) is a latter-day version of the romance quest. It is also a thoughtful work about two contemporary academics researching the lives and romantic relations of two mid-Victorian romantic poets, Randolp Ash and Christine La Motte. Malolm Bradbury comments: "Through a plot of complicated literary detection, and a multiplication of stories and texts, the novel explores the relation between romance and reality, lies and truths, the Victorian conception of the romantic self and the modern notion of the self as 'a discontinuous machinery and electrical message-network of various desires, ideological beliefs and responses, language-forms and hormones and pheromones.'"[9] Similarly, David Lodge's *Small World* is a version of the medieval quest romance, where the heroes and heroines no longer go on plgrimages but on academic conferences.

V.S. Naipaul's *A Way in the World* (1994) contains, like the histories of Ben Yiju and Madmum and Bomma, the histories of Sir Walter Raleigh and his discovery of Eldorado in the early seventeenth century, and Francisco Miranda and his attempts to liberate Venezuela from Spanish rule in the early nineteenth century. Both are written as fiction, both subtitled "An unwritten story," as if they were unused fragments from the narrator's archive. Unlike Naipaul who privileges Europe and European ways at the cost of non-Euroepan, Ghosh privileges both African and Asian ways with unjaundiced eyes which increases the value of *In an Antique Land*.

Foucault elaborates, gesturing towards the possibilities, which arise when such assumptions are called into question: "The present epoch will perhaps be above all the epochs of space. We are in the epoch of simultaneity: we are in the epoch of juxtaposition, the epoch of the near and the far, of the side-by-side, of the dispersed. We are at a moment, I believe, when our experience of the world is less that of a long life developing through time than of a network that connects points and intersects with its own skein."[10]

NOTES

1. William Graves, Introduction to the Garland edition of John Ozell's translation of Baron de Montesquieu's *The Persian Letters* (New York: Garland Publishers, 1972).
2. (Delhi: Ravi Dayal Publisher, 1992).

3. "History and Anthropology," *New Literary Theory*, No. 2, 1990.
4. William Graves.
5. R.K. Narayan, *The Man-Eater of Malgudi* (1961; Harmondsworth: Penguin, 1983), p. 115.
6. Suniti Kumar Chatterjee, "The Basic Unity Underlying the Diversity of Culture," *Indian Culture* (Delhi: The Universal Book and Stationery), p. 53.
7. Michael Ondaatje, *In the Skin of a Lion* (London: Picador, 1988), p. 146.
8. J.B. Priestley, *English Humour* (London: Longmans, Green, 1931), p. 130.
9. Malcolm Bradbury, *The Modern British Novel* (London: Secker and Warburg, 1993), pp. 439-40.
10. Foucault, "Of Other Spaces," trans. Jay Miskowiec, *Diacritics*, 16 (1986), p. 22. Cited in Soja, p. 10.

The Shadow Lines and *In an Antique Land*: Some Thematic Considerations

SHARMILA GUHA MAJUMDAR

The two novels under consideration here—*The Shadow Lines* and *In an Antique Land*—deal with history. World War II, our Independence and the partition of the country have provided Amitav Ghosh with raw material against which he studies the historical truths—the meaning of nationalism and political freedom in the modern world—in *The Shadow Lines*. In the first section of the book, called 'Going Away' the story-teller concentrates on London on the eve of, and during, the war, of which he has only a vicarious experience. His knowledge of war was not gained from books but from the experience of his uncle who exercised the greatest influence upon the adolescent story-teller. Tridib taught him how to use imagination and by using this faculty he conjured up certain vivid pictures which by imperceptible degrees merged into a perception of history. In the subsequent sections the author uses the same method to exercise his historical imagination.

In *In an Antique Land* Ghosh has used the mode of the autobiographical traveller's tale to study the past thousand years' history in the context of two continents—Asia and Africa. Naturally the scope of this book is much larger than the former one in both chronological and geographical distribution. But one thing becomes very clear that in both these books, Ghosh's aim is to bring out the unity of human experience notwithstanding the diversity of context.

World War II was generated by militant nationalism and Ghosh explores the significance of war at two different levels—personal and human. In *The Shadow Lines* the memory of the story-teller shuttles back and forth in time and on his first visit to London he is continuously haunted by Tridib's account of his first visit to London, at 44 Lymington Road where they stayed with the Prices on the eve of the war. In 1939 Tridib's father Saheb, as he was jocularly referred to by his elder sister-in-law, the storyteller's grandmother, took some photographs of Alan Tresawsen, Mrs. Price's brother and his friends. The storyteller recounts in detail what Tridib told him about one of those pictures. It focussed on the tragedy of war as well as on 'exhilaration'—a sense of compassion and fellow-feeling brought about by the shadow of impending death. This sense of exhilaration cut across national borders and both in England and in Germany that was the defence mechanism that people developed to combat the sense of doom. In that picture besides Mayadebi, Mrs. Price and her husband Snipe, there are four others—three young men and a young woman of whom three would be dead within two years. The spectre of war looms large on their lives and "in the foreground of one of those pictures, there is a large, shallow pit. Snipe has been digging that pit for the last two weeks in the back garden. This pit is intended to be the foundation of an Anderson air raid shelter, his second line of defence against the expected German bombs."[1]

With the war hovering on the horizon they knew death was "the most real of their realities." (67) Even before the start of the war they knew that none and nothing of their world would survive. Books, films and photographs are part of history to be studied, analyzed and set aside. But nobody can know the feeling of young, intelligent people who knew they were condemned to death simply because some people have got their priorities wrong.

A couple of pages later there is a vivid description of the house where on that fateful night of September 1940 Dan and Alan died in bombardment. This is a tragedy not only because they were casualties of ruthless nationalism but also because they were people who raised their voices against war-mongering. Ila, who was a member of the socialist movement in Britain, felt proud of being a part of history. She thought Alan and his friends who were witness to the war and fascism, events important in history, must have been as much happy as she was in her political activism. But she never knew that even a small event like a riot did have as much historical importance as a war, as all were results of the politics of hatred, though perhaps on different scales and each provided insight into the personal and human aspects of political violence.

We find a different exposition of the concept of nationalism in a person like the story-teller's grandmother. She was born and brought up in British India. To her, nationalism was a hallowed word, the mainstay of political thinking in the nineteenth and early twentieth century which meant hatred of things British and in her desire to win political freedom she dreamt of killing English officials. She even considered war as a necessary evil which inspired the idea of nationalism and thus strengthened the foundation of a nation. She thought English were a nation because they were reborn in the same pool of bloodshed during wars;

blood of their fathers, brothers or sons; while India was yet to emerge as a nation as blood of near and dear ones shed in a war had not baptized Indians. This firebrand nationalism outlived its utility in the late twentieth century and degenerated into a politics of hatred. What was basically a clash of political aspirations was sometimes distorted into senseless animosity. This limited view of nationalism was shared not only by Indians like the grandmother but also by Irishmen like Mike who thought for a person to be rightfully Indian it was necessary to kill Englishmen.

Thus nationalism and war in the European context, nationalism, freedom and partition in Indian context become related things in the author's historical consciousness.

In 'Coming Home' Ghosh comes back to the Indian subcontinent, to Calcutta and Dhaka where he tries to find out the meaning of political freedom. Indian nationalism which was the chief weapon of the freedom fighters in their struggle against foreign rulers could not even ensure the territorial integrity of the country. After partition—the price we are supposed to have paid for our political freedom—nationalism in the Indian context changed its meaning to exclude people on the other side of the border but could not include everybody on this side of paradise. There are several points of view from which Independence, communal riots and partition are seen.

There are people like the story-teller's grandmother who was born and brought up in Dhaka but came to Calcutta long before partition. Unlike so many of their brethren they did not have to feel the pang of being uprooted and to face the daunting task of rebuilding lives from the debris of history. To them 'refugee' was a term of abuse. But even if they did not suffer materially, their emotional wound took a long time to heal and left a deep scar. When seventeen years after partition, the grandmother was going to visit her sister Mayadebi in Dhaka, she was told by her son that at the airport she would have to fill her nationality, her place and date of birth in the disembarkation card she got visibly nervous. As the story-teller realized years later "that she would have to fill in 'Dhaka' as her place of birth on that form . . . and at that moment she had not been able to quite understand how her place of birth had come to be so messily at odds with her nationality" (152) was the reason for her nervousness. This dichotomy in the situation gave rise to confusion and bewilderment in the minds of people even long after partition became a part of the history of the subcontinent. Emotionally they could hardly accept the Radcliffe line and in their own minds wondered like the grandmother "whether [they] would be able to see the border between India and East Pakistan from the plane"; (151) and when told otherwise failed to understand "what was it all for then—partition and all the killings and everything—if there isn't something in between?" (151)

This is the question to which the author addresses himself. The schism in our national life was formalized by drawing a line on the map right through the homeland. Like war this tragedy also brought out the worst as well as the best in human beings on this subcontinent. There have been crude barbarity and also demonstration of the noblest sentiments on both sides of the border. Lakhs of Hindus had to leave their dream behind to swarm to the suburbs of Calcutta. Not a few Muslims like Saifuddin the mechanic had to suffer the same fate. What did political freedom mean to these people? Who can know the feelings of thousands of innocent people who lost their friends and relatives in the communal frenzy?

We take a few minutes off to take a cursory glimpse into post-partition Bengali literature which abounds in stories of these hapless people, their suffering, anger, desperation and determination. Because many Bengali writers of the time came from across the border. I am referring to one such short story by Prativa Basu, significantly titled "Dukulhara"—people who lost their moorings on the other side of the border but failed to strike root on this side.

Bindubasini who lost her husband and son within a year got over her bereavement in course of time, but could never reconcile herself to the loss caused by partition. She was a witness to rioting, killing, groundless apprehension, exodus by villagers. She could not eat, could not sleep, packed bag and baggage in panic and then unpacked at the assurance from her Muslim subjects. But ultimately she had to leave with her widow daughter-in-law and two grand-daughters, one of whom died on their way to India. The other girl and her mother fell prey to flesh-traders while Bindubasini was killed by their accomplice.

The sense of agony and desperation that pervade the story is turned into anger in the grandmother after Tridib's death in 1964 riots in Dhaka. The personal tragedy transformed the meaning of border for the grandmother. Previously she was skeptical about the line, now it becomes something which defines her nationality. When in 1965 war beween India and Pakistan broke out she saw in it a threat to the freedom of her grandson, the future of the nation. The meaning of freedom comes to include fighting away the Pakistanis who barely twenty years ago were her countrymen.

There had also been people like the grandmother's Jethamoshai (father's elder brother) or Saifuddin's father who decided to ignore the shadow line altogether. They did not think it worthwhile to leave their homes just because some politicians were drawing a line somewhere. As Jethamoshai put it, "Once you start moving you never stop. . . . I don't believe in this India—Shindia . . . but suppose when you get there they decide to draw another line somewhere? What will you do then?" (215)

Many years after all this happened, when he tried to revive his memory of the 1964 riots in Calcutta, the story-teller discovered the irony of the entire political process known as our Independence and partition of the country. As a school boy in Calcutta he had a terrible memory of the 1964 riots. Memory of not what he saw or heard but the far more powerful memory of what he felt in his child's perception of the whole thing. The theft of Hazratbal, a holy relic enshrined in a mosque near Srinagar, triggered off communal riots in Khulna, a town in erstwhile East Pakistan. The riots spread to Dhaka and found its echo in Calcutta. As a Ph.D. student he discovered to his consternation that none of his colleagues who were all brought up in Delhi and had even the faintest memory of the riots. One of them was a bit surprised that he remembered a riot in Pakistan so well. For people of Delhi a riot in Khulna or Dhaka is just a piece of news. But not so for somebody in Calcutta. He realized "the simple fact that there had never been a moment in the four-thousand-year-old history of that map, when the places we know as Dhaka and Calcutta were more closely bound to each other than after they had drawn their lines . . . . a moment when each city was the inverted image of the other, locked into an irreversible symmetry by the line that was to set us free—our looking-glass border." (233)

Robi's loss in the 1964 riot was no less than many others. He was too young to register anything other than fear; fear that haunted him in his nightmares. In his adult consciousness Tribid's death signified the futility of our freedom. He has developed that objectivity which gives him a dispassionate, analytical outlook. He could relate his plight with those of many others in the subcontinent and knew if they could not outgrow the grandmother's hysterical reaction posterity would never forgive them. The country was freed, somebody drew the line and everybody was led to believe that the monster of religious communalism was laid to rest. They hoped peace, stability, things people associate with the right to self-determination of a nation, would come. But as a member of the post-1947 generation he had seen how the euphoria evaporated. He felt that nobody seemed to know the meaning of freedom. If they did there would not have been so many killings in Assam, the north-east, the Punjab, Sri Lanka, Tripura. People who kill or get killed, do so in the name of freedom. The very concept of freedom is a mirage. Robi's words have the ring of truth that has been borne out by our experience in the subcontinent towards the fag end of the twentieth century: "And then I think to myself why don't they draw thousands of little lines through the whole subcontinent and give every little place a new name?

What would it change? It's a mirage, the whole thing is a mirage." (247)

The 1964 riots have been described in *Antique Land* from the other side of the border. The scholar-protagonist's realization does not differ much from the sum-total of that of different characters in the other book. If we remember the unusual provocation for the recounting of riot memories we will at once understand how man's responses to certain things and situations are conditioned by his own history and culture and how tall claims and high hopes borne out by intellectual discourse are belied when the occasions most demand them. In the total Muslim culture of rural Egypt people can hardly conceive of men not circumcised in childhood. For them it is almost as natural as breathing, eating or drinking. So long as people remain outside the purview of the historical process of major cross-cultural conflict and assimilation; so long as they are exempt from undergoing the agony of such a process, physical peculiarities are physical peculiarities, and not symbols. But for a six-year-old who had seen the brutality of riots, the state of foreskin is more than a physical peculiarity sanctioned in a particular culture. It has ever-widening circles of association, completely independent of it, capable of producing an intensely emotional response even in a student of social anthropology. As it happened, Amitav the character, went to attend a marriage at Nabeel's place. He was the only foreigner there. People at Nashawy were always curious about Doctor-al-Hindi. So they started asking him all sorts of questions ranging from the method of disposal of dead bodies to the custom of circumcision in his country. These practices are dictated by religion and in their uni-religious society there is no conflict regarding these things. But to Amitav who has seen Hindu-Muslim riots in the subcontinent where these different practices have been made bones of contentions, these enquiries did not present themselves as innocent curiosity. So he suddenly left the gathering. Nabeel failed to understand why he was so upset about such trivial things. Amitav knows his emotional reaction was conditioned by the memory of a communal riot which he witnessed as the six-year-old son of an Indian diplomat in Dhaka. As he puts it toward the end of the next chapter: "The stories of these riots are always the same: tales that grow out of an explosive barrier of symbols—of cities going up in flames because of a cow found dead in a temple or a pig in a mosque; of people killed for wearing a lungi or a dhoti, depending on where they find themselves; of women disembowelled for wearing veils or vermilion, of men dismembered for the state of their foreskins. . . . I could not have expected them to understand an Indian's terror of symbols."[2]

If the major themes in *The Shadow Lines* were nationalism and political freedom, in *Antique Land* one of the predominant themes is religion—its meaning and practice, the irony inherent in religious traditions—their universality and inter-tradition conflicts that have shaped much of human history. In the wedding-episode Amitav was aware of the punishment of being an Indian; but to be a part of India which has been a melting pot for centuries has its own rewards. The scholar-protagonist of this book gathers parallels in history which reveal the unifying elements in various religious traditions and India is a potent source.

In chapter V of the 'Nashawy' section, there is the story of Sidi Abu-Kanaka, the holy man, whose grave did not yield to the spade of the government engineers who were digging a canal right through the village cemetery. The villagers protested but to no avail. Much to their astonishment and delight the tomb of the much-revered holy man resisted every effort on the part of the government to proceed along the charted line. When the grave was opened the body was found to be still whole and incorrupt and giving a perfumed smell. Convinced of the futility of their effort the authority finally diverted the canal. In gratitude the people of the village built a moqam for the Sidi. There are also stories about how the Sidi wrought miracles to protect the villagers from harm time and again. A similar story is recounted in chapter VI of the 'Mangalore' section; the story of a Bhuta-shrine immobilizing bulldozers that were commissioned to destory it and finally government engineers deciding to divert the project to spare the shrine.

The canonization of local holy men through mystification in folk-imagination is against Islam as Ustaz Sabry points out. The Bhuta-cult is not a part of canonical Hindu practice; it is dismissed by the standard authorities "as mere 'devil worship' and superstition." (264) But one thing is made clear by the two stories; human civilization has moved along the same line even at a distance of a few thousand miles. There is a method in history which may not be as inexorable as physical methods but still powerful enough to establish a pattern in the movement of events.

Preservation of one's religious identity has been the cause of much bloodshed. It is a revelation to know that one's religion may not be such an exclusive prerogative as one may like to think. The concept of exclusivity of one's religion may even be the handiwork of a couple of "enforcers of history." The episode of Amitav's visit to the mowlid of Sidi Abu-Hasira gives us an inkling into the history of development of religious divide. Islam and Judaism have the same semitic origin. They have the same mythological and historical background. They have physical proximity, close linguistic and cultural bonds—factors which in a primitive civilization did forge a kind of acceptance between the two religious groups as is evident from the story of the Sidi who was born of Jewish parents and reportedly converted to Islam when he came over to Egypt. He had followers among both these communities. But "intertwined histories, Indian and Egyptian, Muslim and Jewish, Hindu and Muslim, had been partitioned long ago" (339) and that is why the Egyptian government officials find it so difficult to understand why an Indian who is neither Muslim nor Jewish should have any interest in the mowlid of Sidi Abu-Hasira. To them religion has lost its human face. Socio-political systems do not recognize that human intercourse is a vital part of religion; instead they rigorously classify religious traditions as being mutually exclusive and in a way that best suits the academia, particularly western academia.

The story of the slave of Md H. 6, which initiated this novel comes full circle here. A scholastic search into the derivation of the name of the slave has established him to be a son of one of the several matrilineal communities of Tulunad, i.e. Mangalore in the pre-Brahminical days. Here is also the story of religious assimilation. The local deity of the Bhuta-cult has merged with gods of Sanskritic Brahminical tradition. 'Berme,' the deity of Bhuta-cult becomes 'Bomma' under the influence of 'Brahma' one of the gods in Hindu Trinity; and the slave is named after this mongrel god 'Bomma' which was a common name for boys of the region. Bomma the slave went into the service of Ben Yiju the Jew who migrated from Tunisia via Egypt to India. A trader by profession, he spent seventeen years in the port city of Mangalore. He is a wonderful product of cross-cultural assimilation. Being a part of the Arab-speaking world, the orthodox Jew invoked God by the name of Allah. His relationship with Bomma who practised Bhuta worship was determined probably by the spiritual philosophies of the Muslim Sufi saints and Vachanakara saint-poets of South India. The central metaphor of the devotee being in perpetual bondage to the Lord went a long way in determining various social relationships including that between Ben Yiju and Bomma, a trader and his business agent. Though Bomma was called a slave, their relationship may not have been the same as existing between a master and a slave in the sixteenth-century European colonial system. It was more in the nature of a commitment: "even the most mundane institutions have their life-giving myths and against the setting of that distant backdrop of legend and metaphor, the elements of slavery in the ties that bound an apprentice to a master craftsman, an accountant to a merchant, would have appeared, perhaps, not as demeaning bonds, but rather as links that were in some small way ennobling—human connections, pledges of commitment, in relationships that could just as well have been a matter of a mere exchange of coinage." (263) Man has written history partitioning the past and this has largely been a self-fulfilling process. But the mowlid of Sidi Abu-Hasira which is a small remnant of the world of Bomma and Ben Yiju, probably holds key to the future of humanity.

The most recent developments in the field of religion in India do not escape critical attention in the novel. A newly-prosperous fishing hamlet on the Malabar coast has changed its religious identity from that in the days of Bomma. The villagers who have the benefit of modern education have relegated their Bhuta deity to a lower level and placed Vishnu on the altar. The Bobbariya bhuta the spirit of a Muslim mariner is represented by an image, like a Hindu God. This is how the scholar-protagonist learns the uses of History: "The past had revenged itself on the present: it had slipped the spirit of an Arab Muslim trader past the watchful eyes of Hindu Zealots and installed it within the Sanskritic pantheon." (274) Ironically, on the walls of the newly-built "Hindu" temple there are posters of a "fundamentalist Hindu political organization . . . notorious for its anti-Muslim rhetoric." (273) So this is another side to the story of religion where assimilation leads to confrontation and militancy because these fishing people who had always lived at the periphery of Hindu society try to gain acceptance in the Sanskritic fold by catering to fundamentalism.

Thus the tangent points in the two novels consist in the study of constant interaction between ideas and events and resultant integration and differentiation. Ghosh has drawn parallels between war and riot, Europe and Indian subcontinent to show how all violence whether committed in the name of nationalism or freedom is to be given no other colour. The barriers of nation, country and time dissolve in the consciousness of the author and he reaches a tragic realization of how unscrupulous political forces continue to suffocate human aspirations.

NOTES

1. Amitav Ghosh, *The Shadow Lines* (Delhi: Ravi Dayal Publishers, 1988), p. 60.
2. Amitav Ghosh, *In an Antique Land* (Delhi: Ravi Dayal Publishers, 1992), p. 210.

In an Antique Land: A Traveller's Tale

PRADEEP TRIKHA

Amitav Ghosh describes himself as a traveller interested in men, places and scenery. All the world, as Shakespeare said, is a stage, and this for Ghosh is a key metaphor. In his review Homai Shroff points out that the writer explores "a colourful and warmly human picture of people and places, both medieval and modern."[1] Ghosh seems to think that travel is man's primordial quest to expand his awareness into realization. Perhaps this is the reason he embarks upon tracing the history (journey into the time) of a Jewish merchant, Ben Yiju from Egypt who spent two decades in Mangalore (a trade centre on Malabar coast in India) and his relationship with Indian slave Bomma, who worked for him as a business representative in Aden. Ghosh recedes into twelfth century in order to develop his story.

Ghosh like Vikram Seth believes that travel in "antique lands" is an experience for liberty, "perfect liberty, to think, feel, do just as one pleases."[2] Ghosh's journey reminds one of Hazlitt's "On Going a Journey" as far as the sincerity of description goes. Like Graham Greene's priest in *Power and Glory* and Ernest Hemingway's Old Man in *The Old Man and the Sea*, his spirits remain undaunted till he completes his endeavours.

Curiosity is his first love which enthralls him to go to small villages—Lataifa and Nashawy—South of Alexandria in Egypt. Inquisitive as Ghosh is, he has, to use Samuel Johnson's phrase, a "vigorous intellect" to work patiently for little more than ten years or so to weave story of his novel into a fine texturous fibre. As a social anthropologist he introduces his readers not only to the twelfth century Aden and Mangalore but he also points out that Egypt and India unquestionably belong to a socio-cultural tradition based on the religion of hospitality. This remains a constantly operative factor in the novel, as it could be seen and felt during Ghosh's stay in Lataifa and Nashawy. It could also be seen during Ben Yiju's stay in Mangalore and Bomma's stay in Aden seven hundred years ago.

Incessantly the writer's Columbus-like spirit "ploughed" through the "footnotes of history" to retrace the story of the merchant and his slave. Ghosh's journey is not bed of roses, he carries out his research in the heat and dust of a Synagogue of Ben Ezra near Cairo: "It was here in the forlorn corner of Mass that memories of Abraham Ben Yiju and his slave lay preserved for more than seven hundred years."[3] It is after the seven centuries the author records: "the sweat was dribbling off my face on to my notebooks. I gave up trying to work and sat in my room with the door open, hoping to trap a breath of fresh air." Manuscripts he could lay his hands on were in Judaeo-Arabic and "that there was no accepted method of learning to read the manuscripts except through a long apprenticeship with one of the handful of scholars who had made a lifetime's speciality of the subject." (103)

In an Antique Land has episodic plot, yet it possesses organic unity because it has a beginning, a middle and an end. Events and span of history it covers are so arranged that the organic whole emerges. Ghosh's search in Lataifa and Nashawy is assisted by his neighbours there; Abu Ali, his "gargantuan landlord"; Khamees the Rat "the beady-eyed local wit"; his adversary the Imam; Zaghloul the weaver and "the quiet" Nabeel whose "personal fate—left stranded in Baghdad at the outset of the Gulf War—bespeaks a larger one for Egypt and the 'developing world.'"

Persistently, Ghosh's active and inquisitive mind searches for the relevance of Egypt-India relations over the period of time. Through one of the characters, Ustaz Sabry, a school teacher and scholar, the writer voices his own opinion:

> Our countries were very similar, for India, like Egypt, was largely an agricultural nation. . . . Our countries were poor, for they had both been ransacked by imperialists and now they were both trying in very similar ways to cope with poverty. . . . Our two countries had always supported each other in the past: Mahatma Gandhi had come to Egypt to consult Sa'ad Zaghloul Pasha, the leader of the Egyptian nationalist movement, and later Nehru and Nasser had forged a close alliance. (134)

Ghosh is in Egypt in twentieth century as Ibn Battutat was in India in the thirteenth century. Like Battutat, Ghosh is nostalgic to retrace Ben Yiju's journey eastward which is "the simplest and most natural means of availing himself of the most rewarding possibilities his world had to offer." But unlike Battutat, Ghosh is writing a novel and not a historical treatise. His efforts are to provide "magical, intimate insights" not only into Egypt from the Crusades to Operation Desert Storm, but also into its cross-cultural relations with India.

During his adolescent years Abraham Ben Yiju could decide for himself his vocation to be the Business. Circumstances drew him near his patron Madmum (the Chief Representative of Merchants). Ben Yiju introduced himself in Madmum's "privileged circle" and "curiously enough at some point before A.D. 1132 Ben Yiju moved to the Malabar coast and did not return to Aden for nearly two decades." He had three good reasons: first, his trade flourished and he felt no need to travel back to Aden; secondly his camaraderie with Bomma, his slave, who looked after his trade in the Middle East; and thirdly, what tempted Ben Yiju to stay in Mangalore was a Nair woman Ashu, whom he married and raised a family. Later, when he left Malabar coast, he took his children with him, leaving behind Ashu.

After revealing the story of Abraham Ben Yiju, Ghosh returns to Mangalore, meets Prof. Vivek Rai, a historian, who helps him to decipher the mystery surrounding the second protagonist of his story Bomma; Ghosh now links "the matrilineally descended Tulu and the patriarchal Jew who would otherwise seem to stand on different sides of an unbridgeable chasm." In order to break ennui Ghosh strives to create "fictive ties of kinship between poeple who were otherwise unrelated." He does not try to authenticate just the trade relations of the "antique lands" but also inaugurates the fact that in the medieval world, "slaves were sometimes gradually incorporated into their master's households and came to be counted as members of their families." Interestingly enough he records:

> Perhaps the most elusive aspect of medieval slavery is its role as spiritual metaphor, as an instrument of religious imagination. . . . Slavery was often used as an image to represent the devotee's quest for God. . . . Searching for their master with a passion that dissolved selfhood, wealth, caste and gender. (260-61)

Besides Ben-Bomma story, Ghosh's stay in Egypt and orphic descriptions of contemporary Cairo form integrated part of the narrative. The writer's portrayal of Cairo enthrals the readers. If on one hand Ghosh's description has Wordsworthian sense of reality (to describe Nature) on the other it also has Coleridgean sense of wonder and awe. He intrusively comments here and there on superstitions of the people in Lataifa and Nashawy. At Nashawy, Amm Taha, like Coleridge's Ancient Mariner, fascinates Ghosh because he gives details of "how matter stood behind the walls and talismans, they guarded every house from the envy of neighbours and the Evil Eye."

"Going Back" is the section which concentrates on the writer's second visit to Egypt. It registers socio-cultural change which has occurred in Egypt in recent years under the spell of the Western influence. People in village are no longer ignorant about the city glamour. Popular culture of the day has lured many young and old alike. It is no "surprise that Cairo absorbs outsiders."[4] But "as a rule people here respect one another"[5] and they are hospitable and "serene to foreigners." Thus in spite of the fact that like many other developing countries, Egypt too is attracted towards the Western commercial world, its natives have not yet developed xeroxed mentality of the West.

In an Antique Land does not display the author's intellectual capability or epic sweep. What one discovers is a very minute and shrewd observation of human nature. Therefore, he deals with a unit small enough to manage—a microcosm, whether be it at Lataifa or Nashawy or Mangalore. The book has unadulterated, straight-forward impression of the people the writer came in contact with and the circumstances of the lives of the people during the course of his research. He paints the lively portraits of Abraham Ben Yiju and Bomma on one hand and on the other of Abu Ali, Ustaz Sabry, Sheikh Mussa, Nabeel and Zaghloul. All these characters burgeoned his wanderlust. Travel gave him a sense of freedom and leisure. Ghosh is thrilled to meet people and visit places. He could also get genuine picture of traditional Egypt by living among the villagers. He could get to know about their aspirations and setbacks, their sense of belongingness to their soil and also the young generation's uprootedness because of their search for new pastures green.

Ghosh sustains readers' interest by displaying rich and varied kinds of men and manners. The writer is absorbed by the variety of human types. It seems to him that in Egypt and India the most impressive and the most awe-inspiring monument of antiquity is neither the Citadels, nor the Pyramids, nor the Nile but the man himself. To see human beings closely is Ghosh's chief aim in visiting Egypt. With a convex lens in his hand he tries to penetrate into the people of contemporary world and also the people of antiquity. Their lives have dramatic situation and their dialogues have dramatic intensity. Each section of the book and each chapter add to the reader's clarity to understand the plot. *In an Antique Land* thus is a travel book for it records people and their manners. Ghosh has an artist's eye, his perceptions are sensitive and observations are acute. In the prologue he confesses that before getting the clues about the letters of Ben Yiju, he "had never heard of the Cairo Geniza . . . but within a few months, I was in Tunisia, learning arabic. . . . I knew nothing then about the slave of MS H. 6 except that he had given me a right to be there, a sense of entitlement." With this "sense of entitlement," Ghosh sets out to quench his quest for more interesting facts. His is "a travellers' tale." Apart from his perfectly pitched prose for vivid images, Ghosh has the travel writer's infallible eye for the quirk that lays bare the soul of a people.

NOTES

1. Homai Shroff, "A Sublime Journey," *The Illustrated Weekly of India*, Dec. 12-18, 1992, pp. 38-39.
2. Vikram Seth, *From Heaven Lake: Travels through Sinkiang and Tibet* (London: Abascus, 1987), p. 33.
3. Amitav Ghosh, *In an Antique Land* (New Delhi: Ravi Dayal Publisher, 1992), pp. 59-60.
4. Peter Theroux, "Cairo—Clamorous Heart of Egypt," *National Geographic*, vol. 183, no. 4, April 1993, pp. 38-69.
5. *Ibid.*

In an Antique Land: A View

LEELA GANDHI

Amitav Ghosh's visionary and somewhat unreadable book *In an Antique Land* explores the relationship between the grand narrative of history and "those barely discernible trances ordinary people leave upon the world." The former, positioned as the backdrop to Ghosh's narrative, appears variously as the Crusades, the European colonization of India and partitioning of the Middle East, nationalism and fundamentalism, and finally operation Desert Storm. From the margins and corners of this "tornado of grand designs." the author eloquently recovers the minute and ordinary voices of Ben Yiju, a Jewish merchant originally from Tunisia who came to India around 1130 A.D., and his Indian 'slave' Bomma, a native of Tulunad. The more laborious thread of this narrative records the pedantic voice of Ghosh himself scrutinizing the edges of contemporary Egypt and India for evidence of subaltern histories. At its worst moments, *In an Antique Land* collapses under the cumulative weight of its three-hundred and forty-nine endnotes. At its best moments, however, Ghosh's successful manipulation of multiple narratives produces a fascinating dialectic between history and life—even, fact and fiction.

Between the interminable lists and events of 'consequential' history, Ghosh subversively interposes a drunken Bomma cheering Adenese soldiers into battle. Elsewhere, a single dead of manumission is transliterated into a possible marital union between Ben Yiju and Ashu, and Indian slave girl from the matrilineal community of Nairs. "If I hesitate to call it love," the author observes in spite of the enforcers of history, "it is only because the documents offer no certain proof."

If memory facilitates the secret connections between people, places, and cultures in Ghosh's *The Shadow Lines*, his new book privileges imagination as the agency of historical and personal affinities. It is through his imaginative, rather than purely 'academic,' interrogation of the past that the author is able to animate the dead letters of libraries and archives with living voices. His description of an early episode in the Egyptian village of "Nashawy" explicates this methodology. Nabeel, who will eventually disappear into the "anonymity of history" produced by Operation Desert Storm, tries to "feel" the author's experience of loneliness in a strange country. This, Ghosh comments, "was the first time that anyone in Lataifa or Nashawy had attempted an enterprise similar to mine—to enter my imagination and look at my situation as it might appear to me." Unfortunately, the empathy with which Ghosh revitalizes the past is not sustained in his accounts of contemporary Egypt. He remains too self-consciously the social anthropologist "doktor al-Hindi," surrounded, with a few exceptions, by caricatures asking endless questions about circumcision and holy cows.

Nevertheless, Ghosh's sensitive amplification of unrecorded lives and voices successfully *personalizes* history, and makes it more *personable*. The footnotes where Ben Yiju and Bomma's story occurs is simultaneously the site of innumerable small and forgotten reconciliations: "Indian and Egyptian, Muslim and Jewish, Hindu and Muslim." Ghosh's pursuit of his cross-cultural protagonists becomes the more meaningful search for "human connections," and systems of counter-belief capable of accommodating pluralistic forms of worship. In Mangalore, where Ben Yiju forges his connections with Ashu and Bomma, Ghosh follows the trail of the Magarivas—low caste Hindu fisherfolk whose distinctive identity is registered in a "deity known as the Boobariya-Bhuta, deemed by legend to be the spirit of a Muslim mariner who died at sea." Ironically, the walls of the Boobariya-shrine Ghosh visits in Mangalore are plastered over with the posters of a fundamentalist Hindu political organization, notorious for its anti-Muslim rhetoric. In the collision between political interest and long standing traditions of pluralism, the Magarivas, Ghosh observes, were "now laying claim to the future . . . by discovering a History to replace the past." At a time when the *sangh parivar's* version of history invites contemporary India to forget the sanctity of its shared and inter-communal past, *In an Antique Land* invites resistance. The Vachanakara song Ghosh imagines Bomma overhearing at the 'antique' site of the recently reconstituted Boobariya-shrine also supplies a fitting epitaph to the demolition at Ayodhya:

> With a whole temple
> in this body
> where's the need
> for another?
>
> No one asked
> for two.

The article was first published in *In-between*, 2 (March 1993), pp. 67-68.

In an Antique Land: A Counter-Narrative of Coloniality

NILANJANA GUPTA

Standing here, addressing a conference on "Commonwealth Studies" is a poignant reminder of the conquerors, the rulers, the imperialists who determined the history of the world and changed the events of our lives with a disjunctive violence. It is also a reminder of the fact that imperialism was more than economic exploitation and political domination. Coloniality and imperialism are relationships that have had a cultural, intellectual and social impact which is even more insidious than the naked fact of political domination. As the term postcolonial suggests, the fall-out of colonialism is still very much with us.

In Salman Rushdie's famous phrase, this present historical moment is when "the Empire writes back"; the periphery is speaking and the centre is listening. However, the intellectual power centre is still to shift. In Aijaz Ahmad's words, there is still only a limited range of "authorised questions" set by the intellectual centre that may be answered in the works of postcolonial literature and one of the central issues that may be addressed is that of the concept of "nationhood." As Ahmad comments, even to a sensitive and liberal critic like Frederic Jameson, "The essential task of a 'Third World' novel, it is said is to give appropriate form (preferably allegory, but epic also, or fairy tale, or whatever) to the national experience. The range of questions that may be asked of the texts . . . must predominantly refer, then, in one way or another, to representations of colonialism, nationhood, post-coloniality, the typology of rulers, their powers, corruptions and so forth."[1]

We can see the implications of this position when we look at the valorized or canonized Third World novels—Chinua Achebe's trilogy, Ngugi's novels, Garcia Marquez's *A Hundred Years of Solitude* and of course Rushdie's *Midnight's Children* and *Shame*. Much of Indian writing in English has been concerned with the construction of nationhood like Shashi Tharoor's *The Great Indian Novel* or even in a different way, Vikram Seth s *A Suitable Boy*. Most of these writers attempt to create an epic vision of the past by multiple narratives, the use of myths, fantasy, allegory. All are concerned with political equations in some way, yet they are focussed on the ruling classes or coteries. The people, if they do appear at all, are usually disassociated from the political process, or are shown as defeated, disillusioned with the corrupt, power-hungry new rulers. Most of these novels are indictments of the postcolonial condition; often they also seem to be implicitly suggesting that the new corrupt rulers are no better than the foreign rulers—they may even be worse. Naturally these are sentiments that the metropolitan west finds reassuring.

It is in this context that Amitav Ghosh's *In an Antique Land*[2] deserves our attention. This novel focusses on the interrelationships of the people rather than of nation-states and their rulers. There are three important spatial tropes—India, Egypt and the 'West.' While India and Egypt have ancient ties which are myriad, the West is represented as the powerful interventionist in the relationship between the two. More importantly, the West, its rhetoric, its ideologies, its ways of thinking have been superimposed on the histories of the two 'antique lands.' Ghosh tries to show that the intervention of the West has destroyed the processes of dialogue, exchange, assimilation and syncreticism of the peoples of the two nations. Instead, there is the metaphysic of domination, classification and violence which Ghosh characterizes as 'Western.' He describes how in 1500 A.D. a Portuguese fleet came with a letter from the King of Portugal to the Hindu ruler of the city-state of Calicut demanding that he expel all Muslims. As the Hindu ruler remained obstinate in his refusal to comply, the Portuguese fleet attacked and conquered what is today part of Gujarat. A hastily put together army of the Muslim potentate of Gujarat, the Hindu ruler of Calicut, and the Sultan of Egypt could offer little resistance. "As always, the determination of a small, united band of soldiers triumphed easily over the rich confusions that accompany a culture of accommodation and compromise." (288) A modern parallel is established as Ghosh closes the novel. Almost five centuries later, the Gulf War again disrupts history and this time characters like Nabeel "vanish into the anonymity of History." (353)

The construction of the text is itself complex. There are basically two strands of narrative. In the first, Ghosh looks at the life of a twelfth century Indian slave Bomma who works for an Arab Jewish trader Abraham Ben Yiju and tries to reconstruct his history, while the second portrays simultaneously his own experiences as an Indian researcher in an Egyptian village. Let us look at the strand of the narrative which deals with the ancient times first. Ghosh's choice of the Indian slave as the focal centre of the narrative is itself significant. He is literally a person who inhabits the footnotes of history. To quote the opening lines: "The slave of MS H. 6 first stepped upon the stage of modern history in 1942. His was a brief debut, in the obscurest of theatres, and he was scarcely out of the wings before he was gone again—more a prompter's whisper than a recognizable face in the cast." (13)

From this anonymity, Ghosh attempts to rescue the life of this slave who was so much part of Ben Yiju's household that his friends would enquire after Bomma in their letters. In tracing this fascinating history, Ghosh makes us aware of how ancient the links are between what is today Egypt and what is today India. The cross-dissemination of cultures, religions, and traditions is brought to light through the existing correspondence of Ben Yiju with his family and friends, as well as by Ghosh's 'digressions' which describe the historical events of the past. All these coalesce marvellously to highlight the syncretism of culture. To take just two examples: first the passage which traces the history of the home of Abraham Ben Yiju, master of Bomma—a Roman fortress called Babylon. The fort was built in 130 A.D. by the emperor Trajan on the "site of an even earlier structure." Of the two massive towers of the entrance to the fort, one has been incorporated several centuries ago into the structure of a Greek Orthodox Church. In Ben Yiju's time, it was a port which was busier than Baghdad and Basra combined. Through this gateway entered the Arab general in 641 which was the decisive event that marked the Muslim victory over the Christian powers in Masr or Egypt. He laid the foundations of a new city which soon replaced Alexandria as the country's capital. Three hundred years later, a general in the army of the Fatimid dynasty who was formerly a Greek slave, conquered the Egyptians and marked the boundaries of a new township, al-Qâhira. "It was this name that was to pass into European languages as Cairo, Le Caire and the like." (36) The passage recreates for us a time when these antique lands of the Middle East and the East were the centres of trade and commerce, of production and of culture. To quote:

> With the pivotal ascendancy of the Fatimid Empire, it [Al-Qâhira] had come to play a pivotal role in the global economy as the entrepôt that linked the Mediterranean and the Indian Ocean: the merchandise that flowed through its bazaars came from as far afield as East Africa, Southern Europe, the Western Sahara, India, China and Indonesia . . . the juncture of some of the most important trade routes in the known world and the nucleus of one of the richest and most cosmopolitan centres of the world. (37-38)

Today this ruin is "a gigantic open refuse-pit, an immense rubbish dump" (38) but "incredible as it may seem, excavations in this suppurating wasteland have yielded huge quantities of Chinese pottery and other riches: it was here that some of the earliest and most valuable fragments of Indian textiles have been found." (39) This passage makes us aware of, among other things, the history, geography and economics of a world before colonialization, of the perpetual shifts in religious powers, of globalization of trade before GATT. This ancient centre is now a "suppurating wasteland." Cairo (and Egypt) like all the countries or regions mentioned in this passage—East Africa, Southern Europe, the Western Sahara, India and China—are among the poorest, least productive countries in the postcolonial world. This passage also shows us the multiplicity of cultures that created the city. The Greeks, Muslims, Jews, the Orientals and the Christians all contributed in the building of Cairo and Cairo is, the author tells us, "Egypt's metaphor for itself." (32)

The other passage I would like to look at is the one where Ghosh is trying to unravel the true name of the slave. He discovers that it was probably "Bomma" (in the ancient Judeao-Arabic script it was represented by the three characters BMH). His search takes him into the history of the South Indian tribe, the Tulus and the process of Sanskritization of their myths—where some of the "deities would occasionally appear within the mists of high Sanskritism, while others fell from favour and vanished into the nether world." (252) Thus Ghosh is astonished to discover that the Tulu Brahma is not the four-headed, four-armed image accompanied by a goose of the classical iconography, but a warrior deity with curling moustaches, holding a sword in one hand. He learns that this was the principal figure in the Tulunad-Bhuta pantheon originally called Berme or Bermere. "Over time, with the growth of Brahminical influence the Tulu deity Berme had slowly become assimilated to the Sanskritic deity 'Brahma.'" (254) Again, the syncreticism of religions and cultures is revealed in the search for the slave's true name. The processes of assimilation and the difficulties of knowing or even recognizing these seams of history and culture become evident.

The narrative which is interwoven with that of Ghosh's anthropological and archaeological researches is that of his experiences of the present. He goes to the villages of Latâifa and Nashawy to learn the language and culture of the Egyptians. Whereas the narrative mentioned earlier stresses the inter-relationships between countries and peoples, this strand of the narrative seems to concentrate on the tendency towards exclusion. Some of the most humorous passages in the text are those when the fellahs (peasants) of Egypt react to Ghosh's account of India and Hinduism. These are a few of the exchanges: Ustaz Mustafa who has "read all about India when I was in college in Alexandria" says:

> "There is a lot of chili in the food and when a man dies his wife is dragged away and burnt alive."
> "Not always," I protested. . . .
> "And of course you have Indira Gandhi and her son Sanjay Gandhi, who used to sterilise the Muslims. . . ."
> "No, no, he sterilized everyone," I said.
> His eyes widened and I added hastily: "No, not me, of course, but . . ."
> "Yes," he said, nodding sagely. "I know." (46)

Later Ghosh admits that he is a Hindu, reluctantly because for him it is "a religious identity largely by default" (47) to which Ustaz Mustafa says:

> "What is this 'Hinduki' thing? . . . If it is not Christianity nor Judaeism nor Islam what can it be? Who are its prophets?"
> "It's not like that," I said. "There aren't any prophets. . . ."
> "So you are like the Magi?" he said, bright-eyed. "You worship fire then?"
> I shook my head vaguely, but before I could answer . . . he said smiling coquettishly, "I know—it's cows you worship—isn't that so?"
> There was a sharp, collective intake of breath as Jabir and the other boys recoiled, calling upon God in whispers, to protect them from the Devil. (47)

Scenes like these become distressingly familiar to the narrator in the text, but these exchanges serve to highlight two important aspects of modernist ideology—first, the ease with which the 'Other' is constructed and rejected as 'impure' or abnormal. Secondly, we the Indian readers, also receive a jolt along with the writer when we come face to face with the observers's vision of India and Hinduism.

Ghosh also shows us how one of the strands of ideology shared and revered by the two 'Antique Lands' is the concept of modernity. There are two scenes which show this poignantly. In the first, Ghosh is summoned by his neighbour to tell him if the 'Makana Hindi' (the Indian machine) he has bought is good. It turns out to be a water-pump. Ghosh is aghast. "I knew nothing at all about water-pumps; indeed I could not recall ever having noticed one before coming to Latâifa." (72) But he has to pronounce the machine 'excellent' to the great relief of his friend. As a result, Ghosh regains some of his stature in the village. This incident deeply disturbs him.

> I stayed up a long time that night, marvelling at the respect the water-pump had earned me; I tried to imagine where I would have stood in Jabir's eyes if mine had been a country that exported machines that were even bigger, better and more impressive—cars and tractors perhaps—not to speak of ships and planes and tanks. I began to wonder how Latâifa would have looked if I had had the privilege of floating through it protected by the delegated power of technology, of looking out untroubled through a sheet of clear glass. (74)

Even more poignant is the scene which finds Ghosh and the Imam "delegates from two superseded civilizations, vying with each other to establish a prior claim to the technology of modern violence." (236)

> It seemed to me that the Imam and I had participated in our own final defeat, in the dissolution of the centuries of dialogue that had linked us: we had demonstrated the irreversible triumph of the language that had usurped all the others in which people once discussed their differences. We had acknowledged that it was no longer possible to speak, as Ben Yiju or his slave, or any one of the thousands of travellers who had crossed the Indian Ocean in the Middle Ages might have done. . . . Instead . . . we had both resorted . . . to the very terms that world leaders and statesmen use at great, global conferences, the universal, irresistible metaphysic of modern meanings. (237)

Ghosh is prodded out of his despair by the good-natured laughter of Eid and Khamees who tell him "Do not be upset, ya doktor. Forget about all those guns and things" and promises to visit him in India, even to live with him. Thus, the possibility of dialogue in the language of friendship and community is re-established.

The West is also shown as the imperial power in the world of knowledge. Bomma's story ends in Philadelphia where the manuscripts are kept. The manuscripts are scattered far from their origins, in England, the United States and Russia. The history of these peoples has been appropriated, classified and housed in the 'West.' Facts are distorted "in the process of shaping them to suit the patterns of the Western academy." (342) Yet the novel ends with the discovery that "in defiance of the enforcers of History, a small remnant of Bomma's world had survived" (342) in the form of the tomb of Rabbi Abu-Hasira of Morocco.

This novel makes us rethink our notions of Time and Space as the title itself suggests. The choice of the word 'Land' rather than nation or even country undermines the modernist project of nationalism. While the word 'Antique' is destabilized by the implied present of the phrase *In an Antique Land*. The title posits the text as one of "the counter-narratives of the nation that continually evoke and erase the totalizing boundaries both actual and conceptual—disturb those ideological manoeuvre through which 'imagined communities' are given essentialist identities."[3]

One way in which this is done in the text is to focus on the process of migrancy. While the 'migrant intellectual' has been valourized by writers like Bharati Mukherjee and Salman Rushdie, in this novel, Ghosh examines many other kinds of migrancy. Discussions of nationalism often ignore its 'Other' that is the creation of the exile, the migrant, the refugee. By accepting the nation as the 'given,' we overlook the fact that this is a relatively modern conceptual construct and that partitions and boundaries are, as Amitav Ghosh's earlier novel suggests "Shadow Lines."

The travels of Ben Yiju are motivated by economic concerns similar to those of the fellaheen who go to work in Iraq. Amitav Ghosh himself is on a search for knowledge while the German, British and American 'Orientalists' had already travelled these same roads. Edward Said points out that one way of challenging the very basics of every art and theory of government is to challenge the principle of confinement because "to be governed, people must be counted, taxed, educated, and of course ruled in regulated spaces." The nation-state cannot understand or accept those who do not fit into the neat categories it has created. Thus the police officer at the tomb of Sidi Abu-Hasira is confounded when he sees Ghosh's passport and finds he is not Israeli. Nor is he Jewish, Muslim or Christian—naturally he assumes that "There had to be something odd afoot." (335) The senior officer is at pains to maintain his distance from Ghosh's companion Mohsin, by denying "the protective bonds of neighbourhood and kinship . . . the accustomed terms of communication—those immemorial courtesies of village life, by which people strove to discover mutual acquaintances and connections." (337) It is, according to Said, these migrant workers, refugees, immigrants, students and other such groups who "constitute a real alternative to the authority of the state."[4] The creation of the frameworks, the boundaries of nations, has also automatically created the margins, the outsiders. Ghosh seems in agreement with Frantz Fanon's sentiment that "national consciousness, which is not nationalism is the only thing that will give us an international dimension."[5]

Ghosh's tendency towards syncreticism and breaking barriers is reflected in the construct of the text itself. Breaking away from the traditions of both realism and magical realism, Ghosh's text is a combination of autobiography, history, anthropology, travelogue and fiction.

In this text, Ghosh seems to be responding to Said's call in *Culture and Imperialism:* 'The major task is to match the new economic and socio-political dislocations and congifurations of our time with the startling realities of human interdependence on a world scale. We need to go and to situate these in a geography of other identities, people, cultures, and then to study how, despite their differences, they have always overlapped one another, through unhierarchical influence crossing, incorporation, recollection, deliberate forgetfulness, and of course, conflict."[6]

Ghosh seems to me to be one of the few novelists who is today offering an alternative to the postcolonial trend of narrating the nation. *In an Antique Land* presents us with a truly subversive look at history, while suggesting possibilities of an alternative discourse of dialogue, rather than domination.

NOTES

1. A. Ahmad, *In Theory* (London: Verso, 1992), p. 124.
2. Amitav Ghosh, *In an Antique Land* (Delhi: Ravi Dayal Publisher, 1992).
3. Homi K. Bhabha, ed., *Nation and Narration* (London: Routledge, 1990), p. 300.
4. Edward Said, *Culture and Imperialism* (London: Vintage, 1994), p. 395.
5. Quoted in Bhabha, p. 4.
6. Said, pp. 402-3.

The Image of Woman in *In an Antique Land*

E. KANAKA BHAGYA VENI

Patriarchy which is the ruling social system almost all over the world ordains that woman's place is the home, her role as a wife and mother is quite often synonymous with her total human existence.

The term "family" derives from Latin "Famulus" which "means a household slave and familia[1] signifies the totality of slaves belonging to one individual" who is the male head, the limitation imposed on woman for her family function is not however confined to the West, despite the Latin philological lineage. In India, in China, and in Greece and Rome, woman has always been relegated to background for her family roles and the task of civilization "has become more and more man's business."[2] One therefore expects the presentation of women in literature, created and dominated by man, to be mere role-fulfilments.

In contrast to Europe, the Indian subcontinent has refused to evolve through successive stages of history and continued an archaic existence[3] and this failure illustrated in the repeated political defeats, economic subjugation, marked sterility in the creative efforts in every field of human knowledge has led to a total ossification of the Hindu psyche. The ancient modes and ideals instead of undergoing revision and transformation in consonance with the changing time, have tended to dominate the ethos in decadent forms. So the ever-obedient, ever-suffering Sita who ended her life in self-immolation has remained the dominant feminine archetype.

Since the totalitarian expertise in destroying the identity, the very soul of human being is now a recognized phenomenon, it should not shock us to see that women steam-rolled and flattened into the family roles, tend to be dehumanized insofar as they are invariably stripped of all the individualizing traits of a sentient being. Shouri Daniels describes the "female incarnate" thus: "She has no shape or form. She is every thing or nothing. She is fluid. Pour her into any mould and she takes it. . . . Ideals and principles lie outside her nature."[4] As she is the void, she becomes a being only insofar as she can be regarded as an object in relation to man who is of course the subject.

In Amitav Ghosh's *In an Antique Land* the word "antique" which means "ancient" is deliberately used to portray woman as "antique" and, in "antiquity," woman as metaphor "land," woman as always passive and submissive like land.

Elaine Showalter in her theory of feminist criticism has talked about the analysis of women according to the three socio-cultural and psychological critical categories of Feminine, Feminist and Female-aesthetic.

Feminine is the concept of womanhood, the traditional role of the woman, in relation to the patriarchal society where she is understood always in connection to the male. She has no identity of her own but is venerated as a mother in relation to the father, as a sister in relation to her brother, as a wife in relation to her husband and as a daughter in relation to her father.

According to Elaine Showalter, "In the Feminist phase or the winning of the vote, women are historically enabled to reject the accommodating postures of femininity and use literature to dramatize the ordeals of wronged womanhood." Feminist is the concept of the theory that they are fighting for their rights, trying to break from the ideological form. Feminist was a stance or tone of women libbers striving for the recognition of their rights and the fight for their identity as individuals in the society.

According to Elaine Showalter, "In the Female phase women reject both imitation and protest—two forms of dependency—and turn instead to female experience as the source of an autonomous art." Female is the concept of the theory that the woman is an individual, woman as herself, the movement towards the understanding of woman as a female, woman as power, woman as an erotic symbol of desire, that within her self she has power, the recognition of power gives her maturity.

In the novel *In an Antique Land* the presence of woman is not felt in most parts of the novel and if present, woman is always mentioned in connection to the male—be it her father, brother, son or husband. The names of all the women characters are not mentioned. One of the women characters whose name is mentioned is Ashu—Ben Yiju's wife. Ben Yiju married Ashu who, according to Goitein, was 'probably beautiful.' Ashu is not mentioned anywhere else in the entire corpus of Ben Yiju's documents, although her children figure in it frequently. Ben Yijû did not once refer to her in his letters or jottings.

Busaina, Khamees's sister's introduction is physical. She is mentioned as tall and sweet-looking. She is referred to have left her husband and moved back to Nashawy with her children. Although she had given her husband two fine, healthy children, the two of them had never really got on. They had quarrelled all the time and in the end things had come to such a pass that her husband had announced that he was going to marry again. She and her husband used to quarrel all day long because she had to have her way in everything. He did not accept this as he might have wanted a submissive woman as his wife, who would never decide anything by herself and would always depend on her husband for everything and accept his decisions.

Khamees's wife didn't have children, and having failed to father any children, he had taken a second wife, but with no result. His wife had walked off in a rage, shouting to the world that·it was his fault that he was childless, not hers. He does not accept that it is because of his fault that he is childless as hinted by his first wife and goes on to take a second wife, but with no result. Amm Taha says that he uses Hoopoe's blood for a spell for women who can't bear children. It signifies that it was considered that if a man could not father children it would only be because of his wife's fault.

Ben Yiju's daughter's name is not mentioned whereas his son's name Surur is mentioned. This indicates that women were not considered important—even to mention their names. Ben Yiju's daughter is mentioned in his letters as "I have left a daughter, his sister." The wives of Imam are mentioned. They are identified as Imam's first wife and Imam's second wife. Sakkina, Shaikh Musa's wife, is portrayed as a shy woman, she was so shy to answer the author that Ahmed had to speak for her. She was very young and her age was a fraction of her husband's age.

For many of the women characters their physical appearance and their clothes speak for them, as is the case with the three women in Shaikh Musa's house—one in the first bloom of her adolescence with a gentle, innocent face and a rosy complexion, she was a pale, pretty, self-possessed young woman, dressed in a long, printed skirt, the other was dark and thickest, and she was wearing a black fustan and the author goes on to say that her clothes and her bearing spoke of a college, or at least a high school education. The author knocks at the door of Ustaz Sabry's house and a woman dressed in the severe black robes of an elderly widow appears. She is described as a thin lady with thin, fine-boned cheeks. The identity of these women is physical.

Women are also portrayed as objects of entertainment. The girl dancer mentioned in Nashawy was young, dressed in a simple, printed cotton dress, with a long scarf tied around her waist whose dance was a source of entertainment to the people gathered.

Most of the women characters perform the duties of a servant. The two women in Shaikh Musa's house come into the room carrying a pair of trays loaded with food, Sakkina appears in the doorway and gives Hasan a tray with three glasses of tea on it, Shaikh Musa's wife ushers the guests into the guestroom, showing them the way with a kerosene lamp and goes back to bring some tea and food, later she gives the lamp a final scrub and opens the door to show another room, the women carry food for their men out to the fields, Imam's first wife brings in a tray of tea, and women walk towards the town balancing baskets of vegetables on their heads. These women are nameless and perform functions.

Abu-Ali would always berate his wife or roar abuse at her. In another context a vendor says that he would rather divorce his wife than sell the fruits for a lesser price in the market. Here women have been portrayed as a commodity.

The other women characters mentioned in the novel are Ahmed's mother, Nabeel's mother, Ismail's mother, Ali's mother, Amm Taha's first wife and his second wife, Eid's wife, Amitav Ghosh's mother, Hasan's wife, the headman's daughter etc.

To conclude, Amitav Ghosh is being provocative, he is drawing attention to this antiquated attitude of the patriarchal society towards women.

NOTES

1. F. Engels, *The Origin of the Family, Private Property and the State* (1884; Moscow: Progress Publishers), p. 58. Before Engels, John Stuart Mill in the *Subjection of Women* (1869; London: O.U.P., 1966) denounced "the legal subordination of one sex to the other" as "one of the chief hindrances to human improvement," advocated "perfect equality." (p. 427) For Mill also, "Home" was "domestic slavery." (p. 46)
2. Sigmund Freud, *Civilisation and Discontents*, trans. James Strachey (1930; London: Hogarth Press, 1963), p. 73.
3. This 'archaic' existence' has for its metaphysical principle a cyclical recurrence which is deemed eternal, hence development in linear pattern—that we find in 'modern world dominated by Judeo Christian concept of time as straight line—may not be found in the 'archaic' ethos. (See for details, Mircea Eliade, *The Myth of the Eternal Return or Cosmos and History*, trans. W.R. Trask (Princeton, 1949), p. xii and also Mircea Eliade, *Myths, Dreams and Mysteries: The Encounter between Contemporary and Archaic Realities*, trans. Philip Mairet (London: Harvill Press, 1960), p. 23.
4. Shouri Daniels, *The Salt Doll* (New Delhi: Vikas, 1978), p. 12.

Enigma as Ontology in *The Calcutta Chromosome*

BABLI GUPTA

In a recent article for the *Times of India*, Ashok Mitra joins the debate on modalities of civilizational advance in contemporary India and by way of putting a question mark on the uncritical enthusiasts of Globalization, observes, "Development itself is a ferociously, value-based phenomena." (22.5.96) The renewed stress on giving centrality to social values as the basis of assessing progress, rather than relying on the aggregation of material wealth and power as the sole determining criteria for social advance, overriding concern for human values, forms the core of the debate which has gained urgency amongst social historians, activists and political formations of the radical variety. The literary arena, in a matching response has thrown up a new breed of writers like Amitav Ghosh, Mukul Kesavan, Rohinton Mistry who combine their professional skills as social historians, with a literary flair to compose works of art which are profoundly concerned with civilization and history, share a common propensity of deconstructing, often overturning the models and assumptions of western civilizations with their awesome pretensions and misplaced confidence about guiding, with paternal care, the destiny of postcolonial nations. The prevailing mood amongst writers "The Raj strikes back" gives us the backdrop for understanding, if only partially the core of Amitav Ghosh's latest work *The Calcutta Chromosome: A Novel of Fevers, Delirium and Discovery* (1996). Written in the form of a mystery novel, it remains mysterious in more ways than one.

Attempts to unravel the enigmatic design of this book are as successful as unpeeling an onion to find the core. If readers and critics go ahead to discover patterns and meanings unintended by the author, Ghosh has only himself to blame for the muddle.

A certain amount of subjectivity notwithstanding, this essay attempts to devise a pattern by tracing the link between Ghosh's two works, *In an Antique Land* (1992) and this latest novel of 1996, and see the latter as a deliberate inversion of the earlier masterpiece. It is almost as if Ghosh is exorcising the gloom which had crept upon him in the writing of *In an Antique Land* where he recounts the tales of two ancient civilizations, Egypt and India, and chronicles their inevitable decline. In both books, the chance discovery of marginal figures, lost in time, becomes the occasion for researching the historical past of ancient civilization with their richness and complexities, to trace their inevitable destruction at the hands of the European conquerors, who were more able and organized but not for that reason more civilized than the ancients. "As always, the determination of a small united band of soldiers triumphed easily over the rich confusions that accompany a culture of accommodation and compromise." (288)

In the later novel, Ghosh, eager to shake off this sadness and bitter wisdom, looks in the direction of magic, conspiracy and silence to overturn the logic of Europe's conquest of the East. What if the conquered races were to draw a circle of silence around themselves impregnable to the rationalism and science of the west? Would they succeed in resisting and at times even overcoming the conquistador, to have the last laugh? It is a dangerous but tempting line of argument, and Ghosh abandons his characteristic narrative style, to sample these magically derived conclusions.

The two worlds of science and counter-science, European rationality and Indian mythos are brought together against the backdrop of Calcutta's streets, markets and monuments. The narrator discovers a forgotten monument in Calcutta, built in the memory of one Sir Ronald Ross, awarded the Nobel Prize for his discovery of the Malaria parasite. The marble arch of the monument is inscribed with Ross's versification in self-celebration:

This day relenting God
Hath placed within my hand
A wondrous thing; And God
Be praised. At his command

Seeking his secret deeds
With tears and toiling breath
I find thy cunning seed
O million murdering Death. (35)

This is provocation enough for a rebuttal from L. Murugan, the self-appointed biographer to Ronald Ross, who gleefully parodies this high sounding moral sententia with bitter humour to expose how these scientific achievements barely touched the lives of the millions living at the edge of death.

Half stunned I look around
And see a land of death—
Dead bones that walk the ground
And dead bones underneath;

A race of wretches caught,
Between the palms of need
And rubbed to utter naught,
The chaff of human seed. (35)

So much for disinterested service of science for the benefit of mankind! Besides as Murugan explains, the sudden interest of all European countries in finding a cure for malaria was not to save human lives as much as to ensure unrestricted expansion of virgin territories: "The mid-nineteenth century was when the scientific community began to wake up to malaria. Remember this was the century when old Mother Europe was settling all the Last Unknowns: Africa, Asia, Australia, the America's even uncolonized parts herself." (47)

A part of the novel then fits in conveniently with the Third world counter narrative to the Raj enterprise, but Ghosh goes ahead to give a complicated twist story and constructs a secret history of medical research. Sir Ronald Ross it appears had been manipulated all along to make the necessary deductions, while the actual guiding sprit operating behind the scene was a low-born scavenger woman called Mangala hand-picked and trained as an assistant by Ross's predecessor Dr. Cunningham to help him in his laboratory.

What follows is a dark and disturbing chronicle of how Mangala, as the presiding Deity and her accomplice Laakhan—modelled on the mythic Lakshman, loyal second-in-command to Rama, manage to outwit, unseat and annihilate those who could stand in the way of Ronald Ross inheriting the mantle of prized laboratory of Dr. Cunningham. This includes their benefactor Cunningham, a host of other scientists, missionaries or curious individuals who accidentally stumbled upon their stealthy designs. Is Ghosh working at alternatives or suggesting that both are equally manipulative and suspect?

The narrative becomes increasingly dense with complicated patterns working at cross purpose. On the one hand we have the politically correct and gender friendly slant which fits in ever so nicely with the subaltern perspective. Ghosh makes an elaborate case for those forgotten underlings who do the spade work for all those grand discoveries, which are then credited to their superior masters. The author goes into intricate details of medical history to make a credible case for the illiterate Mangala accomplishing the impossible. This is not so far fetched as it seems at first glance. The author is in fact relying on current trends in the field of social medicine as more and more scientists, and social workers are coming around to the view that scientific investigations, specially those related to social medicine, health, hygiene and control of epidemics can be conducted with more economy and efficiency by those who are born and brought up indigenously rather than by those experimenting in remote, sanitized laboratories with little knowledge of the nitty-gritty of actual conditions.

In Murugan's words, "We are talking about a microscopy which was still an artisanal kind of skill at that time. Real talent could take you a long way in it . . . unlike Ross she didn't need to read a zoological study to see that there was a difference between Culex and Anopheles, she'd have seen it like you or I can see the difference between a dachshund and a doberman." (203) Ghosh however does not limit his talents for writing a mystery novel with political overtones. The linear pattern is intersected at many points with counter patterns which completely overthrow the earlier assumptions. Instead of forwarding an alternative theory of science, which has a place for the subalterns, the author goes ahead to argue against all scientific conceptualization. Theory itself becomes the main stumbling block to knowledge, "She was not carrying a shit-load of theory in her head, she didn't have to write papers or construct proofs." (203)

This is a world of mysteries rather than rationality, where Mangala's real talents become those of magician rather than of an artisan. The counter-sciences may have extraordinary powers to overturn science but their motives like that of their counterparts are self-seeking rather than humane. Ghosh is subtly working out the complicity of the two different kinds of quests with similar motives, a search for power, self-aggrandizement and ironically, for permanence in this uncertain world. The grisly scenes where Mangala decapitates pigeons shivering with artificially induced malaria as a last-ditch effort to cure or at least mitigate the effects of syphilitic paresis tells only half the story. The other half concerns the diabolic secret aspirations for a kind of immortality acquired through a technology of interpresonal transference of intelligence through the chosen people.

The female extraordinary, we are told, has stumbled upon the unique combination of genetic chromosomes and special intelligence which produce the rare Calcutta Chromosome. The unique Chromosome makes it possible for information to be transmitted chromosomatically from one body to another thereby ensuring the preservation and continuity of their lineage from the pre-Christian era into the future. Ghosh's accomplishments in the technique of writing can be seen in the way he marshals arguments and data to make this bizarre theory sound almost believable. The narrative is densely packed with information painstakingly gleaned from the study of Computer Science and Microbiology to make the impalusible sound convincing enough, at least to sustain our interest in the story. The medical history helps to underscore the thematic relevance of the novel. Microbiology and Cybernetics are areas in Science, all set to overhaul the face of the twenty-first century. The intelligence of Master-Computers and inventions in Genetic Engineering have accomplished thaumaturgic feats, more amazing than Mangala's primitive rites. In 1927, we are informed, Julius-Von-Wagner the Austrian psychologist and scientist was awarded the Nobel Prize for his discovery made along the same lines as Mangala's intuitive insights: "In fact, until antibiotics, the Wagner-Jauregg process was pretty much a standard treatment: every major VD hospital had its little incubating room where it grew a flock of anopheles. Think about it: hospitals cultivating disease! But on the other hand, what could be more natural than fighting fire with fire? . . . This is the only instance known to medicine of using one disease to fight another." (205)

Whether this tongue-in-cheek account is a fact or humorous exaggeration, is besides the point. It serves the purpose of redefining attitudes to practices and rituals which are normally frowned upon as regressive primitivism and blurs the boundary lines between science and magic. Mangala and Julius-Von-Wagner become unlikely partners in their scheme for the manipulation of malarial fever for inducing a state of dementia which could stage miracles. The delirium, which is a form of dementia opens the road to discoveries which plumb the unconscious, is a twin-edged weapon. It can lead to cure or for perpetuation of obsessions of a dangerous kind. The Mangala's creed uses it to transpose thoughts and intelligence of one human being into another, by bending the walls of the mind through the fever. Any resemblance of this to modern techniques of controlling the brain is intentional to the author's design of pulling-out the dividing line between the conscious and unconscious, sane and insane, known and unknown depths of the human mind.

The strategy to draw a number of parallels, which converge and countermand each other, creating the aura of ambivalence and indeterminacy, becomes the preamble for investigating the world as mystery. The line of argument in this essay is to establish how this description of the world as enigma follows from an ontological position, adopted for the first time, which brings the author dangerously close to mysticism and its first principles, Philosophic Idealism.

Philosophic Idealism begins with the postulate that the essence of nature and existence remains outside the bounds of human reason. The dualism in Idealist Ontology postulates that perfect knowledge is unattainable because of the insurmountable dualism between the knower and the known. Human reason and its accessories, science, theory, even language itself become obstacles, to knowing as epistemology changes the truth in the very act of apprehending it. The Counter-Science acolytes have a cutting edge over others as they begin with an intuitive grasp that reality cannot be known. Murugan explains to Antar, the Egyptian born, New York based Computer-Scientist slated to be the next-in-line Laakhan:

> Maybe this other team started with the idea that knowledge is self-contradictory; maybe they believed that to know something is to change it; therefore, in knowing something, you've already changed what you think you know so that you don't really know at all, you know only its history. Maybe they thought that knowledge couldn't begin without acknowledging the impossibility of knowledge. (88)

The desire to escape tyranny of knowledge and yearnings to experience the truth beyond knowledge—through intuition, spiritualist séances, or medically engineered dementia, found in full measure in this mystery tale is evidence of a definite incline towards mysticism, with shades of Neo-Platonism brought in to bind the ancient with the modern. The post-Aristotelian conception, conceives the world as an emanation from the one with whom the soul is capable of being reunited in trance or ecstasy. Buttressed with layerings of ancient regimes, Ghosh repeats the same line of thought to the last comma, dot and smudge of ink: "For them the only way to escape the tyranny of knowledge is to turn it on itself. But for that to work they have to create a single perfect moment of discovery when the person who discovers is also that which is discovered." (252)

One explanation for this surprising tilt could be that the anthropologist in the writer scans the movement of civilization through the centuries and comes up with a series of negations. In spite of material advance, and dazzling possibilities afforded by science, technology, the author seems to say, mankind has not really added to the sum of wisdom, self-knowledge and still remains floundering in the dark of mental and moral ignorance. While the best bits of humour and ironic insights are reserved to express his disenchantment with the bourgeois social order, the author does not endorse any other alternative. The practitioners of magic are an equally disappointing lot. They are just as self-seeking and ruthless as their civilized counterparts and their motives are even more confusing. Mangala achieves a certain amount of success when she works through the British scientist Ronald Ross, for the success of his enterprise. On her own, she achieves little, which makes us wonder what all this bustle about detecting, selecting and perpetuating the chromosomatic lineage was all about. Suppose that the magic-people gain a kind of immortality for their line, what do they hope to do with it, or did they aim for immortality, read power, without a purpose? These are some of the questions deliberately left unanswered in the book.

The anti-climactic back-slide undermines interest in the narrative that centres on the elaborate preparations for Urmila's reincarnation as Mangala. Urmila is also the name of the mythic Lakshman's much-neglected wife. She is a typical middle class Bengalee elder sister, sacrificing herself for her traditional male-dominated household, till she rebels and takes upon herself aspect of the vengeful goddess Kali. The suspense surrounding her 'Avtar' and the possibilities of developing her into a full-fledged character are wilfully negated as the narrative comes to an abrupt halt on the eve of her reincarnation. It is never known how she used her new found powers, if she had used them at all. Murugan, the companion who helped to instigate her revolt and assisted the preparations for her transmogrification had pleaded with Urmila to save him from impending madness, minutes before his disappearance: "'Don't forget me,' he begged her, 'If you have it in your power to change the script, write me in. Don't leave me behind. Please.'" (253) But Urmila as deity was either helpless, or worse, had punished Murugan for daring to investigate and illumine the enigmas of the dark world. It is Murugan's sudden departure which leads Antar to reconstruct his story on his Computer and ultimately discover him locked in a mental asylum. The Computer and its fancy gadgetry have the wizardry to transpose Murugan's grotesque visage across the continent, into another world, but cannot find an answer why the man should have ended the way he did—naked, covered with his excrement, with maggots in his hair and permanently hand-cuffed. Moreover, how can a mad man in this helpless condition have the power to control Antar's movements, unless he had acquired magical powers himself What are we as readers, to make of a world where the mad cannot change their own destiny but still can make scientists dance to their tune? Is Murugan warning Antar about his impending fate or merely indicating the powerlessness of the powerful?

The selection of the Egyptian Antar, belonging to the new generation of scientific-technically trained immigrants, working for a faceless company in New York, as the next Laakhan incarnate, carries the tussle of the parallel worlds into the heart of western civilizations. It is Antar's living conditions, more than the sights and smells of Calcutta streets which set the tenebrous tone of the novel. His lonely life with only a Computer for company and the isolation of all his companions (mainly from the Middle East, and central Asia) who shuffle out a dreary existence, living at the fringe of the glittering metropolis, in a world apart, which constitutes the lasting impression of the novel.

The combined effect of scattered strands of plot and tonal arrangements put together underscore the parallel existence of contrary forces, countermanding each other. The author compels us to think about what is lacking in the world, which creates this atmosphere of bewilderment and utter futility. At this point, it would be useful to go back to the citation made at the beginning of this essay, emphasising the appropriate value frame which is needed to give meaning to human life and civilizations. It is the presence or absence of human values which eventually determines the worthiness of a civilizational order. In its absence human activity is reduced to meaningless bustle, with contrary impulses working to annul each other. Mankind, the author seems to say, may have refined its abilities of manipulating the outer layers of reality but inwardly it remains the same primitive being, self-seeking in design and bestial in ways. Instead of a linear advance towards a progressively higher stage of civilization, we could be moving in circles, ending more or less where we began, centuries ago.

In all his earlier novels Ghosh has made known his commitment to a broadly defined, secular-humanist frame of values. The present work may become the turning point in the reverse direction indicating a shift towards an uncertain non-rationalistic view of life, wavering between the two poles of nihilism and mystical transcendence.

There is yet another more positive way of explaining this uncharacteristic turn in a rational way, by taking the help of literary analogies, to clarifying meaning. There are striking resemblances between Ghosh's *The Calcutta Chromosome* and E.M. Forster's *A Passage to India*. Forster presents India as a land of mysteries which can be solved and muddles which elude understanding, defy resolutions and generally suggest that the essential meaning lies outside the bounds of rational constructs. One can take the mystical overtones in Forster as well at face value, except that it would be out of place in an iconoclast known for his hostility to blind faith. And one who had elevated skepticism into a personal creed. Alternatively this interweaving of mystery and muddle can be taken as an acknowledgement of the relativism inherent in all epistemological frameworks to counter absolutism and dogmatism of thought. *A*

Passage to India makes a more relevant and meaningful reading, when interpreted as a timely admonition administered to both the erstwhile British rulers and their successors in the then newly Independent India, that no single institution, way of living or looking at things can possess perfect infallibility. There is evidence, of a kind, to support a socio-historic interpretation, in the Forsterian mould, for Ghosh's ontological positions, his habit of riddling the reader with unresolved mysteries, and subversive questioning, of western institutions of learning and charity. This is however an inadequate and partial explanation of the novel taken as a whole. The new directions of his thought, the tonal emphasis and techniques of form bring it close to the Drama of the Absurd.

The form in Absurd drama is valorized to authenticate the meaning. Dialogue, characterization, and plot unfolding, the most important vehicles of meaning in Aristotelian drama are relegated to a secondary position. The formal aspects of dramaturgy are enlarged to include mime and gesture, music and drama; means of communication other than dialogue. Thus the meaning of theatrical experience is conveyed obliquely through suggestions rather than statement. Absurd drama explores the language of silence fervently sought in *The Calcutta Chromosome*. The quest for a new language which pierces through the fallacy of words brings the author close to the world of Samuel Beckett with special reference to the play, *Waiting for Godot*.

The structure in Beckett's play takes the form of a circular rotation, to end where it begins. It finds an echo to the circular movement of civilization in Ghosh's work where the primitive exists simultaneously with the modern. Beckett constructs two parallel sets of characters, which at times complement and at others contrast with each other, without making the nature of their relationship explicit. The form in Beckett's drama thus, helps to give a literary precedent for the counter-worlds in Ghosh's novel with both authors exhibiting a peculiar knack of constructing carefully crafted, random configurations in preference to neatly fabricated designs to mirror the arbitrariness of the universe. The resemblance comes closest in their common distrust of language as a means of communication. Dialogue in Beckett's play aims to confuse rather than clarify, culminating in two sets of speeches by Lucky which give a practical demonstration of Apasia, that is the impairment of the power to use words. In later works, Beckett has stripped language to the bare minimum replacing it with mime, gestures and the elongated pauses on stage to experience the sounds of silence.

There are points of divergence within the given similarities. Ghosh's mistrust of language has a past history as well as a specific background. In *In an Antique Land* for example, he conveys the sense of being "trapped by language" in sad and humorous episodes. It is understandable, in a social anthropologist to become wary of language as there are ample occasions to witness how language, which acquires its connotations from its use by specific communities, races and cultures, is weighted down with its own prejudices. Thus a specific word denoting a specific activity or custom comes to have an opposite meaning for people located differently. In spite of their friendship with "Dr. Amitabh" (Ghosh) the villagers of Nashawy and Lataifa in Egypt are horrified by the agnostic doctor from a Hindu family, when he tries to explain the practice of cremation prevalent amongst the Hindus which is considered barbaric because amongst other things, he is forced to use the equivalent of the verb "to burn" which has a different meaning altogether for his friends. Similarly the practice of circumcision in Islam, is looked upon as an act of purification by the Muslim, a view which may not be shared by their uncircumcised brothers of the non-Islamic world. For Ghosh, languages had become, "an explosive barrier of symbols":

> "Tell me, is it true what they say, that in your country you burn your dead?" . . . My heart sank: this was a question I encountered almost daily, and since I had not succeeded in finding a word such as 'cremate' in Arabic, I knew I would have to give my assent to the term that Khamees had used: the verb "to burn," which was the word for what happened to firewood and straw and the eternally damned.
>
> "Yes," I said, knowing that I would not be able to prevent the inevitable outcome. "Yes, it's true; some people in my country burn their dead."
>
> "You mean," said Khamees in mock horror, "that you put them on heaps of firewood and just light them up?"
>
> 'Yes,' I said quickly, hoping he would tire of the subject.
>
> It was not to be. "Why?" he persisted. "Is there a shortage of kindling in your country?"
>
> "No," I said, "you don't understand."
>
> There was a special word, I tried to explain, a special ceremony, certain rites and rituals it wasn't like lighting a bonfire with a matchstick. But for all the impression my explanation made, I may as well have been silent. (168)

There are additional difficulties for the writer of the novel. Unlike theatre, the genre of novel does not have alternative strategies of communication at hand. The novelist must take recourse to language, to convey the futility of the same.

The Calcutta Chromosome has a specially designed character to convey the authorial viewpoint. He is the focal point in a parallel plot which is not allowed to grow. Saiyad Murad Husain, eminent writer and National Award winner, who takes on the tribal name "Phulboni" to make explicit the nature of his allegiances could be Amitav Ghosh himself. But Phulboni like Urmila, is made to disappear abruptly from the scene, after having fulfilled a specific function. That is of voicing, the author's innermost anxieties, and secret longings: "For more years than I can count I have walked the innermost streets of this most secret of cities, looking always to find her who has so long eluded me: Silence herself. I see signs of her presence everywhere I go, in images, words, glances, but only signs, nothing more. . . . By every means available, I have sought her, the ineluctable, ever-elusive mistress of the unspoken, wooed her, begged to join the circle of her initiates." (189)

Ghosh makes explicit the philosophic foundations of these mystical yearnings as arising from the Metaphysics of eternal dualism: "Mistaken are those who imagine that silence is without life; that it is inanimate, without either spirit or voice. It is not: indeed the Word is to this silence what the shadow is to the foreshadowed, what the veil is to the eye, what the mind is to truth, what language is to life." (40)

The line of thinking is converging into an unabashed variety of transcendentalism, running in a different direction to Beckettian Nihilism which negates all belief, specially of the spiritual kind. The author goes back to the teachings of Valentines, the Alexandrian philosopher of early Christian era, to link Phulboni's wanderings to the primeval quest. In Valentian cosmology, the ultimate deities are Abyss and Silence, "One being male and the other female, one representing mind and the other truth." As Abyss and Silence are not complementing polarities, but aspects of the same negation, a quest which searches for meaning between the two is foreclosed to doom. Even in mysticism Ghosh does not offer transcendence.

In conclusion, *The Calcutta Chromosome* ends in an ontological deadlock. Essentially a novel of ideas, it works like a brain teaser undermining conceptual certainties and reads the world as a mighty conundrum, where questions and problems are given conjectural answers. Closest to the Theatre of the Absurd, in attitudes and the use of form, it is nevertheless rooted in a very different historical and intellectual climate.

The conceptualizing of the Absurd took place in Europe, at the time of the rise of Fascism. It was essentially a reflection of the dismay and disillusionment of the intellectual and cultural avant-garde to the crumbling down of European democracies, and the institutions of its ligitmism, when they come face to face with the fury of the senseless violence unleashed by the Fascist advance. An alternative response was available even at that time, witnessed in the commitment and activities of those who joined the Resistance movement, and worked alongside the socialist forces, which contributed decisively to the anti-Fascist as well as the National Liberation struggle in the colonies. It was the time when the self-conception and esteem of the bourgeois was at its lowest, while socialism, as the inspirational force for the radical movement was in its prime.

Ghosh is writing his novel in the aftermath of the post-Presteroika watershed; following the dissolution of the Soviet Union and all that it had signified in the triangular struggle between capitalism, socialism and nationalism. For capitalism, however, this is its most favourable movement, as it regroups itself for a global offensive against the erstwhile colonies, which had slipped out of its hands since the end of the second world war.

It is the ascending phase of Capital's advance, rather than the moment of its decline which prompts the sense of entrapment, intrigue and dread in Ghosh's writings, indicating that his allegiances, in the ultimate analysis are in reverse direction to the ideological moorings of the Absurd which is essentially Eurocentric and hostile to politics. Ghosh on the other hand, remains a politically conscious writer in spite of the change in his mode of writing.

The Calcutta Chromosome merits attention as a seminal work, touching raw contemporary issues. Even its obscurities and muddles are symptomatic of the tendential response which may come to be shared by writers in the future, faced as they are with the predicament at hand; the ideological impasse. which makes the choosing difficult and the greater imperative therefore of breaking the impasse, if only to come to grips with the real world.

The present work is in the nature of an interregnum, a prolonged moment of interrogation and re-adjustment in thought from where the writer may emerge with renewed belief and reaffirmation of his earlier commitments; which in its turn will mould his narrative choices. The other, more dismal possibility is also there. Ghosh in his mood of pessimism may let down his defences and seek integration with the literary imagination of High Modernism. He could become yet another illustrious member, among the ranks of the Ideologs of Immigration with post-Modernist persuasions. The problem of choosing would be overcome by elaborating at length of the redundancy of choice and impossibility of stable belonging. The ideologies of High Modernism which insist that there is nothing outside the fabrication of power and therefore nothing to choose between alternative systems of power, can come convenient in explaining away the present imbroglio-situated in history, into the ontological condition of being, and permanently bestow upon the world a profound and bleak sense of human entrapment. Then, there would be nothing left except to submit himself to the interminable whisperings of discourse, mysterious both in origin and fate.

The list of Ghosh's enthusiasts and admirers, this writer included, would like to believe that the scales are evenly held in balance. Against the ominous signals given by the latest work, they would place their belief in the writer who made explicit his narrative and political choices and wrote sensitive masterpieces one after the other, imbued with his sincere humanist outlook and concern for real life and real people. The rest would be crystal gazing. We can at best wait; with fingers crossed and bated breath.

Quest and Subversion: The Empire Strikes Back in *The Calcutta Chromosome*

URBASHI BARAT

In an introductory note to *Passenger to Frankfurt*, Agatha Christie explains her choice of the thriller format for this novel as her response to the realities of the time. The fears, the suspense and the dangers of the thriller, remote from the even tenor of everyday life though they may seem, are in fact an appropriate metaphor for the contemporary human situation. Thus, her story may be 'in essence a fantasy,' which is all 'it pretends to be.' "But most of the things that happen in it are happening, or giving promise of happening, in the world of today. It is not an impossible story—it is only a fantastic one."[1]

Christie's comment about *Passenger to Frankfurt* might have been made about Amitav Ghosh's much later novel *The Calcutta Chromosome.*[2] The two novels, Christie's and Ghosh's, stand at very different levels of achievement and project very different views of life, but like all thrillers they both suggest that the contemporary world can best be understood through the objective correlative of bizarre incidents and unexpected turns of action. For this is a world in which there is no safety or security, not even in the most commonplace situations; everything contains the seeds of terror, everything is subject to sudden change. As Graham Greene once explained why he wrote thrillers, "It sometimes seems as though our whole planet had swung into the fog belt of melodrama," and to write truthfully about this planet is inevitably to write a thriller,[3] with all its apparently incredible action and simplistic characterization.

When Amitav Ghosh turns to the thriller for the first time in *The Calcutta Chromosome,* then, he is not merely trying his hand at something new, he is making a social and philosophical statement through his choice of form itself, which posits danger and destabilization of existing modes of thought and belief as the essence of living. The thriller captures more swiftly and accurately the chaos and the violence of everyday life than any other form of fiction, and relates them more clearly to the inner realities of human existence through its ubiquitous pursuit-motif, its archetypal and symbolic *l'homme traqué*, its mysteries and brutalities that lie beyond rational explanation and categorization. Where the detective-story, with which it has so much in common, is an intellectual puzzle to be solved by the dispassionate detective, who stands outside the action, the appeal of the thriller is not cerebral but instinctive and elemental, and its characters, whether hunter or hunted, have their very existence at stake at every moment. Indeed, everyone and everything in the thriller must be interlinked; no-one can stand apart and remain an observer, but has to become part of the quest in a world in which there are more things than are dreamed of in your philosophy. Ghosh's choice of the thriller pattern for his novel becomes especially interesting when it is seen as an ironic take-off on the way in which stories of medical and scientific discoveries and inventions are popularized in children's books, science-fiction tales, *Reader's Digest* and the like as whodunits and chases. Where these celebrate cerebration and dissemination—*science* is knowledge—*The Calcutta Chromosome* puts forward the paradox that life finds sustenance through 'counter-science,' through secrecy and silence and rejection of rationality.

Anyone who has read *Passenger to Frankfurt* will immediately recall it when s/he goes through *The Calcutta Chromosome*; sometimes, in fact, Ghosh seems to be deliberately parodying its conventions and assumptions. Both novels open and unfold in similar ways, with the action triggered off accidentally—or so it seems on the surface—and extends into the past, encircles the present and reaches out into the future, until the underlying conspiracy behind each mystery, each incident, is revealed and the matter resolved each in its own fashion. Both novels mingle fact and fiction, hammering their narrative intensity out of journalist materials and documentary data and setting their action in a wide arena that encompasses East and West, carefully and realistically etching out the background, with local colour and colloquial dialogue to establish immediate credibility[4]: indeed, Ghosh's novel sometimes even reads like a *roman à clef*. Both novels are based on science and refer to medical discoveries that changed the nature of human life, in both a woman lies at the centre of the mystery, which in both is unravelled mainly at the centre rather than at the end.

Both novels, furthermore, make considerable use of the film techniques of crosscut and dissolve so popular in the thriller. *The Calcutta Chromosome* is in fact structured entirely on these two devices. They have always formed Ghosh's favourite narrative method, from *The Circle of Reason* onwards, employed in order to convey the sense of the interpenetration of past and present and all time and all space. But in *The*

Calcutta Chromosome they do more. Meenakshi Mukherjee points out that time and space are so deliberately jumbled in the novel that the "discontinuity itself becomes meaningful."[5] The constant cuts and displacements contribute to the fear and suspense, to the feeling of inexorability, so integral to the thriller; the constant shifts in points of view and time-sequence erase the boundaries between hunter and hunted and make them equally part of the same mystery, the same conspiracy, the same quest; the constant juxtaposition of different times, places, characters and kinds of pursuit extend the scope of each from the specific and the particular to the universal. The deliberate rejection of the conventional narrative line of the thriller here, moreover, indicates both its greater complexity of scope and meaning and its rejection of the world of this characteristically Western genre. The traditional thriller or detective-story moves through a well-worn pattern of discovery of the crime or statement of the problem and builds up the chase through clues, ratiocination and climactic action finally to unravel the mystery and sort out the problem. *The Calcutta Chromosome*, however, only plays with this movement even as it seems to follow it, so that the apparently climactic moments are not really the turning-points in the quest at all, and the various strands or quests really part of the one great quest for life itself; the mystery must continue and there is no final solution. The novel may come to an end but not its story. Because Ghosh is a fabulist rather than a raconteur, his thriller is effectively a quest-narrative that even in its structure challenges some of the fundamental concepts of the Western philosophical, historical and literary traditions. The colonial world examined in a post-colonial setting turns conventional assumptions about itself, about history and science, inside out and upside down. Ghosh uses the thriller form, in other words, only to subvert it.

The novel begins some time in the early twenty-first century, when Antar, an Egyptian computer programmer and systems analyst in New York, suddenly finds the ID card of an old colleague flashed on his computer screen. As he recalls the name of its owner, he is aroused by something more than ordinary curiosity, and begins his search for L. Murugan, who, he finds he had noted himself in a file, had suddenly disappeared from Calcutta on 21 August 1995, one day after he had reached the city, which was, coincidentally, perhaps, but appropriately, called World Mosquito Day. Murugan was a man obsessed with the early history of malaria research, and especially with the career of Ronald Ross, who had won the Nobel Prize for his discovery in India of the life-cycle of the malaria parasite. Murugan's own conviction was that there was some "Other Mind," some person or persons who had guided Ross towards his discoveries and away from other avenues of thought. (31) After all, records show that Ross had never been academically inclined or research-oriented, and had started on his quest for the malaria vector only after Dr. Patrick Manson had urged him to test his [Manson's] ideas about how the world's oldest and most widespread disease is transmitted. All Ross's discoveries were in fact serendipitous, and were always made, by a strange coincidence, only when Lutchman, a helpful 'dhooley-bearer,' was present. The inevitable conclusion, believed Murugan, was that Ross 'thinks he's doing experiments on the malaria parasite. And all the time it's he who *is* the experiment' (67) conducted by poor illiterate natives of a colonized country—a reversal of conventional wisdom about scientific thought and progress and an ironic glance at the popular Western images of Oriental inscrutability and menace in Fu Manchu and his ilk. Note, too, the subversive demolition of science, scientific jargon and scientific argument (and the tongue-in-cheek humour) when Murugan earnestly attempts to explain the relationship between science and counter-science by an analogy with matter and anti-matter—and rooms and ante-rooms.

Murugan's brash ways and his single-minded pursuit of his subversive hypothesis had alienated him from the scientific community and had caused concern among his friends and colleagues. But he had managed to persuade his employers to let him go to Calcutta, the place of his own birth and childhood as well as of Ross's discovery, in order to pursue the truth. The quests that belong to different times and places and which are motivated so differently are thus juxtaposed from the beginning itself: Antar's for Murugan, Murugan's for the truth behind Ross's research, which too was just as much a quest as Antar's and Murugan's quests are research. Indeed, all the characters in the novel, unalike as they are, are entangled through their individual quests and connected in other devious and subterranean ways with one another and with the one greater quest of all life, for immortality: hence the device of the story-within-a-story and the quest-within-a-quest. The most striking characteristic of these inextricably interlinked characters is, paradoxically, their alienation from their immediate surroundings; for any quest to succeed, it seems that the hunter must be free from the bondage of conventional social relationships and must survive poverty, disease, exploitation, marginalization, anything and everything that might weigh down the human spirit. Thus, Antar is a Coptic Christian from Egypt in New York, orphaned early and a childless widower, working alone from home; Murugan is obviously a South Indian Hindu born and brought up in Calcutta and—in a sly glance at the common colonial habit of anglicising Indian names—calling himself Morgan; he is a divorcé and another lonely researcher with Life Watch. Is there also a satiric echo in his slangy speech of the brash Indianization of the English spoken by Quick-Gun Murugan of popular television? For Murugan seems to out-American the Americans in his breezy speech-patterns, so that the Empire strikes back, again, through him.

Urmila Roy and Sonali Das may be Bengali Hindus in Calcutta, one a reporter searching for the meaning of Phulboni's 'Laakhan' stories and the other an actress and writer, but Urmila is an outsider even at home, used and exploited there, and Sonali's parentage and lifestyle are anything but conventional; the revelation of the identity of her father at the end of the novel—thriller-fashion—makes her own participation in the conspiracy inevitable. Phulboni is a Bengali Muslim born in Orissa, and a writer; as such, there is considerable irony in making him a devotee of the Mistress of Silence. There is, moreover, no cultural divide on the basis of—witness, for example, Kazi Nazrul Islam's *Shyama-Sangeet*—religion alone among Bengalis, but Westerners prefer to believe in stereotypes; the character of Phulboni becomes thus an attack on colonial attitudes.

Then there are the foreigners, such as Mrs. Aratounian, an Armenian Christian, erstwhile owner of a nursery shop and later of the guest house near Ross's house in Calcutta, in which Murugan puts up; historical figures such as Ross, Grigson and Cunningham, Englishmen engaged in their own kinds of quests, and the American Farley, who wants to find out more about Cunningham's research and meets such a mysterious end at Renupur station, where Phulboni manages to survive a similar experience; and the Finnish spiritualist Madame Liisa Salminen of Madras, whom C.C. Dunn/D.D. Cunningham visits and with whom he shares an apparently supernatural experience. Mme. Salminen had, moreover, been the inspiring spirit behind the Polish Countess Pongrácz's pioneering archaeological work in Asia and Egypt—where she had met and similarly influenced the young Antar—and her study of the teachings of Valentinus, the ancient Alexandrian philosopher, for whom the Abyss and the Silence were the greatest deities. The foreigners embody the continuing interest of the West in the spiritual quest of the East; the colonized world asserts its superiority over its colonizers in what is their greatest pride and professed weapon, matters of the intellect.

The links between these apparently disparate people are carefully made, so that by the end of the novel the vastness, the all-inclusiveness, of the conspiracy is established and becomes a sign of the reality of its existence, and the fantastic, as Christie had remarked in *Passenger to Frankfurt*, is no impossibility. As in the typical thriller, clues and hints abound, embedded in the text, every detail, however incidental and peripheral it might seem at first, being significant, so that everyone and everything seems caught up in one monstrous design, and even the colonial exxperience becomes part of the pattern, and hunter and hunted become one. In the silence and the secrecy of the search for immortality there is no baying of the Hounds of Heaven; every step forward leads the characters back into the past and then to the future, further and further into the abyss of mystery and incomprehension, until they realize that they have been enmeshed in the great web long before they knew it.

Thus, for example, Antar and Murugan are both expatriates in New York, working at different kinds of research for the same organization; their countries were both once colonized by the same imperialist power, and their home now is another, and the greatest, imperialist power. While Antar has had malaria, Murugan has had syphilis, which used to be cured by the introduction of the malaria parasite into the system—which is the object of Ross's search and the subject of Murugan's own. If Antar hunts for Murugan, Murugan too hunts Antar; as it turns out, the lost ID card that turned up on Antar's computer screen was no accident but a carefully planned operation that brings Antar, too, into the web of conspiracy. This is the pattern that repeats itself in every quest. The connection between each is revealed in an exchange between Antar and Murugan in a New York restaurant, for what they say here recurs in many guises throughout the novel:

> 'Tell me Ant,' Murugan said, fixing his piercing gaze upon Antar's face. 'Tell me: do you think it's natural to want to turn the page, to be curious about what happened next?'
>
> 'Well,' said Antar, uncomfortably. 'I'm not sure if I know what you mean.'
>
> 'Let me put it like this then,' said Murugan. 'Do you think that everything that can be known, should be known?'
>
> 'Of course,' said Antar. 'I don't see why not.'
>
> 'All right,' said Murugan . . . 'I'll turn a few pages for you: but remember, it was you who asked. It's your funeral.' (50)

Note the aptness of the flippant remark at the end, and especially in a novel that challenges conventional Western notions about knowledge, death, immortality and reincarnation.

It also strikes at popular Western notions about literary creativity, beginning with its subversive attack on the logocentrism derided also by twentieth-century deconstructionists. If secrecy is the 'first principle of a functioning counter-science,' communication, or putting ideas into language, is, as Murugan explains, establishing 'a claim to *know*—which is the first thing that a counter-science would dispute.' Knowledge in the conventional, Western, sense is impossible, for 'to know something is to change it, therefore in knowing something, you've already changed what you think you know so you don't really know it at all: you only know it's [sic] history.' (88) Phulboni, a great writer himself, quite emphatically rejects the common belief that words can communicate experience or truth or help to discover the meaning of life when he suggests that 'the Word is to this silence what the shadow is to the foreshadowed, what the veil is to the eyes, what the mind is to truth, what language is to life.' (24) That is why he has always wondered: "Does a story come to be in the words that conjure out of my mind or does it live already, somewhere, enshrined in mud and clay—in an image, that is, in the crafted mimicry of life?" (189) He had once written a fictional tale about a drowning woman being saved by a small polished grey stone with a small white mark on it that made it look like an eye; and many years later, to his astonishment, he had discovered a similar image being worshipped in a small shrine and was also told a true story about a drowning woman identical to the one he had thought he had only imagined so long ago. (190) So which is more true, fiction or fact, and which comes earlier? And what is the nature and the value of mimetic representation? Phulboni's views, born of experience, add a new insight into the old Western controversy, summed up by Plato's, Aristotle's and Plotinus's arguments.

Behind all the characters and all the varieties of quest is the elusive unseen presence, whom Phulboni acknowledges as his Muse and his spiritual guide, (27) and who is imaged in clay as Mangala-bibi the goddess and worshipped in secret by only those who are part of her continuing quest for an immortality achieved not through death and entry into the after-life but through the transference of the Calcutta chromosome through the 'fevers, delirium and discovery' transmitted by the malaria parasite. Mangala is the woman who works in Cunningham's laboratory, whom Farley antagonizes; but then Farley unaccountably disappears. She adopts different forms and personae as she crosses over from one body to another through the years; she is Mrs. Aratounian in Murugan's Calcutta and she becomes Urmila, though the latter does not realize that she has been chosen to receive her, Murugan discovering the secret the day he, too, disappears; and she becomes Tara in New York, helping Antar to cross over as well. Murugan might now live in a shelter run by the Department of Alternative Inner States—the twenty-first-century Newspeak equivalent of an asylum—but he seems to know what he is saying and doing, and his condition questions the meaning and nature of madness in Western terms and its relation to knowledge, truth and expression.

Assisting Mangala is Lutchman/Lachman/Laxman/Laakhan/Lokkhon, appropriately named after Rama's brother in the *Ramayana*, and as historical a figure as Mangala, Ross, Farley, Grigson or Cunningham, and so another mark of the blend of fact and fiction that distinguishes both the method and the meaning of the novel. The variations on his name as he appears and reappears through the novel form again an ironic comment on the paradoxical relationship between language and reality and on Western notions of scholarship as exemplified in Grigson's linguistic research. Like Mangala, he adopts different personae through the ages, appearing even in Phulboni's fiction, and he continues her hunt in various ways. He guides Ross to his discoveries, he frightens away Grigson, who might have posed a threat to Mangala-bibi's experiments, he manages to dispose of Farley, he is with Phulboni at Renupur station from where Farley had disappeared, he is Sonali's servant and Urmila's fishmonger, and appears in Antar's life in New York as well. Who is the protagonist of the novel, then? Is it Antar, or Murugan, or Urmila, or Laakhan, or Mangala? The two-part division of the novel, that suggests that its action takes place over two days, might indicate that it is Murugan, or, because it begins and ends with him, Antar; but just as the contents of the two parts spill over into one another and include more than one day and one centre of consciousness, so that the division is effectively misleading, so also there can be no one definitive protagonist. Indeed, the common Western notions of protagonist, of character development, and of good and evil have disappeared here, so that *The Calcutta Chromosome* suggests the superficiality and inadequacy of these ideas as its projects the validity of traditional Indian literary norms, summed up by R.K. Narayan in 'The World of the Story-Teller' as follows:

> Everything is interrelated. Stories, scriptures, ethics, philosophy, grammar, astrology, astronomy, semantics, mysticism, and moral codes—each forms part and parcel of a total life and is indispensable for the attainment of a four-square understanding of existence.
>
> The characters in the epics are prototypes and moulds in which humanity is cast, and remain valid for all times.

Consequently, the story is 'part of human history rather than fiction,' and 'the curtain never comes down *finally*' [6] in any narrative.

Contrast this with *Passenger to Frankfurt* which reflets the quintessential imperialist/colonial complacency and certainty about the rightness of its view of life. That is why it ends cosily on a domestic scene of preparation for the protagonist's wedding and with the restoration of the normality of everyday life. Only the quest of the scientist remains, and it is a goal he will soon achieve, for he merely needs to revive and go over what he has already done earlier. As the financier tells him, 'knowledge is knowledge. What you have given birth to—what you have made come to life, you should not destroy.' (185) *The Calcutta Chromosome*, however, ends very differently. There is no such thing as normality, and the conspiracy does not end: those who attempt to destroy it are themselves destroyed. The spies of *Passenger to Frankfurt* are killed, arrested or imprisoned, but those of Ghosh's novel only spread out their tentacles and their area of action, 'like ripples expanding concentrically,' as Narayan puts it.[7] After all, the quest is not for a drug that will induce universal benevolence but for the renewal of life itself. There can, accordingly, be no comforting rounding-off, but rather only a step further towards the realms of the non-rational and the ineffable—realms that are accessible especially to the poor, the marginalized, the colonized, the survivor. There are no simplistic statements about human nature; there is, instead, the belief in the infinite possibility of the transcendence of human limitations and human mortality. That is why the conspiracy never ends; the cult of Silence and secrecy spreads to territories governed by the Word and reason. Western knowledge and science had once conquered the East, but inevitably the Empire must strike back. Through its subversive quest, *The Calcutta Chromosome* celebrates the eternal, celebrates the triumph of the spirit over all that bogs it down in the mire.

NOTES

1. (Glasgow: Fontana/Collins, 1982), p. 9.
2. Amitav Ghosh, *The Calcutta Chromosome: A Novel of Fevers, Delirium and Discovery* (Delhi: Ravi Dayal, 1996).
3. Graham Greene, "The Catholic Temper in Poland," *Atlantic Monthly*, March 1956, p. 39.
4. Amitav Ghosh's re-creation of the ambience of the Calcutta of the 1990s is remarkably accurate, and his ability to reproduce Bengali idiom in English without sounding exotic or forced is refreshing. The occasional misprint of names and places, therefore, unnecessarily hurts the ear; perhaps more careful proof-reading would be advisable.
5. Meenakshi Mukherjee, "Spine Chiller," *India Today*, May 15, 1996, p. 163.
6. R.K. Narayan, "The World of the Story-Teller," *A Story-Teller's World* (New Delhi: Penguin, 1990), p. 5.
7. *Ibid.*, p. 7.

The Continuity of Life, Mission and Mystery in *The Calcutta Chromosome*

MADHUMALATI ADHIKARI

It would be too facile to contemplate that Amitav Ghosh in *The Calcutta Chromosome* has attempted to inscribe a simple scientific thriller on the fever, delirium and discovery of the malarial parasite. More appropriate it would be to recognize that he has contrived to introduce a maze of ideas criss-crossing each other to project the profound meaning and mystery of life through a visibly insignificant facade of a 'spine-chiller' that negates the rational view of science and the universe. To excavate the treasure of concepts one must 'read the novel a second time'[1] and also read between the lines. The intricate relationship of time, place and characters, often mind-boggling, propels the reader to embark on a journey of an uncircumscribed domain of the past, present and future. Initially, the thematic originality and complexity bewilders the reader but a close scrutiny discloses that like his earlier novels, *The Circle of Reason* (1986), *The Shadow Lines* (1988) and *In an Antique Land* (1993), Ghosh in *The Calcutta Chromosome* (1996) has universalized the specific through the concept of quest and journey. The notion of delirium, fever and discovery superficially associated with malaria is extended to the meaning of life having identical symbolic and symptomatic significance.

Amitav Ghosh's novels, a discourse on human quest, project characters engaged in individual search for truth, self-identity and self-knowledge. The spiritual and corporeal exploration, the promise of alternative worlds and visions, invariably compel them to shuffle between different geographic locations and points of time. The personal odyssey takes shape through individual memory and recollections of others. In *The Circle of Reason*, the progress is carried on through the stages of *Sattva, Rajas* and *Tamas*, and finally the circle is completed by a return to *Sattva* or Reason; in *The Shadow Lines* one moves through the bomb-scarred London, riot-torn Calcutta and Bangladesh to view the outside world that affects the inside world and to learn the true value of man; the story of education and journey continues in a different ensemble in *In an Antique Land.* To Ghosh journey is a metaphor and symbol of life that man must undertake in search of truth and fulfilment.

I

The verbal felicity of the engrossing novel *The Calcutta Chromosome*, moves with a rapid pace and often makes one forgetful of the vacillation of time and place that separates and yet cements the major characters of the novel: Ronald Ross a British scientist in Calcutta (1895-99), Murugan a Calcutta born researcher working in New York and Calcutta (1990-95) and Antar the Egyptian computer clerk in New York (1970-early twenty-first century). The constant shifting between three points of time—past, present and future—common in cinematic technique, enables one to visualize a sequence and a simultaneity in action that in turn blends the theoretical conjectures of fact and fantasy. The willing suspension of disbelief resolves and dissolves the differences between perception and imagination. The co-mingling of realism with romanticism demonstrates the extraordinary but eternal continuity of life.

The bane and the most challenging problems of mortal existence lie in human isolation. Man's knowledge of being an island is painful and yet, Amitav Ghosh suggests that despite this inevitability there is happiness, security and companionship if sought sincerely. The continuity of life exists in the pattern of fission and fusion. Antar, a widower leads a solitary life in his apartment with shadow-like neighbours. Ava the computer is his sole companion and is linked with the other individuals of this scientific world through his machine; Murugan a divorcé has no companions, only some acquaintances like Antar, Urmila, Sonali, Mrs. Aratounian; Urmila theoretically has a family but practically she is an alien to be exploited; Sonali the illegitimate child of Puhlboni and an actress lives all by herself; Mrs Aratounian does not seem to have any family or close friends; Phulboni the writer is also a loner, often seen walking the Calcutta streets companionless; Laakhan and Mangala are above their community to be revered but not to be accepted as a close associate; Ronald Ross the scientist has a family in the background but in the world of research he too is emotionally estranged from all other co-creatures and yet the novel closes with a word of consolation for the frightened and lonesome Antar, coming from an assemblage of people. He can feel their presence in his room in New York, "They were saying 'We're with you; you are not alone; we'll help you across.' He sat back and sighed *as he hadn't sighed in years.*"[2] (256, emphasis added) The sigh of relief confirms his return to a state of wholeness, happiness and friendship. Initially, the fragmentation of human association is highlighted and a nominal kinship is established either through Malaria or Syphilis connoting a diseased human correlation. But the final impression as already mentioned, is of a closely bonded community.

The story revolves around the idea of 'matter and anti-matter,' 'science and counter-science. . . . The first principle of a functioning counter-science is secrecy.' (88) The central actor in the drama is not Ross but Murugan or Morgan who narrates, interacts and interprets a significant section of the adventures. It is vital to discover that Murugan is the other name of Kartik, the son of Goddess Durga, reputed for swift movement in Indian mythology. Mangala's resurrection through different female forms as the representative of the great mother Kali, the archetypal nurturer and the 'terrible mother figure,' is implicitly stated. The unobtrusive manoeuvering by Mangala as the emissary of the great mother is subsumed in the search of the figurine in the Kalighat episode by Murugan and Urmila. (188-95) Ghosh employs the Goddess metaphor to insist on the necessity of coming back to life. No Indian reader can overlook the idea that Mangala is one of the names of Goddess Kali. Ghosh in fact, re-formulates the old myth.

Murugan for the sake of convenience, often introduces himself as Morgan (a sea-dweller) to his non-Indian acquaintances. Not accidentally but deliberately, Ghosh gives him an alternate name to signify his proficiency in diving deep into the mysteries of life. His specific presence as the prime seeker of truth demands our consistent attention.

The history of malarial research is unfolded through a compressed or extended, circular or repetitive movement of incidents, contextually different, to allow a zigzag motion through 'reality' and 'fiction' that can be apprehended only by an appropriate 'reading process.'[3] This quality of metafiction permits Ghosh to experiment with vision-mixing: the hard realistic and detailed picture of Robinson Street, Calcutta, suddenly dissolves into the mysterious world of Laakhan and Mangala (134-40); Sonali becomes a witness to a metaphysical 'interpersonal transference' (90) of Laakhan's spirit into the body of Romen Haldar with the help of Mangala's words, 'The time is here, pray that all goes well for our Laakhan, *once again*.' (140, emphasis added) Here, Ghosh introduces a belief system that accepts interpersonal transference as a regular affair. Life's continuity is maintained through this mysterious process. Much later, we are informed that the entire show was conducted not by Mangala but Mrs. Aratounian, another beneficiary of the system. Ghosh often employs the technique of suspended action to intensify the mystery and also to convey the feeling of simultaneity. Discontinuity of time and space becomes meaningful[4] and ultimately offers contemporary relevance.

The world and life of matter projected through Ronald Ross, Antar and Murugan is juxtaposed with another super-terrestrial world and life of anti-matter represented through Laakhan, Mangala and their emissaries in succeeding generations. Despite the weird and bizarre atmosphere accentuated by inhuman rites with human bodies and decapacitated birds, the novel closes with an epiphanic recognition of life's continuity and the spirit of fraternity. In *The Circle of Reason*, Ghosh through Mrs. Verma communicates a comparable message: 'If there's one thing people learn from the past, it is that every consummated death is another beginning.'[5]

II

The novel documents a series of interrelated moments wherein each character feverishly attempts to reach the core of his quest, his mission: Antar the Egyptian computer clerk, sometime in the early 21st century, struggles to trace the adventures and diappearance of L. Murugan; Murugan's search is centred around the missing links of malaria research conducted by Ross between 1895-99; Ross becomes a symbol of scientific research that happily culminates in a discovery; Urmila's 'little research' (93) on Phulboni and his fictional character Laakhan guides her to reach the eye of a greater mystery; Sonali's quest for Romen Haldar ceases with the unveiling of Laakhan's mystery (241); Grigson's exploratory mission to establish Lutchman/Laakhan's true identity remains unaccomplished as he realizes that the knowledge would endanger his life (80); Farley's discovery of Mangala-Lutchman mystery remains buried as he disappears in a 'rarely used station; Renupur' (129); Mangala and her subordinate Laakhan's search for 'immortality' (90) is rewarded though its continuity is suggested; Mangala's experiments with counter-science through the principles of 'silence and secrecy' (177) practised in India and Egypt, is of course, the primary quest presented in the novel. Mangala's mission meticulously manipulates other quests and characters. The mysterious progress of her experiment negates all 'direct communication' (90) of the discovery. The truth has to be discovered by someone totally unrelated with the exercise. Ultimately Urmila becomes the chosen person. Murugan enlightens her, 'Don't you see?' he said. 'You're the one she's chosen.' (254) Having performed her role successfully Mrs. Aratounian moves towards her final destination, Renupur. Urmila takes on the role of Mangala and Mrs. Aratounian. The fictional reincarnation reflects the Goddess myth. Despite the story of the complex quest one gets the feeling that all the characters are controlled by the spirit of the Great Goddess, the archetypal mother revered by all forms of life. The chain reaction initiated by Mangala is continued by Mrs. Aratounian and then Urmila, a never ending process. For once Ghosh has assigned a superior role to women. The sustained note heard through the allegory insists the presence of a secret spirit that acts through different chosen people to unravel the mystery: disease and its cure, problem and its solution. It is congenially tuned to man's betterment. The message of Indian philosophy pertaining to the eternal human quest has been woven into the fabric of the novel by Ghosh.

III

All performers are explorers of some mystery; consciously or unconsciously, they move towards a preordained direction of truth. The interest of the novel, however, lies neither in the mystery and discovery of a scientific truth nor in the ancient confrontation between good and evil but in the hidden signs that powerfully evoke the superiority of one particular culture. The novel suggests the conflicts, the problems but not all the solutions. Despite the eerie atmosphere, one must avoid labelling Laakhan and Mangala as dangerous elements. They do not represent evil. Persons like Farley or the upper-caste station master of Renupur or Countess Pongracz disappear in a perplexing manner because they are out to interfere with the mysterious life of the central characters, Laakhan and Mangala. Ghosh enigmatically suggests that the repositories of truth and higher knowledge can be a dhooley bearer and a sweeper woman. He demolishes the ancient myth of inter-dependence between class superiority and a right to knowledge. Becuase of this radical social view, the offensive station master is annihilated either by Laakhan or the guardian supervisor of secret knowledge for opposing Laakhan/knowledge. Twice in the course of the novel, Laakhan is portrayed as a lantern bearer or metaphorically, a knowledge carrier. (80, 229) Phulboni's adventures of Renupur dissolve the boundaries between the real and the unreal. It is difficult to ascertain the veracity of the encounter and yet, the authentic ambience of the entire drama is accepted by the Hindus (Murugan, Sonali, Urmila), Muslims (Saiyad Murad Hussain alias Phulboni and Antar) and Christians (Mrs. Aratounian and Countess Pongracz). In fact, Ghosh universalizes the theory of transmigration of souls and the right to knowledge irrespective of class, creed and cultural separation. Ross endeavours to solve the mystery of malaria through reason or science (45); Mangala attempts to find a cure for syphilitic paresis through counter-science or faith. (204) The author seems to conform with the Indian philosophical thought that emphasizes the realization of True Knowledge/Being either through *Tarka*—analysis and reason—or *Bhakti*—faith and devotion. Ross is the leader of the former method while Mangala and Laakhan are of the latter.

The mystery of the novel accentuated by the use of Magic Realism dissolves the boundaries between the physical and spiritual truths and explores the possibilities of existence of various levels of consciousness. The power of folk medicine acquired through trial and error and practised by Mangala is ratified by Ghosh. The rustic infiltration into the world of knowledge to control 'the ultimate transcendence of Nature,' (90) is an endeavour to improve the theory of migration of soul. According to Indian faith, human soul migrates from one body to another but the movement is controlled by a superpower. Mangala, a human, attempts to carry out the same exercise on her own, 'because she thinks she's a god and what that means is that she wants to be the mind that sets the thing in motion. The child in the Kalighat episode informs Urmila, 'Today is the last day of puja of Mangala-bibi. Baba says that tonight Mangala-bibi is going to enter a new body.' (194) This conscious exercise surely grants greater power to man. The author draws upon the Indian myth of Ganesha (206) to explain the theory of 'transposition of personality.' (206) Thus in the novel, the ancient and yet a probable theory has been applied. Here, we not only have a balance commingling of hard scientific facts with folklore, Valentinal philosophy of Abyss and Silence, spiritualism of the Theosophical Society, Hinduism and the faith of Coptic Christians but also a covert suggestion of Indian supremacy in the world of knowledge and science. The frequent indication of successful research on malaria and syphilitic paresis cannot be ignored. Amitav Ghosh as a novelist dominates over the social anthropologist. His fictional universe is a microcosm of the real universe ordained, controlled and guided by the Spirit (female in nature), that nurtures and destroys, symbolized by the clay doll, a figurine with painted eyes, a pigeon on one side and microscope in the other hand. (37) In fact, this is not a 'mystery thriller'[6] but a philosophical novel to entertain all and enlighten a few. Like Milkman of Toni Morrison's *Song of Solomon*, we come to 'realize that only by knowing the past can [we] hope to have a future.'[7] *The Calcutta Chromosome*, literally and figuratively rekindles our awareness of the rich Indian heritage to make our future progress inevitable.

NOTES

1. Meenakshi Mukherjee, "Spine Chiller," *India Today*, 15 May 1996, p. 163.
2. Amitav Ghosh, *The Calcutta Chromosome* (Delhi: Ravi Dayal Publisher, 1996).
3. Patricia Waugh, *Metafiction: The Theory and Practice of Self-Conscious Fiction* (London: Methuen, 1984), p. 16.
4. Mukherjee, p. 163.
5. Amitav Ghosh, *The Circle of Reason* (London: Hamish Hamilton, 1986), p. 414.
6. Mukherjee, p. 163.
7. Toni Morrison, *Song of Solomon* (New York: Knopf, 1977), p. 93.

Disappearances and Discovery: A Study of *The Calcutta Chromosome*

INDIRA BHATT

"Malaria strikes back' scream the headlines in newspapers, periodicals, scientific journals. Teams of research-journalists re-record the details from the past—the historical facts about malaria and the scientist Sir Ronald Ross who was awarded the Nobel Prize for his findings on malarial fever. This sets off the creative artist into the jungle of science-laboratories, scientific vocabulary, the methods of investigation and the scientists. Amitav Ghosh in his novel *The Calcutta Chromosome*[1] takes up this issue of the malarial fever colouring it with mysticism and mystery, supernatural and superstition, calling it the theory of science and counter-science:

> "Let me put it like this," Murugan said. "You know all about matter and anti-matter, right? And rooms and anterooms and Christ and anti-Christ and so on? . . . Now let's say there was something like science and counter-science? Thinking of it in the abstract, wouldn't you say that the first principle of a functioning counter-science would have to be secrecy? The way I see it, wouldn't just have to be secretive about *what* it did (it couldn't hope to beat the scientists at the game anyway); it would have to be secretive *in* what it did. It would also have to use secrecy as a technique of procedure. It would in principle have to refuse all direct communication, straight off the bat, because to communicate, to put ideas into language would be to establish a claim to *know*—which is the first thing that a counter-science would dispute." (88)

Murugan further explains:

> Not making sense is what it's about, conventional sense that is. Maybe this other team started with the ideas that knowledge is self-contradictory, maybe they believed that to know something is

> to change it, therefore in knowing something, you've already changed what you think you know so you don't really know it at all: You only know its history. Maybe they thought that knowledge couldn't begin without acknowledging the impossibility of knowledge. (88)

Thus he arrives at the working hypotheses: "If it's true that to know something is to change it, then it follows that one way of changing something—of effecting a mutation, let's say—is to attempt to know it or aspect of it." (88) With this Amitav Ghosh emphasizes secrecy, mystery and self-contradictory knowledge and confronts what he calls conventional science with the ingenious knowledge and method of the uneducated Indians. This paper attempts to examine how this theory of science and counter-science is presented and with what purpose.

It is Murugan the Indian scientist working in New York's Life-Watch, an expert on Ronald Ross and malarial fever who narrates the story to Antar the Egyptian technologist working alone from his flat in New York with his computer Ava as per the instructions of his employer, the International Water Council. Murugan and his story are screened, shown to Antar who has simply to push some buttons and Ava goes hunting all the details about Murugan, his movements, his ideas, his beliefs, his suppositions and inferences. This happens cinematographically, Antar watching sort of a film as we do, so often on TV screen. Only this is the twenty-first century and the method and manner of the show is quite different. The novel opens sometime in early twenty-first century in Antar's flat in New York with the appearance of an ID card on Ava's screen which tripped her system and she wouldn't stop till she found out all about the subject: Like why? What? When? Where? How? She has some sort of a simulated urge for self-improvement. Ghosh describes this system of the future minutely: "Anything she didn't recognize she'd take apart on-screen, producing microscopic structural analyses, spinning the images around and around, tumbling them over, resting them on their side, producing ever greater refinements of details," (3-4) and further he clarifies that "she had been programmed to hunt out *real-time* information, and that was what she was determined to get. Once she'd wrung the last, meaningless detail out of him, she'd give the object on her screen, final spin, with a bizarrely human smugness, before propelling it into the horizonless limbo of her memory." (4)

This sets the tone of the novel and provides explanations of all sorts of details made known to Antar (and to the reader) surmised and inferred by Murugan, about the events that happened in 1995 in Calcutta as also some hundred years ago in Calcutta and Hyderabad. Ghosh has used this device of computer-system of the future, like H.G. Wells' Time-machine, to move in time-past, recent past and present for Antar. For the reader it is past—the last decade of the nineteenth century, the present days of August 1995 and the future sometime in early part of the twenty-first century. He has manipulated the time-span, as Malcolm Bradbury explains: "an exploitation of relation between antecedent and present, between the time-span, of what is told and the time it takes to tell, between narrated time and narrational time, between matter attended to scenically and in detail and matter scanted or sketched."[2] It takes only a few hours for Antar to watch Murugan's experiences of two days in Calcutta and what Murugan explains of experiments of Ronald Ross and others, a few years of the nineteenth century. It is at three levels of time that the story is revealed to the reader, unfolded as it is through Ava. It also involves a high degree of 'fictional faking' and the novelist tries to create a sense of mystery and a special insight into the oriental sense of spiritualism, belief in birth and rebirth, transposition and transcendence which is no more than a numinously dramatic satisfaction, "a building up of the so-called myth for its own splendid sake."[3]

Against the background of the historical facts of Ronald Ross's discovery about malarial fever, the novelist presents the supernatural power of Mangala, an assistant to D.D. Cunningham. She is portrayed as a gooddess-like figure who has found a so-called cure for siphilis but has also acquired knowledge of transcending life beyond life. The two parallel events are described: Mangala sometime in 1893 performs certain rituals (recorded in a letter by Farley): "What he [Farley] saw was this: the woman Mangala was seated at the far end of the room, on a low divan, but alone and in an attitude of command, as though enthroned. By her side at the far end of the room were several bamboo cages, each containing a pigeon . . . they were all slumped on the floors of their cages, shivering, evidently near death . . . on the floor by the divan, clustered around the woman's feet, were some half-dozen people in various attitudes of supplication, some touching her feet, others lying prostrate. Two or three others were huddled against the wall, wrapped in blankets . . . they were syphilitics, in final stages of the terrible disease." (125-26) Farley the western scientist understands this clearly and wants to warn them not to waste their hopes on "Whatever" quackery it was that the woman offered, to expose the falsehoods that she and her minions had concocted to deceive those simple people. (126) But his curiosity makes him stay where he was, unobserved by Mangala and sit through Mangala's performance of rituals. Finally he returns to his own experiment and demands to see the slides 'the transformations that

Laveran described.' Only after that he is given the slides smeared with the dying pigeon's blood: "it was then that he saw Laveran's rods appear, hundreds of them, tiny cylindrical things, with their pointed penetrating heads piercing the blood miasma." (128) This was to be the future invention of his team-mates. His knowledge proves his doom. He is promised by Mangala through the young boy assistant to reveal everything "if I would but accompany him to his birth place, fortunately the place of which he spoke is not far from the location of my clinic. We are to leave to-morrow." (129) But Elijah Farley never reaches Barich; he disappeared during the journey, never to be seen again. "The police discovered that he had indeed boarded the train at Sealdah, as scheduled but had disembarked before his destination—a remote rarely used station called Renupur, in severe monsoon weather. A guard was said to have reported later that a young man had been seen carrying his luggage." (129) He is denied knowledge. His glimpse into Mangala's knowledge is the cause for his disappearance—death. Even the letter he wrote from which Murugan constructs the story of Farley's and Mangala's encounter, disappears and there is no scientific proof of Farley's knowledge and experiment as also about the existence of the letter. Cleverly the novelist constructs mystery both about Farley's knowledge and his disappearance.

A similar event takes place in 1995. It is Sonali who goes looking for Romen Haldar to the old house at Robinson street which Romen had shown her. Her experience and observation of the rituals are recorded:

> She caught a glimpse of tops of dozens of heads, some male, some female, young and old, packed in close together. Their faces were obscured by the smoke and flickering firelight. . . . Then there was a stir in the crowd and Sonali forced herself to look down again. A figure had come out of the shadows: it was a woman and she was dressed very plainly—in a crispy-starched saree, with a white scarf tied around her hair. Her figure was short and matronly and Sonali took her to be in late middle age . . . she had a cloth bag slung over one shoulder, an ordinary cotton jhola, in her left hand she was carrying a bamboo bird-cage. She seated herself by the fire and placed the bag and the bird-cage beside her. She took out two scalpels and a pair of glass plates. Then she reached out, placed her hands on whatever it was lying before the fire and smiled. Raising her voice, the woman said to the crowd, in archaic rustic Bengali: 'The time is here, pray that all goes well for our Laakhan once again' . . . there was a flash of bright metal and a necklace of blood flew up and fell sizzling on the fire. (139-40)

The body on which the rituals are performed is that of Romen Haldar and the woman is Mrs. Aratounian who does not speak, to Sonali's knowledge, Bengali. Romen Haldar who was to meet Sonali that evening, suddenly and inexplicably disappears. The novelist does not explain his death or what he keeps on calling, disappearance. These two events separated by hundred years adds to the mystification of the plot in the novel. In the case of Farley, it is his knowledge which is to be kept secret that brings about his disappearance—death. In Haldar's case, nothing is mentioned, except that in the Calcutta of 1995 such mysterious rituals are performed in the name of some special knowledge of transcendence. Then there is the mention of a station-master who gets killed at Renupur (where Farley had been killed in 1894) on a moonless Amavasya night possibly in the year 1900, at the hands of a boy called Laakhan. In 1933 or so Phulboni miraculously saves himself from getting killed by the train at Renupur. Way back in 1895 in Secunderabad Grigson had also with great difficulty saved himself from getting killed just like Phulboni in 1933. Both of them were followed by the railway station lantern and could not see who was trying to kill them, though Lutchman and Laakhan are mentioned. Phulboni in his stories mentions Laakhan and the ghost-trains that he himself had seen, the ghost-station-master that he had come across. The characters Lutchman, Laakhan, Lucky of the nineteenth, the twentieth and the twenty-first centuries appear and disappear. Are we to suppose, according to the novelist's theory voiced through the character of Murugan, that they are improvements on their earlier life? There are no such indications in the novel. In fact these characters are not even fully presented three dimensional characters. There is also a hint that the boy who appears at Urmila's doorstep with fish wrapped in papers from which Murugan connects up the story is the same one Laakhan. So it seems. Since in all these incarnations of the boy, the novelist describes one common thing—the boy has a deformed thumb. Even Haldar has this deformity. There is neither a physical improvement, nor the intellectual improvement in all these personalities of the boy.

Through these parallel events, the mystery of the plot gets thicker and denser. When one asks the questions of why and in what direction the events lead to, one feels baffled. A mystery novel would have clues that lead to the solution. Here the novelist has wonderfully and vividly created the mysterious happenings and has attempted to relate them, only to arrive at nothingness. At the end, Ava shows Murugan, Urmila and Sonali rushing to the station Sealdah, where they are told Phulboni and Mrs. Aratounian have gone. This is the place from which Murugan has been recorded as missing, since August 1995 and is not heard of till his ID card appearance on Ava screen. What happens to the rest of them is left to the imagination of the reader. But Sealdah is the station from where Mangala and Laakhan were hired; it is the place that plays vanishing tricks causing most of the characters to disappear. One moment they are all rushing to the station in 1995, with Urmila saying that she would save them and take them across, the next moment we find Antar hearing voices, finding resemblance between Tara and Urmila and Maria and Sonali, talking to him, as if they were all with him in his room, "a voice whispering in his ear, 'keep watching; we're here; we are all with you.'" That is Tara along with the rest of the characters saying, "we'll help you across." (256)

The question is from what he is to be saved and where he has to go across. This mystery with its mysticism remains almost unexplained and unrelated. Ghosh tries to explain this with his theory of counter-science and secrecy thereof, and contradictions of knowledge. He mentions the search for the ultimate transcendence of nature, of immortality: "What I'm really talking about is a technology for interpersonal transference," (90) explaining the failure of the body and migration therefrom. This technology he calls the Calcutta chromosome. The oriental belief of life beyond life, births and rebirths, the novelist attempts to explore. Herein we find the echoes of the *Bhagvad Gita*, about body being a sort of garment to be discarded when it turns old and torn to acquire a new, fresh garment for the soul. The end-result of the application of this theory to the characters in the novel is far from satisfactory. Rushdie-like, Ghosh has picked up the topical issue of the recurrence of the malarial fever, and in the feverish delusion, he has presented a secondary world in space and time, though highly imaginative, yet it very unconvincingly remains unfelt. Sprinkling of metaphysical concepts does not enhance in any way the deeply felt moral or aesthetic convictions. They make the novel readable but do not create an impression of wholeness, of some special perception and experience of the primary world. As Meenakshi Mukherjee remarks: "To prise them out one would have to read the novel a second time."[4] Jaya Banerji consideres it 'far-fetched' and compares it to the grandma's 'Bengali braid,' with the thread of malarial research running through the novel: "If Ghosh ever drew his storyline on a blackboard he would end up with real granny's knot of a plot—each character's life intertwined with the others in some way or the other. As for direction, he proceeds in ever decreasing circles until he comes to the centre which is where he started in the first place."[5]

There are certain passages which are beautiful and vivid especially the Phulboni stories narrated by Urmila and Phulboni's anguished cry for the goddess of silence. Calcutta has been celebrated as the city of joy: portrayed as the voices, and now we have a city craving for the goddess of silence. Is Ghosh too much with too many words: "The word is to silence what the shadow is to the foreshadowed, what the veil is to the eyes, what the mind is to truth, what language is to life." (24) Is it a search for the words of silence? Since the words do not make any sense: "maybe none of this makes sense." (88) Since this is a novel from the author of *The Circle of Reason* (1986) and *The Shadow Lines* (1988), one is tempted to search for the hidden meaning. Instead what we find is something of "an exoticisation of India," to use Meenakshi Mukharjee's words, "How does a writer avoid the allegation of neo-orientalism for such as exoticisation of India?" Against all the inventions and terminology of the new technology, what we find is the characters appearing and disappearing from the screen and life itself without making any impression on the reader's mind as it usually happens with thrillers. Nor do they arrive at any discovery. Shakespeare can best sum up this as "a tale told by an idiot, full of sound and fury, signifying nothing." Is it anything more than "cacoethes scribendi,"[6] disappointing and disillusioning the readers' expectation from Amitav Ghosh?

NOTES

1. (New Delhi: Ravi Dayal, 1996).
2. Malcolm Bradbury, *Possibilities: Essays on the State of the Novel* (London: OUP, 1973).
3. Ann Swinfen, *In Defence of Fantasy* (London: Routledge and Kegan Paul, 1984).
4. Meenakshi Mukherjee, Review in *India Today*, May 15, 1996.
5. Jaya Banerji, Review of *The Calcutta Chromosome* in *Indian Review of Books*, Vol. 5, Number 9 June-July 1996.
6. Editor, *Indian Review of Books*, Vol 5, number 9, June-July, 1996.

History and Anthropology in *The Calcutta Chromosome*

SHYAM S. AGARWALLA

In recent years, we have seen a new genre of writing novel, that of combining the recipes for the novel-about-writing-a-novel. One might call it the romance of the researcher, in which the latter stands in for the old quester-hero, following the lure of a fragmented text into distant times and places. The personal adventure of the quester in these stories (I think of recent ones by Umberto E. Co, Julian Barnes, Antonio Byatt, Paul Auster, Margaret Drabble, Bharati Mukherjee and V.S. Naipaul) is a fictional play to frustrate the discursive bind which always confines our world.

Amitav Ghosh, like Byatt, Naipaul, Mukherjee and David Lodge, is an academic, in search of a past full of romance but history also. The method of all these novelists is the same: to dive deep into some texts or archives to discover some remote past, to find some connection with the present. Ghosh's *In an Antique Land* and *The Calcutta Chromosome*, if deconstructed, are steeped in history and social anthropology. The first is spun around ancient Indo-Arab trade links where history and myth interweave and which are further elaborated in a prologue of notes. The second, subtitled "A Novel of Fevers, Delirium and Discovery," deals with medical history (Ronald Ross's discovery of the malaria puzzle in Calcutta in 1889), computer applications, religious cults set against the background of nineteenth and twentieth century India.

With history begins social anthropology. Clifford Geertz writes about the impact of anthropology, the science, upon History, the discipline. In his perspective and revolutionary article titled "History and Anthropology," Geertz gives a fine distinction between these two subjects: "There seem to be some historians . . . who think that anthropologists . . . present static pictures of immobile societies scattered about in remote corners of the inhabited world, and some anthropologists . . . who think that what historians do is tell admonitory, and then, stories about one another episode in Western civilization: 'true novels' (in Paul Veyne's phrase) designed to get us to face—or outface—facts."[1] Another quarrel, according to some, is about Big and Little. Historians write and act big and anthropologists write of small, well-bounded communities. Historians accuse

> anthropologists of nuancemanship, of wallowing in the details of the obscure and unimportant, and to anthropologists accusing historians of schematicism, of being out of touch with the immediate . . . of actual life. . . . Or perhaps it is about High and Low, Dead and Living, Written and Oral, Particular and General, Description and Explanation, Art and Science. . . . To the historical imagination, 'we' is a juncture in a cultural genealogy, and 'here' is heritage. To the anthropological imagination, 'we' is an entry in a cultural gazette, and 'here' is home. . . . What has undermined them has been a change in the ecology of learning that has driven historians and anthropologists, like so many migrant geese, onto one another's territories. (321-24)

These geese turned vagrant by such inducements are not limited to anthropologists and historians. They have been joined by others, novelists and literary theorists among them. Amitav Ghosh is one such novelist.

Ghosh, through his character Murugan, shows the motifs that animate the plot of *The Calcutta Chromosome.*[2] Murugan demonstrates through his reading of the journals of the Nobel Prize winning bacteriologist, Ronald Ross, what looks and sounds like pathbreaking scientific research, is actually its mockery. In Murugan's reconstruction of the 1890s, Ross is progressing in his research because some people are helping him through the maze. I shall come to these people later in this writing.

Ross discovered the cause of malaria in Calcutta. "In the small laboratory seventy yards to the southeast of this gate Surgeon-Major Ronald Ross I.M.S. in 1898 discovered the manner in which malaria is conveyed by mosquitoes." (20)

Murugan was born in Calcutta, although he left it at an early age. It was as a graduate student of Syracuse that Murugan first discovered the great love of his life: the medical history of malaria. When he was in New York in a small college, he pursued his study of the early history of malaria research. After leaving the college he joined Life Watch and his research went on uninterruptedly. He found that Ross was born in India in 1857. He was awarded the Nobel Prize in 1906 for his work on the life-cycle of the malaria parasite.

Before coming to India in 1895 for further research on Ross, Murugan tells Antar, his colleague in New York, that Ross "wasn't a Pasteur or a Koch: he just didn't have as much variety to his game. His stuff on malaria was about the only cutting-edge work he ever did. And even that was a freak one-off thing. . . . The actual research, the hands-on stuff, took just three years, door to door; three years spent entirely in India. He kicked off in the summer of 1895, in a little hole-in-the-wall army camp in a place called Secunderabad and ran the last few yards in Calcutta in the summer of 1898." (43-44) Then Murugan tells Antar about another psychologist-cum-bacteriologist Julius von Wagner—Jauregg, an Austrian. "He was born the same year as Ronnie Ross, but in Austria. He was a psychologist: had a couple of serious run-ins with Freud. But the reason his name is up there in the bright lights is that he discovered something about Malaria that Ross couldn't even have begun to guess at." (46) He discovered that artificially induced malaria could cure syphilis—at least in the dementia paralytic stage when it attacks the brain. He got the Nobel Prize in 1927. Recalling the history of malaria Murugan tells Antar that the mid-nineteenth century was the period when the scientific community began to wake up to malaria. This was the time that new sciences like bacteriology and parasitology were beginning to make a splash in Europe.

Elaborating on the research work in malaria, Murugan says that the nineteenth century's biggest break-through in malaria research had happened in the 1840s. Way back in the 1840s a man called Meckel found microscopic granules of black pigment in the organs of malaria patients—black spots, some round, some crescent-shaped, tucked inside tiny masses of protoplasm. For forty years no one could figure out what this stuff was. In 1880, Alphonse Laveran, a French army surgeon in Algeria, found it to be a critter, a protozoan—an animal parasite. This work of Laveran was advanced further by Camillo Golgi in 1886. He showed that Laveran's parasite grows inside the red blood cell, eating its host and shitting black pigment; that the pigment collects in the centre while the bug begins to divide; he demonstrates that the recurrence of malarial fevers is linked to this pattern of asexual reproduction." (59)

So far as Ross's research project on malaria was concerned, he was avoided by the people in Secunderabad. He offered two and three rupees for a single finger prick but the people thought that it was witchcraft. According to Murugan, Ross was progressing because some people were helping him through the maze. Abdul Kadir came first. Then a man called Lutchman walked into Ronnie's life. He volunteered to drink Ronnie's cocktail. Lutchman, as far as Ronnie knew, was a "dhooley-bearer," a government servant to shovel shit.

In April 1897, at Ootacamund, Lutchman succeeded in planting a crucially important idea in his head: that the malaria vector might be one particular species of malaria. Unaware of the indirect help of Lutchman, Ronnie was supplied more of the anopheles. They were "about a dozen big, brown fellows, with fine tapered bodies and spotted wings, hungrily trying to escape through the gauze covering of the flask which the Angel of Fate had given to my humble retainer." (66) On August 20, 1897 Ronnie made his first major breakthrough: he saw the placement of plasmodium zygotes in the stomach sac of Anopheles Stephensii. "Eureka" he says to his diary, "the problem is solved." "Whew" says Lutchman, skimming the sweat off his face, "thought he'd never get it."

Lutchman was quite high up in the pecking order. Ronnie gave him a big room in his bungalow. J.W.D. Grigson discovered that the actual name of Lutchman was Laakhan.

Amitav Ghosh, in a parallel study of history, reveals that at the time of Ronnie's stay in India there was a secret religious society which tried to conceal its own identity. Laakhan/Lutchman is a member of this secret society. While the novel never clearly identifies the beliefs and goals of this secret society (for that could break the code of secrecy), it is obvious that its members are the devotees of the cult of silence.

What if, the narrative suggests, this group of people believed in counter science? This group "started with the idea that knowledge is self-contradictory; maybe they believed that to know something is to change it, therefore in knowing something, you've already changed what you think you know so you don't really know it at all: you know its history. Maybe they thought that knowledge couldn't begin without acknowledging the impossibility of knowledge." (88) This group was working with plasmodium falciparum but in a different way. They made a certain amount of progress. Now, they were stuck, maybe for want of right equipment. So they chose Ronnie.

This group, according to Murugan, wanted to achieve the ultimate transcendence of nature. It was a technology in which all information could be transmitted chromosolly, from body to body. "When your body fails you leave it, you migrate—you or at least a matching symptomology of your self. You begin all over again, another body, another beginning. Just think: no mistakes, a fresh start . . . a technology that lets you improve on yourself in your next incarnation?" (91-92)

Amitav Ghosh narrates the story of Mangala who, like Laakhan, was in this group of people of silence. It is linked with the story of Elijah Monroe Furley who arrived in Calcutta in the 1980s. He wanted to work in the laboratory of Dr. Cunningham. He had two assistants: a sweeper woman Mangala and a young man who came from Renupur. Farley noticed that Mangala and the young man were not ordinary assistants in a laboratory. He noticed some half-dozen people in various attitudes of supplication before Mangala, some touching her feet, others lying prostrate. Two or three others were huddled against the wall, wrapped in blankets. They were all syphilitics, in the final stages of the terrible disease.

The story switches to Ronnie once again. With Ronnie comes Lutchman. In Calcutta Ronnie began working with a related avian species, halteridium—a bird version of malaria. Lutchmen kept a large flock of infected birds for him.

The aesthetic of silence is described vividly by Murugan. Its proponent was Madame Salminen, in Madras. She ran her little outfit called the Society of Spiritualists. Her disciple, Countess Pongraez, claimed in her diary that it was Mme Salminen who had revealed to her the truth of the Valentian Cosmology, in which the ultimate deities are the Abyss and the Silence, the one being male and the other female, the one representing mind and the other truth.

With this, the role of history ends and anthropology enters. In 1995, in Calcutta, Phulboni, to mark his 85th birthday, pays homage to silence: "Mistaken are those who imagine that silence is without life; that it is inanimate, without spirit or voice. It is not: indeed the word is to the silence what the shadow is to the fore-shadowed, what the veil is to the eyes, what the mind is to truth, what language is to life." (24) This public tribute to silence lends credibility to Murugan's speculations about the cult of silence; it also emphasises the mystical quality of silence. Phulboni is clearly a member of the secret society and he has accepted silence as his religion.

Phulboni's quest for silence—his literary muse—is expressed in language. How do the members of the secret society of silence seek to resolve this essential contradiction? Murugan contends that this marginal group of people are really trying to develop a technology for interpersonal transfer whereby knowledge could be spread chromosomally. The Chromosome that allows transmigration of personalities without biological reproduction is the Calcutta Chromosome.

Some characters in the novel are incarnations of one another, Laakhan/Lutchman and Mangala, the two mainstays of the secret society, lived in the 1890s, but continue to exist through their 1995 incarnations. This secret is revealed by Sonali Das to Urmila and Murugan in chapter Forty-One. It was just a coincidence that Sonali went to Robinson Street in search of Romen Haldar. She found there the smoke, the people, the boy, the woman in the saree, the fire, the body of Romen. The woman was Mrs. Aratounian, the incarnation of Mangala. She touched the body that was lying in front of the fire and called him Laakhan. Phulboni wrote a number of short stories titled *The Laakhan Stories*. The stories are very short and they all feature a character called Laakhan. In one he is a postman; in another he is a village schoolmaster. People dismissed these stories by saying that it was some kind of elaborate allegory. Urmila suspected that there was something more to it. Mrs. Aratounian advised her to borrow the book from the National Library. They discuss the stories. Mrs. Aratounian says that the stories are a message to someone; to remind him of something—some kind of shared secret.

Laakhan and Mangala and their different selves—Romen Haldar and Mrs. Aratounian—are pivotal to the plot since they play the role of Fate or chance. The delineation of the plot and characters of the novel are controlled by the members of the secret society. Chance meetings are rarely so; the reality is that the secret society has decided upon a certain sequence of events. Murugan says this to Urmila: "Someone's trying to get us to make some connections; they are trying to tell us something; something they don't want to put together themselves, so that when we get to the end we'll have a whole new story." (179) When they come to the end, the story of Phulboni, Romen Haldar and Mrs. Aratounian reveals that, like the people of the secret society in the 1890s, they are also planting carefully selected clues to the chosen people—Urmila and Murugan. This group supplied some legal-size photocopy of a page of very fine English newsprint to Urmila. It was *The Colonial Services Gazette*, in which she read about Colonel D.D. Cunningham and his false name, C.C. Dunn, how Cunningham took five days' leave in the middle of January 1898, boarded a Madras-bound train in the false name of C.C. Dunn. The book also reveals how he met Mme. Salminen. Similarly, Murugan has also been able to piece together the puzzle because the society has provided him with evidence as they had done with Ross.

Anthropologists do not merely note down facts of what they observe; rather, they construct accounts of their experience of other people's experience. And these accounts "are thus fictions; fictions, in the sense that they are something made, something fashioned—the original meaning of fiction—not that they are false, unfactual, or merely 'as if' thought experiments." Geertz says: "In the end, it may be in a deeper understanding of the 'and' in 'History and Anthropology,' accouplement that progress lies." (334) Amitav Ghosh, in *The Calcutta Chromosome*, joins history and anthropology to produce a fiction. This feat marks him off from other Indian novelists writing in English.

NOTES

1. Clifford Geertz, "History and Anthropology," *New Literary History*, No. 2, 1990, p. 321.
2. (New Delhi: Ravi Dayal, 1996).

A Journey to the Unknown: A Quest for Immortality in *The Calcutta Chromosome*

TAPAN K. GHOSH

After the remarkable success of *In an Antique Land*, Amitav Ghosh has planted yet another milestone in the fast expanding landscape of Indian English fiction. *The Calcutta Chromosome* (1996), an experimental work that combines literature, science, philosophy and fantasy is a novel not only of 'fevers' and 'delirium' but also of 'discovery,' although the object it discovers remains an alluring but elusive mystery.

'A medical thriller, a Victorian ghost story and a scientific quest'—this is how the blurb describes the book. Although a fairly accurate description, the title—*The Calcutta Chromosome: A Novel of Fevers, Delirium and Discovery*—is rather inadequate for a work of such erudition, painstaking research and, what is more important, thrill. It warns the reader of a dreary and learned treatise on the chromosomal traits of the inhabitants of Calcutta who are susceptible to all sorts of fevers (including political fever) and delirium—a highly specialized subject meant for medical students. What Amitav Ghosh has written is, in fact, a complex, fascinating and highly imaginative story of quest and discovery that weaves past, present and future into an intricate texture and is narrated, despite its burden of erudition, in a crisp, racy and crystalline prose that grips the reader's attention till the end.

On the face of it, the book is about malaria—a retelling of the story of Ronald Ross's discovery of the life-cycle of the malaria parasite much of which is available in medical history and in Ross's own memoir. The story of Ross, the Nobel Prize winning British bacteriologist, is a familiar one to Indians—it is often included in school texts—and his memorial arc at the entrance to the P.G. Hospital is a common sight to the pedestrians in Calcutta. In spite of that epoch-making discovery in the late nineteenth century, the disease still remains a curse in our life, continuing to take its annual toll of thousands of lives. It is one of the reasons why the story of Ross evokes at once a fascination and a sense of regret in our minds. One wonders whether these mixed feelings had stirred the imagination of Amitav Ghosh and inspired him to rewrite Ross's story at the fag end of the twentieth century when other killer diseases like cancer and AIDS top the priority list of scientists and writers of science fiction.

But Amitav Ghosh has largely deviated from the well-known account of Ross's discovery on August 20, 1897, and has cast it in an altogether different vein. His aim is not to write a scientific treatise on malaria but to present an alternative version of the story and, through it, hint at an alternative reality. The book is divided into two sections: (a) 'August 20: Mosquito Day,' and (b) 'The Day After.' The major part of the narrative takes place in Calcutta in 1995. On August 20, the World Mosquito Day, L. Murugan—a person obsessed with malaria and Ronald Ross—arrives in Calcutta on a search for the clues to the enigmatic Calcutta Chromosome. The next day he mysteriously disappears. At the heart of the narrative lie the events of these two days. Connected with these are the medical history of malaria, Ross's research and discovery, the experience of Antar, Murugan's former colleague at Life Watch in New York, and some scattered incidents in Calcutta. The novel traces the adventures of Murugan and the strange truth of what actually took place on those fateful days in August 1995, and years before in the laboratory at P.G. Hospital where Ross had made his final breakthrough. Wrapped in mystery the narrative stretches across time and space to cover a hundred years. It ranges from an unspecified time in future to the late nineteenth century and trails the history of the intriguing but elusive Calcutta Chromosome through a wide assortment of characters and a mind-boggling set of events. Here 'each character is both the hunter and the hunted, his or her life woven into an intricate pattern with the lives of the others. The ribbon that touches each life is a sinister, mysterious belief in the supernatural.'[1] The story moves from the god-forsaken village of Renupur in north India which abounds in ghosts and ghostly trains, through a little Egyptian hamlet on the western edge of the Nile Delta with its 'brilliantly sunlit vision of sand and mud-brick and creaking water-wheels'[2]—which is believed to be 'the most sacred site of the ancient Valentinian cult: the lost shrine of silence,' (177) to New York in the twenty-first century where Antar tries to solve the puzzle of Murugan's disappearance with the help of his garrulous supercomputer called Ava. Mystery, adventure, espionage, electronic surveillance, hologram, planchette, black magic, spiritualists, counter-science, plasmodium falciparum, syphilitic paresis, re-incarnation, esoteric cult of silence and a mind-bending theory of immortality—all these are cooked in a huge melting pot until the different strands are closely interwoven to reveal 'a frightening vision of a world repeating itself over and over again despite apparent change.'[3]

The novel, set in the future, delves into the past. It begins at the New York apartment of a computer-bound Egyptian archivist named Antar, who works for the International Water Council, a global organization that explores and examines 'the depletion of the world's water supplies.' (6) His is an inconsequential 'at home' job. What he is required to do is tagging, naming, numbering and propelling into the 'horizonless limbo' (6) of Ava's phenomenal memory the routine inventories that the IWC throws at him with 'metronomic regularity.' (4) One morning Ava Ferrets out a lost and badly damaged ID card with a small metal chain attached to it. With her astounding resourcefulness Ava reconstructs, at Antar's command, the lost card that has originated in Calcutta, and creates a holographic projection of the man to whom the card once belonged. Antar recognizes the card and identifies the man as L. Murugan, the principal archivist of Life Watch, 'a small but respected non-profit organization that served as a global public health consultancy and epidemiological data bank' (7) where Antar had once worked. Murugan (Morgan to friends)—'a cocky little rooster of a man' (29) with thin and discoloured hair, bright black eyes, moon-like face, a boxer's nose, and a trimmed goatee in an aggressively jutting chin—was known for his combativeness, obstinacy and 'unstoppable fluency.' (30) Murugan, the principal narrative thread and also the most entertaining character in the book, is, by his own admission, the world's only expert on Ronald Ross, the great love of his life being the medical history of malaria. Murugan, Antar remembers, has been missing since August 21, 1995. He was last seen in Calcutta and all subsequent attempts to track him ended in failure.

Antar launches a computer-aided search for the missing Murugan who, the readers learn, is engaged in a search of his own. He believes that Ronald Ross, who was awarded the Nobel Prize in 1906 for his work on the life-cycle of the malaria vector, had been handed the information on a plate. It was not his discovery at all. Someone else had planted the idea that malaria parasite might be one particular species of mosquito in his head. Years ago, Murugan had written a summary of his research in an article entitled 'Certain Systematic Discrepancies in Ronald Ross's account of Plasmodium B' which received very hostile reception from the scientific journals to which it was submitted. It only 'served to brand Murugan as a crank and an eccentric' (31) and cost him the membership of the Science Society. His ostracism from the scholarly community resulted in an 'increasingly erratic and obsessional behaviour.' (31) And he began to talk publicly about his notion of the

"'Other Mind': a theory that some person or persons had systematically interfered with Ronald Ross's experiments to push malaria research in certain directions while leading it away from others." (31) Murugan was convinced that there was a conspiracy afoot in 1895. Ross was completely on a wrong track. Like his mentor, Patrick Manson, the noted Scottish bacteriologist who had written a book on filaria, Ross thought that the malaria parasite was transmitted from mosquito to man orally, via drinking water. But almost overnight he changed his tack and on August 20, 1897, he found the connection between plasmodium zygotes and Anopheles stephensil. Murugan found it hard to swallow and he wanted to know what actually happened and how. The conspiracy theory had become such an idee fixe that he was determined to leave for Calcutta in search of the missing links which, he thought, could enlighten him and the world about the century-old puzzle. The persuasions of the friends and well-wishers to give up the wild-goose chase were of no avail. He reached Calcutta on August 20, 1995, and the very next day he vanished. In a simultaneous replay of their lives, Ross is seen stumbling on his discovery and Murugan researching Calcutta on the World Mosquito Day to prove his hypothesis that Ross had been literally led by the nose to enlightenment by force beyond his comprehension. What drives the narrative forward is Antar's curiosity and Murugan's scepticism which is fuelled by the author's highly imaginative concept of an alternative reality.

In Calcutta Murugan finds out the missing links and the brain that had masterminded the conspiracy behind Ross's discovery. The conspiracy that led to the discovery of the 'Calcutta Chromosome' and that stitches up various parts of the narrative into a coherent whole, covers the past, the present and the future. The conspirators are eternal: they led Ross where they wanted him to go, they confuse Murugan and trap him into their experiment, and at the end of the story drag Antar into their fold. The funniest thing is that writers, journalists, film stars, and businessmen of late twentieth century Calcutta become part of this secret scheme.

But what is this conspiracy about? What is the aim or purpose of this secret team? In a nutshell, a journey to the unknown and a quest for immortality. Amitav Ghosh holds that science not only reveals reality but also, at times, creates it. What is known is knowledge. At the other end of this scientific knowledge lies the unknown, the unarticulated truth. Mixing science, philosophy, literary theory and fantasy, Amitav Ghosh creates a group of silent researchers whose main objective is not only to invent something but also to conceal their invention. The source of their strength is silence, the concealed truth. (This is exactly opposite of

Michel Foucault's dictum that 'knowledge is power.') Phulboni, 'the greatest living writer' (23) of Bengal and the winner of the National Award, is the chief exponent of this cult of silence. The team consisted of 'fringe people, marginal types,' (89) some of whom had been picked up by Dr. D.D. Cunningham (at whose laboratory in the P.G. Hospital Ross discovered the malaria bug) from railway stations to serve him as research assistants. They started with the idea that "knowledge is self-contradictory . . . they believed that to know something is to change it, therefore in knowing something, you've already changed what you think you know so you don't really know it at all. You only know its history . . they thought that knowledge couldn't begin without acknowledging the impossibility of knowledge." (88) Hence the hypothesis "if it's true that to know something is to change it, then it follows that one way of changing something—of effecting a mutation . . . is to attempt to know it, or aspects of it." (88) These believers in counter science used secrecy as a technique of procedure. For them silence was a religion. However incredible it may sound, these people had developed 'the most revolutionary medical technology of all time.' (90) They were already ahead of Ronald Ross on malaria research. In 1927, an Austrian Clinician and Psychologist named Julius Von Wagner-Jauregg won the Nobel for his discovery that artificially induced malaria could cure, or at least mitigate, syphilitic paresis, although very little was known at that time about the process in which it worked. But much earlier than that, in 1890s, the secret Indian team, under the leadership of an enigmatic woman called Mangala, had achieved remarkable success in this field of research. Mangala herself was a victim of hereditary syphilis whom Dr. Cunningham had found at Sealdah station and trained as a laboratory assistant. Murugan believes that Mangala was a genius and she was 'way ahead of Cunningham in her intuitive understanding of the fundamentals of the malaria problem.' (202) He even hazards a guess that she was the 'demi-urge' (188) of Ross's discovery. While using a variant of Wagner-Jauregg process, Mangala noticed that malaria worked on paresis through a different route, the brain. Like syphilis, malaria causes irreparable damage to the brain; it 'muddies up the blood/brian barrier.' (205) It can be 'more hallucinogenic than any mind-bending drug.' This is one of the reasons why the primitive people often thought of malaria as 'spirit-possession.' (205) Mangala had developed a particular strain of malaria that could be cultivated in pigeons. And she found some way of making the bug cross over to the patient from the bird. She secretly started treating syphilitic patients in Cunningham's laboratory and her treatment often produced strange side-effects which looked like weird personality disorders. She at last discovered that they were not really disorders but transpositions, 'a cross-over of randomly assorted personality traits, from the malaria donor to the recipient,' (206) via the pigeon. It hinted at a freak chromosome, freak because it eluded standard techniques of detection and isolation. Moreover, unlike other chromosomes, it was not present in every cell because it was not 'symmetrically paired' and was not 'transmitted from generation to generation by sexual reproduction.' It developed 'out of a process of recombination' and was 'particular to every individual.' (206) It was only found in the non-regenerating tissue, the brain, and could be transmitted through malaria. It is this stray DNA carrier that Murugan calls 'the Calcutta chromosome'—'a biological expression of human traits that is neither inherited from the immediate gene pool, nor transmitted into it.' (207) What Mangala and her associates had succeeded in doing was, in short, 'the ultimate transcendence of nature' or 'immortality' (90) through a technique of inter-personal transference of human traits. As Murugan puts it to Antar: "Just think, a fresh start: when your body fails you, you leave it, you migrate—you or at least a matching symptomology of your self. You begin all over again, another body, another beginning . . . a technology that lets you improve on yourself in your next incarnation." (91-92)

Murugan is convinced from his extensive research that Ross's discovery was only a minor subset of this experiment with the Calcutta Chromosome. By 1897, Mangala had run into a dead end. After a number of abortive attempts at stabilizing the chromosome during the process of transmission, she concluded that the existent strains of malaria would not take her any further. She required new information about the malaria bug. That is why, she became desperate to have Ross figure out the whole thing: "Because she actually believed that the link between the bug and the human mind was so close that, once its life-cycle had been figured out, it would spontaneously mutate in directions that would take her work to the next step." (208)

To know something is to change it! She had done it by planting carefully selected clues in Ross's head and expertly manipulating his research in directions she had wanted it to take. As Murugan puts it humorously: "He thinks he's doing experiments on the malaria parasite. And all the time it's he who is the experiment on the malaria parasite. But Ronnie never gets it; not to the end of his life." (67) This fantastic theory may sound preposterous, even far-fetched. But in Amitav Ghosh's immaculate art of story-telling it appears all too plausible. He has succeeded in imparting to this erudite theory a human interest and a semblance of truth and procuring for it 'a willing suspension of disbelief.'

Did Mangala and her henchmen succeed in their quest? There are characters and incidents in the novel that testify to Murugan's conviction that they did. Lutchman alias Laakhan is a living example of interpersonal transference of Calcutta chromosome. This weird, sometimes sinisterly malevolent, character with a deformed hand is "all over the map, changing names, switching identities." (74) Murugan even suspects that he was the 'pointman for whoever was the real brain behind the scheme.' (74) He crops up across time and space and his name is mentioned throughout the story. He walked into Ross's head that malaria vector might be one particular species of mosquito. He staged a train accident to kill Elijah Monroe when the latter came to detect the clandestine experiment in Cunningham's tropical laboratory. Ross's friend, J.W.D. Grigson, was also rewarded with a near fatal accident in Secunderabad when he figured out that 'something isn't quite Kosher about their Lutchman kid; something doesn't fit," (76) and that he showed a little more scientific inclination than become a 'dhooley-bearer.' Even Phulboni, who had written a set of stories called 'the Laakhan Stories,' came across this inscrutable person, or rather his spirit, in the deserted railway station of Renupur thirty-six years after Grigson's encounter with him, and narrowly escaped death in a train accident apparently manipulated by Laakhan. One suspects that Laakhan is not one man but many men who have inherited or imbibed the personality traits of original Lutchman through interpersonal transmission of Calcutta Chromosome. Mangala, too, figures in a number of places across the time. In Cunningham's laboratory in 1890s she treated syphilitic patients under the guise of a sweeper woman. People who came to Mangala looked upon her as a goddess and believed that she had a cure. Murugan discovers, on August 20, 1995, an esoteric cult of image worship in Calcutta and learns that the image is that of Mangala. She is called 'Mangalabibi' and people offer puja to commemorate her re-incarnation. Phulboni writes a story about the image ('a clay figurine, a semi-circular mound with two painted eyes. On one side of the mound was a tiny pigeon, and on the other a semi-circular instrument' [188] that looks like an old-fashioned microscope) and all aspects of the coming of that image into the world.

Despite touches of science and philosophy, fantasy and reincarnation theory, it is difficult to find any deeper significance in this highly innovative science fiction. The novel is written in a light mood. The narrative often distracts the mind which spills over with questions that remain unanswered. The disappearance of Phulboni and Mrs. Aratounian, both of whom are inextricably linked to the secret religious cult that Murugan finds himself up against, remains shrouded in mystery. The identity of the gap-toothed, emaciated boy who walks in and out of Murugan's and Sonali's life, also remains an unresolved puzzle. There are also some factual errors. Urmila, the reporter of *Calcutta*, says: "Ma Shoroshoti would play a note or two on her sitar." (192) But Saraswati's instrument is Veena, not sitar. These minor blemishes notwithstanding, *The Calcutta Chromosome* is a highly readable novel. The judicious mix of fact and fiction, philosophy and science, mystery and humour, the memorable portraits of nineteenth and twentieth century India (Farley, Grigson, Cunningham, Phulboni, Mrs. Aratounian, film star Sonali Das and her lover Romen Haldar, and Urmila the journalist), the enviable scholarship and painstaking research that have gone into the story, and the felicitous use of American colloquialisms ('grab-a-bite,' 'dickhead,' 'cocky little rooster,' 'Are you kidding?' etc.) and Bengali phrases ('shorshe-ilish,' 'dhakai parotha,' 'urmi-pishi-kirmi-pishi' etc.) have made it a delightful novel that moves the reader's mind and orients his thoughts in a new direction. Finally, the intrusion of the supernatural into the practical world of science and technology adds an extra interest to the book. ". . . everything is other than what it appears to be, a phantom of itself," (129) writes Elijah Farley, the baffled American missionary doctor from Calcutta to his erstwhile colleague Eugene Opie in John Hopkins University hours before his disappearance. Whatever their outward appearances may be, it is possible, the book suggests, to imagine familiar incidents and characters as something different, something even monstrous and dreadful. There are worlds at the periphery of this one about which we know very little until we are catapulted in them. Amitav Ghosh has cast the incidents of everyday life in a vortex of Gothic imagination that transforms and transplants them into a weird, uncanny and unfamiliar world.

NOTES

1. Jaya Banerji, "Bengali Braid," review of *The Calcutta Chromosome*, *Indian Review of Books*, Vol. 5, No. 9, June-July 1996.
2. Amitav Ghosh, *The Calcutta Chromosome: A Novel of Fevers, Delirium and Discovery* (New Delhi: Ravi Dayal, 1996)
3. Swati Ghosh, "The Man with the Missing Thumb," review of *The Calcutta Chromosome*, *The Statesman*, 12.7.96.

The Calcutta Chromosome: A Literary Touchstone

PRADEEP TRIKHA

Amitav Ghosh has added another feather in his literary cap with his latest novel *The Calcutta Chromosome*. The book is likely to become a literary touchstone for its content and technique. As he did in his earlier books, Ghosh once again approaches human affairs from unconventional points of view like anthropology, medical science, psychology, history and sociology and has been able to discover a considerable body of information that furnishes the basis for a provisional understanding of human beings.[1] Ghosh represents 'the past' which he reconstructs from the tit-bits of 'memory' and of course 'memory' is not the individual property, it is a complex cultural and historical subject to revision and amplification to zoom in on human experiences. *The Calcutta Chromosome* is peppered with "a breath-taking intensity and variety."[2] It represents "history, science, Egypt, Bengal, the fluid interflow between rural and urban, between cultures and civilizations, the play of ideas."[3]

Like V.S. Naipaul and Salman Rushdie, Ghosh is perceptive towards the proclivities of a new world which is still in the making in which historicity and contemporaneity are germane. Ghosh too, like them, discerns experiences of the past and the present to explore lives of men and women in his novels. His *Shadow Lines* (1989), *In an Antique Land*[4] (1994), and *The Calcutta Chromosome* redeem a gap between 'worlds' of the rulers and the ruled. These novels have immediate as well as historic relevance because they deal with history and politics. They reconstruct the past, not from the chronological order of events, but scattered events which are more quizzical and ironical. Naipaul's *The Mystic Masseur* (1957), *The Suffrage of Elvira* (1958), *Miguel Street* (1959) and *The Way in the World* (1995) and Rushdie's *The Moor's Last Sigh* (1995) are rare paradigms of complex cultural and historical phenomenon. Ghosh, Naipaul and Rushdie revive and amplify the memory. Roger Bromley is of the view: "Narratives particularly represent our ideas about everyday life by producing cultural images and stereotypes of it. They thus have an important function in representing the past, because they provide crucial forms in which memories are made. Memory is not simply the property of individuals, but a complex cultural and historical phenomenon constantly subject to revision, amplification and forgetting. Memory is therefore a construction. Memories are actively inocuted and reinvented by cultural interventions."[5] No doubt Bromley is writing in British context but one can read it with a sharper focus on contemporary novel writing in general especially with reference to writers like Ghosh, Naipaul and Rushdie who represent our 'ideas' by producing cultural images and stereotypes through the past. They have an important function in delineating the past because they provide crucial forms in which memories are insulated. In Orwellian sense they control both the past and the present.[6]

Ghosh is a novelist who conformingly writes about a vanished era. In his recent novels *In an Antique Land* and *The Calcutta Chromosome* he traces the past like a social historian and chronicler. He might have written differently had he lived among his characters and yet his claim of being a modern writer is in no way diminished because modernity is not a matter of surface detail: "it belongs to the depth and quality of response that a writer makes to the society in which he lives and if these are present it hardly matters in what period the actual 'fable' is cast."[7] Most of the characters, situations and passions Ghosh deals with belong to no particular age or society, though it is true that he is aware of their bearing in the world in which he lives. His use of detail is fully woven in the tapestry of the novel. *The Calcutta Chromosome* can be read on many levels because it has layers of meanings, characters and events; it stretches across the period of 100 years or so, and circumrotates around missing person(s), the atmosphere is cloaked in mystery and suspense, supernatural and metaphysics.

II

The Calcutta Chromosome has the content of 'cerebral excitement' because it is swathed in mysteries and secrets; many explanations are buried in the text and it is not easy to have all answers. After all life does not easily capitulate all its esoterics. The novel has two sections: "August 20, Mosquito Day" and "The Day After." The story set in future, delves into the past; it opens in not too distant future where Antar, a computer bound Egyptian clerk with Lifewatch (now the part of International Water Council) in New York inadvertently comes across and abandons identity card on his computer screen of a former colleague, L. Murugan. The latter was a self-professed authority on Ronald Ross, the scientist who cleaved the malaria conundrum in 1898 in Calcutta. Murugan, completely obsessed with an arcane malarial theory of his own had himself disappeared in 1995 in Calcutta under weird circumstances.[8] Murugan's obsession was: "An alternative interpretation of late nineteenth century malaria research: Is their a secret history?" He had once explained to Antar over a cup of tea at a Thai restaurant:

> You know all about matter and anti-matter, right? And rooms and anterooms and Christ and anti-Christ and so on? Now, let's say there was something like science and counter-science? Thinking of it in the abstract, wouldn't you say that the first principle of a functioning counter-science would have to be secrecy? The way I see it, it wouldn't just have to be secretive about *what* it did (it couldn't hope to beat the scientist at that game anyway), it would also have to be secretive *in* what it did. It would have to use secrecy as a technique or procedure. It would in principle have to refuse all direct communication, straight off the bat, because to communicate, to put ideas into language would be to establish a claim to *know*—which is the first thing that a counter-science would dispute.[9]

Murugan believes that 'to know something is to change' is the idea of knowledge which is self contradictory. He is convinced that weird marginal group helped Ronald Ross in his research on malaria.

Antar initiates a search for Murugan and finds himself embroiled in a bizarre tale defying all explanations. The story rolls back to Ronald Ross's tropical laboratory in Calcutta. Though Ross won the Nobel Prize in 1906 for discovering that malaria is contracted through mosquito bites, he had been handed the information on a platter. Someone, called D.D. Cunningham had donated his labour, laboratory and research to Ross and from the margins of counter-science several forces (men and women) had been directing the scientist's malarial quest. Unsolicited intruders in this arena of wisdom had no other way except board a one way train to oblivion.[10] Murugan douses headlong into the situation to decipher the multilayered mystery of malaria research. He is more interested in knowing about the men and women of Indian origin who helped Ross from the margins of counter-science. In August 1995 Murugan's peregrination begins, fortuitously; he confronts many people and sometimes he makes contemplative moves to meet them as if they were holding their horses for him. He fathoms that most of them "are irredeemably subordinated to the mysterious Calcutta Chromosome."[11] He is convinced that "marginal group" helped Ross to achieve what he yearned for, "immortality," "the ultimate transcendence of nature." Murugan surmises that while Ross worked on malaria theories, his lab assistants (Lakhan and Mangala) worked on 'inter-personal transference,' transmission of personality: "when your body fails you, you leave it, you migrate—you or at least a matching symptomology of yourself. You begin all over again, another body another beginning. Just think: no mistakes, a fresh start. What would you give for that Ant: a technology that lets you improve on yourself in your next incarnation?" (91-92)

Murugan is keen to see the veritability of the philosophy in which he believes now and Mangala practises once. Ross in his research drove home spread of malaria to mosquitoes while Mangala secretly cultivated particular strain of malaria in regions which produced "strange personality disorders. Except they weren't disorders but transposition" of personality traits from malaria donor to the recipient. This strain is Calcutta Chromosome, "a biological expression of human traits that is neither inherited from the immediate gene pool nor transmitted into it." In the long run, Mangala fails because she is unable to gather new information regarding malaria bug. The only way to gather the information was to make the bug mutate and know its life-cycle. Another research was conducted by Wagner Jauregg in 1927, which fetched him a Nobel Prize for proving that the paralytic symptoms of syphilis can be mitigated by malaria and also that malaria does irreparable damage to the brain. Mangala on the other hand crochets that patients suffering from the disease often were possessed by spirits. That is why strange personality disorders take place.

III

The novel opens like a slow moving art film but gradually picks up momentum and becomes whodunit which oscillates between centuries. The plot is 'episodic'[12] having some 'organic unity.'[13] It revolves around a missing person or persons. The narrative is quite conventional; it gives more details of the atmosphere as compared to the details of its characters. Consequently the characters have little space to fully evolve themselves. They enact many episodes: an arresting ghost story in a remote railway station, a dark ritual in a dilapidated neo-Gothic bungalow[14] and the consecration of silence. As Phulboni, a great writer (or through him Ghosh), says:

> Mistaken are those who imagine that silence is without life; that it is inanimate, without either spirit or voice. It is not: indeed the

word is to this silence what the shadow is to the foreshadowed, what the veil is to the eyes, what the mind is to truth, what language is to life. (24)

The silence of the city . . . has sustained me through all my years of my writing, kept me alive in the hope that it would claim me too before my ink ran dry. For more years than I can count I have wandered the darkness of these streets, searching for the unseen presence that reigns over this silence, striving to be taken in, begging to be taken across before my time runs out. The time of the crossing is at hand, I know, and that is why I am here now, standing in front of you: to beg—to appeal to the mistress of this silence, that most secret of deities, to give me what she has so long denied: to show herself to me . . . (24-27)

Perhaps Ghosh gives an account of his personal experience in the city of joy, Calcutta, through Phulboni; he venerates 'silence' because he feels that the world is full of sound and fury signifying "nothing" and to extol "silence" would restore some meaning in life. Ghosh synthesizes his scholarship and imagination and "employs the detective mode with elegant panache to make his novel a roller coaster ride through the arcane meadows of memory, the software of future, the hard ambiguities of the instant. A scientific thriller a metaphorical whodunit."[15] Characters in the novel appear and disappear, without prior notice or intimation. It is not to say that there is lack of coherence but they do have unity of time and place because whenever they meet and wherever they are, their inter-personal relations become sagacious even though they are shrouded in mystery.

Uncertainties of day-to-day life are Ghosh's main concern in his novels. Like in his other novels, in *The Calcutta Chromosome* too, Ghosh voices 'living uncertainties' because abstinence permeates all over; there is hardly anything which has continuity and the writer is of the view—'to know something is to change it.' Antar strives to trace his missing colleague Murugan and soon finds himself lost in the lives of men and women with whom he had no direct link; discontinuity creeps in his life and he moves on and on in search of the real goal. For the sake of convenience, characters of the novel can be divided into two groups—one belonging to the 90s of the nineteenth century and others who come in contact with Murugan. The common denominator in the two groups is their search for immortality; their movement in the novel is concentric which can be substantiated through a graph. The graph on one hand reveals the characters, their relations and their movement, on the other hand it depicts layers of meaning Ghosh introduces in his novel[16]:

CIRCLES OF MYSTERY

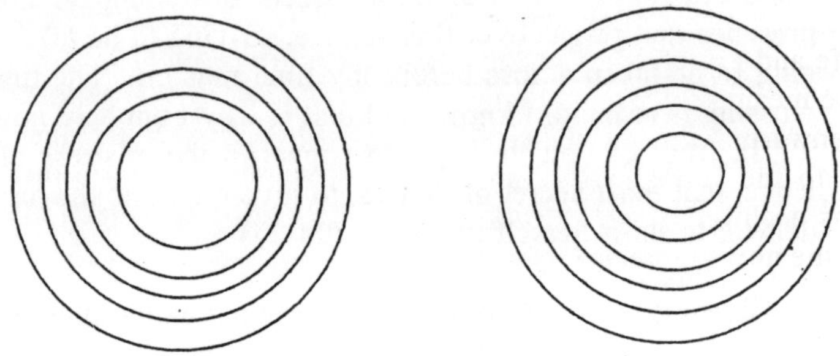

Circle A (1898-1902) Circle B (1995-)

Ghosh undertakes the task of a historian and depends on his intuition in order to identify the subject of study and his individual judgments over the central issue of the novel. For him, like for Bergson, the concrete, the immediate and the vital are more important. Life is 'unceasing,' continuous, undivided process, a sort of cosmic movement of which we are expressions rather than parts.[17] There can be a possibility that there is discontinuity in events of an individual's life but the existence of life as a whole is a continuous process.

IV

'Journey' is a periodic theme in Ghosh's novels; for him it is not merely a passage through space, but rather an expression of the urgent desire for discovery and change that underlies actual movement and experience of travelling. *In an Antique Land* describes Ghosh as a traveller interested in men, places and scenery; he thinks travel is man's primordial quest to expand his awareness into realization.[18] Both Antar and Murugan in *The Calcutta Chromosome* have an urgent desire for discovery and they undergo profound experiences during the course of their researches, even Ronald Ross expands his awareness when he works in Cunningham's laboratory. Hence, to study, to inquire, to seek or to live with intensity through new and profound experiences are all modes of travelling, or spiritual and symbolic equivalent of journey.[19] Antar and Murugan are travellers in that they are restless. 'Travelling,' Jung observes is an image of aspiration of an unsatisfied longing that never finds a goal. It is a 'quest' that starts in darkness of the profane world and gropes towards light.[20] If Antar initiates the journey, Murugan completes it in the end.

The novel can be described as the narrator's journey both forward and backwards in time and space in order to decipher intenser meaning of life and existence. The concentric plots in the novel give vivid effect to the meaning. It is an attempt to impose pattern on experience. Ghosh has enwarped the variety of characters and their lives, whether they belong to the contemporary society or to the nineteenth century. He remains a chronicler of events, men, places and social environment and thus the novel becomes a literary touchstone.

NOTES

1. Louise M. Rosenblatt, *Literature as Exploration* (N.Y.: Nobel and Noble Publishers, 1976), p. 138.
2. Tarun J. Tejpal, "Circle of Mysteries," *Outlook*, Vol. 2, No. 24, June 12, 1996, p. 76.
3. *Ibid.*
4. Pradeep Trikha, "Amitav Ghosh's *In an Antique Land*, A Traveller's Tale," *Indian Literature Today*, ed. R.K. Dhawan (New Delhi: Prestige, 1994), pp. 185-89.
5. Roger Bromley, *Lost Narratives* (London: Routledge, 1988), pp. 1-2.
6. In his *Nineteen Eighty Four*, George Orwell wrote: "Those who control the present, control the past . . . those who control the past, control the present." The works of the authors under consideration often stretch across the period of few hundred years and culminate the events in the present.
7. Gilbert Phelps, "The Novel Today," *The Modern Age*, ed. Boris Ford (Harmondsworth: Penguin, 1961), p. 478.
8. Tejpal.
9. Amitav Ghosh, *The Calcutta Chromosome: A Novel of Fevers, Delirium and Discovery* (New Delhi: Ravi Dayal, 1996), p. 88.
10. Jaya Banerjee, "Bengali Braid," *Indian Review of Books*, Vol. 5, No. 9, 16 June-15 July 1996, pp. 2-3.
11. S. Prasannarajan, "An Echo of Eco," *Biblio*, Vol. 2, No. 4, May 1996, pp. 10-11.
12 T.S. Dorsche, ed., *Classical Literary Criticism* (Harmondsworth: Penguin, 1965), p. 41.

13. *Ibid.*
14. One is reminded of the opening scenes of Indian films like "Madhumati" (1959) and "Sahib, Bibi aur Gulam" (1962).
15. Prasannarajan.
16. Circle A depicts the period from 1898 to 1902 and circle B from 20 August 1995 to the early years of the 21st century. The centripetal force is constantly working in the lives of characters shown in circle A and B, each tries to reach the centre (in order to gain immortality).
17. Morton White, *The Age of Analysis* (N.Y.: Mentor, 1955), p. 67.
18. *Ibid.*
19. J.E. Cirlot, *The Dictionary of Symbols* (N.Y.: Philosophical Library Press, 1962), p. 157.
20. *Ibid.*

The Calcutta Chromosome: A Postmodernist Text

SUBHASH CHANDRA

Postmodernism has been nomenclatured as a mood or a state of mind rather than a movement and this mood has been generated by the collapse of the Cartesian certitudes which assumed a conscious, thinking and autonomous subject. The Cartesian subject functioned as a fulcrum of perceiving, deciphering and ordering the objective structures of reality and the whole business of making sense of the universe. This exercise came to be labelled as a humanistic enterprise, which in turn, resulted in a stable, organically progressive, chronological and transcendent history with fixed categories and totalizing statements—unambiguous and unchallengeable. However, in this changed mental state (Postmodernism) "the autonomous subject has been dispersed into a range of plural, polymorphous subject positions inscribed within language. . . . Instead of certainty of progress associated with 'the Enlightenment Project,' (of which, Marxism is a part), there is now an awareness of contingency and ambivalence."[1] Thus dissolution of the autonomous subject has been responsible for "epistemological scepticism" which in turn points to the instability and insubstantiality of history.

Even though Parsa Venkateshwar Rao, Jr., in his review of the novel has called *The Calcutta Chromosome* a "science mystery thriller," (which does not take the novel away from the postmodern category, as Leslie Fiedler stresses the breakdown of barriers between the high and low—detective, science and pornographic fiction—literature) one witnesses some major postmodern tenets at work in the book. The most important postmodern feature operating in the text is the questioning attitude towards the obvious historical fixities. The following inscription precedes the opening of the novel:

This day relenting God
  Hath placed within my hand
A wondrous thing: And God

Be praised. At his command,
Seeking His secret deeds
With tears and toiling breath,
I find thy cunning seeds,
O million-murdering Death.
Sir Ronald Ross (Nobel Prize for Medicine, 1906)

Ghosh begins to build the edifice of the novel on research conducted committedly and obsessively by a major character, Murugan, into the medical history of malaria. The area of examination progressively narrows into "the early history of malaria research," and later into further specialized subject, "the research career of British poet, novelist, and scientist, Ronald Ross." Murugan's discovery of certain systematic discrepancies in Ronald Ross's account of "Plasmodium B" led him to researching the subject more deeply and preparing an article, "An Alternative Interpretation of Late 19th Century Malaria Research: Is there a Secret History?" The hostile response from journals to which he sent the article, the rejection of his proposal to the History of Science Society to seat up a panel on early malaria research for the Society's next convention, and finally his expulsion from the membership of the Society embody the entrenched antipathy of the forces of the establishment towards the "Other Mind," or the "Other Voice," Murugan's theory claimed that "some person or persons had systematically interfered with Ronald Ross's experiments to push malaria research in certain directions while leading it away from other,"[2] turning Ronald Ross into a goaded and manipulated agent rather than his being a successful scientist who "discovered the manner in which malaria is conveyed by mosquitoes," as inscribed on the medallion, and the portrait of Ross, located in the arch, built into the Presidency General Hospital, near the site of Ross's old laboratory in Calcutta. Upset and frustrated Murugan decides to come to Calcutta for a first-hand enquiry into the details at the cost of his job and career. Ghosh projects through Murugan's anger and frustration the postmodernist "rage against humanism and the Enlightenment legacy" which permitted a unipolar perception. Murugan's efforts also allegorise the sceptical, questioning mental attitude which needs to be adopted by the self-satisfied, smug, but manipulated masses who consume unconsciously all that has the aura of truth about it. In this sense, Murugan, besides being a character in the novel becomes a symbol of the postmodern cynicism about the binary opposition of truth/falsehood. Murugan is eventually proved right in his research findings about the "malarial maze," validates the viability of looking at things by looking through them.

It is significant that the person on whom is bestowed the Nobel Prize for medicine "doesn't know a goddam thing about mosquitoes: he's never even heard the word anopheles." (66) Ross succeeds, because "they" want him to, and it is "they" who first dry up malaria patients for Ross and then give him Abdul Kadir and later Lutchman to steer him along the right track. It is, in fact, Lutchman, who besides being his patient (guinea pig) and retainer also becomes Ross's guide, planting useful ideas in his head. Ross, instead of doing experiments on the malaria parasite, becomes "the experiment on the malaria parasite." And what does this other team or "they" want? What is their interest in leading Ross on in his research? They are after a much bigger project. Their agenda consists of immortality—inter-body migration—through the mutation of the parasite. One reason of Murugan's coming over to Calcutta is to partake of the immortality.

It is significant that as against the research conducted by the trained scientists like D.D. Cunningham, Elijah Monroe Farley and later Dr. Ronald Ross, we have the team of Mangala and Lutchman (who are illiterate), carrying on their own enquiry into the various strains of malaria, of course with a different and higher purpose of eventually isolating and developing what Murugan calls "The Calcutta Chromosome." What is this Calcutta Chromosome? A unique type of chromosome—it is a chromosome by extension because it does not possess the usual properties of chromosomes—which could enable the transposition of certain personality traits. And thus if developed, it could enable migration from one body to another with a fresh start, without earlier blemishes. We have, thus, counter-science posited against science and the novelist seems to prioritize the counter-science which includes in its fold areas and phenomena, considered invalid by the proponents of science, but which are difficult to wish away, just because the processes of conventional science cannot verify, codify, and generalise such phenomena. Postmodernism's distrust of the meta-narrative, or grand-narrative and the concept of "progressive liberation of humanity through science," are apparent in the text. The novel, in favouring the continent, as against the metanarrative in the form of historical discourse, effectively critiques the "universal knowledge and foundationalism."[3]

How is this subversion of history achieved? It is through the forces of anti-rationality and contingency. The micro-events hold sway in the narrative and Postmodernism believes that society functions better in terms of micro-events. Jean Francois Lyotard, the precursor of Postmodernism, "turns towards the Kantian sublime as a means of devaluing cognitive truth-claims and elevates the notion of the *unrepresentable* (that is to say, intuitions that cannot be "brought under" adequate concepts) to absolute pride of place in the ethical realm."[4] One finds is the novel the intuitive approach in solving the scientific riddles, and getting out of the scientific cul-de-sacs. Mangala and Lutchman embody the validity of intuitions in the realm of practical science and Ghosh is unequivocal in demonstrating the value of intuitiveness in a world dominated by reason and rationality, which get de-constructed in the novel. It is the "dark-drives" which propel actions and not reason and rationality, which if anything, become blinds to cover and camouflage the "real." Murugan functions as another deconstructive force in the book. He discounts the foolproofness associated with science generally and becomes instrumental (though it is "they" who want him to make connections and join the threads) in bringing to light the "submerged aspects" and the "forgotten actors" in the drama of malaria research.

An important tendency of Postmodernism is its reduction of experience to "a series of pure and unrelated presents." The past loses its pastness and is made to fuse in the present becoming some aspect of the present. The dissolution of the temporal boundaries may also include foreshortening of the future. The tale of *The Calcutta Chromosome* begins in the 21st century in New York, when technology has taken over private and professional realms and the experiential reality has taken the form of "images" on the screen. Antar, an Egyptian, working for the International Water Council, stumbles on the Murugan's (his erstwhile colleague at Life Watch) ID card on his super computer, AVA/IIe and succeeds in establishing contact with him. Murugan tells him about the whole affair. Jean Baudrillard calls this reality as hyper-reality in which in the characteristic Postmodern style we witness disappearance of distinction between illusion and reality. Antar sees on the Sim. Vis. System (Simultaneous Visualization Headgear) Murugan "standing in the lobby of a large auditorium and two women were running up the stairs." (256) Who are these women? Are they Sonali and Urmila? They were the ones who were with Murugan. Or are they Tara and Maria, as they appear to be. But they are living in New York,-Tara living in the same building as Antar. But then how come Tara and Maria are wearing sarees. The merging of the illusion and reality is best described in the closing lines of the book:

> He [Antar] felt a cool soft touch upon his shoulder and his hand flew up to take off the Sim Vis Headgear. But now there was a restraining hand upon his wrist, and a voice in his ear. Tara's voice, whispering: "Keep watching: we're here; we're all with you."
>
> There were voices everywhere now, in his room, in his head, in his ears, it was as though a crowd of people were in the room with

> him. They were saying; "We're with you; you're not alone; we'll help you across." (256)

What is the purpose of undercutting the reality about to be revealed to Antar? In fact, the ending puts a question mark on the whole novel, which constitutes a probe into the metanarrative prefixed as prologue to the book. What does Ghosh want to achieve by doing this? One of the answers can be that Ghosh does not want Murugan's truth, which in turn will become Antar's truth, to become final, transcendent, negating the possibilities of being further questioned, investigated into by others, who might come up with "their" truths. The novelist is in tune with the Postmodernist temper in stressing the tentativeness of truth, as Postmodernism reduces all truth-claims to the level of rhetorics and discounts the possibility of a single claimant.

The seeming ambiguities and contradictions in the novel resolve themselves into a comprehensible, compact work, if the book is approached through the prism of Postmodernism.

NOTES

1. Madan Sarup, *An Introductory Guide to Post-Structuralism and Postmodernism* (New York: Harvester, 1991), p. 130.
2. Amitav Ghosh, *The Calcutta Chromosome* (New Delhi: Ravi Dayal, 1996), p. 31.
3. Sarup, p. 132.
4. *Ibid.*, p. 150.

Telling and Showing: The Cinematic Narrative Technique in *The Calcutta Chromosome*

MADHUMALATI ADHIKARI

Fiction more often than not uses the 'artificial device of story-telling'[1] wherein the author (like Thackerary and Wells), keen about *telling* the reader what to think of the character rather than letting the character *show* himself (like Henry James and Joseph Conrad), ignores the characteristic view. Fortunately, the rise of the cinematic technique has compelled the fiction writer to take cognizance of its artistry and include motifs, communicative modes omitted from conventional inscriptions, for self-enrichment. In recent times, the penetration of the cinematic technique into literature has enabled the writer to manipulate the complex strands of story-line, his design and ideologies more expertly and satisfyingly than ever.

Amitav Ghosh's application of the cinematic technique in *The Calcutta Chromosome* (1996) is not a mere excuse to experiment with a fashionable literary exercise but to defamiliarize reality and 'to make it seem strange, and as a result [to] renew our perception of what lies around us.'[2] The novel is not a simple 'spine-chiller' or a science fiction that revolves round the hypotheses of anti-science, anti-matter and immortality but a 'broader enquiry about life.'[3] The fictional record mingles fact and fiction unobtrusively. The reader is voluntarily rushed through a time span of some hundred years that moves into a labyrinth of cultural variety that bridges the distance between America, England, Egypt and India. For Ghosh, the cinematic devices of narration and point of view become very convenient: "to expand or compress the actual time period of an event; to show the simultaneity, emotional contrast, or equivalency of corresponding events to insert a repeated visual (and sometimes aural) comment that anchors a series of shots to a motif or idee fixe (as in a refrain); and to fill in or project pieces of plot by inserting scenes from the past or the future."[4]

The novel has three different strands of story-line; the first narrates the life-story of Antar an Egyptian computer clerk, working all alone on his super-intelligent machine Ava, sometimes in the early twenty-first century, to locate the adventures of an India-born American scientist L. Murugan who had incomprehensively disappeared in Calcutta in August 1995; the second, historically true, revolves around Ronald Ross the British scientist who in 1902 had discovered 'the manner in which Malaria is conveyed by mosquitoes'; and the third, a mysterious illogical account that chronicles Ross's investigation as to be a subordinate research only, controlled by a larger and more potent power through its two agents: Mangala a sweeper woman and Laakhan/Lutchman a 'dhooley bearer.' The novel manipulates British, Egyptian, Armenian and Indian characters appearing in the different decades of the twentieth and the early twenty-first century. The question that is to be answered in this paper is, 'How and why Ghosh employs this uncommon technique?'

Ghosh positions and moves his 'camera-eye' to project distinct fields that would explore the psyche of the individual character and evoke specific emotional reactions in the viewer. The movement is never linear but is punctuated by *cross-cuts*, *contrast-cuts* and *jump-cuts*. The novel opens with Antar's story: his apartment in New York, his lonely, desolate life-style, his hopes and fears, his friends, his passage down the memory lane. (12-16)[5] The *flashback* builds up the character, gives substance to his personality and familiarizes the reader with his history. The segment narrating the story of the Hungarian lady archaeologist al-Magari, is a flashback and also a contrast-cut to amplify the present isolated and sad condition of Antar and his happy days of childhood. The emotional rise and fall of the character well illustrated by the device jumps from the Egyptian days, back to the present American life and the other details of his existence are edited for the time being, to be recorded in a suitable place in the future. All *cuts* demand an expert manipulation of events.

Constant 'compression, repetition and extension' of facts provide recurring images and motifs that reduce the distance between the reader/spectator and the text/screen. Murugan narrating Ross's story to Antar states, 'I'll turn a few pages for you; but remember it was you who asked. It's your funeral.' (58) Later the image of the funeral is repeated again. (255) The explanations of 'technology for interpersonal transference' is given to Antar (90) and then to Urmila by Murugan. (178-183) Lutchman's lantern appears in Grigson's episode (79) and Phulboni's narration. (218, 229) The repetition unites symbols or images or motifs to extend, to add new dimensions to the fictional truth and to create the cinematic sense of still images slightly altered that offers the impression of movement witnessed by a reader. This increases the credibility of the text. V.F. Perkins has noted, 'the credibility of the movies come . . . . from our habit of placing more trust in the evidence of our eyes than in any other form of sense[ory] data: a film makes us feel like *eye-witness* of the events which it portrays.'[6] Ghosh employs the cinematic technique for conveying the experience of 'witnessing' the events pertinent for willing suspension of disbelief in relation to such a fantastic and bizarre tale.

One very interesting fact that immediately attracts the attention of the reader in *The Calcutta Chromosome* is the space and time montage. Disruption of time and space enables us to visualize and seek the complexities of plot structure and admire a conglomeration of ideas. The reader may flit between the physical and the psychological time of different characters that progress either simultaneously to different geographical places or remain in the same physical location but at different spots of time. While Sonali is witnessing Mangala-bibi's magical attempts to transfer Laakhan's spirit into Romen Haldar's body, (140) almost at that very moment Murugan is having a peculiar experience of seeing 'faces round his bed . . . rippling like reeds, behind the surface of the mosquito net' (131) in Mrs. Aratounian's flat. The visual cuts, the non-linear progression presented through a meandering story-line narrated by four different speakers—Murugan, Antar, Urmila and Sonali—from multifarious angles, thrusts the reader into a compelling confusion wherein he remains unaware of the author's guidance. As a result, for interpretation, the reader's intelligence and imagination are the two tools by which he can deconstruct and reconstruct the text for a proper comprehension of the mysterious message subsumed in the design of the book. Ghosh never spells out clearly the idea that he wishes to convey but the experiences of the different characters make the reader realize that he is not looking into the problem of malaria research but being informed about a great design of the Female Spirit that conrols the Universe to preserve the continuity of life through her agents, Laakhan and Mangala/Mrs. Aratounian/Urmila/Tara.

The use of a series of strongly visual images accentuates the feeling of visibility and subdues the realization of aural reception. Ghosh is very adept in handling the language that makes *transitions* either smoothly and abruptly or expectedly and unexpectedly through a *metaphorical dissolve* which synthesizes two different actions or images by their implied meanings. Phulboni's mysterious experience in Renupur is a characteristic illustration of *metaphorical and form dissolve*. The blood curdling "scream, a raging inhuman howl [tears] through the stormy night. It hurled a single word into the wind—'Laakhan'—and then it was silenced by the thunder of the speeding train." (227) The 'inhuman howl' and silence, an example of *abrupt transition* is juxtaposed with a smooth dissolve projected through the 'stormy night' and the 'speeding train.' The effect of the raging howl, the stormy night and the speeding train dissolves metaphorically to represent fear, death and mystery. The *form dissolve* that links up two images with the same shape or colour is carried out very often by the computer Ava whose memory reconstructs and deconstructs images for Antar's convenience. Ghosh himself very often experiments with *vision mixing*: Urmila recalls and reports to Murugan that as a child she often had a dream, 'I dreamt I would open the front door of our flat one day and find a small group of Gods and Goddesses outside.' (192) The description in the very next paragraph begins with, "she paused at the open door of a workshop . . . and found [her self] staring into a teeming crowd of smiling flesh coloured faces.' (192) The faces disappear behind a six foot dancing Ganesha and then an elderly man materializes suddenly in front of her. The parallel drawn between the ordinary front door of her flat and the workshop door, the faces of the gods and goddesses and the crowd of smiling faces, the figure of Ganesha and the old man, is very palpable. Clearly, Urmila's dream of childhood dissolves into the reality of an idol-maker's workshop at Kalighat. The reader, to investigate and to appreciate the beauty of the various types of transition, must move slowly through the text.

Amitav Ghosh often uses the technique of the *establishing shot* that in fact, gives the long range view of a scene. It is commonly used to 'allow the viewer a territorial framework in which to understand subsequent action.'[8] The views from Antar's window in New York, the details of Lower Circular Road and Robinson Street in Calcutta give us the exact positioning of the character and his contextual relationship with the immediate environment. While making use of the establishing shot, Ghosh expertly exploits the power of a *deep focus shot* that enables the viewer to see the background, middle-ground and fore-ground clearly. He applies this method in relation to Antar, Murugan, Urmila, Sonali and even Ronald Ross. We are not only informed about the general ambience of society—colonial or postcolonial, Western or Eastern—but also the circle of friends and foes, material objects and psychological presences surrounding the characters. This offers a complete picture to the reader and extends the satisfaction of visualising the whole.

The novel records a web of interconnected moments that focuses not on the idea of a scientific research but on the search for immortality: 'a fresh start. When your body fails you, you leave it, you migrate—you or at least a matching symptomology of yourself. You begin all over again, another body, another beginning.' (91) Events and moments of the text presented through the varied perspectives of different characters emerge as points of awareness reflecting forms which at first sight may appear as inversions, parodies and repetition. Supplication before Mangala-bibi witnessed by Farley in Calcutta, (125) Lucky's amazing behaviour of prostrating himself before Tara and touching her feet with his forehead in New York, (185) and Murugan's act of touching Urmila's feet (254) are not mere instances of repetition but a form of inversion of time and place that connects the separate scenes. This compels the reader/spectator to compare the different actions all the time, one strengthening the other. Vsevolod Pudovkin in 'Form and Discipline' terms the process as *'relational editing.'*[8] (125) Ghosh has relied heavily on editing to maintain the suspense in the novel and also to connect the various sections of the plot structure.

Like many Art-films, Ghosh raises countless questions but keeps silent about their solutions. The beauty and the pleasure of the book is in searching for the solutions and delving deep into its mysteries created by bio-physical, meta-physical, geo-physical and trans-temporal images. It is not easy to etch such qualitatively different images meaningfully. But Amitav Ghosh accomplishes the near impossible by the artistry of the audio-visual technique. The most significant reason for employing this method is to give credibility to our world that contains the voice of logic and illogic, matter and anti-matter, science and anti-science. Ghosh is determined to establish that truth is stranger than fiction. It is not difficult to assert confidently that not a lure of an affectation but a genuine artistic need had motivated Ghosh to opt for the cinematic narrative technique in *The Calcutta Chromosome*.

NOTES

1. Wayne C. Booth, *The Rhetoric of Fiction* (Chicago: University of Chicago Press, 1983), p. 3
2. Wallace Martin, *Recent Theories of Narrative* (Ithaka: Cornell Univ. Press), p. 47.
3. Meenakashi Mukherjee, 'Spine Chiller,' *India Today,* 15 May 1996, p. 163.
4. J.A. Cuddon, *A Dictionary of Literary Terms* (London: Penguin, 1982), p. 47.
5. Amitav Ghosh, *The Calcutta Chromosome* (Delhi: Ravi Dayal Publisher, 1996).
6. V.F. Perkins, 'Form and Discipline,' *Film as Film: Understanding and Judging Movies* (Baltimore: Penguin, 1972) p. 62, emphasis added.
7. Cuddon, p. 50.
8. 'From Film Technique,' *Film Theory and Criticism: Introductory Readings,* ed. Gerald Mast, Marshall Cohen and Leo Braudy (New York: U.P., 1992), p. 125.

Traumatic Evolution of Nations: A Study of *Dancing in Cambodia, At Large in Burma*

D.K. PABBY

The latest book by the eminent Indian English novelist Amitav Ghosh titled *Dancing in Cambodia, At Large in Burma*, published by Ravi Dayal, Delhi (1998), gives a rather misleading impression to the reader who glances at its title. It seems that it is Ghosh's narrative description of his travels through these two countries after these achieved independence from their colonial rulers. But as one progresses along, the first impression soon gives way to a serious realisation that the book defies conventional literary classification of a 'travelogue' or 'travel-writing.' In fact, it is an imaginative rendering of complex responses of a scholarly researcher and sensitive writer of the agonizing process of the evolving of a nation for two South Asian countries Cambodia and Burma in their postcolonial phase. These responses make, no doubt, a fascinating reading having been rendered in elegant and rhythmic prose revealing the harsh realities of the political, socio-cultural, economic and ethno-regional problems that these countries were confronted with after throwing off the yokes of slavery. In sooth, these countries are still grappling with the problematic of evolution of their distinct national identities; and the writer appears to hold a mirror to the other nation-states in the region and the continent. This thought-provoking and disturbing book is divided into three chapters with first and third chapters covered in about 50 pages each and the middle-one genuinely sandwiched into only eleven pages.

Chapter one titled 'Dancing in Cambodia,' starts with an anthropological description of the sea-journey of King Sisowath along with his entourage of several dozen princes, courtiers, officials and most importantly a troupe of nearly a hundred classical dancers and musicians from the royal palace at Phnom Penh. For the king, the journey that started on 10 May 1906, at two in the afternoon, aboard a French liner called *Amiral-Kersaint*, was the fulfilment of a lifelong dream and desire to visit France. For others it was a cherished opportunity to step out of their own land and to stage the first ever performance of Cambodian classical dance in Europe, at the Exposition coloniale in Marseille, an immense fairyland of an exhibition centred on the theme of France's colonial possessions. The 'colonised' situation of the dancers is sensitively portrayed in these tantalizing snippets of information of which the Marseille newspapers were often full: "it was said that the dancers entered the palace as children and spent their lives in seclusion ever afterwards; that their lives revolved entirely around the royal family; that several were the King's mistresses and had even borne him children; that some of them had never stepped out of the palace grounds until this trip to France." (3)

Accompanying these smart dancers, as their supervisor and head, was the eldest of the King's daughters, Princess Soumphady, whose royal manners and style of dress had an electrifying effect on the Marseillais crowd. Though she admired very enthusiastically the clothes and hats of the Frenchwomen, yet she politely declined the suggestion to wear clothes like those. This was perhaps an indication of the sense of pride that she and other Cambodian women felt about their distinctive attire suited for their variety of dances. Ghosh learns the remaining story of King Sisowath and Princess Soumphady's 1906 journey to France through Chea Samy, a sister-in-law of Pol Pot and a teacher at the School of Fine Arts in Phnom Penh, in 1993. The car-journey with his friend Moylka who was a mid-level Civil servant and a poised, attractive woman in her early thirties, was quite a hazardous one, as it was four months before the countrywide elections to be held under the auspices of United Nations's Transitional Authority in Cambodia. The personal interview and encounter with Chea Samy reveals the latter's connection with the royal palace as also with the renowned revolutionary Pol Pot who never showed any favours to his relatives during the period of his rule. Amitav Ghosh describes the situation thus:

> Chea Samy was working in a communal kitchen at the time, cooking and washing dishes. Late that year some party workers stuck a poster on the walls of the kitchen: they said it was a picture of their leader, Pol Pot. She knew who it was the moment she set eyes on the picture.
>
> That was how she discovered that the leader of the terrifying, inscrutable 'Organization,' Angkar, that ruled their lives, was none other than little Saloth Sar (Pol Pot). (14)

After 'breaking' of Cambodia by the Vietnamese in 1979, the country became "like a shattered slate: before you could think of drawing lines on it, you had to find the pieces and fit them together." (16) In the post-revolution period, when the Ministry of Culture launched an effort to locate the trained classical dancers and teachers who had survived, one of the well-known surviving dancers described their sensitive position in these words: "I was like a smoker who gives up smoking. . . . I would dream of dance when I was alone or at night. You could get through the day because of the hard work. It was the nights that were really difficult; we would lie awake wondering who was going to be called out next. *That was when I would dance, in my head.*" (17) As if to reinforce the significant role of culture and art in the process of national reconstruction even in the most trying circumstances, Amitav Ghosh tells the readers:

> Like everyone around her, Chea Samy too had started all over again—at the age of sixty, with her health shattered by the years of famine and hard labour. Working with quiet, dogged persistence, she and a handful of other dancers and musicians slowly brought together a ragged, half-starved bunch of orphans and castaways, and with the discipline of their long, rigorous years of training they began to resurrect the art that Princess Soumphady and Luk Khun Meak had passed on to them in that long-ago world, when King Sisowath reigned. Out of the ruins around them they began to create the means of denying Pol Pot his victory. (18)

Shifting the narrative back and forth, Ghosh highlights the problems of Cambodia's colonisation by France as also the rise of Pol Pot, Khmer Rouge, other minority groups resorting to Guerrilla war-tactics, and attack by Vietnam, through the strategies of contrast and comparison. Thus the complexity of the political, social, economic, cultural and ethnic problems gets concretized with the help of analytical portrayals of Norodom Sihanouk, Minister Thiounn and his grandson Thiounn Mumm, Pol Pot and his brother Loth Sieri, King Sisowath, Son Sann, Hun Sen, Khieu Samphan, Rodin, et al. In spite of all the political turmoil and chaotic-anarchic situations, one thing that kept the spirit of the 'nation' alive in Cambodia is its rich cultural heritage of music and dance. This becomes evident from the vivid description of the cultural festival that was held in Phnom Penh in 1988 amidst the destruction of social, economic, cultural and political fabric of the country:

> But people flocked to the theatre the day the festival began. Onesta Carpene, a Catholic relief worker from Italy was one of the handful of foreigners then living in Phnom Penh. She was astonished at the response: the city was in a shambles; there was debris

> everywhere, spilling out of the houses on to the pavements, the streets were jammed with pillaged cars, there was no money and very little food—'I could not believe that in a situation like that people would be thinking music and dance.' But still they came pouring in, and the theatre was filled far beyond its capacity. . . . When the first musicians came onstage, she [a relief worker] heard sobs all around her. Then, when the dancers appeared, in their shabby, hastily-made costumes, suddenly, everyone was crying: old people, young people, soldiers, children—'you could have sailed out of there in a boat.' . . . They could not stop crying; people wept through the entire length of the performance.
> It was a kind of rebirth: a moment when the grief of survival became indistinguishable from the joy of living. (52)

In the second chapter entitled 'Stories in Stones,' Amitav Ghosh explores the significance of an important cultural symbol of the twelfth-century temple 'Angkor Wat' in the cultural life and ethos of Cambodia. Speaking of Angkor Wat as 'a monument to the power of the story,' Ghosh writes:

> This is true in a perfectly literal sense: with every step a visitor takes in this immense twelfth-century Cambodian temple he finds himself moving counters in a gigantic abacus of story-telling. The device is a vast one—it is said to be the largest single religious edifice in the world—and it provides its own setting as well as a cast of galactic dimensions. The setting is Mt Meru, the sacred mountain of ancient Indian myth, whose seven carefully graded tiers provide the blueprint for the temple's form. The cast is the entire pantheon of gods, deities, sages and prophets with which that cosmos is peopled. (54)

Ghosh then tells us about a discovery that he made about the paradoxical character of Angkor Wat being a uniquely powerful symbol of the romance of lost civilizations and ancient glory devoured by time for many people around the globe; whereas for Cambodians it serves as no less a vivid symbol of modernity:

> Angkor Wat is, for example, undisputedly a temple, yet it never figures in anything to do with religion, or indeed in any context that might be called 'traditional' or old-fashioned. Its likeness appears instead on certain factory-produced commodities, like beer; it is stamped on uniforms, civil and military; it figures on the lo-

> gos of large corporations, like banks; indeed, the erstwhile Kampuchea Airlines even succeeded in transforming this most earthbound of structures into a symbol of flight, by lending it a pair of wings. (56)

As an anthropologist that Ghosh is, he found out that the legend of the accidental discovery of Angkar Wat by the nineteenth-century French explorer Henri Mohout is a kind of myth no more and no less true than any of the others inscribed upon the temple. And commenting on the story of the 'restoration' of the temple by applying the most scientific methods available, with help from Indian archaeologists also, the writer reinforces the paradoxical stance of this central cultural symbol of Cambodia:

> The story is a familiar one, for in this century many other parts of the world have seen their present being technologically and symbolically superseded by the relicts of their past. But in Cambodia the process went further than elsewhere. For an entire generation of Cambodians, including politicians as different in ideology as Prince Sihanouk, Son Sann and Pol Pot, Angkor Wat became a symbol of the modernizing nation-state. It became the opposite of itself: an icon that represented a break with the past—a token of the country's belonging, not within the medieval, but rather the contemporary world. Thus the beer, banks, airlines and of course, flays. (60)

The third and concluding chapter of Amitav Ghosh's book is titled 'At Large in Burma.' It is an attempt to explore the history of his 'roots' by listening to the stories of other countries: 'places my parents, and relatives had lived in or visited before the birth of the Republic of India, in 1947.' He writes:

> To me, the most intriguing of these stories were those that my family carried out of Burma. I suspect that this was partly because Burma had become a kind of lost world in the early '60s, when I was old enough to listen to my relatives' stories. It was in 1962 that General Ne Win, the man who would be Burma's longtime dictator, seized power in a coup. Almost immediately, he slammed the shutters and switched off the lights: Burma became the dark house of the neighbourhood, huddled behind an impenetrable, overgrown fence. It was to remain shuttered for almost three decades. (65)

Memories of Burma were mainly kept alive by Ghosh's family through an aunt and her husband nicknamed 'Prince' who left Burma for Calcutta in 1942, in the last, panic-stricken weeks before the Japanese Army marched into Rangoon. Though the Prince spoke nostalgically about the magnificence of Burma and called it 'the richest country in Asia except for Japan' where people were very generous and hospitable to the strangers, the author discovered that 'Burmese nationalism practically started with anti-Indian riots.' (67)

Amitav Ghosh then analyses like a true anthropologist as to what went wrong and how that made Burma, after fifty years, one of the United Nations's ten least developed nations on earth, and a byword for repression, xenophobia and civil abuse. The decline started, he was told, with the assassination of Aung San on 19 July 1947, though he was the country's acknowledged leader and the hero of its independence movement. Suu Kyi, eminent human rights activist and a 1991 Nobel Peace Prize Awardee, still living in a kind of house arrest in Rangoon, is Aung San's worthy daughter and she was only two at the time of her father's assassination. Since it attained its independence in January 1948, Burma has seen civil wars, communist uprisings, military coups and continual fightings amongst its sizable minority groups—the Karen, the Rakhine, the Shan, the Mon, and several smaller groups. The Burmans are otherwise predominantly Buddhist and form two-third of the country's population. During the colonial times, the British recounting policies favoured minority groups over the ethnic Burmans. The British Burma Army was thus formed largely of the units such as Karen Rifles and the Kachin Rifles. Consequently, after independence, civil war was inevitable with insurgents outnumbering the government troops who in any case were inexperienced. Interpreting the subsequent events of civil strife and political turmoil, Amitav Ghosh writes:

> It takes a military dictator to believe that symbols are inert and can be manipulated at will. Forty years after his assassination, Aung San had his revenge. In a strange, secular reincarnation, his daughter, Suu Kyi, came back to haunt those who had sought to make use of his death. In 1988, when Burma's decades of discontent culminated in an anti-military uprising, Aung San Suu Kyi emerged from obscurity as one of the country's most powerful voices, the personification of Burma's democratic resistance to military rule. (74)

Peaceful resistance to the rule of the Military Junta still continues to be the mainstay of Suu Kyi's non-confrontist struggle. She holds regular public meetings at her residence in the University Avenue. She answers questions from the public on all subjects ranging from food and health to politics and literature. But it appears to Ghosh that in spite of her mass appeal, SLORC (State Law and Order Restoration Council) has succeeded in keeping its hold on power as they have succeeded in creating systems of surveillance that are unparalleled in the scope of their inclusiveness. In mustering resources and the expertise required to operate complex systems of social control, Burma's military rulers are an exception and that appears to be the reason why they have been able to hold on so long to power in spite of Suu Kyi's popular appeal and mass base.

Suu Kyi is not even aggressively critical of Burma's 'observer status at the ASEAN' which seems to some an endorsement of the military regime. Her basic conciliatory approach and tone permeates through her response:

> I don't quite understand why one talks about constructive engagement as being such a problem. Each government has its own policy, and we accept that this is the policy of the ASEAN nations. I sometimes think that this problem is made out to be much bigger than it really is. . . . Just because [these governments] have decided on a policy of constructive engagement, there is no need for us to think of them as our enemies. *I don't think this is a case of us and them.* (112, my italics)

This Gandhian approach of Suu Kyi, it seems, equips her with much-needed moral strength to weigh things objectively. Her optimism reflected in an answer to Ghosh's question epitomizes the philosophy of a leader committed whole-heartedly to the ideals of peace, non-violence and achievement of objectives through noble means, however delayed these may be: 'I have always told you . . . that we will win . . . that we will establish a democracy in Burma, and I stand by that. But as to when, I cannot predict. I've always said that to you.' (113-14)

In the perceptive analysis of the socio-politico-cultural crises in Cambodia and Burma, presented in extremely readable and elegant prose, Amitav Ghosh has presented, by implication, a prophetic vision for India also in the context of the complex process of national reconstruction.

The Politics of Isolation and Resurgence in *Dancing in Cambodia, At Large in Burma*

NOVY KAPADIA

Cambodia made international headlines in April 1998, when the Khmer Rouge leader Pol Pot died of heart attack at the age of 72. Born Saloth Sar, he grew up in a relatively prosperous farming family in Kompong Thong province—the heartland of the then French protectorate. He studied radio electronics in Paris, when he won a scholarship in 1949. His political career took off when during the 1950s he scaled the ranks of the fledgling underground Communist Party and became secretary-general in 1962.

Pol Pot came to power in 1975 and quickly set about transforming the country into his vision of an agrarian Utopia by emptying the cities, abolishing money, private property and religion and setting up rural collectives. Pol Pot became notorious by ruthlessly trying to impose his vision of a perfect society. He was considered the architect of Cambodia's brutal killing fields regime from 1975-79 and has been held responsible for the deaths of two million Cambodians, in his attempt to turn the country into an agrarian Maoist Utopia between 1975-79. Such is his infamy that even after his death, the President of the USA, Bill Clinton, spoke "a time to remember his murderous reign of terror and to pursue justice against other Khmer Rouge leaders who share the guilt."[1] Weeks before his death, the USA had sought Chinese help to put Pol Pot on trial as reported in *The Hindu*, Sunday, April 12, 1998, p. 6.

The death of the deposed tyrant has aroused an international hue and cry. It has also led to many pertinent queries about Pol Pot's motives, his politics of social engineering and the milieu in which he perpetrated one of the worst genocides in the twentieth century. An answer to such queries and an understanding of the factors which led to Pol Pot's politics of isolation are found in Amitav Ghosh's latest book, *Dancing in Cambodia, At Large in Burma* (1998). The demise of Pol Pot and the questions that it has raised about his regime has made Amitav Ghosh's book an important political document. It is no longer just a travelogue and the impressions of a sensitive author about exotic South-East Asian nations. With an astute eye for detail and in fluent prose, the author blends fact and observation to create an important work of history, sociology and politics.

Without resorting to morbidity or glib sensationalism or excessive moralizing, Amitav Ghosh aptly reconstructs the cruel social experiments of Pol Pot and the misery imposed on the ordinary people. The travelogue is not about Pol Pot and his misdeeds but a travel writer's observations on Cambodia and Burma, both countries which practised the politics of extreme isolation in the recent past. As a perceptive author and a politically alert observer, Amitav Ghosh tries to comprehend the social scenario during the regime of isolation. Conversation with associates of Pol Pot is a major device adopted by Amitav Ghosh to describe some of the cruelties of the late dictator. For instance, the Khmer Rouge's undisguisedly racist nationalism whose principal targets are "Vietnam and Cambodia's own Vietnamese minority," (25) is conveyed through the conversation of a defector. Amitav Ghosh describes how this Khmer Rouge defector in 1992 told United Nations officials about the indoctrination he had received at political camps:

> As far as the Vietnamese are concerned, whenever we meet them we must kill them, whether they are militaries or civilians, because they are not ordinary civilians but soldiers disguised as civilians. We must kill them whether they are men, women or children, there is no distinction, they are enemies. (25)

Amitav Ghosh astutely suggests that Pol Pot's proximity to the "elitist, racially exclusive culture of the court may have had a formative influence on some aspects of their political vision." (25) Ghosh even cites historian Ben Kiernan in support of this theory.

The author also shows how terror was essential to the exercise of power by Khmer Rouge leaders like Pol Pot and Khieu Samphan. The latter was the head of state and is "believed to have played an important role in planning the mass purges of that period." (50) Ghosh presents the mindset of such brutal leaders, who consider terror and cruelty as a morally cleansing weapon: "It [terror] was an integral part not merely of their coercive machinery, but of the moral order on which they built their regime." (50) Ghosh shows that Pol Pot's hero was Robespierre. The aspect of Robespierre which Pol Pot admired was aptly described by the prescient playwright Buchner, quoted in this book, "Terror is an emanation of virtue." (50) Analyzing the nature of such a regime, the author shows that the proclaimed revolution gradually began "to devour itself." (49) Friends and associates with moderate views were gradually eliminated. Ghosh documents the assassination of Hou Yuon and Hu Nim who even briefly served as Minister of Information, because their moderate views "were sharply at odds with the ultra-radical, collectivist ideology of the ruling group." (49) There is a vivid description of the torture chambers at Tuol Sleng in Phnom Penh, yet another example of the cruelty of the Pol Pot regime.

Pol Pot's vision of social Utopia was influenced by his life with hill tribes in remote north-eastern Cambodia. These original Khmers were self-sufficient in their communal living, had no use of money and were untainted by Buddhism. In the opening section of his travelogue, Amitav Ghosh shows how Pol Pot and his associates targetted the middle class in their attempts at social engineering. Again, Ghosh brings variety to his narration by the manner in which he depicts the uprooting of the middle classes. This aspect of the Khmer Rouge revolution is described as the memory of his friend Molyka, "a mid-level civil servant, a poised, attractive woman in her early thirties, painfully soft-spoken, in the Khmer way." (7) Molyka's family was from the social group that was hardest hit by the revolution, the urban middle class. Molyka as a thirteen-year-old was evacuated with her whole extended family, fourteen in all, to a labour camp in the province of Kompong Thom. This was part of the process of re-education and social cleansing. She was separated from the others and sent to work in a fishing village, on "Cambodia's immense freshwater lake, the Tonlé Sap." (9) She worked as a servant and nursemaid for a family of fisherfolk. She did not return to Phnom Penh till 1979 when the Vietnamese over-ran the Khmer Rouge. Of the fourteen people, from her family who had been evacuated, ten were dead. Using the example of a colleague and friend, Ghosh generalizes on the plight of the urban middle class:

> City people by definition, they were herded into rural work-camps; the institutions and forms of knowledge that sustained them were abolished—the judicial system was dismantled, the practice of formal medicine was discontinued, schools and colleges were shut down, banks and credit were done away with; indeed the very institution of money, and even the exchange of goods and services, was banned. (10)

Using examples from history, Amitav Ghosh shows that no previous regime had made such systematic and sustained attacks on the middle class. Ghosh also related Cambodia's civil war to contemporary politics. He expresses the view that "Cambodia's was not a civil war in the same sense as Somalia's or the former Yugoslavia's, fought over the fetishism of small differences: it was a war on history itself, an experiment in the re-invention of society." (10)

Conversing with people who relate anecdotes about their family history, is another device used by Ghosh to convey his impressions. It also gives the discourse, the form of a story. For instance Ghosh learns the story of King Sisowoth and Princess Soumphady's journey to France in 1906 through Chea Samy, a sister-in-law of Pol Pot and a teacher at the school of Fine Arts in Phnom Penh in 1993. The interview with Chea Samy reveals her connection with the royal palace and Pol Pot. It is learned that when the Khmer Rouge seized power in 1975, Chea Samy and her family, despite being related to Pol Pot were shown no favours.

> They were sent off to a village of 'old people,' long-time Khmer Rouge sympathizers, and along with all the other 'new people,' were made to work in the rice-fields. For the next couple of years there was a complete news blackout and they knew nothing of what had happened and who had come to power; it was a part of the Khmer Rouge's mechanics of terror to deprive the population of knowledge. (14)

It is learnt that Chea Samy only came to know that her brother-in-law Pol Pot was leader of the Party, when in 1978, some party workers stuck a poster on the walls of their communal kitchen. Propaganda, the creation of a personality cult and other such techniques to consolidate Khmer Rouge's mechanics of terror. In the opening section of this book, Amitav Ghosh cleverly documents the politics of isolation by the Khmer Rouge and its consequences.

Analytical portrayals of Prince Norodom Sihanouk, Minister Thiounn and his grandson Thiounn Hol, Pol Pot and his brother Loth Sieri, King Sisowath, Khieu Samphan, the French painter Rodin give a human dimension to the unfurling of the socio-political history of Cambodia from May 1906 till 1993. The dates are significant, as in 1906 Sisowath and a hundred classical dancers set sail from Saigon to stage the first ever performance of Cambodian classical dance in Europe, at the Exposition Coloniale in Marseille. The year 1993 is significant as it was the year that countrywide elections were held under the auspices of the UN's Transitional Authority in Cambodia known by its acronym, UNTAC. The elections, the will-power of the people during duress and their supreme love for music and dance represent the possible resurgence and redemption of Cambodia. Amitav Ghosh cleverly shows that despite the political turmoil and prevailing anarchy, the spirit of the nation is maintained by its rich cultural legacy. This is evident from a vivid description of a cultural festival held in Phnom Penh in 1988. She was astonished at the response: "the city was in a shambles; . . . there was no money and little food. . . . But still they came pouring in, and the theatre was filled far beyond its capacity. It was very hot inside." (52) Another foreigner, Eva Mysliwiec, a Quaker relief missionary, recalls the performance: "When the first musicians came onstage she heard sobs all around her. Then, when the dancers appeared, in their shabby, hastily-made costumes, suddenly everyone was crying—people wept through the entire length of the performance." (52) Such a spontaneous expression of joy is a vindication of faith amongst the Cambodian people that their artistic heritage survived despite all the political turmoil and attempted social engineering by the Khmer Rouge. A member in the audience sums up the feelings with an apt phrase, "We thought everything was lost, that we would never hear our music again, never see our dance." (52) Towards the end of the first section of his book, Amitav Ghosh shows that the passion for dance and music symbolized the politics of resurgence in Cambodia. It gave the beleagured Cambodian people an identity and certitude, a badge of authenticity. The author sums up this mood as "a kind of rebirth: a moment when the grief of survival became indistinguishable from the joy of living." (52)

The theme of resurgence is also fully explored in the second chapter entitled "Stories in Stones." It examines the significance of an important cultural symbol, the twelfth century temple Angkor Wat in the ethos of Cambodia's cultural life. It is said to be the largest single religious edifice in the world with "the entire pantheon of gods, deities, sages and prophets with which that cosmos is peopled." (54) In this brief section, Amitav Ghosh shows how this architectural wonder became a unifying symbol for Cambodians, including politicians of different ideologies such as Prince Sihanouk, Son Sann and Pol Pot. Yet, as Ghosh shows, the five towered image of Angkor Wat is not a symbol of religious unity. Buddhism is the dominant religion of the majority of the Cambodians, so the shrine at the main temple of Angkor Wat attracts both believers and tourists. However, as Ghosh shows, Angkor Wat is not as the Golden Temple at Amritsar is to the Sikhs or the mosques at Mecca and Madina are to the Muslims or St. Peters Church at the Vatican to the Roman Catholics, a symbol of spiritual faith and renewal. Paradoxically, for the Cambodians, Angkor Wat never figures in anything religious or in any context that might be called 'traditional or old-fashioned.' It is also not just a "uniquely powerful symbol of the romance of lost civilizations; of ancient glory, devoured by time." (56) Instead, for Cambodia, it serves "as a no less vivid symbol of modernity." (56) Like music and dance, this awesome national monument becomes a symbol of the resurgence of Cambodia, an expression of national pride, an identity by which the world can take notice of this small nation ravaged for centuries by French colonialism and later in the 1970s by American fighter planes and troops as a consequence of the Vietnam War. So it is not just a religious symbol but a symbol of national pride. Ghosh shows how images of Angkor Wat, "appear to be omnipresent." (56) Its likeness appears on products of mass consumption, as if to glorify the latter by their association with a splendid past:

> it is stamped on uniforms, civil and military; it figures on the logos of large corporations, like banks; indeed, the erstwhile Kampuchea Airlines even succeeded in transforming the most earthbound of structures into a symbol of flight, by lending it a pair of wings. (56)

The temple is thus used as a political symbol. As a symbol of resurgence it is also woven into the flags of political parties which contested the 1993 general elections. In this complex, brief but fascinating travelogue, Amitav Ghosh cleverly reveals how the magnificent edifice of Angkor Wat becomes a symbol of national pride and how a national monument can have so much meaning and hope for an entire population.

The use of history and politics in a work of art is familiar territory for Amitav Ghosh. He has blended both history and politics in his earlier novels like *Shadow Lines* (1988) and *In an Antique Land* (1992). In his travelogue, Ghosh has made the past and present merge effortlessly into each other, a technique he has used very effectively in his third novel, *In an Antique Land.* It is a work in which there is a blending of fact and fiction and a coalescing of many areas of human knowledge such as history, anthropology, philology, sociology and religion. K.C. Belliappa in his learned essay shows that in this novel, Ghosh demonstrates, "how an excursion into the past is no escape from the present, but a coming to grips with the present realities of living."[7] Ghosh uses the technique of juxtaposing the medieval and modern worlds of the twelfth and twentieth centuries in two different civilizations of India and Egypt, with their diverse cultures of Christianity, Judaism, Islam and Hinduism. Through this clever fictional discourse, Ghosh illustrates the need for human understanding and religious tolerance, which he considers as imperative in a world full of strife due to religious obscurantism and fanaticism. As Belliappa shows, the reconstruction of history by Ghosh has made *In an Antique Land* "a brilliant metaphor of our times." (65)

The trend of blending history and politics in travel writings was set by V.S. Naipaul, over three decades ago. Ghosh has emulated this trend in *Dancing in Cambodia, At Large in Burma.*

V.S. Naipual's motive for travel writing varies with each phase and in each decade. A travel scholarship from the government of Trinidad allowed him to tour West Indies, at a time when Indian-black tensions were running high and resulted in *The Middle Passage* (1962) the first of his travel books. Frustrated at the communal divide in Trinidad, Naipaul travelled to India, the land of his origins and his forefathers. His first sojourn in India led to dismay and disillusionment, expressed in *An Area of Darkness* (1964).

Throughout Naipaul's first travelogue on India, there is a sense of humiliation, of personal frustration that the India of his secret imagination, dreams and longings is a mere mirage. The country of his origins is neither a spiritual nation nor does it possess a scientific outlook to life. Naipaul views India as another oriental third world nation despite its size and ancient history. In this book he expresses anger at the dirt, decay, incompetence, passivity and corruption prevalent in India and the way Mahatma Gandhi has been turned into a saint for personal benefits. So his initial quest for finding solace in India's ancient culture and a home away from home ends in despair. At this stage, Naipaul's travel writing reflects the confusions of decolonization, with its suspicions and humiliations.

In the 1970s, in what is termed as the third phase of Naipaul's writings, he examines the ambiguities of freedom in the decolonized world. This results in *India: A Wounded Civilization* (1977), a critique of the period of Internal Emergency declared by the late Prime Minister, Mrs. Indira Gandhi. Three years later, Naipaul writes a fascinating book *Among the Believers: An Islamic Journey* (1980) which deals with several prevailing paradoxes amongst newly Independent nations in the decolonized world. In this book he highlights the essential illogicality of many national movements which desire the material benefits of modernisation while rejecting the civilisation and thought processes that have made such production possible. This facet animates much of the writing of this period. In this book, Naipaul reveals his concept of a Universal Civilisation, which he believed was represented by Europe, the United States of America and Japan. He felt, they offered the kind of tolerant society and comforts most people of the world want. Naipaul showed that even in orthodox Islamic societies, there is a desire for such freedom and goods. However the author perceptively shows that many people in decolonized and orthodox societies desire not only freedom but also want the imagined securities of the past. Such paradoxes result in irrational rage or fantasies. Naipaul's remedy is for cultures to creatively adapt to changing circumstances.

Naipaul's third book of Indian travels, *India: A Million Mutinies* (1991) is full of vigour and confidence in the future of India. The book is filled with the voices of a wide variety of people and has limited authorial comment. It shows that notions of freedom and self assertion have moved from the elite to a broader range of society and a sense of identity and a notion of India has been aroused. This travel book can be termed as the postcolonial with its acceptance of energies, cultural achievements, conflicting claims and freedoms that have developed in the modern world. Amitav Ghosh shows a similar trend in his latest travelogue on Cambodia and Burma in which he shows the impact of colonization and all the paradoxes of a postcolonial phase. Creditably both Naipaul and Amitav Ghosh use history as a backdrop to their novels and travel writings, without diminishing the artistic and literary appeal of their works. Both have shown that the novel can flourish by the use of history.

Ever since the historical novel popularized by Sir Walter Scott came into vogue, a ceaseless debate has arisen about whether it is hazardous to infiltrate too much history into the plot of a novel or to have too many historical figures among the leading characters. This dilemma is tackled in different ways by various authors. Salman Rushdie in his novel *Midnight's Children* (1981) blends the autobiography of the narrator Saleem Sinai with the collective experience of a people and the history of nation from the Jallianwalla Bagh massacre to the Emergency promulgated by Mrs. Indira Gandhi. The essence of Rushdie's novels is his ability to play with history, to blend memory and facts. Similarly Amitav Ghosh in *The Shadow Lines* (1998) uses the twin ingredients of memory and imagination to blend his presentation of historical facts. Using the narrative technique of unfurling events, by reading old newspaper reports, Amitav Ghosh shows how communal violence spread in Calcutta and cities of erstwhile East Pakistan in 1964. Amitav Ghosh's novel, *The Shadow Lines* is very contemporary and relevant as it shows how communal fanatics thrived on the spread of rumours which intensified feelings of anger and triggered off violence. The bland newspaper reports and memory technique of Amitav Ghosh remove the impact of time and show that riots are contemporaneous, following a similar pattern of suspicion, distrust and rumour activating conditioned minds.

The earlier novels of V.S. Naipaul deal with the triple problems of marginality, exile and insecurity and the confusions of decolonisation. His book *The Loss of El Dorado* (1969) examines the early history of Trinidad and is part of Naipaul's attempt to merge journalism, reportage, history and fiction into a form appropriate to his own analysis of the colonial world and its aftermath. The two central stories provide a wider panorama of Trinidadian history than the usual story of slavery. There is a similarity in the novels of Naipaul and Amitav Ghosh in their portraits and analysis of the postcolonial world and their concerns about the nature of freedom, commitment and authenticity in relation to experience and giving purpose to life. Ideas are questioned by actualities. In three of Naipaul's best works of fiction, *In a Free State* (1971), *Guerrillas* (1975) and *A Bend in the River* (1975), the focus is on the hopes, desires and fears of individuals and how insecurity is transformed into violence and tyranny. Personal lives illuminate the political. In a world without stability or purpose, the author is concerned that the law of the jungle prevails. If Naipual is pessimistic about the disorder created by the collapse of the British Empire, Amitav Ghosh expresses concern about how different cultures and communities are becoming antagonistic to a point of no return.

Interest in such contemporary postcolonial issues has led both V.S. Naipaul and Amitav Ghosh to indulge in travel writing. The new phase in Naipaul's work begins with *Finding the Centre* (1984) which consists of a travel article about the Ivory Coast. The focus has shifted from discussion of the problem of freedom and irritation with irrationality to a celebration of the various people and places Naipaul discovers through travel and writing. Similarly, Amitav Ghosh's recent book, *Dancing in Cambodia, At Large in Burma*, is a sensitive insight into the postcolonial experiences and politics of isolation, violence and hatred in two volatile South-East Asian nations, Cambodia and Burma (now Myanmar). This enthralling travelogue is divided into three sections. The opening chapter, "Dancing in Cambodia," is of 54 pages. The next chapter "Stories in Stones" is brief, a mere eleven pages and deals with the renowned Angkor Wat temple ruins of Cambodia. In the final chapter, the author's focus is again political as he examines the struggle to establish democracy in Burma. This section is entitled, "At Large in Burma" and is of 49 pages. Interestingly each section is unique, with contrasting thematic influences, background and narrative techniques.

The opening section "Dancing in Cambodia" is a compact socio-political analysis of the impact of French colonization of Cambodia, the aftermath of decolonisation and its subsequent humiliations and fantasies. The aesthetic nature of the Cambodia population is revealed by their fascination for art and dance, which could not be suppressed even during the ravages and cruel social engineering of their oppressive ruler, the late Pol Pot. Dance becomes the central metaphor for this section. Amitav Ghosh uses the non-linear narrative, which shuttles backward and forward in time with unfurling of layers of memory. This narrative technique shows the impact of the past on the present milieu in Cambodia, struggling to seek an identity as an independent nation.

The brief section on the glories of Angkor Wat, also reveals an important political message. As an anthropologist and social historian, Amitav Ghosh analyses how this magnificent lost twelfth century Cambodian temple, discovered by French explorer Henri Michael in the nineteenth century, "is a monument to the power of the story." (54) Amitav Ghosh cleverly weaves myth, legend and local stories to show the paradox that Angkor Wat had become. Ghosh shows that this restored architectural wonder is a unique powerful symbol. This also reflects a phase of decolonization, confusions and uncertainties, plus a vigorous glorification of the past. Seeking refuge in past glories to compensate for modern inadequacies is a recurrent feature in many newly independent states as is frequently shown in the travel writings of both Naipaul and Amitav Ghosh. Cleverly in this section, Ghosh uses the narrative technique of a story told by a monk to recall the glory and restoration of Angkor Wat.

In the last section, "At Large in Burma," Ghosh mostly uses the linear narrative to depict the struggle for democracy in Burma. Very cleverly the author shows the clash between the forces of orthodoxy and status quo as represented by the military junta ruling as SLORC (State Law and Order Restoration Council) and the forces of change seeking democracy, headed by Nobel Peace prize winner Aung San Suu Kyi and her followers. She spearheaded a peaceful non-resistance mass movement to restore democracy and civil liberties in her country, despite house arrest, mass arrests of her followers and stringent surveillance. This section has strong political overtones. Ghosh relates Suu Kyi's predicament of house arrest to the postmodern dilemma. He says,

> In the postmodern world, politics is everywhere a matter of symbols, and the truth is that Suu Kyi is her own greatest political asset. It is only because Burma's 1988 democracy movement had a symbol, personified in Suu Kyi, that the world remembers it and continues to exert pressure on the current regime [military junta]. Otherwise, the world would almost certainly have forgotten Burma's slain and dispersed democrats just as quickly as it has forgotten many others like them in the past. (83)

This is a very telling political comment by Amitav Ghosh as it reveals the frequent double standards of the developed nations who profess to uphold the values of democracy, freedom of speech and liberty for people of all races, but for the sake of political or economic convenience, support dictatorial regimes.

The section starts on a nostalgic note. By use of the memory technique, Ghosh recalls the childhood tales he had heard about Burma. He confirms that his interest in Burma developed through the tales narrated by his aunt and her husband, nicknamed "Prince." As an anthropologist, Ghosh relates this story telling to an Indian tradition.

> Like many Indians, I grew up on stories of other countries: places my parents and relatives had lived in or visited before the birth of the Republic of India, in 1947. To me, the most intriguing of these stories were those that my family carried out of Burma. I suspect that this was partly because Burma had become a kind of lost world in the early '60s, when I was old enough to listen to my relatives' stories. (65)

Ghosh thus subtly brings several political motives to this section. Besides the obvious struggle for democracy and freedom, this section also reflects several other crucial aspects of contemporary politics. The author raises several questions about development by implication. Can a nation develop in isolation, especially in this last decade of the twentieth century, when the technological revolution has made the world a 'global village.' Later in this section, the position and role of minorities in a decolonized, newly independent country is also raised. This question becomes very relevant, in the aftermath of the bloodbath of Bosnia Herzegovina and Serbia. The desire of national minorities or ethnic groups to seek independence, a political phenomenon which has increased in the 1990s is reflected in this book, by the struggle of the Karens for independence. It is learnt that the Karen army had been fighting against dire odds for fifty years. "Many regarded the war against SLORC as a direct continuation of the war against the Japanese. Some Karenni families had been at war for three generations, and many of their fighters had spent their entire lives in refugee camps." (92) The author makes no political comment, he does not glorify the heroic struggle by the ethnic minority, the Karens against the ruling Burmans. Instead he raises several pertinent, political questions, which makes this travelogue very intriguing, relevant, gripping and contemporary. For instance he says that the struggle of the Karens raises a fundamental question about how ethnic minorities can be accommodated in a multi-cultural democracy. He recalls an anecdote by Thailand's monarch king Bhumibol who said that if Burma became democratic it would have the same effect it had in Bosnia, only worse. The author rightly says, "If this was so, what did it mean for the prospects of democracy in multi-ethnic societies?" (86)

The marginalisation of an Indian migrant in the Burmese civil war is cleverly shown by Amitav Ghosh as an eminently postmodern encounter. Ko Sonny was a regimental commander with the Karenni insurgents. His real name was Mahinder Singh. "His family had been settled in Burma for three generations. His parents were born there; his father was Sikh and his mother Hindu." (89) His plight is due to youthful idealism. Whilst studying physics in the University of Rangoon, he championed the cause of Karenni and other minority students. He was arrested in 1988 and after his release because of police harassment escaped to the border. Sonny's plight is similar to many student dissidents caught in the throes of civil war. Their hopes and aspirations of a normal career have subsided and they are now full time insurgents. Ghosh shows the social impact of such commitment to a cause, through the misfortunes which have occurred to Sonny. His girlfriend, a Burmese in Rangoon, gave up waiting for him and married someone else. In 1994 his mother died of a heart attack and he came to know about it months later. After years of fighting, he has limited options and income. The alternatives are either to join the underworld in Thailand or remain in the jungle. The only hope is restoration of democracy and a process of national reconciliation launched by Aung San Suu Kyi, the only figure who has popular support among ethnic Burmans and minorities like the Karenni, Kachens and Karens. The human cost of insurgency is cleverly shown by Amitav Ghosh in this gripping narrative. Ghosh shows that "all boundaries are artificial." (100) The solution offered is very practical. He says that Burma's best hopes of peace "lie in maintaining intact the larger and more inclusive entity that history, albeit absent-mindedly, bequeathed to its population almost half a century ago." (100)

Inclusiveness, harmony and tolerance seem to be the lessons of history that Amitav Ghosh is trying to impart, through his complex but gripping travelogue. The thought-provoking, stimulating travelogue thus becomes a metaphor of our times and an allegorical political message for all muli-cultural, multi-racial nation states striving for existence in the postmodern world.

NOTES

1. Cited in "Pol Pot's cremation today," *The Hindustan Times*, 18 April 1998, p. 14.

2. Cited in "USA seeks Chinese help for Pol Pot's trial," *The Hindu*, 12 April 1998, p. 6.
3. Cited in David Streath, "Pol Pot dies of heart attaek," *The Telegraph*, 17 April 1998, p. 3.
4. Cited in Thomas Wagner, "Killing Fields victims feel cheated," *The Telegraph*, 17 April 1998.
5. Amitav Ghosh, *Dancing in Cambodia, At Large in Burma* (Delhi: Ravi Dayal, 1998).
6. Amitav Ghosh, *In an Antique Land* (Delhi: Ravi Dayal, 1992).
7. Cited in K.C. Belliappa, "Amitav Ghosh's *In an Antique Land*: An Excursion into Time Past and Time Present," *The Postmodern Indian English Novel*, ed. Viney Kirpal (Delhi: Allied, 1996), p. 65.
8. Bruce King, *V.S. Naipaul* (London: Macmillan, 1993).

The Hungry Tide: A Riveting Novel of Epic Scope and Humane Breadth

TAPAN KUMAR GHOSH

After the tremendous success of, and the controversy[1] over, *The Glass Palace* (2000), an epic saga that spans several generations and continents to describe the little known, intertwined histories of Burma, Malaya and India and to draw attention to the forgotten 'long march' that had taken place at the end of the World War II, Amitav Ghosh crafted another fascinating and ambitious novel, *The Hungry Tide* (2004), about a place that remains remote and exotic to many readers and about a community of people who live on the periphery of the Indian subconscious, the dispossessed of the tide country. *The Hungry Tide* does not have the grand historical sweep of *The Glass Palace*, but it is a layered and moving book in which Ghosh creates a broadly realistic portrayal of the Sundarbans that acts as a counterpoint to the dreamlike, unknowable mangrove swamps found in an allegorical section of Salman Rushdie's *Midnight's Children*. In his masterly story-telling and use of vividly realized details, the mysterious and enchanting Sundarbans—with the mangroves and man-eating predators, fishes and dolphins, tempests and tides, myth, culture and history—come alive. The pre-historic rain forest is not here merely a backdrop of the human drama but a living presence, one of its major characters. In fact, nothing happens in the book but that the Sundarbans makes it happen.

Divided into two broad sections: "The Ebb: Bhata" and "The Tide: Jowar," *The Hungry Tide* is set in the Sundarbans, an archipelago of hundreds of scattered islands, some densely populated while others completely uninhabited, at the *mohona* (confluence) of several rivers in the Bay of Bengal. "The islands are," the novelist says, "the trailing threads of India's fabric, the ragged fringes of her sari, the *achol* that follows her, half-wetted by the sea" (6).[2]

Interposed between the sea and the plains of Bengal this archipelago stretches—for almost three hundred kilometers—from the Hooghly river in West Bengal to the shores of the Meghna in Bangladesh. It is called 'India's doormat, the threshold of a teeming subcontinent' (50). For hundreds of years the foreigners—the Arakanese, the Khmer, the Dutch, the Portuguese, the Malays, the English—have taken this eastern route to the Gangetic heartland. It is an untamed area where the Ganga empties into the Bay, where there is no border to divide freshwater and salt, and the boundaries between land and water are always mutating, creating a diverse natural habitat where tigers and snakes, crocodiles and sharks roam free. This is a place where floods continually inundate the land and whole forests lift their heads above the tides and then disappear. It is a liquid landscape where surging cyclones can wipe out thousands of lives with the flick of one giant wave, where animals and humans, myth and reality imperceptively merge into each other in a ritual struggle for survival. 'Midwifed by the moon' (8) and sculpted by colossal tides and titanic storms, this estuarine region—known variously as the Sundarbans, after the sundari tree, *Heriteria minor*; *Badaban*, after the mangroves, and *bhatir desh*, the tide country—is home to the Royal Bengal Tigers and the Irrawaddy dolphins, *Orcaella brevirostris*. Some even call it *atthero bhatir desh,* the land of eighteen tides. The place was mentioned in the record books of the Mughal emperors and in Francois Bernier's *Travels in the Mughal Empire*. The multiplicity of names for the Sundarbans is a metaphor for its ephemerality. The land itself is inconstant, subject to radical transformation as a result of late summer storms and tide water. Whole islands are washed away by the cyclones that sweep in from the Bay with huge tidal surges. Thousands of human beings and animals routinely die here in natural disaster. As a character in the novel puts it: "*in the tide country, transformation is the rule of life: rivers stray from week to week and islands are made and unmade in days*" (224). Here, for hundreds of years, only the truly dispossessed braved the tigers, crocodiles and sharks to eke out a precarious existence from the mud and the forest produce.

At the beginning of the twentieth century, a rich and visionary Scotsman, Sir Daniel MacKinnon Hamilton, who believed in the dictum 'labour conquers everything,' founded a utopian settlement where people of all races, classes and religions could live together 'without petty social distinctions and differences' (53). He wanted to establish a new society, a new kind of country: "It would be a country run by co-operatives. . . . Here people wouldn't exploit each other and everyone would have a share in the land" (52). The news was spread and people from Orissa, eastern Bengal and Santhal Parganas rushed to the tide country in search of free land. Villages sprouted on the islands and Hamilton gave them names. Everything was provided for them: electricity, telephone, bank and currency. It was a magnificent dream dreamed by a leading capitalist of colonial India: "He dreamed of a place where men and women could be farmers in the morning, poets in the afternoon and carpenters in the evening" (53). But, unfortunately, his dream did not come true. The tide country was not yet ready for Hamilton's progressive ideas. His memory is preserved in the names of the islands given by him and in the estate he had founded.

The tide country is not very far from Calcutta and the mainstream Indian society—only ninety seven kilometers away. Yet it represents another world where it is impossible to tell who is who, and what their castes and religious beliefs are. It is not just the legacy of Daniel Hamilton, but the hostile environment erases all societal strata, since everyone is equal in the struggle to survive in the adverse surroundings. Here people live amidst utter poverty and 'hunger and catastrophe [are] a way of life' (79). It is a difficult life that leaves most women widowed at a young age and land barely arable because of the salt water of the hungry tide that cannot always be prevented from flooding the fields. As in his other novels, Amitav Ghosh shows here an anthropologist's fascination for the place and its people and the stories they tell—the local myths and legends that subvert the official versions of history and religion. The tide country people have an epic narrative of origins which they pass on orally from generation to generation. They have a kind of local religion—they worship a goddess named Bon Bibi, the presiding deity of the Sundarbans and the arch-enemy of

Dokkhin Rai who represents evil. But the epic of Bon Bibi—*Bon Bibir Karamoti orthat Bon Bibir Johuranama* (*The Miracles of Bon Bibi or the Narrative of Her Glory*)—is strongly inflected by Islamic influences, which evince the syncretic nature of the archipelago's culture and religion. *The Hungry Tide* is a powerful evolutionary story of this region and its people. The setting, unlike in *The Glass Palace*, is geographically limited, yet vast in its implications of some wider global concerns, like preservation of endangered species, environmentalism versus survivalism, rights of the homeless and the dispossessed.

Into the transformative sphere of the tide country, where life is lived 'on the margins of greater events' (11), venture two individuals from the outside world. They are Piya (Piyali) Roy, a Bengali-American cetologist from Seattle who cannot even speak her mother tongue, and Kanai Dutt, a prosperous and proud owner of a translation business in New Delhi. The narrative space is taken up by them and a handful of other characters, each on a personal quest through life. Piya is drawn by the tidal water; she has come to study the Irrawaddy dolphin, *orcaella brevirostris*, a rare river dolphin that can negotiate the mix of fresh and salt water. She is trying to unravel the mystery of this marine mammal that lives in the tidal pools, where they travel and why. Kanai, on the other hand, has been summoned to the land by his aunt, Nilima Bose, a renowned social worker who runs a trust—Badabon Trust—that supports the rights of the poor and the underprivileged and offers manifold services—medical, paralegal and agricultural—to a population of several thousands in Lusibari, the most southerly of the inhabited islands of the tide country. He comes to Lusibari on account of a posthumously discovered notebook—a diary of sorts written by his late uncle and addressed to him. He uses this notebook to decipher another mystery, that of his uncle's death. Linking the two narrative strands is Fokir, an illiterate fisherman who knows the watery labyrinths of the Sundarbans better than anyone and is a key to both the quests. The two stories—one of the notebook and the other of Kanai, Piya and Fokir—that make up the narrative structure of the novel, are unfolded in a braided manner in alternate chapters, the former shedding light on, and containing the seed of, the latter.

Kanai's narrative brings to life the character of his uncle, Nirmal Bose, who is dead before the story begins. Nirmal was a teacher of English literature at Asutosh College in Calcutta where he had made a name for himself as a leftist intellectual and promising writer. He was a poet at heart and a very good speaker. Nilima was his student, and she fell in love with Nirmal, being mesmerized by his fiery lectures and impassioned recitations. They were married in a civil ceremony against the opposition of Nilima's family. The couple came to Lusibari in the years following independence when Nirmal's radical politics became too dangerous in Calcutta and got him into trouble.

Appalled by the dire poverty of the tide country people, Nilima organized the women of the island, mostly widows, and founded the Badaban Trust which brought help, medicine and finally a hospital to the place. Over the years her dedicated work immensely benefitted the islanders and brought them a semblance of respectability and financial independence. Her life-long service to the destitute and dispossessed did not go unrewarded. The Badabon Trust was officially recognized as a model NGO in India and Nilima was decorated with one of the country's highest honours by the President. Nirmal spent his career as headmaster of the island's high school named after Daniel Hamilton. He never supported his wife's single-handed efforts to bring about a qualitative change in the lives of the people they lived with. Because, for this erstwhile Marxist, they bore the stigma of social service. But it was Nirmal who gave her trust its name and suggested the construction of a cyclone shelter in the hospital which saved the lives of many islanders. Kanai had been to Lusibari in 1970, sent by his parents to be rusticated for his audacity, arrogance and misbehaviour with teachers.

For a brief period, during his stay in Lusibari, a young and spirited girl named Kusum passed their lives. She became Kanai's mentor and guide in the island and left a deep impression on his mind. He learnt about the Sundarbans and its people through his association with Nirmal, Nilima and Kusum, particularly the former. In fact, the relevant information about the tide country is presented in the novel through the perspective of Nirmal and his social awareness, his knowledge of its history, myth, geology and geography.

A poet at heart, who constantly invoked Rilke's *Duino Elegies* and sought confirmation of his ideas and thoughts in the lines of the German poet, Nirmal approached retirement from service feeling like his life was poorly spent because he had never lived up to his revolutionary ideals. It was at this stage of his life, in late 1970s, he accidentally came across Kusum, now a widow with a five year old son named Fokir. It was through Kusum and her relative, Horen Naskar, Nirmal came to know about, and was ultimately involved in, the unique experiment of a large number of East Bengali refugees to reinvent themselves and establish a classless, egalitarian society in one of the uninhabited islands of the Sundarbans, named Morichjhapi, that falls within the purview of a reserve forest. (Kusum's back story, her mysterious disappearance from Lusibari and reappearance in Morich Jhapi as a member of the squatters' colony occupies a substantial portion of Nirmal's notebook).

The notebook, now left to Kanai, contains a first person account of the events at the end of Nirmal's life, which revolved round Kusum, her son Fokir, her relative-turned-lover Horen, and the catastrophic struggle of the refugees to create a new habitat on the Morichjhapi island. The notebook was written hurriedly over one or two days in mid-May, 1979, hours before the Morichjhapi massacre, in Kusum's hut where Nirmal had taken shelter.

Nirmal's account of the squatters' movement that swept across the tide country in 1978-79, is rooted in a real uprising among a truly dispossessed and uprooted people (mostly east Pakistani refugees who had fled to India after Partition). They ran away from the hostile environment of their resettlement camp in central India (Dandakaranya) and tried to remake their lives in the familiar terrain of the Sundarbans. They were the poorest of the poor who belonged to the lowest strata of the society. But their revolt was quelled by the Left Front government which had always championed the cause of the refugees from erstwhile East Pakistan.

Amitav Ghosh's historically engaged fiction presents the whole episode more or less objectively, even though the specific political actors and discourses that led to the gruesome massacre and forceful eviction of the refugees are downplayed in the novel.[3] The Morichjhapi massacre is a shameful story of betrayal and of state-sponsored terrorism to evict Indian nationals from the land where they felt at home. It goes to the credit of Amitav Ghosh that he has dared to record, in terms of fiction, this little publicized historical event. But one would expect him, despite his aversion to overtly political writing, to at least assign some historical responsibility to particular political players. The state authorities had declared Morichjhapi as a 'protected forest reserve' for tigers, and they proved unbending in their determination to throw out the 'squatters.' Was it possible, one wonders, that the issue of socio-economic class—and caste—was involved in the making of the policy that unduly privileged nature at the expense of human beings? The novelist elaborates: "Was it possible that in Morichjhapi had been planted the seeds of what might become, it not a Dalit nation, then at least a safe-haven, a place of true freedom for the country's oppressed?" (159) And it was something that the self-styled champions of the 'have-nots' who have made hypocrisy and doublespeak their political trademark, could not swallow?

It is true that the Sundarbans is the only habitat where Royal Bengal tigers, with their dwindling number, continue to live in the wild. They are zealously protected by various international environmental groups who apply economic and diplomatic pressures on the Indian and Bangladeshi governments to maintain the tiger habitats by military/ police force. But in the name of tiger preservation human lives are threatened; the tigers routinely maul and kill the islanders and their cattle (see the chapter 'A Killing,' 289-95). Amitav Ghosh questions this human cost of wildlife preservation when he makes Kanai ask Piya, the American marine biologist, who exclaims horror at the killing of a tiger: "Isn't that a horror too—that we can feel the suffering of an animal but not of human beings?" (300-1) The novelist uses this haunting trope of

Romantic literature ('Tiger, tiger, burning bright') to bring the continuing debate between environmentalists and survivalists to a memorable climax. Hours before she was raped and killed by the criminals and gangsters deployed by the people's government of West Bengal to unsettle and dislodge the settlers from Morichjhapi island (on which they had made this home because they felt less unwanted, less of a burden there than anywhere else), Kusum told Nirmal about her experience of the 'siege' and asked: "*Who are these people, I wondered, who love animals so much that they are willing to kill us for them?*" (261-62). Kusum's anguished question sent the former Marxist's head reeling, and without giving any reply he lay down on a mat. In the Sundarbans, Ghosh argues, human lives are valued less than those of tigers.

Nirmal desperately wanted to be a part of the Morichjhapi movement, ignoring the appeal of his practical wife who advised caution and non-involvement, because as a young man he had been in love with the idea of a revolution and he could never let go of the idea even when he had turned his back on his party. The squatters' uprising against the government and their resistance till the end 'was the closest Nirmal would ever come to a revolutionary moment' (119). The refugees' attempt to establish a classless, casteless, secular society and create a new future for themselves seemed to him to be the fulfilment of Daniel Hamilton's dream with the only difference that it was not an individual's dream. The dream had been dreamt by the very people who were trying to make it real. Nirmal whole-heartedly believed in Rilke's idea that 'life is lived in transformation' and to him what the settlers of Morichjhapi 'stood for was the embodiment of Rilke's idea of transformation' (282). It showed him that a man like him could be changed even after retirement, that he could begin anew. His other interest was Kusum for whom he had developed a romantic attachment. Centred on the doomed, utopian settlement in the tide country, the romantic triangle that emerged involving Nirmal, Kusum and Horen strangely prefigures the Kanai-Piya-Fokir story and seems to be its earlier incarnation. But Kusum chose Horen as her lover. On the night before her death, she not only offered her body but also handed her son Fokir to Horen who took him back to safety.

The revolution did not succeed. The settlers were forcibly driven out of the island. Scores of people were murdered.[4] Women were raped and killed. The corpses were thrown either into the rivers to be eaten by crocodiles and sharks or into the tiger reserves. The rest were sent back to Dandakaranya. Their quest to reinvent their lives and make their own future proved futile. So did Nirmal's life-long search for a pure revolution. He did not survive long after the failed uprising. Before the final assault of the government force on the refugees, he hurriedly jotted down his experience in a notebook in the form of an extended letter and addressed it to Kanai in the hope that his nephew, with his mastery over many languages, would be able to carry it to the notice of an unheeding world. The notebook, which was thought to be lost, surfaces again, twenty years after Nirmal's death. Nilima requests Kanai to visit Lusibari to receive the notebook, which Nirmal had bequeathed to him, and decipher its content. In the process of doing so, Kanai's path crosses that of Piya, the American marine biologist of Indian origin, who travels to the Sundarbans to study and document river dolphins.

Kanai is smug, intelligent and a snob who knows six languages and has travelled across the world. He is self-centred and arrogant and is not above using his social status to get his own way. Although he is a bachelor, he has had a number of affairs. His aunt aptly describes him to Piya as "one of those men who likes to think of himself as being irresistible to the other sex. Unfortunately, the world doesn't lack for women who're foolish enough to confirm such a man's opinion of himself, and Kanai seems always to be looking for them" (251). In fact, Nilima warns Piya against her nephew who, she knows, has an eye on the American girl.

Piya, on the other hand, is a reticent, sober, self-reliant and practical scientist who is devoted to her work and yet very sensitive to people and their environment. She is used to the solitude and rigours of life as a cetologist working in the remote fields. She often works in areas where she knows neither the language nor customs and can survive for days on just nutrition bars and ovaltine. While Kanai, like his uncle, is a man of many words, Piya has learned to view speech as 'a bag of tricks that fooled you into believing that you could see through the eyes of another being' (159). She studies the river as though 'puzzling over a codex that had been authored by earth itself' (269). She comes to the Sundarbans in search of the elusive Irrawaddy dolphins. Her search takes her along the meandering waterways of the tide country until events land her in a small boat belonging to Fokir, a young fisherman who catches crabs with his son. (In fact, Fokir saves her from drowning when she is knocked into water by a dishonest forest guard).

Fokir is a son of the soil, perhaps the truest soul of the tide country. He is illiterate but possesses more knowledge of the rivers and the wildlife of the Sundarbans than all the outsiders who do not understand him. Piya and Fokir are as different as two such persons could be, persons who cannot exchange a word with each other and have no idea of what is going on in one another's head. Yet they seem to understand each other perfectly, even without words. Piya feels an affinity for Fokir and his life which is attuned to the rhythm of his environment. Over the days, as Fokir takes her through the mazy waterways that crisscross the Sundarbans and to the tidal pools where the Irrawaddy dolphins take shelter, they develop a latent but live sympathy for each other. They cannot speak a word of each other's language, yet through the reciprocal anticipation of simple needs, they achieve an intimacy beyond words. Fokir's knowledge of Sundarbans' rivers proves invaluable to cetologist Piya and with his help she collects valuable data about dolphins.

Piya's discoveries about dolphins' activities and behaviourial patterns constitute an astonishing piece of research in the book. The nature of the tides and the nature of the dolphins' movement to and from the tidal pools as well as the symbiosis between human beings and this cetacean population comprise the essence of the tide country in this novel. We also learn a number of scientific details about cetology, climatology, Global Positioning System and depth sounding. These detours add an extra authority to the narrative and are much better integrated into the story than in his previous novel, *The Glass Palace*.

It is Fokir who brings Piya to Lusibari where the paths of Kanai, Piya and Fokir all merge. Piya is introduced to Nilima, Kanai's aunt, and Moyna, Fokir's educated and ambitious wife, who works as a nurse in Lusibari hospital, and she learns about idealist Nirmal and his relationship with Kusum and Horen. Kanai decides to accompany Piya and Fokir as an interpreter on a trip to the estuarine terrain to track down the Irrawaddy dolphins. The three of them embark on a motorized boat into the heart of the Sundarbans which brings lasting changes to their lives.

Kanai, attracted to Piya and envious of Fokir who is able to establish an emotional contact with the foreigner despite the communication barrier, constantly harps on the difference between the two: "You shouldn't deceive yourself, Piya: there wasn't any thing in common between you then and there isn't now. Nothing. He's a fisherman and you're a scientist. What you see as fauna he sees as food" (268). Kanai, about whom the novelist says: 'Language was both his livelihood and his addiction' (4), fails to fathom the mind of Piya (or of Moyna with whom he tries to flirt), while the illiterate Fokir is able to enter the emotional tide of her heart. He has to go through an ordeal by water to realize the hidden nature of this emotionally wrought relationship and the inefficacy of language to unlock the mystery of the human heart (321-31). As Moyna, who senses trouble in Fokir's intimacy with the unmarried American, correctly says to him: "words are just air, Kanai-babu . . . when the wind blows on the water, you see ripples and waves, but the real river lies beneath, unseen and unheard" (258).

As Piya pursues her dolphin study even deeper into the mangrove swamps, she and her fellow travellers put themselves at great risk. They encounter a cyclonic storm that brings a huge tidal wave in its wake. Piya and Fokir, dissociated from the larger vessel and its crew, take shelter in an island. While Kanai returns to the safety of Lusibari with the help of Horen and his son, Fokir is killed in an attempt to save Piya from the devastating *Jhor*. Their unusual relationship finds a weird consummation in the form of a dying Fokir breathing heavily down Piya's neck as, watched over by a tiger, they sit tied together by a sari to the trunk of a tree when the eye of the storm passes. The climax is reached in a terrific manner and its haunting quality leaves a lasting imprint on the memory.

The Hungry Tide is a stunning novel of humane breadth which is epic in scope, sophisticated in its observations of people and their milieu, poetic in its evocation of the 'terrible beauty' of the Sundarbans and astute in its analysis of the geographical and socio-cultural forces that have shaped this region. Although the book focuses on certain issues of global concerns, it offers no easy solutions. Amitav Ghosh seems, as always, to be more interested in people than in issues. His book is about the people of the Sundarbans and their heroic struggle for survival. His greatest strength lies in the way he maps the geography of the human heart and examines the nature of man's identity. The questions asked by the refugees of Morichjhapi: "Who, indeed, are we? Where do we belong?" (258) strike the mind of sensitive readers as the existential queries of a bewildered humanity. Despite hunger and poverty, disease and disaster (both natural and man-made), which are a way of life for the islanders of the tide country, none of his characters loses his/ her faith in the essential grandeur of existence. Buffeted by their adventures and experiences, their sufferings and consequent realizations, both Kanai and Piya return to Lusibari, to the refuge of Nilima's towering personality whose Trust has erected a solid bulwark against the vagaries of nature and life on the unsteady soil of the chimerical island, the former to rewrite his uncle's story for a larger audience and the latter to fulfil her life's mission: studying and documenting the riverine dolphins. Nor do they forget the victim and his family. Piya's sincere effort brings financial assistance for Fokir's widow and orphaned son from other corners of the world. In an adverse environment where life is fragile and uncertain, the essence of man, the book suggests, is reduced to its very core. Amitav Ghosh allows the country of the hungry tide to break down the barriers of his characters and their society.

The erosion of borders between nations and/ or genres emerges as a recurring feature of Amitav Ghosh's writing. *The*

Hungry Tide, like his previous novels *The Circle of Reason* and *The Calcutta Chromosome*, challenges the conceptual boundaries that have been erected to separate academic disciplines. The book intermingles marine biology, geography, geology, myth, history, climatology, economics, environmental studies and anthropology in a masterly but effortless manner. While talking about the defeated 'historical materialist' Nirmal to Piya, Kanai says: "For him it meant that everything which existed was interconnected: the trees, the sky, the weather, people, poetry, science, nature. He hunted down facts in the way a magpie collects shiny things. Yet when he strung them all together, somehow they did become stories—of a kind" (282-83). That seems to be a fitting description of Amitav Ghosh's unique story-telling skill in this exquisitely researched novel.

In an interview with the *Outlook* in 2002, Ghosh had remarked: "My fiction has always been about communities coming unmade or remaking themselves."[5] *The Hungry Tide* is the story of one such community of people who, having come unmade from their ancestral roots, try to remake themselves in a place where, as Nirmal writes in his notebook, 'transformation is the rule of life.' After finishing this riveting novel, the readers too feel that they have made an imaginative journey to the tide country and that the experience has remade them.

NOTES

1. The controversy was caused by Amitav Ghosh's withdrawal of the novel from the competition for the Commonwealth Writers Prize, 2001. In an open letter to the prize's organizers, he expressed his unease with the term 'Commonwealth,' which smacks of the old power structure of colonialism, and criticized the prize for excluding Commonwealth writers who chose to write in languages other than English.
2. *The Hungry Tide* (New Delhi: Ravi Dayal, 2004).
3. It is a historical fact that the Marxists of West Bengal had politically resisted Chief Minister Bidhan Chandra Roy's sincere efforts to resettle the East Bengali refugees, who came to India after partition, in the Andaman and Nicobar islands and in Dandakaranya, and that the

refugees had undertaken the 'great march to the east' in 1978 at the expressed promise of some eminent Marxist leaders—who had visited their camp in Madhya Pradesh—that they would be welcomed in West Bengal if the Left Front came to power, Ghosh writes, "Earlier that year a Left Front ministry had taken power in West Bengal and the refugees may have assumed that they would not face much opposition from the state government. But this was a miscalculation" (119). Fact is, it was not at all a 'miscalculation.' Their assumption was based on the earlier promise of the Bengali Marxists who have always used the refugees in the state as their vote bank and have received their uninterrupted political support that immensely helped them to come to power in 1977.

4. The exact number was never brought to light.
5. Sheela Reddy, 'Writing through Turmoil,' *Outlook*, New Delhi, August 19, 2002.

Amitav Ghosh's *The Hungry Tide*: Analyzing Its Complex Range of Concerns

SANTWANA HALDAR

Amitav Ghosh's fictional work moves effortlessly across political and national boundaries and also across generations in time, introducing issues which are central to the postcolonial debates. With a piercing insight, he explores historical events that were sidelined in government records and upholds the issues related to imperialism and multiculturalism. An active member of the Subaltern Studies Project[1], Ghosh likes to present those events from the perspectives of the subalterns. *The Hungry Tide*[2] reveals his concerns for the marginalized who are ignored both by the government and the non-government institutions. The novel also records its author's concerns for other related issues such as the preservation of animals at the cost of human lives, duplicity of the government in power, validity of political and national boundaries, obliteration of facts from officially recognized history and such others.

The plot of the novel is woven out of complex threads of events ranging from past to present, the past exposed through the descriptions of planned massacre in Marichjhapi, a fact obliterated from official record but recorded in the diary of the retired headmaster Nirmal—the diary is read by his nephew Kanai after thirty years of his death—and the present through the process of discovering a rare species of dolphins in Sundarbans area by Piya, an America born cetologist, who knows no other language but English though her parents were Bengalis.

The novel starts with an accidental meeting of Kanai, an interpreter by profession settled in Delhi, and Piya, the American, on their way to Canning. Kanai goes to his aunt Nilima, Nirmal's widow, who has been famous for her social activities through a Trust at Lusibari in Sundarbans. Kanai offers Piya the address of

Nilima who may be contacted if necessary and Piya is compelled to go there after her first expedition in a government boat in search of dolphins (Orcaella) fails, thanks to the greed of the local police men who were supposed to help her. Though the past event and the present one are not related to each other, both depict the tragedy of the marginalized: Kusum was one of the landless rebels who sacrificed their lives in the unequal battle against the state power for acquiring land in Marichjhapi, an island reserved for tigers by the government, and her son Fokir saves Piya from a severe storm at the cost of his life. An undercurrent of love, blurring the differences of language, caste and creed, holds the plot tight. The present article seeks to highlight some of the concerns expressed in this unique story of the ebb and flow of passion set in contemporary history.

The novel is set in the Sundarbans, the delta in the northern part of the Bay of Bengal, stretching across coastal India and Bangladesh from the Bhagirathi (Ganga) in West Bengal to the shores of Meghna in Bangladesh. The region, a natural habitat for the Bengal tigers, is declared by the government as a reserved area for the engendered species and some of the islands are demarcated as prohibited areas. The local people follow the mythical demarcation, the entire Sundarbans area being divided in the myth into two kingdoms, one occupied by Banabibi, the protector of the wretched human beings and the other occupied by Dakshin Ray, the protector of the tigers. Both the people and the tigers trespass each other's area, often unaware, when they are driven by hunger. In fact, it is almost impossible to demarcate areas in the Sundarbans. "The rivers' channels are spread across the land like a fine-mesh net, creating a terrain where the boundaries between land and water are always mutating, always unpredictable. . . . There are no borders here to divide fresh water from salt, river from sea" (7). Such a setting helps the writer highlight his concern for the arbitrariness of the cartographical shadow-lines that separate one country from the other, and also for the lines of demarcation that separate present and past, self and image, the rich and the poor. Thus the differences of language, culture and social status do not work when Piya listens to the tune sung by Fokír on the boat under the bright moon. The melody

> mirrored her mood and she felt a sense of perfect contentment as she sat there listening to his voice, against the percussive counterpoint of the dolphins' breathing. What greater happiness could there be than this: to be on the water with someone you trusted, at this magical hour, listening to the serene sound of these animals? . . . The thought of experiencing your surroundings in that way never failed to fascinate her: the idea that to 'see' was to 'speak' to others of your kind, where simply to exist was to communicate . . . wasn't it better in a way, more honest, that they [Fokir and Piya] could not speak? For if you compared it to the ways in which dolphins' echoes mirrored the world, speech was only a bag of tricks that fooled you into believing that you could see through the eyes of another being? (157-59)

John C. Hawley's observation that *The Hungry Tide* "shares Ghosh's concern for the individual against a broader historical—or even, in this case, geographical—backdrop"[3] may be relevant in this context.

Concern for the Subalterns

The Hungry Tide reveals Ghosh's concern for the helplessness of the marginalized when they are compelled to fight against the cruel natural surrounding, the empathetic society and the vindictive government. The Sundarbans area is covered by mangrove forest where there are no ferns, no wild flowers, no chattering monkeys or cockatoos. The people who live there have to depend on collection of honey and firewood, for which they have to make their way through the tough and leathery leaves and the impassably dense forest, often at the risk of their lives. "At no moment," Ghosh writes, "can human beings have any doubt of the terrain's utter hostility to their presence, of its cunning and resourcefulness, of its determination to destroy or expel them. Every year dozens of people perish in the embrace of that dense foliage, killed by tigers, snakes and crocodiles" (8). The palm-thatched huts and bamboo-walled stalls and shacks, laboriously built by the people, desperate for having a ground beneath their feet, are at constant risk of being damaged, if not submerged, during the time of cyclone. The people have no illusions about the surrounding water, the basis and foundation of their lives, that turns a stranger overnight. Used to the natural calamities of the region, the people have learnt to cope with misfortunes and even developed intimacy with the tide country. That is why refugees from the delta region in Bangladesh preferred Sundarbans to their resettlement camp in Dandakaranya in central India, where they had been taken, being put into trucks and buses by the central government. Those refugees, originally from Bangladesh—some had come to India just after Partition while others had trickled over later—had been "among the poorest of rural people, oppressed and exploited both by Muslim communalists and by Hindus of the upper castes" (118). The 'resettlement camp' was more like a concentration camp or a prison, as the refugees were surrounded by security forces and forbidden to leave. The soil was rocky and the environment was nothing like they had ever known. The local people—the refugees did not know their language—treated them as intruders, attacking them with bows and arrows and other weapons. They put up with this situation for many years and then in 1978 some of them organized themselves and broke out of the camp. They might have assumed that the Leftists would support them and the Left Front ministry that had taken power in W.B in 1977 would not oppose their move. But this was a miscalculation on their part. The authorities showed an unbending attitude and stuck to their former declaration that the status of Morichjhapi as a protected forest reserve should be maintained.

Among the refugees from Bangladesh who came to settle in Morichjhapi there were some local landless persons, too, like Kusum. After Kusum's father had been killed by tiger, her mother was trapped by a local pimp who took her away from the village, alluring her with the promise of a secure job in town. A rare example of a courageous woman among the downtrodden, Kusum went to Dhanbad where her mother had been taken and succeeded in tracing her mother in the most humiliating condition. By sudden good luck she met a good man Rajen, a lame hawker, in the railway station who married her and also rescued her mother. But the unfortunate girl lost both her mother and her husband and had to remain alone with her little son Fokir in a place far from the tide country where she was born.

One day she caught sight of a great march to the east—the ghost-like persons with children on their shoulders and bundles on their backs were shuffling beside the rail tracks. Seeing that an old woman had stumbled, Kusum rushed to her for help and learnt that they were heading for Morichjhapi. Kusum was delighted to see that those people shared her tongue and also her dream. She took no time to join the march. Nirmal writes in his diary,

> *In my mind's eye I saw them walking, these thousands of people, who wanted nothing more than to plunge their hands once again in our soft, yielding tide country mud. I saw them coming, young and old, quick and halt, with their lives bundled on their heads, and knew it was of them the Poet had spoken when he said: 'Each slow turn of the world carries such disinherited ones to whom neither the past nor the future belong.'* (165)

Rilke's lines reveal the utter helplessness of the displaced who repeatedly fail to grasp a solid ground for their survival. Through such attempt to locate experiences in particular time and place (in Marichjhapi during 1978) Ghosh contributes to the Projects of recuperating subaltern history.[4]

That the educated middleclass people including the persons devoted to social service hardly bother about the displaced subalterns is made clear through Nilima's objection to any sort of medical help for the settlers in Marichjhapi. Nilima said to Nirmal, "*Those people are squatters; that land doesn't belong to them; it's government property. How can they just seize it? If they're allowed to remain, people will think every island in the tide country can be seized. What will become of the forest, the environment?*" (213). Nirmal answered that the area of Lucibary where they were residing also belonged to the government once upon a time. Sir Daniel Hamilton was allowed to take it over and his experiment is proved to be successful. Nirmal raised the most relevant question: "*What was the difference, then? Were the dreams of these settlers less valuable than those of a man like Sir Daniel just because he was a rich shaheb and they impoverished refugees?*" (213)

The question raised by Nirmal at once focuses on the post-colonial subaltern issues. Nilima cannot refute the argument: "*What's been said about the danger to the environment is just a sham, in order to evict these people who have nowhere else to go*" (214). But she sticks to her point that she cannot be a dreamer like Nirmal, that she has to stay on the right side of the government to run the hospital she has established with much trouble. The attitude of the established persons in the society, who are not social workers, is hardly different. A visiting psychiatrist from Kolkata expresses his callousness to Nilima after he learns of Nirmal's attachment to the refugees in Morichjhapi: "*Oh these refugees! . . . Such a nuisance. But of what concern is this to your husband? Does he know anyone on that island? What are they to him and he to them?*" (275). Nirmal's concern for the refugees was not understood in the educated society to which he belonged. Even Nilima developed a doubt that he was attached to Kusum. Nirmal's failure to communicate with his class is recorded in his diary:

> *How could I explain to her that there was nothing I could do for the Trust. . . ? But as for Morichjhapi, Rilke himself had shown me what I could do. Hidden in a verse I had found a message written for my eyes only, filled with hidden meaning. It remained only for the time to come when I would receive a sign and then I would know what I had to do. For the Poet himself had told me:*
>
> "***This** is time for what can be said. **Here** is its country. Speak and Testify.*" (274-75)

It was Horen who understood that Nirmal was different from others, and that he could at once feel the sufferings of the real destitute without bothering about the pros and cons of his involvement in their causes. It took a long time for Kanai to feel that for Nirmal, Kusum was an embodiment of rebellion visualized by Rilke and at the end of his life Nirmal found the real space for rebellion.

In order to show that the educated urban people treat the subaltern as the 'Other,' Ghosh describes in detail the incident of how Kanai fell in the mud and how he was infuriated to see Fokir smiling at his mud-smeared body.

> Suddenly the blood rushed to Kanai's head and obscenities began to pour from his mouth. . . . His anger came welling up with an atavis-

> tic explosiveness, rising from sources whose very existence he would have denied: the master's suspicion of the menial; the pride of caste; the townsman's mistrust of the rustic; the city's antagonism to the village. He had thought that he had cleansed himself of these sediments of the past, but the violence with which they came spewing out of him now suggested that they had only been compacted into an explosive and highly volatile reserve. (326)

Kanai is able to analyze his own self and Nirmal's diary increased this capacity in him. He feels that the instrument of language enabled him to see through another set of eyes, "to filter the world through a mind other than his own" (327). As he looks at Fokir he feels that Fokir sees in him a representative of the outside world, "someone standing in for the men who had destroyed Fokir's village, burnt his home and killed his mother" (327). He had become, he feels, a token for a vision of human beings in which a man such as Fokir counted for nothing, a man whose value was less than that of an animal. Kanai is still unable to gauge Fokir's mind and fears that Fokir might have planned to kill him. After a while he modifies his view and feels that Fokir has brought him to that lonely place because he wants him to be judged. That Fokir's mind is untouched by such complexity is revealed later, when he comes back with Horen and Piya only to find Kanai senseless out of the fear of an attack by a tiger. This apparently insignificant incident tells a lot about the attitude of the well-off persons in the society towards the marginalized. Fokir's tragic death while saving Piya from the cyclonic storm is a fitting reply to all sorts of doubts grudged against him. It is learnt from Piya that in the last hour of the storm—he was protecting her from the blows of the storm in the open—he had been hit by something very big and very heavy, an uprooted stump. It had hit him so hard that she too had been crushed against the trunk of the tree they were sitting. Piya heard him utter the names of his wife and son (Moyna and Tutul) before the breath faded on his lips. Burdened by guilt and responsibility, and also by love that obeys no barrier, Piya tried her best to explain the causes of Fokir's death during the cyclone to her friends and colleagues in America who responded to Piya and appreciated Fokir's contribution to the discovery of the habitat of the Gangetic dolphins. It is now possible for Piya to raise funds for Moyna and Tutul and to attach Fokir's name with the project she has taken up. With the help of an imaginative incident, Ghosh tries to offer the subalterns the honour they deserve. Every expedition, be it the conquest of the Everest or the discovery of the actual habitat of a rare species of sea animal, owes its success to the illiterate local persons who remain unmentioned in the record. Ghosh points at the possible way of removing such social injustices.

In 'Author's Note,' attached to *The Hungry Tide,* Ghosh writes: "Around the time of its occurrence the Morichjhapi incident was widely discussed in the Calcutta press, English as well as Bengali. Today the only historical treatment available in English is an article by Ross Mallick, *Refugee Resettlement in Forest Reserves: West Bengal Policy Reversal and the Marichjhapi Massacre* (*The Journal of Asian Studies*, 1999, 58: 1, pp. 103-125). . . . Annu Jalais's article, 'Dwelling on Marichjhapi' is also yet to be published" (402). Annu Jalais's article is now available on net,[5] but Ghosh's concern for the indirect way of suppressing unpleasant facts still holds good. In the chapter entitled 'Crimes'—the entire chapter is designed as part of Nirmal's diary—Ghosh records 'rumours' as there is no record of the well-planned criminal act of killing and evicting the settlers in Morichjhapi.

> *The siege went on for many days . . . All we heard were rumours: that despite careful rationing, food had run out and the settlers had been reduced to eating grass. The police had destroyed the tubewells and there was no potable water left; the settlers were drinking from puddles and ponds and an epidemic of cholera had broken out.*
>
> *One of the settlers managed to get through the police cordon by swimming across the Garal river—an amazing feat in its own right. But not content with that, the young man had somehow made his way to Kolkata where he talked at length to the newspapers. A furore broke out, citizen' groups filed petitions, questions were asked in the legislature and finally the High Court ruled that barricading the settlers was illegal; the siege would have to be lifted.*
>
> *The settlers, it seemed, had won a notable victory.* (260)

But hopes were belied. The settlers were forcibly evicted from the island. Nirmal did not have the opportunity to record the details of eviction in his diary. He finished writing just hours before the assault started and gave the writing to Horen who left Morichjhapi earlier that day with Moyna's son Fokir. Kanai learnt from Horen, who was trusted with the charge of handing over the diary to Kanai, that the gangsters who had been assembling around the island were carried over in boats and 'dinghies' in the island. They burnt the settlers' huts; they sank their boats and laid waste to their fields. A group of women, probably including Kusum, was taken away by force. People say that they were used and then thrown into the rivers, so that they could be washed away by the tides. Hundreds of the settlers were killed that day and the rest were sent back to Madhya Pradesh from where they had come. Nirmal, too, was put on a bus with other refugees and was left on the way; he was later found stranded and unconscious in Canning. He died eventually as the shock was beyond his tolerance.

It was really shocking for Kanai when he lost Nirmal's diary. The writing, carefully wrapped up in plastic, was swept out of his hands when he slipped in water full of current. That he could at least go through the writing was a sheer chance. For, it had been lost from Horen too, and was found out again after a long time. This time Horen gave it to Moyna who had access to Nilima's home and Moyna slipped it into the study where Nirmal would spend his time after retirement. Nilima discovered the writing on the cover of which Kanai's name was mentioned and asked Kanai to come to Lucibary and accept the writing of his dead uncle. Thus it was this writing that brought Kanai into the tide country and after he has gone through the entire writing, he becomes a completely new person. He is now determined to write the story of Nirmal's notebook—the writing is preserved in his memory, he is sure—as he feels the urgency of Nirmal's concern for preserving the facts about Morichjhapi.

A disappointed Marxist, Nirmal was compelled to leave his job in Calcutta and then accepted the life of a headmaster in a school in Lucibary. He remained completely dissociated from his party and comrades for years. But, much to the surprise of Nilima, he got involved with the revolution in Morichjhapi. Nilima failed to understand why Nirmal wanted so desperately to be a part of the revolution and even doubted if Nirmal had any relationship with

Kusum. After Kanai has gone through Nirmal's writing, he begins to share Nirmal's concern for preserving the records of the revolution—the efforts of the committed revolutionaries to liberate people from oppression—which was a part of subaltern history and which has been ignored by the rulers as well as the historians. He is now able to understand that to Nirmal Kusum stood for an embodiment of Rilke's idea of transformation (282). Nirmal was surprised to find that the illiterate men and women in a remote corner of the tide country could resist the powerful government for so long a time. He was so impressed by their commitment that the spirit of committed revolutionary within him immediately recognized their rebellion as the true one and he felt an urge to circulate the event in the greater world. Kanai is infected by the same concern that left Nirmal insane some thirty years ago. And that is why he has restructured his company to take some time off so that he can devote him to the rewriting of Nirmal's diary. The seriousness of Kanai's purpose reveals the writer's concern for recapitulating the subaltern history.

Ghosh has successfully introduced the debate on the issue of preserving wild animals at the cost of human lives in *The Hungry Tide*. Kusum, a courageous leader of the settlers in Morichjhapi, argues in favour of the landless people, occupying the island preserved for tigers.

> *The worst part was not the hunger or the thirst. It was to sit here, helpless, and listen to the policemen making their announcements. . . . "This island has to be saved for its trees, it has to be saved for its animals, it is a part of a reserve forest, it belongs to a project to save tigers, which is paid for by people from all around the world." . . . Who are these people, I wondered, who love animals so much that they are willing to kill us for them? Do they know what is being done in their names? Where do they live, these people, do they have children, do they have mothers, fathers? As I thought of these things it seemed to me that this whole world has become a place of animals, and our fault, our crime, was that we were just human beings, trying to live as human beings always have, from the water and the soil. No human being could think*

> *this a crime unless they have forgotten that this is how humans have always lived—by fishing, by clearing land and by planting the soil.* (261-62)

During his conversation with Nilima, Nirmal utters almost the same words and argues that the way the refugees settled in Morichjhapi had been the only way of establishing human settlement in different parts of the world. Nirmal feels that the plaintive cry of the refugees wafting across the water was not merely a shout of defiance, but a question asked on behalf of bewildered humankind.

The other side of the debate—that the wild animals, too, have their right to be preserved—is put forward by Piya. She expressed her genuine concern when she found a dolphin calf seriously injured by a motor boat used by enthusiastic officers engaged in preserving wild animals of the area. The incident of setting a trapped tiger on fire, described in detail in the chapter entitled 'A Killing,' reveals Piya's attitude better than her argument. Without bothering about the result she rushed to the mob and plunged into the throng. She snatched the blood-stained spear with which the men tried to kill the tiger and broke it. She was rescued from the angry mob by Fokir, who, much to her disappointment, was taking part in the killing. As Fokir says that she should not be upset, Piya replies, "How can I not be upset? There is the most horrifying thing I've ever seen—a tiger set on fire." Fokir replies that when a tiger comes into a human settlement, it's because it wants to die. Piya covers her ears with both her hands and proposes to leave the spot. It is in fact impossible for her to understand the way of life in the Sundarbans areas where the inhabitants believe in the demarcation of land as per the myth of Bonbibi.

The conversation between Kanai and Piya that follows the killing of tiger may be quoted as an example of how Ghosh introduces the debate on the issue of preserving wildlife:

> 'That tiger had killed two people, Piya,' Kanai said. 'And that was just in one village. It happens every week that people are killed by tigers. How about the horror of that? If there were killings on that scale anywhere else on earth it would be called a genocide, and yet here it goes almost unremarked; these killings are never reported,

> never written about in the papers. And the reason is just that these people are too poor to matter. We all know it, but we choose not to see it. Isn't that a horror too—that we can feel the suffering of an animal, but not of human beings?'
>
> 'But Kanai,' Piya retorted, 'everywhere in the world dozens of people are killed everyday—on roads, in cars, in traffic. Why is this any worse?'
>
> 'Because we're complicit in this. . . . Because . . . people like you . . . push to protect the wildlife here, without regard for the human costs. And I'm complicit because people like me—Indians of my class, that is—have chosen to hide these costs, basically in order to curry favour with their Western patrons. It's not hard to ignore the people who are dying—after all they are the poorest of the poor. But just ask yourself whether this would be allowed to happen anywhere else? There are more tigers living in America, in captivity, than there are in all of India.' . . . 'The difference, Kanai,' Piya said slowly but emphatically, is that it was what was *intended* . . . by nature, by the earth, by the planet that keeps us all alive. Just suppose we crossed that imaginary line that prevents us from deciding that no other species matters except ourselves. What will be left then?' (300-1)

That her concerns for the preservation of wildlife are genuine is clear from her decision to live in Sundarbans area which she calls her 'home,' explaining that for her "home is where the Orcaella are" (400). She is so much involved in the animal world that she takes no special care about her safety. Her sincere belief that as a human being she is only entitled to share this earth with other animals is hardly appreciated by persons belonging to her class, though the marginalized, who are closer to nature, learnt the art of dividing areas among animals and human beings and believe in co-existence. That is why Fokir said that when a tiger enters human habitat it must die, just as a man has to lose his life if he happens to enter in the deep forest (area of Dakshin Roy) meant for tigers. Ghosh offers his readers a scope to participate in the debate so that the real issues introduced both by the environmentalists and the friends of the subalterns may be focused.

The Hungry Tide thus records Ghosh's concerns for the subaltern—their struggle for survival in an unsympathetic world where they are less valued than animals and where their existence is ignored—and for other related issues. The writer's hold on history, geography, anthropology, myths and contemporary political activities is once again highlighted.

Notes

1. Amitav Ghosh contributed an essay entitled 'The Slave of MS. H. 6' to *Subaltern Studies,7: Writings on South Asian History and Society*, ed. Partha Chatterjee and Gyanendra Pandey (Delhi: OUP, 1992),159-220.
2. Amitav Ghosh, *The Hungry Tide* (Delhi: Ravi Dayal Publisher, 2004).
3. To quote the entire passage, "If much of Ghosh's writing meditates on the arbitrary and vexing nature of national borders, this book is surely obsessed with more personal divisions between men and women. One of the major elements of this novel's plot is the story of Kanai's growing relationship with Piya. Another is Piya's developing understanding of Fokir. A third is Kanai's gradual transformation through his reading of his uncle's account of the "Morichjhapi incident" from some thirty years ago. . . . The book is divided into two sections—The Ebb, and The Flood—and is set in the Sundarbans. Measuring over ten thousand square kilometers, this delta is the world's largest mangrove ecosystem. . . . The tide comes in twice daily, resulting in a constant reshaping of the land and an uprooting of anything permanent. Such a setting makes an apt symbol for the ebb and flow of history and the uprooting of populations, both of which have come to be seen as "Ghosh-ian" themes. Furthermore, just as the natural tides of the area tend to obliterate the sense of permanent division between land and sea, Ghosh's characters gradually learn to recognize the transient nature of the divisions between individuals—of whatever social class" (*Amitav Ghosh: An Introduction*; Contemporary Indian Writers in English series; Foundation Books, New Delhi: 2005), pp. 131-32
4. Ghosh's concern for the subalterns in his other works has been widely acclaimed. While focusing on the murderous consequences of Partition in *The Shadow Lines*, he offers a vivid

description of the death of the rickshaw-puller in Bangladesh who becomes a prey to communal riots. Pursuing the fugitive traces of an eleventh century slave to be found in the letters of a Jewish merchant, the owner of the slave (*In an Antique Land*), Ghosh contributes to the rewriting of the subaltern history.

5. Annu Jalais, 'Dwelling on Morichjhapi,' EPW Special Article, April 23, 2005. www.epw.org/in/show/Articlephproot 2005 Annu Jalais finds it amazing that the incidents of Morichjhapi are yet to appear in histories (para. 15). Her documentation reads: "Thirty police launches circled the island, thereby depriving the settlers of food and shelter, they were also teargassed, their huts razed, their boats sunk, their fish and tube wells destroyed, those who tried to cross the river were shot at . . . several hundred men and women and children were believed to have died during that time and their bodies thrown into the river." (para 17)

Against the Tide: Reading *The Hungry Tide*

SARVAJIT MUKERJI

Tillie Olsen writes in *Silences* (1978) about 'those mute inglorious Miltons: those whose working hours are all struggle for existence; the barely educated; the illiterate; women. Their silence is the silence of the centuries as to how life was, is, for most of humanity.' Silences are from 'circumstances of being born into the wrong class, race or sex, being denied education, becoming numbed by economic struggle, muzzled by censorship or distracted or impeded by the demands of nurturing'

A fact that Olsen seems to have overlooked, is that sometimes these 'mute inglorious' and marginalized people possess a wisdom won through generations of living in close association with nature, which is preserved in their folklore, myth and stories. Fokir, the enigmatic boatman of *The Hungry Tide* is both an illustration of Olsen's contention and its disapproval. Fokir appears early in the novel, as the savior of Piyali Roy, the cetologist from Seattle who is in the Sundarbans--the 'tide country' to further her research on the Gangetic dolphin.

> he was of about her own age, in his late twenties. His frame was not wasted but very lean and his long stringy limbs were almost fleshless in their muscularity. . . . His face was narrow and angular and its gauntness seemed to emphasise the size of his eyes. . . . Yet there was a defiance in his stance at odds with the seeming defencelessness of his unclothed chest and protruding bones.

Piyali's fall into river delivers her from the clutches of the forest guard and brings her into contact with Fokir who is to be her friend and guide till his death and perhaps beyond. Fokir is an unlettered fisherman whose only possession is his country boat and his enormous knowledge of the tide country acquired in the course of wresting his livelihood from the feral islands of the Sundarbans. The ebb and flow of the waters of the tide country match the flow of blood in his veins. He knows its rivers, creeks, mangroves, tides and storms. He knows its crabs, crocodiles, tiger, fish and dolphins. The sky, the winds and waters are his teachers. What he has learnt from observation and experience is reinforced by the myths of the Sundarbans. Piyali Roy is his modern counterpart. She is a scientist, intelligent and hardworking, her mind honed by her education and wide experience in fieldwork. She is supported by state of the art technology. Yet she is humble in a way that only the highly intelligent can be, and depends upon Fokir's expertise to prove her theories. She develops an affinity for him which is noted and resented by Moyna, Fokir's wife and Kanai, the man who hopes to possess her.

Fokir is a victim in a way that none of the women are—except for Kusum, Fokir's mother. Fokir, like most denizens of the Sundarbans, has suffered under state hegemony. He survived the Morichjhapi massacre only because he managed to escape in time with Horen. His mother was raped and killed in the same incident. He owns nothing but the country boat that is his home and the source of livelihood and his skill. When on land, he lives in the hospital quarters that have been given to Moyna, who is educated, and training to be a nurse. Interestingly, instead of the classic situation of a woman trapped in an unhappy marriage, we see the illiterate Fokir chafing under the gibes of his educated and employed wife.

Tillie Olsen's perceptive comment marks out women as just one of the categories of the silenced and marginalized. In *The Hungry Tide*, Fokir is mostly silent. With Piya there is the language barrier. Fokir speaks no English and Piya, no Bangla. In the case of Moyna, his silence is the silence of resistance. For Moyna, the future belongs to the educated and the economically sound. When Piya comes to pay Fokir, it is she who receives the money. She is impatient with her husband and determined that their son Tutul is not going to grow up an uneducated fisherman like his father. And yet she is very fond of her husband. Fokir himself is no doormat when he is in his elements—on his boat, among the channels and creeks and rivers of the tide country, Piya notices his defiant stance when he is challenged and then robbed by the forest guard. He deserts Kanai for ten minutes on the uninhabited island of Garjontola, when he senses his contempt and rivalry. That experience is enough to rid Kanai of his superiority complex forever. Interestingly, in the tide country, as Ghosh imagines it, the women are stronger. They are the decision-makers and achievers, while the men are on the margins—dreamers like Nirmal or dispossessed like Fokir.

Ghosh rarely uses the name Sundarbans in *The Hungry Tide*. He almost always refers to it as the 'tide country' emphasizing the element of water rather than forests and, by extension, land, that the original name implies. Another fisherman, Santiago, in *The Old Man and the Sea* thinks of the sea as a woman capable of granting great favours rather than as an adversary. The Sundarbans are more water than land. At high tide many an island disappears and only the tops of the mangroves are visible. The inhabited islands have high dykes built all around them to keep the inundating tides at bay. This is the tide-country and the rise and fall of the waters dictates all activities here. Perhaps that is why *The Hungry Tide* is divided into two parts: The Ebb: Bhata and The Flood: Jowar. Even the myths of the tide-country underscore its woman-centredness. The presiding deity of the region is Bonbibi. Her birth in the holy city of Medina and her journey to the Sundarbans with her brother Shah Jongoli, her victory over the man-eating demon Dokkhin Rai and his imprisonment in one part of the Sundarbans, her prompt succour to those in danger, especially in the jungles, are enacted annually. Her exploits are recited in the form of a long poem and she is worshipped in shrines scattered around the islands. Her cult is a unique amalgamation of the Hindu and Islamic cultures.

On a more mundane level, Kusum, Nilima, Moyna and Piya are women in control of their lives. They are the practical ones. They contribute to the survival and the welfare of the community. They know where they are going and what they want. Nilima, who has summoned Kanai from New Delhi to Lusibari, is the founder of the Badabon Trust. Through sheer grit, determination and hard work she has built a hospital and cyclone shelter on the island of Lusibari. Universally known as *Mashi-ma* (Aunt), she is a well known figure, both in the islands and to the powers that be, in Kolkata. Moyna works in the hospital in Lusibari. Unlike Nirmal, the arm-chair revolutionary, Nilima sets out to make a difference in the lives of the islanders. Like her, Moyna too is a forward-looking woman and has no time for her husband's traditional way of life, his singing and fishing. Unlike Fokir who depends on capricious Nature for his next meal, she has a job and provides for her family. But Piya recognizes Fokir's worth. She is a scientist who deeply respects his knowledge of the tide country. Indeed, he becomes indispensable to her research, familiarizing her with the habitats and behaviour of the dolphins. Though an autonomous woman, deeply involved in her work, she is subtly attracted to him as well.

At the end of the novel, Piya returns to Lusibari, to live there and continue her research under the aegis of the Badabon Trust, thereby ensuring its continuity. Evidently, the mantle of Nilima falls on her. She begins to inculturise herself, learning the Bengali language and forging links with Moyna after Fokir's death—so much so that clad in the colourful saris that Moyna can no longer wear, Nilima mistakes Piyali for Moyna. Interestingly, Piya's GPS has preserved all Fokir's knowledge of the tide country, and Piya intends to name her organization after him.

Fokir's life and death can be seen in relation to the women in his life. His story is seen in the matrix of the stories of the women. Of his grandmother sold to a brothel, his mother Kusum whose search for her mother leads her to Dhanbad and Fokir's father, her eventual return to Morichjhapi where she is raped and killed. In fact, Fokir dies shielding Piya with his body during the cataclysmic cyclone in which both Piya and he are trapped. However, Fokir is the most vibrant of the male characters. Of the others, Nirmal is a Shelleyan 'ineffectual angel' who mistakes the resistance by the settlers at Morichjhapi as the beginnings of a Revolution. He does not survive its failure either. And Kanai, lady-killer and alpha urban male returns to the Sundarbans chastened and subdued to pursue a literary career. Significantly, this is going to be based on Nirmal's diary. He may be considered to be Nirmal's successor, much as Piya is Nilima's. What has wrought this enormous change in Kanai is again Fokir. Fokir is the most vibrant because he is not an outsider like Nirmal or Kanai. In fact he is a local who has suffered at the hands of outsiders, be they the hoodlums who ransack Morichjhapi or the forest guard who robs him of his earnings. His animosity flashes out when he abandons Kanai for a brief while at Garjontola, thereby shattering Kanai's city-bred arrogance and class consciousness forever. He views himself through Fokir's eyes:

> and he [was] seeing not himself, Kanai, but a great host of people—a double for the outside world, someone standing in for the men who had destroyed Fokir's village, burnt his home and killed his mother; he had become a token for a vision of human beings in which a man such as Fokir counted for nothing, a man whose value was less than that of an animal.

This quotation raises the question—is Ghosh politically correct? In the novel there is an undercurrent that seems to work against the concerns of environmental groups. The eviction of the squatters from Morichjhapi, while brutal and extreme in its methods, is to prevent the degradation of the Sundarbans through indiscriminate colonization. The forest guard who misuses his authority is in fact there to preserve the flora and fauna of the region. And in the frequent human-animal conflicts, the animals suffer as well as the human beings. But the sub-text of the novel seems to suggest an irreconcilable conflict between the human and the natural and underscores the naiveté of those who side with the natural world. Ghosh also seems to indicate that women, whether educated or not are the stronger sex.

By the end of the novel Fokir is dead, but he lives on, immortalized by Piya's project that is to be named after him. Nirmal too lives on through his diary that is to be made the basis of Kanai's masterpiece. But the denizens of the tide-country need more than stories to survive. They need practical, tangible things like hospitals, cyclone shelters and money. Paradoxically, it is here that the women triumph. And together, the tangible and intangible, the male and the female, the natural and the human, form the rainbow of the future.

Bibliography

Amitav Ghosh, *The Hungry Tide* (New Delhi: HarperCollins, 2008).

Wilfred L. Gurren et.al., *A Handbook of Critical Approaches to Literature* (O.U.P., 2005);

Betty Friedan, *The Second Stage* (Summit Books, 1986).

R.K. Dhawan, ed., *The Novels of Amitav Ghosh* (New Delhi: Prestige, 1999).

Sea of Poppies: An Overview

TAPAN KUMAR GHOSH

Amitav Ghosh has always a surprise for his readers. With each book, he startles them with a novel theme and a new setting. And in each text, he experiments with a new genre. In *Sea of Poppies* (2008), the first volume of an intended epic trilogy, he, however, revisits, in amazingly detailed and impressive ways, some of the thematic concerns of his earlier novels, like the mass migration of people from one country and continent to another, the incessant movements of trade, commerce and empires that have travelled over the Indian ocean since antiquity, and the lives of ordinary men and women whose stories, framed against the grand historical narrative, call for different ways of looking at past, culture and identity.

Divided into three sections: 'Land,' 'River' and 'Sea,' *Sea of Poppies* is a historical novel set in 1830s, against the background of the first set of opium wars. Incredible though it may sound now, Britain was once engaged in drug-trafficking. The country was the world's biggest opium producer and supplier, not unlike today's Afghanistan that produces poppies to illegally supply heroin to Europe and America. It is an established fact which the British version of history glosses over. About two centuries ago, when the East India Company, the forerunner of the empire, was spreading its stranglehold on the subcontinent, British fortune-seekers in India amassed fabulous wealth—that sustained the colonial rule—by turning the banks of the Ganga into a sea of poppies to grow opium and export it illegally to China. The trade was monopolized by the British merchants under the seal of the company. Peasant farmers of Bihar and parts of Bengal were forced to turn over their fertile agricultural lands to the company's agents for opium production. And this caused widespread poverty and hunger because lands that had once provided sustenance were now swamped with the rising tide of poppies. Moreover, the Chinese rulers were determined to stop a trade that was rapidly undermining the country's economy by turning millions of people into opium addicts. Despite the emperor's decrees that banned the trade, British merchants went on shipping out barrels of refined opium, produced in the company—run factory at Ghaziabad, to Canton, relying on the growing number of addicts to defy his order. In the end, they used force, decrying the Chinese restrictions on free trade, and persuading the British Crown to wage the notorious opium war. Fought in 1839-42 between British East India Company and a weakened China under the Qing dynasty, its ostensible purpose was 'free trade,' i.e. access to China's huge market for British merchants.

By this time, Britain had abolished slavery and the Empire's plantations in far East and the West Indies needed workers who were slaves by another name—'*girmitiyas*,' indentured labourers with a signed contract or '*girmit*' (a corrupted derivative of English 'agreement'). Shiploads of coolies travelled the Indian Ocean under horrible conditions to escape the dismal poverty and deprivation in their native land and to supply cheap labour for the British sugar planters on such islands as Mauritius, Fiji and Trinidad. The novel centres round these two broad economic themes of the 19th century: the compulsory cultivation of opium as a cash crop in Bihar and parts of Bengal for the Chinese market and its disastrous consequences, and the origins and transport of the first batch of Indian Diaspora.

Against this historical backdrop, *Sea of Poppies* paints a moving picture of the human devastation caused by British colonial rule and its lopsided policies. With an unusually sharp eye, Amitav Ghosh looks through the spectacular historical trends at how these trends moulded ordinary human lives. Instead of being drawn towards the narration of the political intrigues of the opium trade itself, the novel keeps its focus on creating its large cast of characters, and letting history tell itself through their lives and stories which are shaped and influenced by socio-political forces beyond their control.

At the heart of this epic saga is a ship, the *Ibis*. Originally built in America as a 'blackbirder,' for transporting slaves from Africa, it has undergone a transformation after the abolition of slavery. The schooner is sold out to a British shipping company and trading house, Burnham Bros., which has extensive interests in India and China. The new owner, Benjamin Burnham, who has his business headquarters and principal residence in Calcutta, has acquired the naval vessel with an eye to refitting it for a different trade: shipping opium to China and transporting indentured labourers to British colonies in the Caribbean islands. The ship has a British captain—Mr. Chillingworth, who is an opium addict, and a first mate—Mr. Crowle who is a rogue. Its second mate—Zachary Reid—is a mulatto freedman who has sailed with it from Baltimore. Son of a white American and his black slave, Zachary is a daring seaman who knows no boundaries but who will always be bound to the brutal history of colonialism and the stigma of colour. By dint of luck and labour he has moved up the ladder to find himself commanding the ship's lascar crew. There is mutual distrust between the two mates who do not like each other. The ship picks up its lascar crew in Cape Town on its way to Calcutta where it will be refurbished to transport a horde of coolies to the sugar plantations in Mauritius. The lascars have come from places which are far apart and they have nothing in common except the Indian Ocean. The crew comprises Chinese, East Africans, Arabs, Malays, Bengalis, Goans, Tamils and Arakanese. They use a delightful lingo, picked up in Asian and East African sea-ports, as their shipboard vocabulary. Their leader, Serang Ali, is a man of formidable appearance, with a 'face that would have earned the envy of Genghis Khan' (14).

The action starts with the arrival of the *Ibis*, and the dropping of her anchor, near Gangasagar island in the second week of March, 1838. As the ship waits for the pilot boat to take it to Calcutta port, the story begins in a riverside village in eastern Bihar where Deeti, the first victim of enforced opium cultivation in the book, is introduced. Deeti, who sees the *Ibis* in a vision, lives on the outskirts of Ghazipur town. Her husband, Hukam Singh, is an *afeemkhor* who works in the Sudder Opium Factory. Mother of a very young daughter named Kabutri, Deeti, like other rural folk is forced to cultivate poppy as part of the colonial policy of the British whose appetite for opium seems never to be satiated. As the narrator says: 'Come the cold weather, the English sahibs would allow little else to be planted; their agents would go from home to home, forcing cash advances on the farmers, making them sign *asāmi* contracts. It was impossible to say no to them' (29-30). As a result, the fertile lands of the Gangetic plain bloom only with poppies, beautiful but deadly, denying the farmers the traditional crops to sustain them, and indebting them to moneylenders and landowners or compelling them to sign the '*girmit*.' They have no control over their opium produce either, because it is procured by the company-run factory at arbitrary prices.

The readers learn, beyond the brilliant colours of the flower, the grim realities of enforced poppy cultivation, the ways of collecting sap from the pods, the activities in the processing factory and its pernicious influence. Poppy becomes a symbol for an entire way of life that wreaks havoc with the centuries-old agricultural traditions of rural India. One of the memorable parts of the novel is a detailed and spell-binding description of the Ghazipur Opium Factory (90-98) through the awestruck eyes of Deeti, who goes there in search of her dying husband with Kalua, a low-caste driver of ox-cart with colossal strength and resourcefulness. On the way to the factory, they watch the march of a large group of *girmitiyas*, 'a hundred strong or more; hemmed in by a ring of stick-bearing guards . . . trudging wearily in the direction of the river' (70) from where they will be ferried in a boat to Calcutta.

The description of the Sudder Opium Factory at Ghazipur is based on a realistic account published in 1865 by its one-time superintendent, J.W.S. MacArthur. It is said that there are only twenty copies of the book in the world, and Amitav Ghosh has put it to brilliantly imaginative use. The narrative sees Deeti running through every single shed of the factory where at different stages poppy flowers, sap and trash are processed into refined opium, the most lucrative of the Empire's products, which travels the seas, via Calcutta port, to Maha-Chin. Outside the factory, groups of monkeys, who drink from the open sewers that drain the factory's effluents, lie perpetually stoned, while inside, in dark chambers, 'bare bodied men sunk waist deep in tanks of opium, tramping round and round to soften the sludge. Their eyes were vacant, glazed, and yet somehow they managed to keep moving, as slow as ants in honey, tramping, treading' (94-95). The description is Dickensian in its evocation of horror and pity. That factory still exists, as the world's largest legal opium manufacturer for pharmaceutical industry.

Hukum Singh dies soon and Deeti is bullied into being a *sati* by her in-laws who have an eye on her property. She is rescued from the flames of self-immolation by the loyal and robust Kalua whose cross-caste elopement starts a massive man-hunt along the banks of the Ganga. Deeti, who has left her daughter behind, marries her rescuer on the river bank and conceives his child. Near the river ghat of Chhapra they catch up with the boat carrying *girmitiyas* to Calcutta and, in order to escape their fate, sign the contract and join the coolies in their journey to an uncertain future.

As the migrants' boat sails on the Ganga and the schooner is refurbished to receive its human cargo in the dry dock of Kidderpore, the novelist skilfully, and seemingly randomly, assembles other key figures and those who will set sail in his narrative of the *Ibis*. Before getting them on board, he explores, in numerous subplots, the sequences of exploitation and suffering that these characters undergo in which the role of the new rulers and of older prejudice is clearly discernible. These are insightful portraits, not simply of the individual characters but of the social classes they are drawn from. At the same time, we find a compelling account of what life in mid-nineteenth century Calcutta and its rural hinterland might have been like. The administrative and trade centre of the East India Company—with its royal palaces, colonial mansions, police headquarters, jails and brothels, courtrooms and temples, river and port—is resuscitated in vivid and realistic details. Calcutta, in this book, is a polyglot and multi-racial city teeming with the seductive chaos and activities that come with rampant capitalism.

Here we meet Raja Neel Rattan Halder—the young, dreamy-eyed, cultured zamindar of Raskhali—who speaks chaste English, flies kite with his son, frolicks with his kept woman (Elokeshi, a minor but vividly drawn character), and has more knowledge of

Hume, Locke and Hobbes (118) than about his own financial condition. In their heyday, the Raskhali Zamindars were sought and courted by company officials and British traders to obtain finances for opium trade with China. Neel has been lured into the business by the hope of huge profits, but when there is a crackdown by the Chinese, he becomes insolvent. Benjamin Burnham, who earlier sought his, and his father's favours, brings a charge of forgery against Neel which leads to his arrest, trial and sentence of deportation to the penal settlement of Mauritius in a racially skewed justice. (This trial is based, as Ghosh writes in his 'acknowledgements,' on the 1829 forgery trial of Prawnkissen Holdar in the Supreme Court of Calcutta). With him we also meet, in Alipore Jail, another convict awaiting deportation. The man is Ah Fatt, the illegitimate son of a Parsi trader in Canton and a Chinese woman, and a living witness to the terrible human wreck caused by the opium trade. There is Paulette Lambert, the free-spirited daughter of a French botanist. She is raised by a Bengali wet nurse whose son Jodu (Azad Naskar is his real name) is almost her twin. (Jodu is another key figure who plays an important role in expediting the climax of the narrative). After her father's death, Paulette is forced back into European pretensions of class and snobbery in the household of Benjamin Burnham, an unscrupulous merchant and archetype of British rule. She boards the *Ibis* in the guise of an Indian coolie in order to escape her British benefactor, who is a man of filthy habits and who tries to marry her off to an aged Supreme Court judge. We meet Babu Nobokrishna Panda (NobKissin Pander in faulty British pronunciation), Burnham's Bengali *gomusta*, the agent responsible for the transport of indentured coolies. Nobokrishna is an efficient, witty, bowel-obsessed bureaucrat who undergoes a strange spiritual transformation under the influence of a holy woman (his own aunt). He begins to hover between the genders and feels that he 'had become the key that could unlock the cages that imprisoned everyone, all these beings who were ensnared by the illusory differences of this world' (503). Despite his eccentric behaviour, he renders great service to the advancement of the plot.

Then there are the Englishmen and their wives with their nasty business and racial prejudice, dirty manners and grand parties, conversing in a mouthful of Anglo-Indian words and phrases typical of the Raj. They are not just Indian stereotypes but credible individuals drawn imaginatively and forcefully. The novel is nowhere weighted down by the burden of anti-colonial sermonizing, although the author has no illusions about the hypocrisy, greed and cruelty that underpinned colonial rule. The company agents in the book have the impertinence to call the slave trade 'the greatest exercise in freedom since God led the children of Israel out of Egypt' (79) and refer to Hindi and Urdu, two major languages of the subcontinent as 'nigger talk.' They look upon free trade as 'a right conferred on Man by God' (115) and believe that the impending war with China will be fought not for opium but for 'a principle: for freedom—for the freedom of trade and for the freedom of the Chinese people' (115). But the native Indians are also oppressive in their own right and many of them end up as cogs in the cruel imperial machinery. The Empire was responsible for the opium trade but there were complicit players both in India and China, the book seems to suggest. At the same time, one finds conscientious Englishmen like Captain Chillingworth who could see through the pretensions of the company's buccaneers. During a discussion about the prospect of a war with China in Burnham's party, he says to Justice Kendalbushe: "The truth is, sir, that men do what their power permits them to do. We are no different from the Pharaohs or the Mongols: the difference is only that when we kill people we feel compelled to pretend that it is for some higher cause. It is this pretence of virtue, I promise you, that will never be forgiven by history" (262). What Amitav Ghosh has, in fact, achieved in the novel is a complete reversal of perspective. Unlike European writers—like Rudyard Kipling, E.M. Forster and Joseph Conrad who wrote about the colonies and placed the white men at the centre of their narratives, Ghosh relegates the British imperialists to the margins of his story, giving the pride of place to the neglected subjects of the colonial enterprise.

The narrative pace quickens, and darkens, as the novelist musters his characters in Calcutta and brings them aboard. As the *Ibis* embarks on its journey, the novelist starts creating, with renewed fervour, this self-contained floating world. Among the ship's passengers are people of all nationalities and cultures, languages and beliefs. Some of them—like the *girmitiyas*—are crossing the sea to escape the destitution at home, and some, like Neel and Ah Fatt, are being transported as convicts. There are also soldiers and guards, subedars and silahdars, apart from the ship's crew and officers. Once on the ship, the migrants forget their social, religious and caste differences. The boundaries of class and race blur unobtrusively and they become, in the words of Paulette, '*jahāz-bhais* and *jahāz-bahens*' (356)—ship- siblings—to each other. All of them become children of the ship who will invent new identities and history for themselves in an unknown land across the black waters where they are being taken. In the on-board 'chokey,' the bankrupt raja, who has been brought up in utmost Bengali refinement, forges brotherhood with the abominable Chinese opium addict. All of them, like Ah Fatt and the ship's captain, have stories to tell and secrets to conceal. And their stories, very much like the sketches of people which Deeti finger-paints as keepsakes for her 'shrine,' tease the reader's mind with discontinuities and suggestiveness. Their narratives begin to overlap and together their experiences form parts of the larger canvas of the East's colonial past.

As their voyage across the Indian Ocean gets under way, the social codes which separated these individuals on land are gradually washed away. On the *Ibis*, a new community begins to form among the migrants. Relationships are forged (e.g. between Jodu and Moyna, Neel and Paulette). A wedding (between Ecka Nack and Heeru) takes place that temporarily brings back the carnivalesque atmosphere of their lost village in which the *girmitiyas*, exiled from home forever, forget their quarrels and plight. There are also individual acts of bravery, defiance and deception that enable the migrants and the convicts to break free from what they see as their fate. Events develop at great speed. On-board intrigues begin to turn the migrants against the crew and even the crew against themselves. The climax is reached through a series of encounters and discoveries which inevitably push the narrative to a crisis. By a cleverly wrought co-incidence Deeti's vengeful relative—the uncle of late Hukam Singh—appears as a subedar on the ship. It is this relative—Bhyro Singh—who eventually captures Deeti and Kalua which leads to torture, murder, revolt and desertion. The narrative closes with the *Ibis* tossing in mid-ocean amidst a storm. Tyrannical Bhyro Singh and villainous Mr. Crowle are killed by Kalua and Ah Fatt respectively. Serang Ali, the leader of the crew, abandons the *Ibis* in a boat, along with the convicts—Neel and Ah Fatt—and the condemned, Kalua and Jodu. Of the main characters, only Deeti and Paulette, Zachary and Nobokrishna are left on board, watching from the rain-drenched deck the disappearance of the long boat behind a ridge of water. The first volume of the trilogy ends neither in despair nor in resolution; it leaves the readers wishing for more.

As an evocative and scholarly re-creation of a by-gone era and its forgotten history, *Sea of Poppies* is brilliant. Amitav Ghosh's remarkable achievement in this novel is a judicious and harmonious blend of history and fiction. What is more important, he once again reminds his readers that history is composed not of spectacular events and heroic characters but of ordinary individuals and their destinies. His book is, as always, more about people than about issues. It is this concern with living individuals that takes the novel away from the dry discourse of historiography and brings it closer to fictionalization of history. His characters are not historical figures, like those of Victor Hugo and Leo Tolstoy, but unremarkable men and women—imperialism's neglected victims—who are caught in the intricate web of history which is beyond their comprehension.

Ghosh's success as a historical novelist depends as much on the distinctiveness of his characters as on his enviable gift of story-telling. He conjures up each character with meticulous care, etching even the minor figures in the reader's mind with deft touches. These are bolstered by a solid mass of specialist information and painstaking attention to social and economic details. The novel represents an incredible feat of research without sacrificing its narrative and characters. It brings vanished experiences of a lost world to life, from the evocatively imagined opium cultivation in eastern Bihar, and the nostalgically itemized *carte du jour* on the luxurious dining table of the time, to the detailed descriptions of the *Ibis*, its nautical niceties and tumultuous journey across the Indian Ocean. In fact, the book provides an encyclopedic knowledge of early nineteenth century Indian food, dress, religious worship and funeral rites, sea-faring and trade, botany and horticulture, sexual practice and criminal justice. It has been remarked by many reviewers that the sea-board sections of *Sea of Poppies*, with their welter of maritime details, rival those in the novels of Joseph Conrad, Melville and James Clavell.

Another dazzling aspect of the novel is the clash and mingling of people, cultures and languages. There are Indians and Westerners, Asians and Africans in the story, and this confluence of people on one of the world's greatest rivers appears to be a spirited disavowal of colonial Kipling's magisterial dictum that the 'East is East and the West is West/ Never the twain shall meet.' They fill the narrative with sprinklings of Bhojpuri, Bengali, Lascari, Hindustani, French, American, Anglo-Indian words and phrases, and a fantastic spectrum of English—from the pidgin of the seafarers to the comically garbled English of Bengali Babu Nobokrishna and Indian 'foreigner' Paulette Lambert—that result in what Peter Parker has called, in his *The Sunday Times* review, 'a glorious babel of a novel.' This wonderful literary device, by which as many languages as people inhabit the text, creates a sense of living voices and of linguistic resourcefulness of the people of diaspora. Amitav Ghosh has ransacked the nineteenth century dictionaries and lexicons of nautical commands, soldiers' slangs, Babu English and colloquial Anglo-Indian words for his characters. Two most important of these sources are Henry Yule's *Hobson-Jobson: A Glossary of Colloquial Anglo-Indian Words and Phrases* (1886) and *English and Hindostanee Naval Dictionary of Technical Terms and Phrases*, published in 1811 by Lt. Thomas Roebuck. But this multifarious language that marvelously captures the multilingual perspectives of the characters, is so well integrated into the text that the book remains accessible to the readers, no matter how obscure and obsolete some of its words are. With its broad canvas, grand historical sweep, vast panorama of characters, linguistic exuberance and superb story-telling style, *Sea of Poppies* is sure to become an enduring masterpiece of 21st century English fiction.

Exposing the Ugly Face of Colonialism: A Study of *Sea of Poppies*

SANTWANA HALDAR

Amitav Ghosh's *Sea of Poppies* is a unique fictional creation based on a wide research not only on various aspects of the colonial rule in the Indian subcontinent but also the sea-routes of the time, the technical know-how of piloting ships, the typical language of the 'laskars' in a ship and so on. In an interview given in 2002, Ghosh said, "I don't think there's a big difference between writing fiction and writing non-fiction. When you're writing non-fiction there's real world out there that has to be taken seriously which means that you have to take step outside the confines of what happens in your head and engage with the real world. But my fiction is also founded on very extensive research. The world interests me. Sometimes the world interests me as fiction and sometimes it interests me as non-fiction and I don't see a distinction."[1] The statement is applicable to all his works including *Sea of Poppies* where hitherto unrevealed aspects of colonial oppression, inflicted by a section of white men who were desperate to make up the loss caused by the abolition of slavery, are exposed through the rendering of how the business of carrying slaves in ships were replaced with the business of opium and of indentured labourers.

The sea forms the background of the novel and the ship the *Ibis*, which had earlier been used for transporting slaves and was now remodelled for the new transport, is at the centre. The novel is divided into three parts: 'Land,' 'River' and 'Sea.' In the first section 'Land,' the characters who were somehow related to the ship are introduced along with the ship. The second part 'River' centres on the activities of the owner of the *Ibis* in Calcutta and also some of his friends. The third part 'Sea' is concerned with the inmates of the ship as it leaves Calcutta and moves on towards its destination. Even before the actual ship is described, it is visualized in the very beginning of the novel by a Bhojpuri woman Deeti, the wife of a worker in Ghazipur's Opium Factory, a poor, illiterate woman who did not have the chance of witnessing a ship when she visualized one.

> She had never seen the sea, never left the district, never spoken any language but her native Bhojpuri, yet not for a moment did she doubt that the ship existed somewhere and was heading in her direction. The knowledge of this terrified her, for she had never set eyes on anything that remotely resembled this apparition, and had no idea what it might portend. (8)

That she was fated to be in that ship is suggested through her premonition, and surprisingly, the picture of the ship that she drew to clarify her vision to her daughter, "was an uncannily evocative rendition of its subject" (10). Later, it was accepted by the seasoned sailors that the vision of the ship was granted to Deeti by the sacred river Ganga. "In time among the legions who came to regard the *Ibis* as their ancestor, it was accepted that it was the river itself that had granted Deeti the vision: that the image of the *Ibis* had been transported upstream, like an electric current, the moment the vessel made contact with the sacred waters. This would mean that it happened in the second week of March 1838, for that was when the *Ibis* dropped anchor off Ganga-Sagar island, where the holy river debouches into the Bay of Bengal." (10)[2] The real ship is described as it was perceived by Zachary Reid, the American who joined as a carpenter but soon became the second mate of the ship on its way from Baltimore to Calcutta.

> The *Ibis* was a schooner of old-fashioned appearance, neither lean, nor flush-decked like the clippers for which Baltimore was famous. She had a short quarter-deck, a risen fo'c'sle, with a fo'c'sle-deck between the bows, and a deckhouse amidships, that served as a galley and cabin for the bo'suns and stewards. . . . One thing Zachary did know about the *Ibis* was that she had been built to serve as a 'blackbirder,' for transporting slaves. This, indeed, was the reason why she had changed hands: in the years since the formal abolition of the slave trade, British and American naval vessels had taken to patrolling the West African coast in growing numbers, and the *Ibis* was not swift enough to be confident of outrunning them. As with

> many another slave-ships, the schooner's new owner had acquired her with an eye to fitting her for a different trade: the export of opium. In this instance the purchases were a firm called Burnham Bros., a shipping company and trading house that had extensive interests in India and China. (11)

While refitting the ship Zachary discovered that "the 'tween-deck, where the schooner's human cargo had been accommodated, was riddled with peepholes and air ducts, bored by generations of captive Africans" (12). Zachary's conversation with Monsieur d'Epinay, who handed him a letter that was to be delivered to the owner of the ship in Calcutta, throws more light on the new trade of indentured labour. He told Zachary, "My canes are rotting in the field. . . . . Tell Mr. Burnham that I need men. Now that we may no longer have slaves in Mauritius, I must hav coolies, or I am doomed" (21).

After Zachary met Mr. Burnham, the owner of the *Ibis* in Calcutta, the latter confirmed him that the vessel was going to do just the kind of work she was intended for. When Zachary reminded him that English laws had outlawed the trade in slaves, he justified the system of slavery with a typical colonial logic: "the Africa trade was the greatest exercise in freedom since God led the children of Israel out of Egypt. Consider . . . the situation of a so-called slave in the Carolinas—is he not more free than his brethren in Africa, groaning under the rule of some dark tyrant?" (79). Finally, Burnham made it clear that it was not 'slaves' but 'coolies' that was to be transported this time. He said, "Have you not heard it said that when God closes one door he opens another? When the doors of freedom were closed to the African, the Lord opened them to a tribe that was yet mure needful of it—the Asiatick" (79). He was happy because a good ship was available in Baltimore, and because a hold that was designed to carry slaves would serve just as well to carry coolies and convicts.

Sea of Poppies depicts how the small farmers and agricultural labourers in colonial India were forced by circumstances to be coolies and deported in Mauritius and other places. The portrait of the Bhojpuri woman Deeti who had the vision of the *Ibis* in the very beginning of the novel is a typical example of such oppressed farmers. The novel shows how after losing her husband, who served in the opium factory and whose land had been forcibly used for opium plantation, Deeti is ready to die in her husband's pyre only to save herself from the lust of her brother-in-law, but is rescued by a lower class man Kalua, who marries her in secret and then takes her to the ship to be coolies in some other land.

Amitav Ghosh reveals areas of colonial oppression that were not much highlighted earlier along with the much talked-about topic of the oppression of the poor by local moneylenders.[4] The British businessmen wanted to earn easy money from cash crops and to meet their greed the Indian farmers were compelled to produce crops according to the liking of the colonials, depriving themselves of wheat and paddy that they needed most to support themselves. The cultivation of Indigo ('neel') that was thrust upon the farmers in Bengal was highlighted in Bengali writings of the period[3] and was included later in the agenda of National movements, but the cultivation of opium was little focussed. Ghosh sincerely reveals the plight of the farmers who fell in the clutches of the English businessmen and began poppy plantation. Before poppy plantation was introduced, the fields were heavy with wheat in winter, and after the spring harvest, the straw could be used to repair the hut's roof. "But now, with the sahibs forcing everyone to grow poppy, no one had thatch to spare—it had to be bought at the market, from people who lived in faraway villages, and the expense was such that people put off their repairs as long as they possibly could" (29). Earlier poppies were grown in small clusters between the fields that bore the main winter crops such as wheat and the farmers liked to use poppy seeds as luxury items. As for the sap, it was left to dry to get hard 'akbari afeem' which the farmers could sell to local nobility and were also free to keep some amount for personal use during illness. But now the 'chandu' opium was made and packaged in the English factory for business and the farmers who supplied the poppies were ill paid and were not even allowed to keep some parts of the harvest with them for free selling or for personal use. Having done a lot of research on poppy plantation, Ghosh shows how the unwilling farmers were forced to plant poppy and face loss:

> no one was inclined to plant more because of all the work it took to grow poppies—fifteen ploughings of the land and every remaining clod to be broken by hand, with a dantoli; fences and bunds to be built; purchases of manure and constant watering; and after all that, the frenzy of the harvest, each bulb having to be individually nicked, drained and scraped. Such punishment was bearable when you had a patch or two of poppies—but what sane person would want to multiply these labours when there were better, more useful crops to grow, like wheat, dal, vegetables? . . . Come the cold weather, the English sahibs would allow little else to be planted; their agents would go from home to home, forcing cash advances on the farmers, making them sign *asami* contracts. It was impossible to say no to them: if you refuse they would have their silver hidden in your house, or throw it through a window. It was no use telling the white magistrate that you hadn't accepted the money and your thumbprint was forged: he earned commissions on the opium and would never let you off. And, at the end of it, your earnings would come to no more than three-and-a-half sicca rupees, just about enough to pay off your advance. (29-30)

Here is a detailed description of colonial oppression by compelling the Indian farmers, poor and illiterate, to harvest crops in their own land for the benefit of the British businessmen who had support of judiciary with them. After Deeti came in contact with other indentured labourers she came to know that everyone's land was in hock to the agents of the opium factory, and that every farmer had been served with a contract, the fulfilling of which left them with no option but to strew their land with poppies. And when the harvest was over the farmers found that the little amount of grains they could bring home would not be able to feed their families and that they were destined to plunge deeper into debt (91).

The plight of the workers inside the Opium factory—the hazards faced by them and the insecurity of their dangerous job—is also revealed through Deeti's first-hand knowledge of the interior of the factory when she entered there after her husband's illness. Deeti saw that troops of boys were climbing as nimbly as acrobats at a fair to the shelves joined by struts and ladders, and were hopping from shelf to shelf to examine the balls of opium. Every now and again, an English overseer would call out an order and the boys would begin to toss spheres of opium to each other. Deeti wondered, "How could they throw so accurately with one hand, while holding on with the other—and that too at a height where the slightest slip would mean certain death" (96). In front of Deeti one boy indeed dropped a ball, sending it crashing to the floor, where it burst open, splattering its gummy contents everywhere. "Instantly the offender was set upon by cane-wielding overseers and his howls and shrieks went echoing through the vast, chilly chamber" (96). For the profit of the British businessmen the Indian farmers had to produce poppy in their fields denying themselves of bread and other necessities, the poor boys had to be engaged in the factory at the risk of their lives, and there was above all the inhuman torture of the white supervisors inside the factory.

Sea of Poppies also reveals that export of opium to China was the brain child of the British and the American businessmen, and thus the myth of China's hunger for opium since antiquity is broken. In the dinner party offered by the landlord Neel Ratan Mr. Doughty proudly proclaims: "the yen for opium would still be limited to their twice-born if not for the perseverance of English and American merchants. It's happened almost within living memory—for which we owe a sincere vote of thanks to the likes of Mr. Burnham" (112). It is disclosed by Mr. Burnham that they were very much worried as the officials in Canton started to end the inflow of opium into China. He said, "It is the unanimous opinion of all of us who do business there that the mandarins cannot be allowed to have their way. To end the trade would be ruinous—for firms like mine, but also . . . for all of India" (111). He further clarified: "If not for opium, the drain of silver from Britain and her colonies would be too great to sustain" (112). Mr. Doughty commented at this point: "Johnny Chinaman thinks he can return to the good old days, before he got his taste for opium. But there's no going back." (112).

Neel Ratan had little idea that the traffic in opium had no official approval in China. He had seen that in Bengal the trade was not merely sanctioned but monopolized by the British authorities, under the seal of the East India Company and it was beyond his imagination that the Company could run a business in China without the official approval of that country. Mr. Burnham shattered

Neel's idealistic views formed on the study of British literature; it is revealed that the business had already been running in an illegal way: "Trafficking in opium has been illegal there for some time. But they've never made a tumasher about it in the past: their mandarins and chuntocks always got their ten-per-cent desturees and were glad to shut their eyes to it. The only reason they're making a fuss now is that they want a bigger share of the profits" (113).

The colonial policy of putting on façade to camouflage the ugly face of colonialism is revealed in Mr. Burnham's arguments in favour of free trade, which, he said, was likely to be the professed cause behind the impending war against the Chinese. He said to Zachary who was also present in the party,

> The war, when it comes, will not be for opium. It will be for a principle: for freedom—for the freedom of trade and for the freedom of the Chinese people. Free trade is a right conferred on Man by God, and its principles apply as much to opium as to any other article of trade. More so perhaps, since in its absence many millions of natives would be denied the lasting advantages of British influence. . . . British rule in India could not be sustained without opium—that is all there is to it, and let us not pretend otherwise. . . . the Company's annual gains from opium are almost equal to the entire revenue of your own country, the United States? Do you think that British rule would be possible in this impoverished land if it were not for this source of wealth? And if we reflect on the benefits that British rule has conferred upon India, does it not follow that opium is this land's greatest blessing? Does it not follow that it is our God-given duty to confer these benefits upon others?" (115)

When Neel Ratan asked him politely if he was not troubled to invoke God in the service of opium, Mr. Burnham promptly answered with a remark of his friend, "Jesus Christ is Free Trade and Free Trade is Jesus Christ" and explained, "If it is God's will that opium be used as an instrument to open China to his teachings, then so be it. . . . I can see no reason why any Englishman should abet the Manchu tyrant in depriving the people of China of this miraculous substance."[5] (116)

Introducing the conversation of the British and American characters on the topic of their illegal business, Ghosh discloses the shameless colonial policy of making money as well as spreading Christianity through illegal and immoral ways.[6] Ghosh's own ironic comment on the function of the Parliament in England is also provided through Burnham's proud remarks. As Neel Ratan said that he was aware of the function of the parliament in England, Burnham laughed and said, "Parliament? . . . Parliament will not know of the war until it is over. Be assured, sir, that if such matters were left to Parliament there would *be* no Empire" (117-18).

After a period of time when it was learnt that the Chinese rulers had beheaded some half-dozen opium-sellers and their bodies had been strung up for full public view, Burnham and Doughty expressed their opinion that war with China was inevitable. The hypocrisy in their attitude is once again exposed in their remarks. Burnham said that he disliked war more than anybody else, but "there are times when war is not merely just and necessary, but also humane." That time had come to China, he said. Mr. Doughty supported him emphatically with the remark, "Indeed, humanity demands it. We need only think of the poor Indian peasant—what will become of him if his opium can't be sold in China?" (260). After an objective display of the plight of the Indian farmers because of the plantation of poppies, the boastful remarks of the British businessmen expose, ironically, the hollow colonial demand that colonial rule was necessary for the total development of the natives. Ghosh makes Captain Chillingworth, an Englishman, confess the pretension of the colonial rulers: "The truth is . . . that men do what their power permits them to do. We are no different from the Pharaohs or the Mongols: the difference is only that when we kill people we feel compelled to pretend that it is for some higher cause. It is this pretence of virtue . . . that will never be forgiven by history" (262).

The colonial rulers exploited not only the subaltern class but also the well-off Indians, the landlords in particular, who had unshakable faith in the Company's policy and a high regard for the Queen's rule. It was due to their ignorance of reality that the well-off persons like the landlord of Rashkhali, Neel Ratan Halder, were trapped by the British businessmen and got ruined. Neel Ratan was financially exploited by Burnham and being accused of forgery, he was sent to a jail across the black water, as a part of capital punishment. That the British judiciary system was far from impartial is once again proved in his case. When Neel Ratan saw that Mr. Justice Kendulbushe was going to preside over the trial, he doubted his impartiality as he was well aware of the judge's friendship with Mr. Burnham. And the result was according to his anticipation. The judge passed upon him the sentence of the law of forgery and explained to him that it was a crime of the utmost gravity. The colonial pride is expressed in every word uttered by the judge:

> forgery was a hanging offence—a measure which played no small part in ensuring Britain's present prosperity and in conferring upon her the stewardship of the world's commerce. And if this crime proved difficult to deter in a country such as England, then it is only to be expected that it will be very much more so in a land such as this, which has only recently been opened to the benefits of civilization. . . . How is society to judge a forger who is also a man of education, enjoying all the comforts that affluence can bestow, whose property is so extensive as to exalt him greatly above his compatriots, who is considered a superior being, almost a deity, among his own kind? . . . Would it not be the duty of this court to deal with such a man in exemplary fashion, not just in strict observance of the law, but also to discharge that sacred trust that charges us to instruct the natives of this land in the laws and usages that govern the conduct of civilized nations?" (235-37)

Neel Ratan was taken across the black water in the ship the *Ibis* where he had to suffer such humiliation as could never be dreamt of by a man of his status. He was to stay with a man who lay unconscious, making the place full of shit and urine and Neel had to cleanse the place as sweepers do. Gradually, however, he developed a sort of friendship with his cell-mate, Ah Fatt, who had been so much addicted to opium during his first meeting with Neel Ratan that he was almost senseless at the time. Both Neel Ratan and Ah Fatt were harassed by the first mate who took sadistic pleasure in inflicting torture on them in unthinkable ways and towards the end of the novel both of them are seen escaping in a boat along with Serang Ali, Jadu and Kalia. Before the escape Kalua had killed Subedar Bhyro Singh—the man, engaged for looking after the indentured labourers, happened to be a relative of Deeti's in-laws and he whipped Kalua in public apparently to punish him for escaping with a woman of upper class, but actually for taking revenge on him after his failure to have perverted sex relationship with Deeti—and Ah Fatt had killed the first mate. The grudge of the oppressed and the tortured against the agents of colonial rulers is evident in these two murders. The severest criticism of colonial rule is however found in the speech of a French man Mr. Lambert, the director of the Botanical garden in Shibpur, whose daughter Paulette is an important character in the novel—the only white woman in disguise in the *Ibis.* Baboo Nobo Krishna Pander, an employee of Mr. Burnham and also a local money-lender, who had been asked by Mr. Lamburt to arrange money by selling a golden chain and could not contact him because of his untimely death, told Paulette what her father had said in fluent Bengali: "I have raised her (Paulette) to revel in that state of liberty that is Nature itself. If she remains here, in the colonies, most particularly in a city like this, where Europe hides its shame and its greed, all that awaits her is degradation: the whites of this town will tear her apart, like vultures and foxes, fighting over a corpse. She will be an innocent thrown before the money-changers who pass themselves off as men of God" (117). Mr. Lamburt was devoted to the cause of the Garden and the poor people, and had little savings when he approached death. He desperately wanted an amount for the passage money of his daughter who must leave India after his death, he felt. His comment on the British rule in India exposes the rotten condition of colonialism.

A vivid picture of racial conflict is found in the description of the foul weather that the ship faced while heading for Calcutta; it was becalmed a fortnight in the doldrums and the crew became the victims of racism. "With the crew on half-rations, eating maggoty hardtack and rotten beef, there was an outbreak of dysentery: before the wind picked up again, three men were dead and two of the black crewmen were in chains, for refusing the food that was put before them" (12-13). With hands running short, Zachary put aside his carpenter's tools and became a full-fledged foretop man. After the second mate fell overboard and got drowned—he was suspected to be murdered by the black men in the crew who hated him—Zachary was to shoulder the duty of the second mate. Though he had no knowledge of sea and ship, he was chosen as the second mate, thanks to his white complexion. The third part of the novel exposes the grim picture of the physical torture inflicted on the natives in the ship both by the white men and the agents of the white men. Even the Captain of the *Ibis* who appeared a bit liberal, approved of Bhyro Singh's beating Kalua who, he said, had run off with a woman of high caste and deserved punishment. When Zachary appealed to him on behalf of Kalua, arguing that the choice of one's wife might not be the concern of the authority, the Captain reminded him of the practice in America where a Negro was never spared in case he dared to marry a white woman. He also clarified the British policy of 'divide and rule' according to which the class of Indian people that helped the British to continue colonial rule in their country must be supported by the British. He said, "I will not deny these men, who have served us faithfully, the justice they seek. For this you should know, gentleman, that there is an unspoken pact between the white man and the natives who sustain his power in Hindoosthan—it is that in matters of marriage and procreation, like must be with like, and each must keep to their own. The day the natives lose faith in us, as the guarantors of the order of castes—that will be the day, gentlemen, that will doom our rule. This the inviolable principle on which our authority is based—it is what makes our rule different from that of such degenerate and decayed peoples as the Spanish and Portuguese" (482). Though outwardly gentle, the Captain followed the unspoken rules of the colonizer, the rules that helped to keep the colony in control. Persons like the Captain did not appear rude and rough as did the first mate of the ship. They only put on facades of civilization when they spoke of civilizing others; but they sincerely believed in the basic differences among the races and their success as colonizers depended on aggravating the differences among persons. Ghosh has analyzed this mindset of the colonizers and has also exposed the various ways of exploiting the natives to enrich their coffer.

NOTES

1. *The Sunday Statesman, Literary,* Kolkata; p.3, Aug.25, 2002
2. This presentation of the ship through a character's vision before it is actually described and the link between the character's intuition and the fact that follows adds an uncanny charm to the novel. Reference to the actual date of the ship's dropping anchor off the Ganga-Sagar island along with the uncanny charm of Deeti's vision is suggestive of a blending of reality and fancy.
3. Amitav Ghosh has shown how the subaltern issues and the feminist issues were merged with the colonial misrule. When Deeti's husband Hukum Singh was on the verge of death, Deeti went to the opium factory to sell the product of her year long labour and got a couple of silver rupees. She was shown the account book and she learnt that at the start of the season her husband had taken a much larger advance than she had thought. She cried in despair at the thought of the utter impossibility of running her family with such meagre amount. The clerk (muharir) behind the counter told her to do what others were doing: "Go to the moneylender. Sell your sons. Send them off to Mareech. It's not as if you don't have any choices" (155). On hearing that Deeti had no son, he said, "Then sell your land . . . you people always come here and talk about being hungry, but tell me, who's ever seen a peasant starve? You just like to complain, all the time" (155). On her way home, she entered a shop to purchase the bare necessities and was trapped by the shopkeeper. "Her frugality was not lost on the shopkeeper who happened to be also a prominent seth and moneylender. What's happened-ji, O my sister-in-law? He said, with a show of concern. Do you need a few nice bright Benarasi rupees to see you through till the shravan harvest? Deeti resisted the offer till the thought of Kabutri. . . . She gave in and agreed to place the impression of her thumb on the Seth's account book in exchange for six months' worth of wheat, oil and gurh. Only when she was leaving did it occur to her to ask how much she owed and what the interest was. The Seth's answer took her breath away: his rates were such that her debt would double every six months. . . . She tried to return goods but it was too late" (156). The conversation between Deeti and the clerk and that between Deeti and the moneylender-cum-shopkeeper reveal the cruelty of the well-off persons; the poor and the under-privileged had always been exploited by their countrymen and the colonial rule aggravated the situation. It was worse when the oppressed was a female.

4. Deenabandhu Mitra's Bengali play *Neel Darpan* written on the indigo plantation in the soil of Bengal raised commotion in Bengal and aggravated the conflicts between the British rulers and the local rebels. The drama enacted on the stage revealed the torture inflicted on the Bengali farmers who were compelled to produce indigo instead of rice and faced irreparable loss.
5. Mr. Burnham brings out the use of opium for medical treatment and argues that to deny the Chinese people of the opportunities of modern medical treatment is a crime which the British would not tolerate. He says, "it would be well nigh impossible to practise modern medicine or surgery without such chemicals as morphine, codeine and narcotine—and these are but a few of the blessings derived from opium. And if we consider all this, is it not apposite to ask if the Manchu tyrant has any right to deprive his helpless subjects of the advantages of progress?" (116). When asked by Neel what he would say on the addiction and intoxication caused by opium, Mr. Burnham poses to be a religious teacher and argues that these ills are merely aspects of the fallen nature of man. He continues, "the antidote for addiction lies not in bans enacted by parliaments and emperors, but in the individual conscience—in every man's awareness of his personal responsibility and his fear of God. As a Christian nation this is the single most important lesson we can offer to China—and I have no doubt that the message would be welcomed by the people of that unfortunate country. . . . It is tyranny alone that is to blame for China's degeneracy, sir. Merchants like myself are but the servants of Free Trade, which is as immutable as God's commandment" (117). The double face of the colonizers—their greed for money as well as passion for spreading Christianity and their lip service to remove the sufferings caused by the tyrants—is perfectly exposed by Ghosh.
6. That the agents of the East India Company had little ideas about the philosophical thoughts and political theories of Great Britain is humorously exposed in the novel through the revelation of their utter ignorance. When Neel Ratan humbly said that he had read the writings of Hume, Hobbes and Locke, Burnham and Doughty reveal their ignorance in regard to these great thinkers in a way that provokes laughter. "'Please do not speak to me, sir,' said Mr. Burnham, in the chilly tone of a man who wishes to snub a name-dropper, 'of Mr. Hume and Mr. Locke. For I would have you know that I have been acquainted with them since they served on the Bengal Board of Revenue. I too have read every word they've written—even their re-

port of sanitation. And as for Mr. Hobbes, why I do believe I dined with him at my club just the other day.' 'Fine fellow, Hobbes,' Mr. Doughty broke in suddenly. 'Got a sit on the Municipal Council now, if I'm not mistaken. Went pig-sticking with me once. The shikarees scared up an old sow and a brood of piglets. Came charging at us! Scared the Nick's knackers out of the horses. Old Hobbes was tossed—right on a little suckling. Dead on the spot. The piglet I mean Hobbes was unscathed. Damnedest thing I ever saw. Made a fine roast too. Piglet I mean'" (118-19).

The Evolvement of the Concept of Travel in Indian Literature

KHALID S.T. ABDU

Indians have played a prominent role in the development of travel literature. Babur, for example, apart from his military expedition, writes an autobiography, *Babur-Nama* (1482), which depicts the ordinary life in Islamic Central and South Asia during his era. In this regard, Tabish Khair and his coeditors note: "Babur includes descriptions of many of the places he visits and he is interested in flora and fauna and techniques of hunting, fishing, and agriculture; there are also set-piece geographical overviews of Fergana, Transoxiana . . . as well as a twenty-page description of Hindustan" (163).

Generally speaking, Indians have been thoroughly conversant with the theme of travel and migration since ancient times. The journey is a part and parcel of Indians' lives, as they perform pilgrimages to various religious centres all over India. A voyage to sacred places is a very common motif in the works of pioneer writers. But there are many writers who do not restrict their themes to the boundaries of India; they go a step ahead to write about their experience abroad. Dean Mahomet, for example, travels to England in the eighteenth century and opens the gate widely for introducing Indian literature to England. Kate Teltscher confirms that *The Travels of Dean Mahomet* (1794) is regarded as "the first travel account published by an Indian in English" (192). However, in the modern period the novel as a literary form was introduced to the Indian audience by Bankim Chandra Chatterjee via his first novel, his only one in English, *Rajmohan's Wife* (1864). Chatterjee is "considered as the father of the novel in India" (Ravi 11).

Indian writers, especially Bengalis, began to travel to England for scholarly purposes during the British occupation. Bengal is considered as a microcosm of India and Bengalis are stereotypes of Indians with regard to the British visualization of the people, so they make generalization about all Indians through Bengalis. In the article, "Imaging the Real: Reading the 19th Century in Bangla," Mahasweta Sengupta writes: "notions about 'India' were largely based on what the British saw in Bengal, and notions about the 'West' were drawn from what the Bengali people found happening among the British during the early periods of transaction between the two people" (59-60).

Obviously, Indian writers realize the importance of voyages in literature as a result of the European influence, whether by the earlier Portuguese or by the later English presence in the land. Therefore, modern travelogues begin to appear in Indian literature during the last two decades of the nineteenth-century British colonization of India. Indian writers who visited England grew in fame. Rabindranath Tagore is one of them. He is one of the many writers who translated his Bengali works into English. In his study of "In the Land of Masters: Indians Travelogues on England," Sisir Kumar Das indicates that Tagore published his travelogue of *Europe-Prabasir Patra* (1880), which was followed by another one in the form of a diary in 1890. A feature of these travelogues is the presence of two components in them: the voyage from Calcutta to England via one of the ports in the Mediterranean and the experiences of the voyagers in London as well as in the countryside of England (190).

Migration is a phenomenon that has been going on since times immemorial. Immigrant writers celebrate discovering not only the new country, but also the place they have left behind. A new imagination of India has been reformulated in the perceptions of these writers. Amitava Kumar remarks: "In the 1930s, expatriate Indians like Sajjad Zaheer and Mulk Raj Anand had founded the Progressive Writers' Association in London" (XIV). The search for Indian identity is the predominant theme in the fiction of early expatriate writers. Many Indian novelists write about protagonists who travel to the Western countries, either to America or Europe. The journey to the West is the chief preoccupation of novelists through their central characters. Shyamala A. Narayan states:

"Most of the Indian English novelists have written about journeys. One of Mulk Raj Anand's earlier novels, *Across the Black Waters* (1940), the second volume of the trilogy with Lala as a hero, describes his experiences in Europe when he goes there as a soldier in the First World War" (135).

The embodiment of the East-West encounter has become one of the salient features of the literary products of the nineteen fifties and the sixties. Raja Rao is one of the important Indian expatriate writers who represent the East-West encounter through the depiction of his protagonists' interaction with Western society. Rao's *The Serpent and the Rope* (1960) is a complex attempt to explore Indian culture and philosophy through the journey of the central character, Ramaswamy. However, the impact of the West results in much soul searching and a need for Ramaswamy to return to Travancore on a spiritual quest to his guru. Graham Huggan argues: "Indian writing, especially in English, is to a large extent a transnational, diasporic phenomenon, the product of complex collisions . . . between East and West" (66).

After independence in 1947, texts offer a site for interrogation of the writers' own identity. This is exactly the case with the Trinidad-born British resident, V.S. Naipaul, whose many books often trace the roots of his ancestors. Naipaul has written many travel texts and the three important works about India are *An Area of Darkness* (1964), *India: A Wounded Civilization* (1977) and *India: A Million Mutinies Now* (1990). In these three books, Naipaul records his response to India after independence and the social behaviour of the people as well as his experience there. He also portrays the situation during the period of the Emergency which was declared by Indira Gandhi in which civil rights were suspended and political activists were imprisoned. Naipaul also reflects the plight of those people who face the agony of separation as a consequence of partition.

Partition is inevitably the legacy of British colonialism, having separated the subcontinent according to the religious differences of the people. The Hindu-Muslim conflict has led to widespread disturbances, causing enormous displacement for people on both sides. R.K. Dhawan points out that approximately one million people lost their lives. Mass-migration of people took place from one country to another; hence novelists reacted to this event as they depicted the plight of refugees who suffered the partition. Khushwant Singh's *Train to Pakistan* (1956) is one of the significant novels that delineate the miserable situation of people during that era (14).

The decline of colonialism paved the way for postcolonial literary studies. One significant feature of this paradigm is de-centering the metropolitan centre, that is, the West no longer holds the power any more and things are falling apart. This opens the gates wide for the interrogation of Eurocentric discourse of hegemony. Hence, knowledge is not merely associated with the West; instead, it can be performed by the exchange of thoughts. Huggan writes:

> there are clear asymmetries of power in the exchange of knowledge between the First and Third Worlds; publishing is an integral part of this complex neocolonial network. To put it simply, even crudely, many third world writers/thinkers are rewarded, or imagine that they will be, for setting their sights abroad. (78)

Thus movement is not only restricted from metropolis to peripheries; it is directed in the opposite side and destined for everywhere. The movement of people can be classified according to either wilful or forceful motifs. Expatriation and migration belong to the former category, whereas exile and refugees belong to the latter. The four classifications of the movement of people in literature come under the category of diasporic writing. Writers of this paradigm live two lives and are tangled up between two cultures. Expatriate writers, for example, undergo the pain of homelessness, displacement, dislocation and dismemberment. Therefore, new concepts appear in literature such as homogeneity, multicultural society and global village as a result of globalization. Andrew Smith remarks:

> Postcolonial literary studies . . . posited a new relationship between narrative and migration. If human beings have tended to understand themselves as citizens of nations or as blood members of ethnic groupings, migration increasingly exposes the insufficiency of these ways of identifying ourselves. (249)

Therefore, concepts of nation and identity have been reformulated and belonging has been redefined according to the new perspectives of expatriate writers. It is this new environment which grants them a privileged status. T. Vinoda confirms: "This essentially is their appeal to the modern sensibility and with these they have won every international prize there is—the Nobel Prize, the Booker, the Booker of Booker, the Pulitzer, the Commonwealth Prize, the National Book Award" (13).

The expansion of Indians across many countries enlarges their comprehension of the world, and hence it broadens their creativity in the field of literature and arts. This new environment enables them to enrich their experience greatly by moulding their consciousness with new cultures. It is this new milieu of cosmopolitan society which combines two hybrid cultures. The decade of the Eighties witnessed new writers who brought novelty to Indian writing in English, and the eminent figure of this period is Salman Rushdie. Jon Mee argues: "The appearance of *Midnight's Children* in 1981 brought about a renaissance in Indian writing in English" (318). This novel has brought newness not merely to Indian writing in English but to postcolonial literature all over the world. Meenakshi Mukherjee indicates, "*Midnight's Children* had a very important role to play in reversal of the 'centre-periphery' paradigm in English literary culture" (86).

Furthermore, the Indian writers of 1980s deviate from the theme of East-West encounter in favour of a new spirit, which is cosmopolitan identity. It is this new reality which enables the protagonist to travel everywhere and mingle with various cultures according to the requirements of modern life. Ravi points out that Rushdie's contemporaries "Amitav Ghosh and Upamanyu Chatterjee . . . have carved a niche for themselves in the sphere of postcolonial literatures. Like their fellow writers all over the world, they have moved into a transcultural ethos" (34). From the 1980s onwards, Indianness is not the main theme of the novels, and not all writers are interested in it either. Their fictional characters belong not only to India but to many places around the world. In other words, new characters are deregionalised individuals living in a broader world. Mukherjee argues that Amitav Ghosh and Vikram Seth brought the non-Western countries into their work, whether fictional or non-fictional (84-85). Seth's *The Golden Gate* (1991) and *An Equal Music* (1999) are the best examples that depict the cosmopolitan identity, where the traveller does not go back to his roots; instead, he/she acquires a new identity. Seth's *From Heaven Lake: Travels through Sinkiang and Tibet* (1987) won the Thomas Cook award for being the best travel book.

It is evident that throughout history Bengalis are India's greatest travellers. There is also a very vibrant tradition of travel writing in Bengali literature, especially during the colonial period and thereafter, so many Bengali novels deal with travel and journeys. Yet Amitav Ghosh appears to have been very much influenced by this tradition and stream of writers starting from Dean Mahomet and Tagore. These writers set the task upon themselves to reflect not only parochiality in their fiction, but also to represent other locations. In his study, "The March of the Novel through History," Amitav Ghosh argues, "to even perceive one's immediate environment one must somehow distance oneself from it," and that "to locate oneself through prose, one must begin with an act of dislocation" (303). Therefore, his characters do not stay in the same place but they indulge in travel all over the globe. In this regard, Robert Dixon remarks that Ghosh's characters "do not occupy discrete cultures, but 'dwell in travel' in cultural spaces that flow across borders" (4).

Therefore, the political boundaries that separate people of different countries have been crossed by the genre of the novel. This occurs more profoundly, especially from the beginning of the twentieth century. Since then, the novel has gained international recognition for integrating the people of the world. Urbashi Barat contends: "the novel in English in the twentieth century has crossed and recrossed borders: the borders of time and space, of genre and discipline, of centre and periphery, of social and moral values (IV). It goes without saying that contemporary Indian intellectuals and writers, like Amitav Ghosh and his compatriots, have been affected by the literary works of their counterparts. Such writers also owe much to the new phenomenon of globalization, in which the internet enormously narrows down the distances between people. It is this new world where all multicultural, multilingual, and multi-religious people meet and live side by side peacefully without taking into account the differences among them. Ultimately, the credit goes to literature that gives us this opportunity to know other cultures and to mingle with other people worldwide beyond human and natural barriers. It is through the ceaseless efforts of our contemporary travel writers in which we transcend the obstacles of frontiers as well as space and time; hence we celebrate living in this new global village of international bazaar.

Works Cited

Barat, Urbashi. Foreword. *Crossing Borders*. Agra: B.S. Sharma & Brothers, 2005. IV- IX.

Das, Sisir Kumar. "In the Land of Masters: Indians Travelogues on England," *Indian Ode to the West Wind: Studies in Literary Encounters*. New Delhi: Pencraft International, 2001. 186-201.

Dhawan, R.K. Introduction. *50 Years of Indian Writing*. New Delhi: The Indian Association for English Studies, 1999. 9-20.

Dixon, Robert. "Travelling in the West: The Writing of Amitav Ghosh," *Commonwealth Literature*. 1 (1996): 3-23.

Ghosh, Amitav. "The March of the Novel through History: the Testimony of my Grandfather's Bookcase." *The Imam and the Indian: Prose Pieces*. New Delhi: Ravi Dayal, 2002. 287-304.

Huggan, Graham. "Consuming India" *The Postcolonial Exotic*. London and New York: Routledge, 2001. 58-82.

Khair, Tabish et al., ed. "The Travel Memoirs of Babur" *Other Routes: 1500 Years of African and Asian Travel Writing*. Bloomington and Indianapolis: Indiana UP, 2005. 162-72.

Kumar, Amitava. Introduction. *Away: The Indian Writer as an Expatriate*. New Delhi: Penguin, 2003. xiv-xxvi.

Mee, Jon. "After Midnight: the Novels in the 1980s and 1990s" *An Illustrated History of Indian Literature in English*. Ed. Arvind Krishna Mehrotra. New Delhi: Permanent Black, 2003. 318-36.

Mukherjee, Meenakshi. "The Anxiety of Indianness," *Mapping Cultural Spaces: Postcolonial Indian Literature in English*. Ed. Nilufer E. Bharucha and Vrinda Nabar. New Delhi: Vision Books, 1998. 78-93.

Narayan, Shyamala A. "Voyage as a Motif in Indian English Fiction," *New Perspectives in Indian Literature*. Ed. C.R Yaravintelimath, et al. New Delhi: Sterling, 1995. 127-35.

Ravi, P.S. "Origin, Growth and the Development of Indian English Novel," *Modern Indian Fiction: History, Politics and Individual in the Novels of Salman Rushdie, Amitav Ghosh and Upamanyu Chatterjee*. New Delhi: Prestige, 2003. 11-35.

Sengupta, Mahasweta. "Imaging the Real: Reading the 19th Century in Bangla." *Writing the West 1750-1947: Representations from Indian Languages*. Ed. C. Vijayasree. New Delhi: Sahitya Akademi, 2004. 59-71.

Smith, Andrew. "Migrancy, Hybridity, and Postcolonial Literary Studies," *The Cambridge Companion to Postcolonial Literary Studies.* Ed. Neil Lazarus. Cambridge: Cambridge UP, 2004. 241-61.

Teltscher, Kate. "India / Calcutta: City of Places and Dreadful Night" *The Cambridge Companion to Travel Writing* Ed. Peter Hulme and TimYoungs. Cambridge: Cambridge U P, 2002. 191-205.

Vinoda, T. "Introduction." *The Expatriate Indian Writing in English.* Ed. T. Vinoda and P. Shailaja. New Delhi: Prestige, 2006. Vol. II. 9-20.